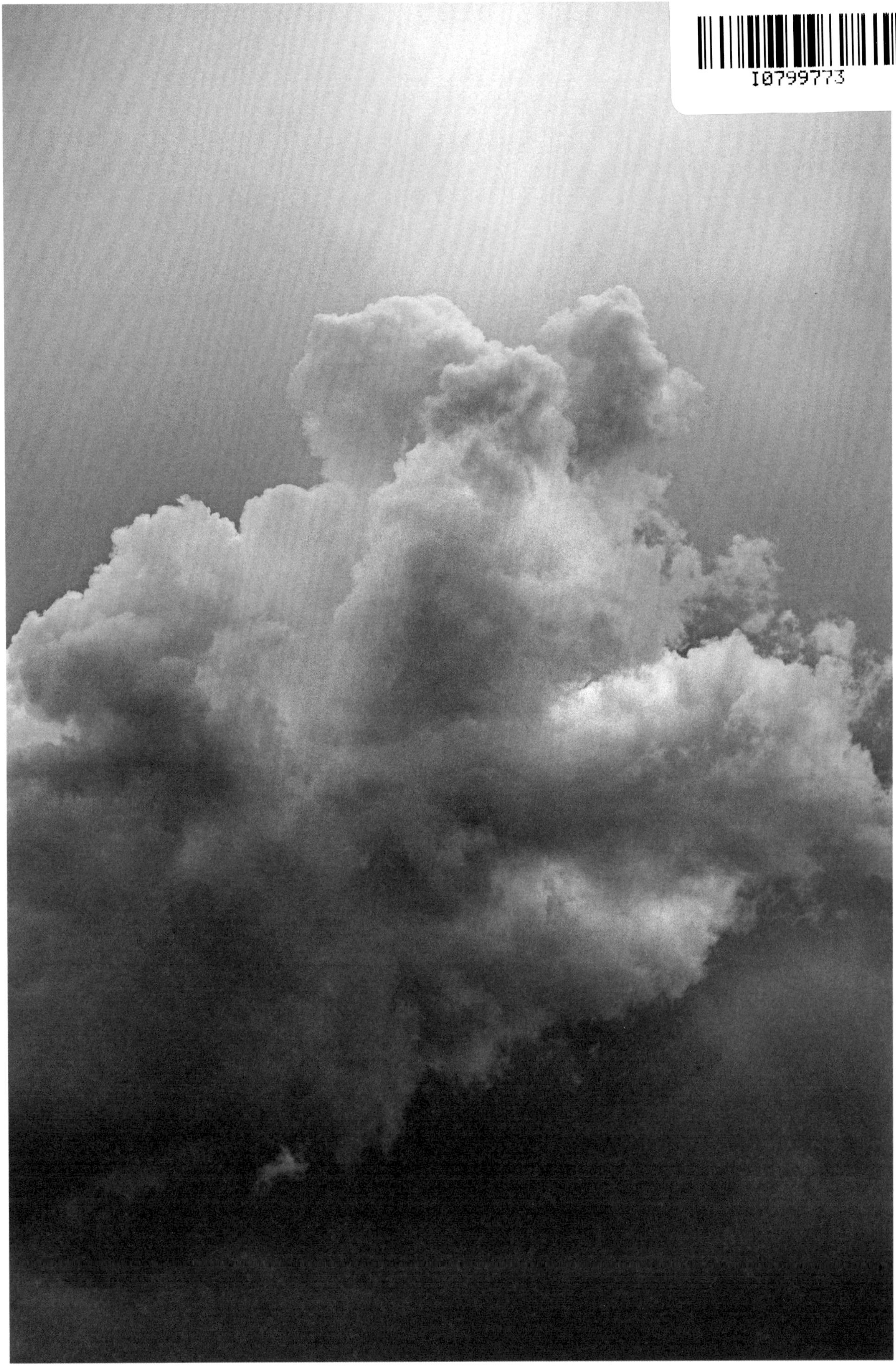

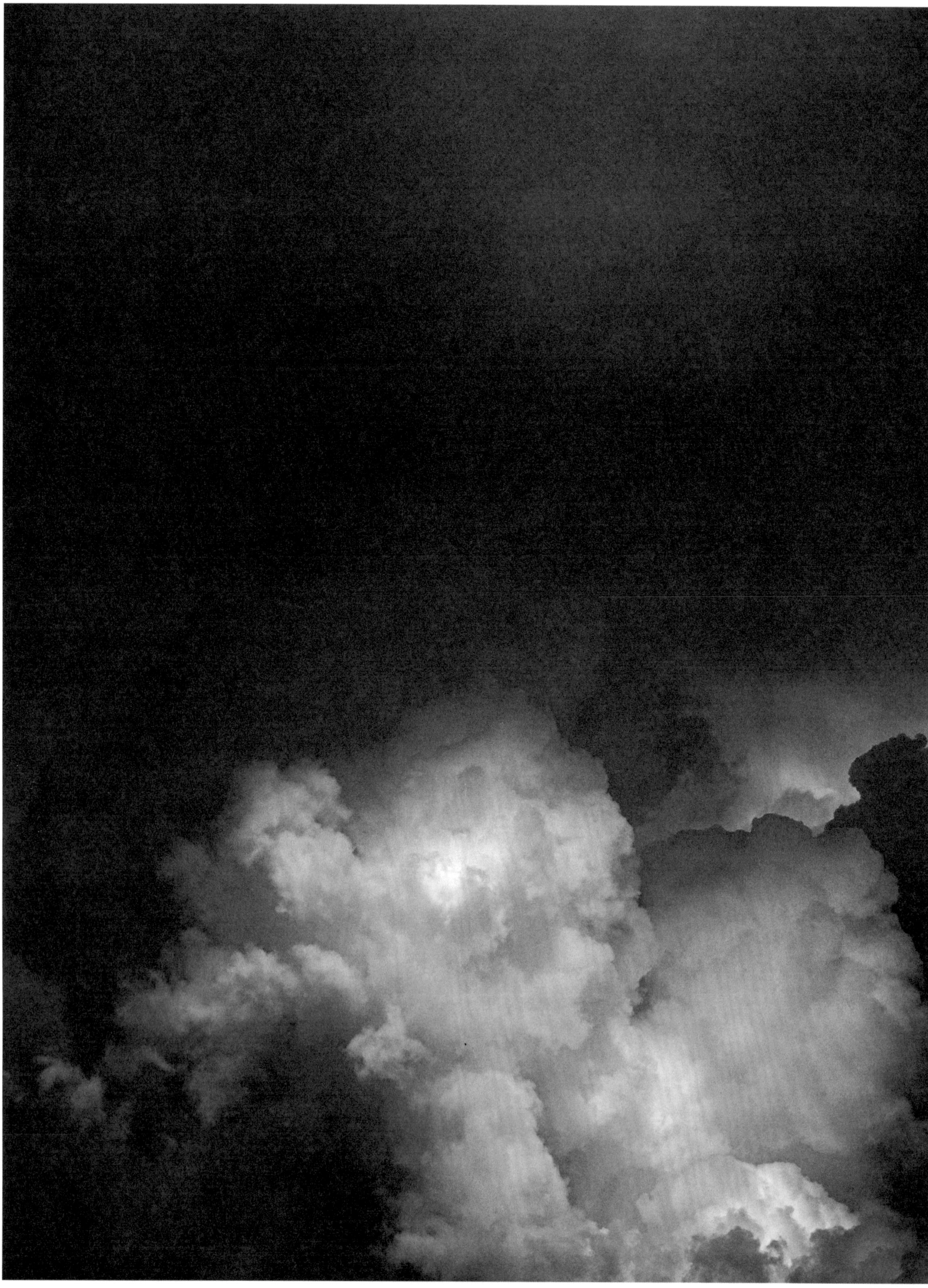

Everything you see has its roots
in the unseen world.
The forms may change,
yet the essence remains the same.

—Rumi

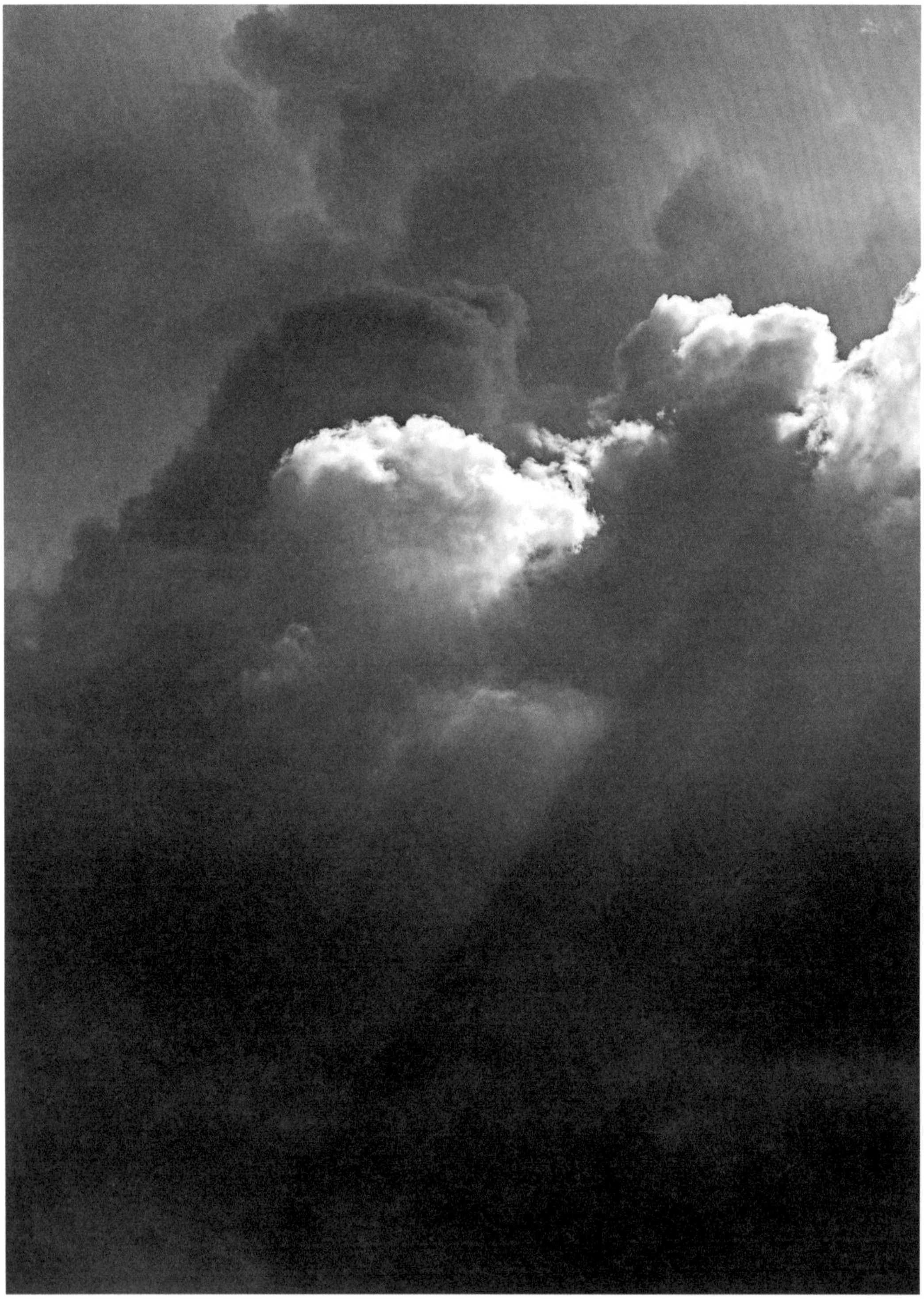

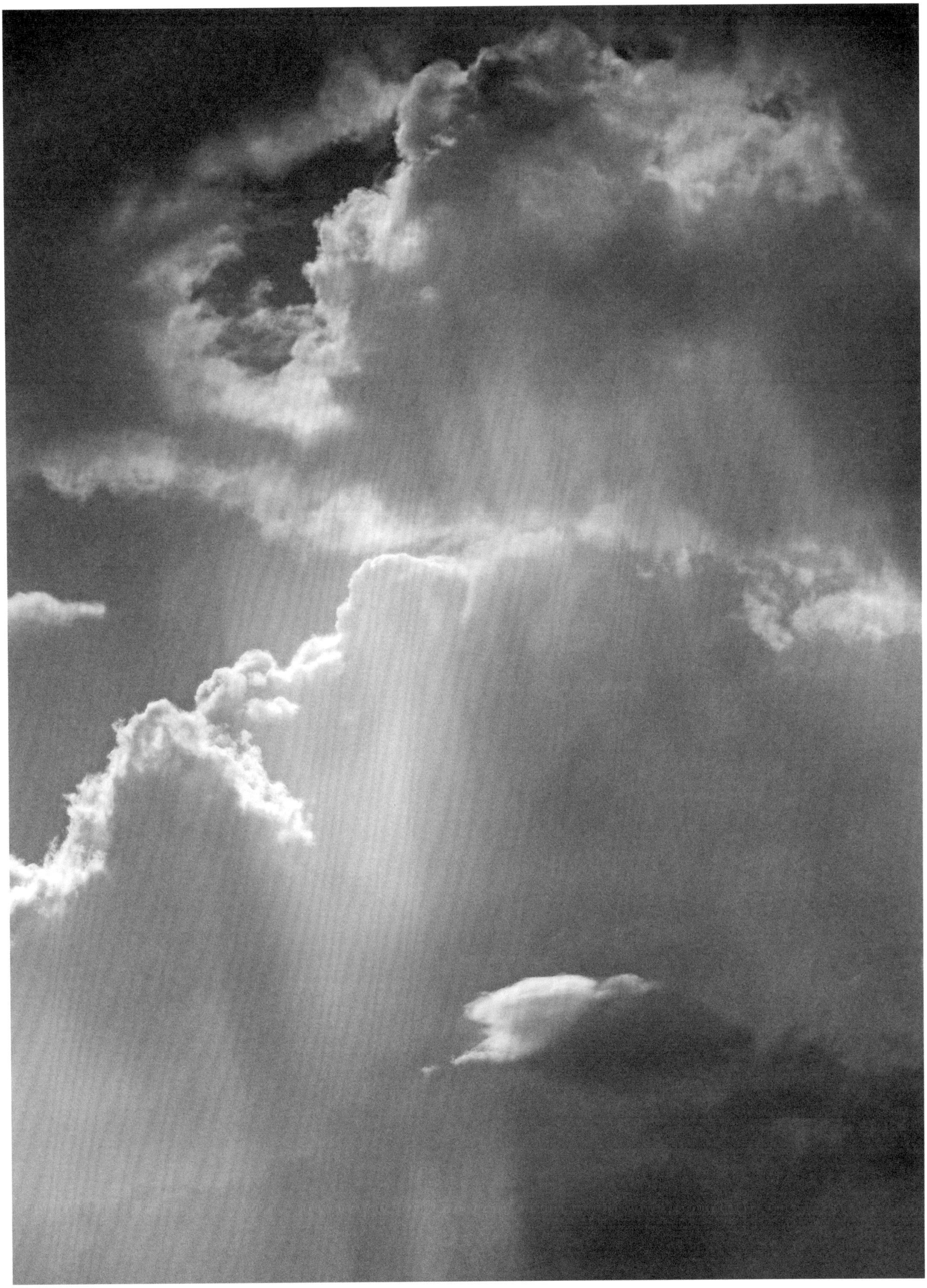

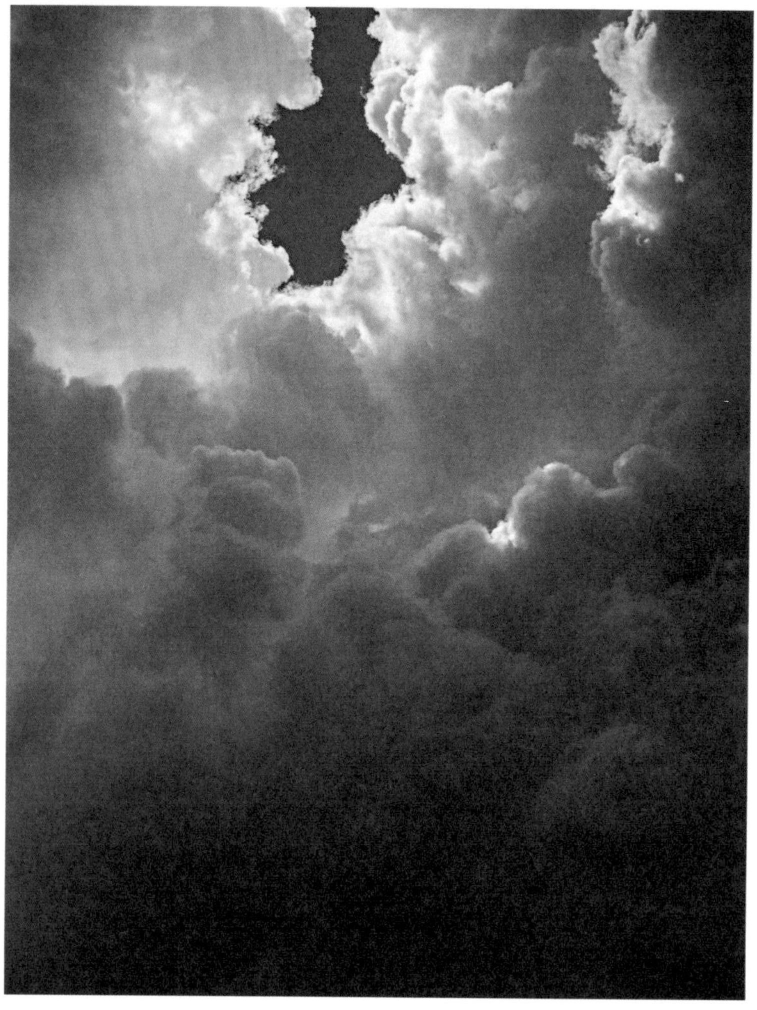

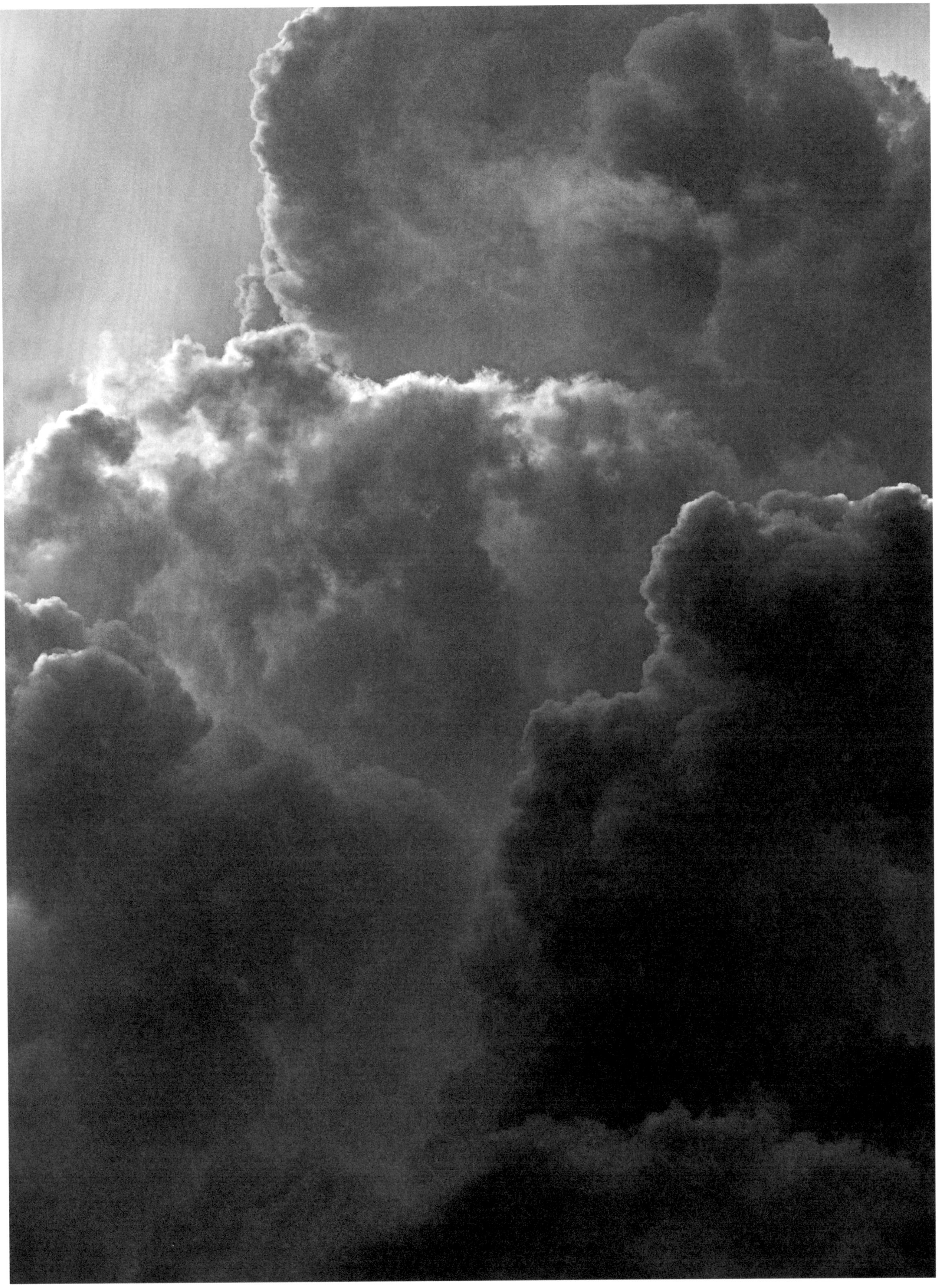

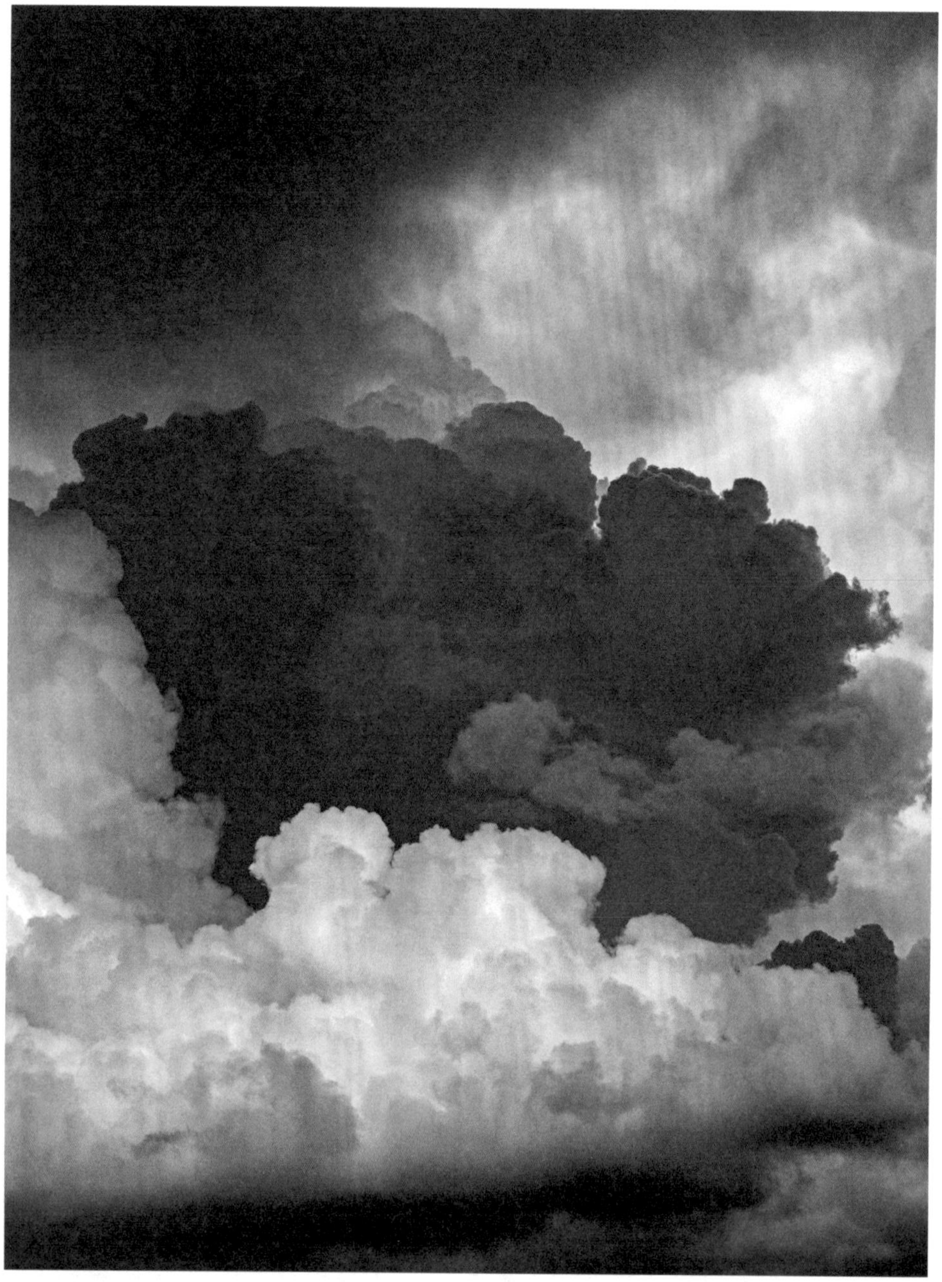

The seasons are a primary gateway connecting the human world with the ongoing revelation of creation, renewal, growth, decay, and death that underpins the cyclical nature of the more-than-human world. Each season, regardless of how it manifests and expresses itself in a specific place, offers a myriad of experiences that can deepen the ties of kinship and reciprocity between the human and the more-than-human, while also creating wonder, awe, fear, and, ultimately, a reverence for the living world.

From the very beginning of the human story, we depended on the seasons for the many life-giving forces that sustained us, be that rain, sun, warmth, growth, or food. Whether we gathered, hunted, or farmed, our ability to nourish ourselves was tied to their rhythms. Generation after generation, the seasons shaped our diverse cultures and spiritual traditions, and our many rituals and ceremonies honored the cyclical nature of creation. Just as each season has unique ways of expressing the nature of a place, each place—and the cultures that emerged from it—had unique ways of enacting these expressions of kinship. These offerings and ways of paying homage were expressions of reverence, helping to align us with many of the rhythms and patterns present within the living Earth.

The modern world, with its mechanization, systemization, and technological prowess has dampened our ability to live attuned to the seasons. Today, most of us live a life insulated—literally and figuratively—from the subtleties and nuances of the cyclical nature of the seasons. The many ceremonies and rituals that deepened our ties of kinship and reverence have mostly become hollow, if celebrated at all. We have imposed a simplified version of the Northern Hemisphere's seasons—Spring,

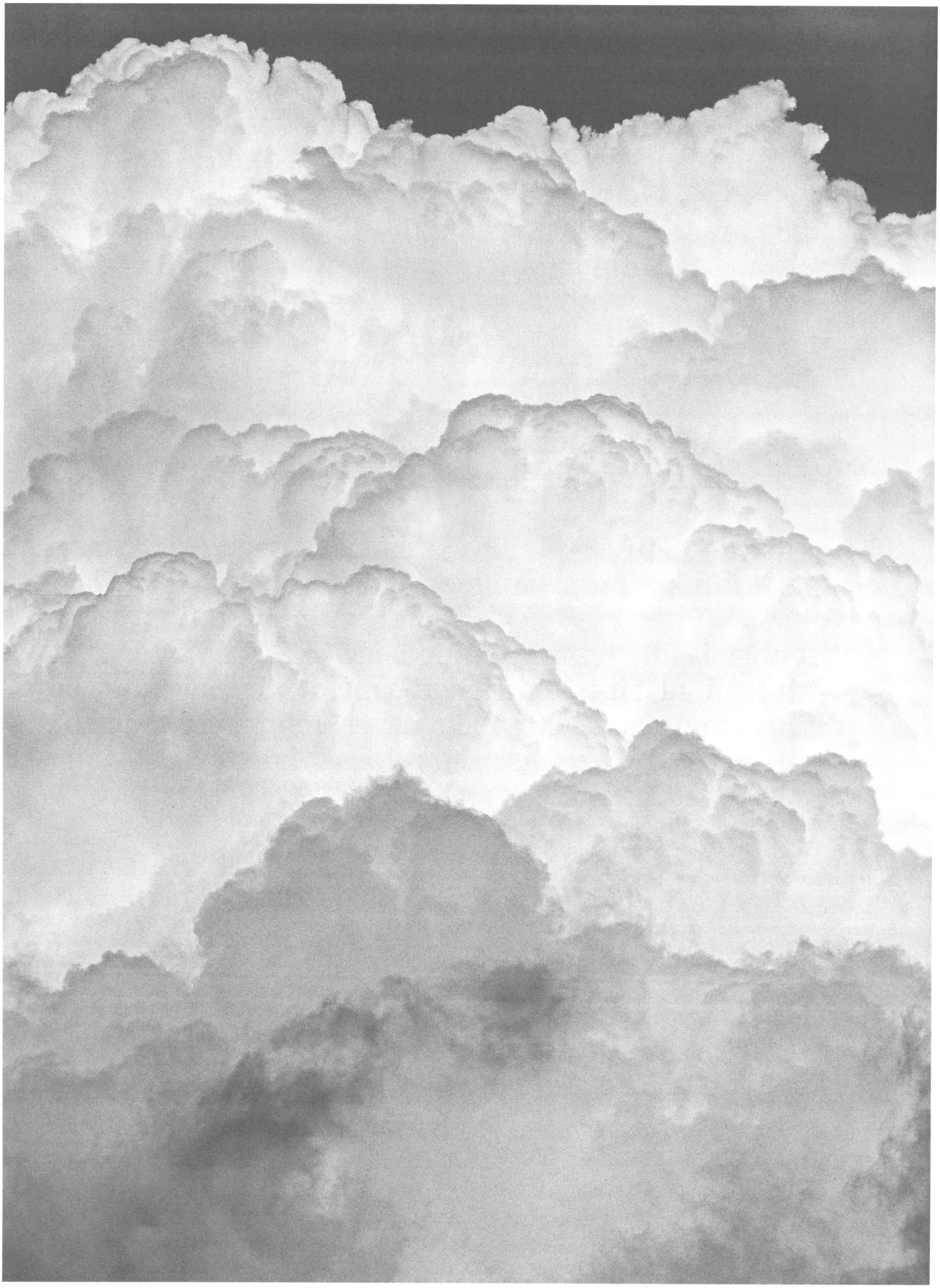

Summer, Autumn, and Winter—with rigid start and end dates, on the rest of the world, adding to the legacy of colonization. Like our relationship with Time, we think of the seasons as something we can control, evident in the draining of our ancient aquifers, the hum of our air conditioners, and the availability of "seasonal fruit" year-round. And amid this reality, sustainability circles, environmental movements, and the farm-to-table food world speak of a return to the seasonal. But what does that even mean anymore? Is it simply replicating the watered-down version of the seasonal celebrations that have survived? And in a world where the birds who once marked the beginning of Spring are silent, where Summers are so hot crops wither and die, where the trees who have shed their leaves in the same land for millennia come Autumn are moving north, where a land of snow has none in Winter, what even *is* a season?

Change is afoot, and yet amid this change the seasons still turn, albeit to a different tune. And despite our best efforts to ignore them, the gateway to kinship they offer still beckons. The seasons, in their unpredictability, in their state of flux, and in their grief are calling to us to pay attention; to again return to a space of receptivity and connection and reverence for the cycles of life they embody. If we hear their call and turn our gaze again towards them, how should we respond? How do we return to an ancient understanding of the nature of seasonality, of place, and of cycles? How do we bear witness to the death that all seasons, not just Winter, now bring? What forms of celebration from the past do we keep? How do we free ourselves from the shackles of imposed seasons that were never tied to place and no longer reflect the world we live in? How should we celebrate cycles and seasons and life in a dying world? What must evolve and change and how?

These are the questions we asked our contributors to consider for this year's edition, offering them space to reflect on our evolving relationship with the seasons through the themes of requiem, invitation, and celebration. And while these themes are presented here as chapters, they unsurprisingly overlap, revealing paradoxes, contradictions, and the complexity of the times we are in. And yet in the midst of this I find myself in a state of awe, for regardless of the great loss that the annual turn of the seasons reveals, the Earth in all Her ever-giving abundance and grace is constantly inviting us to return to Her. This if nothing else is cause for celebration.

Emmanuel Vaughan-Lee
Executive Editor

An unseasonably warm day in February.

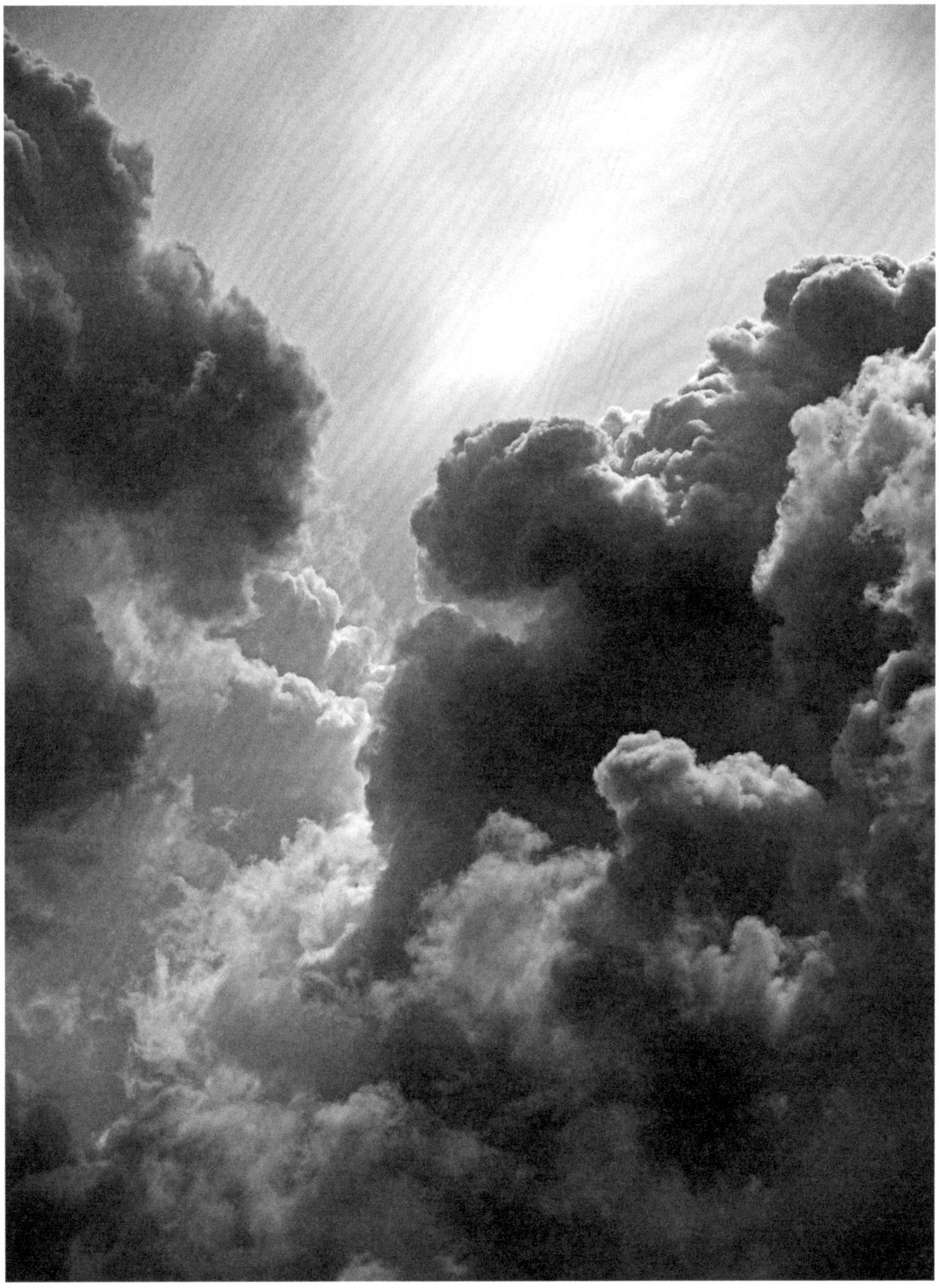

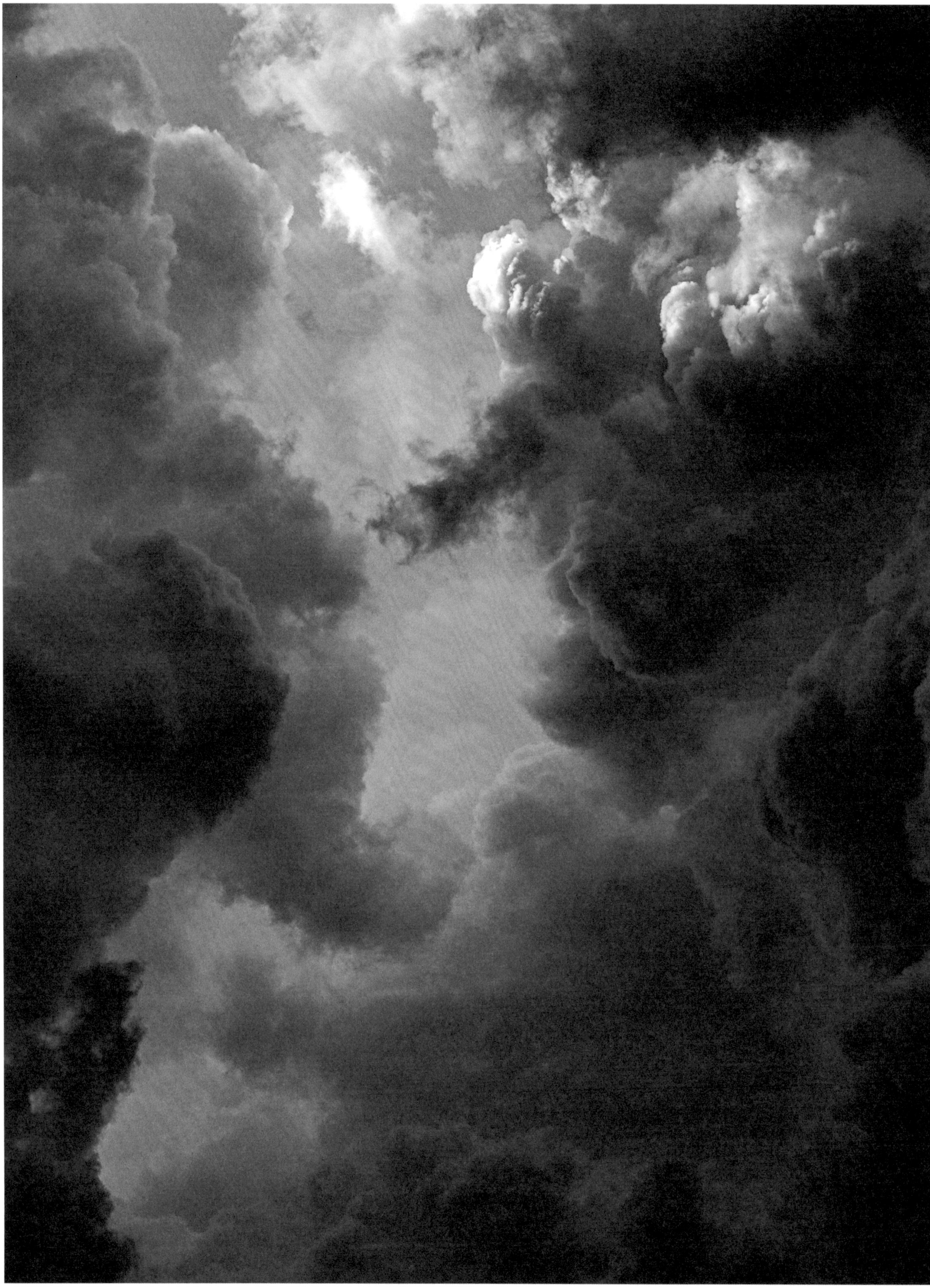

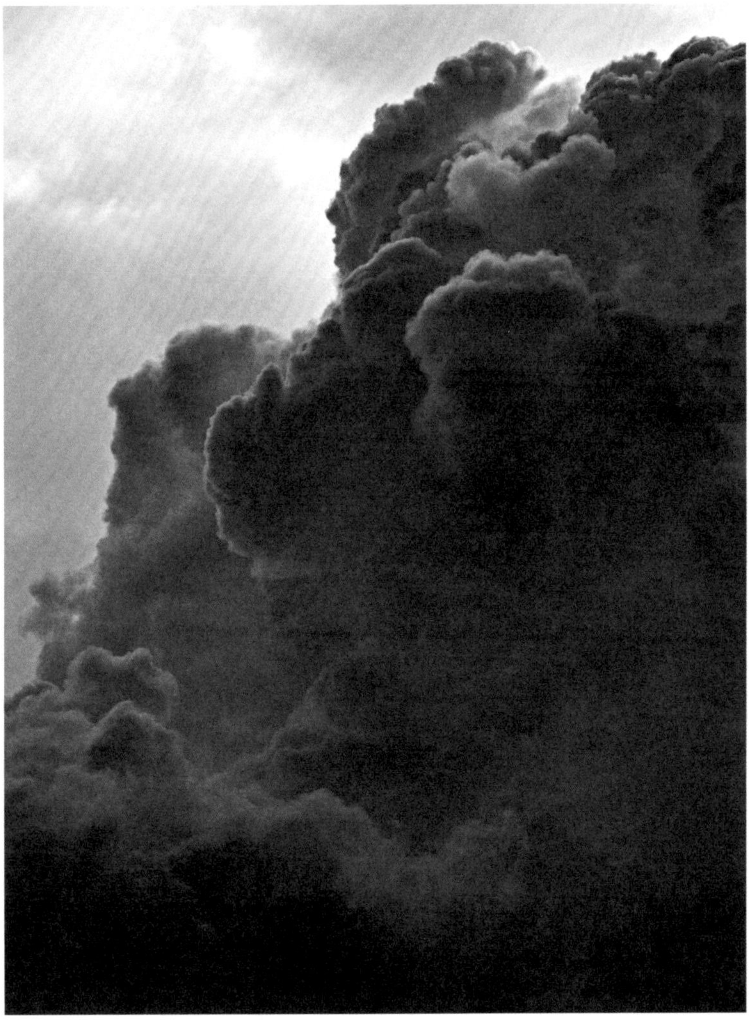

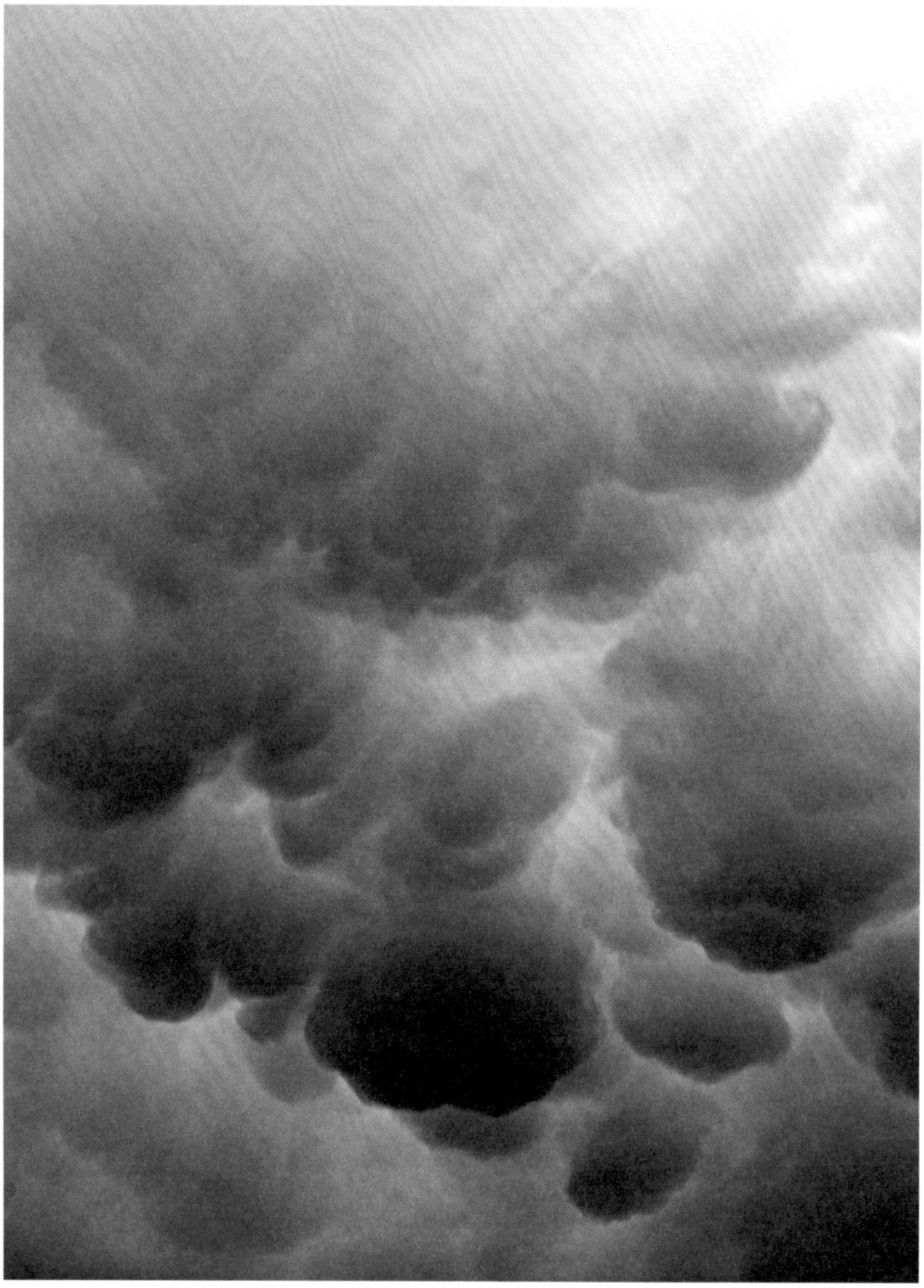

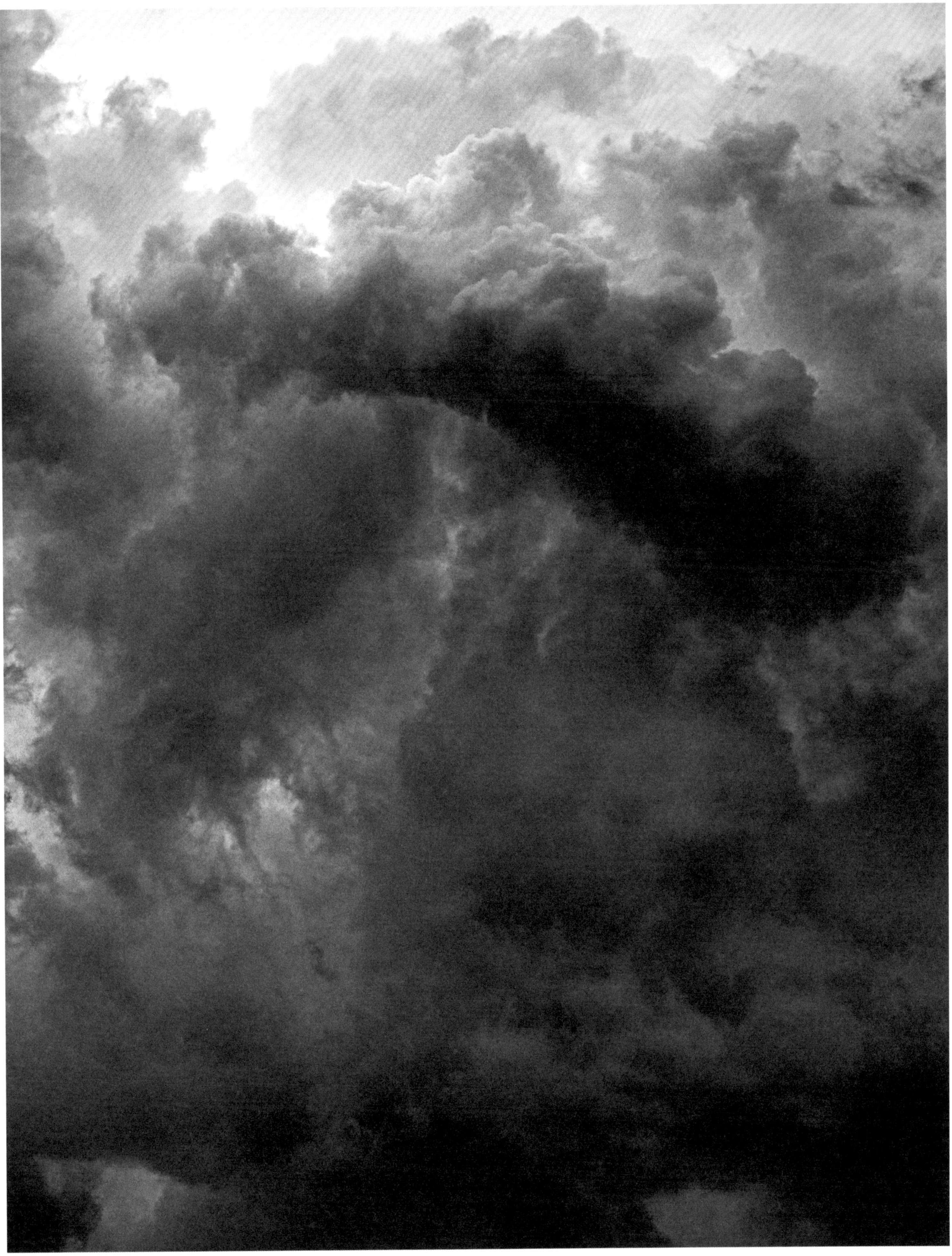

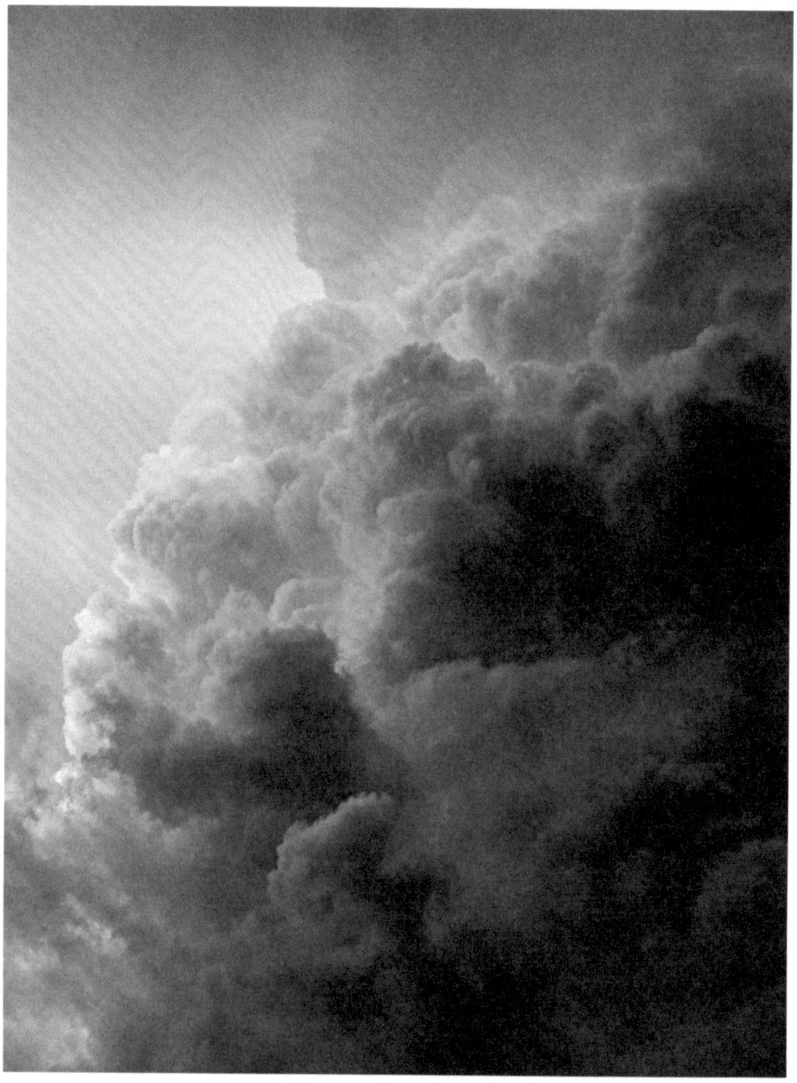

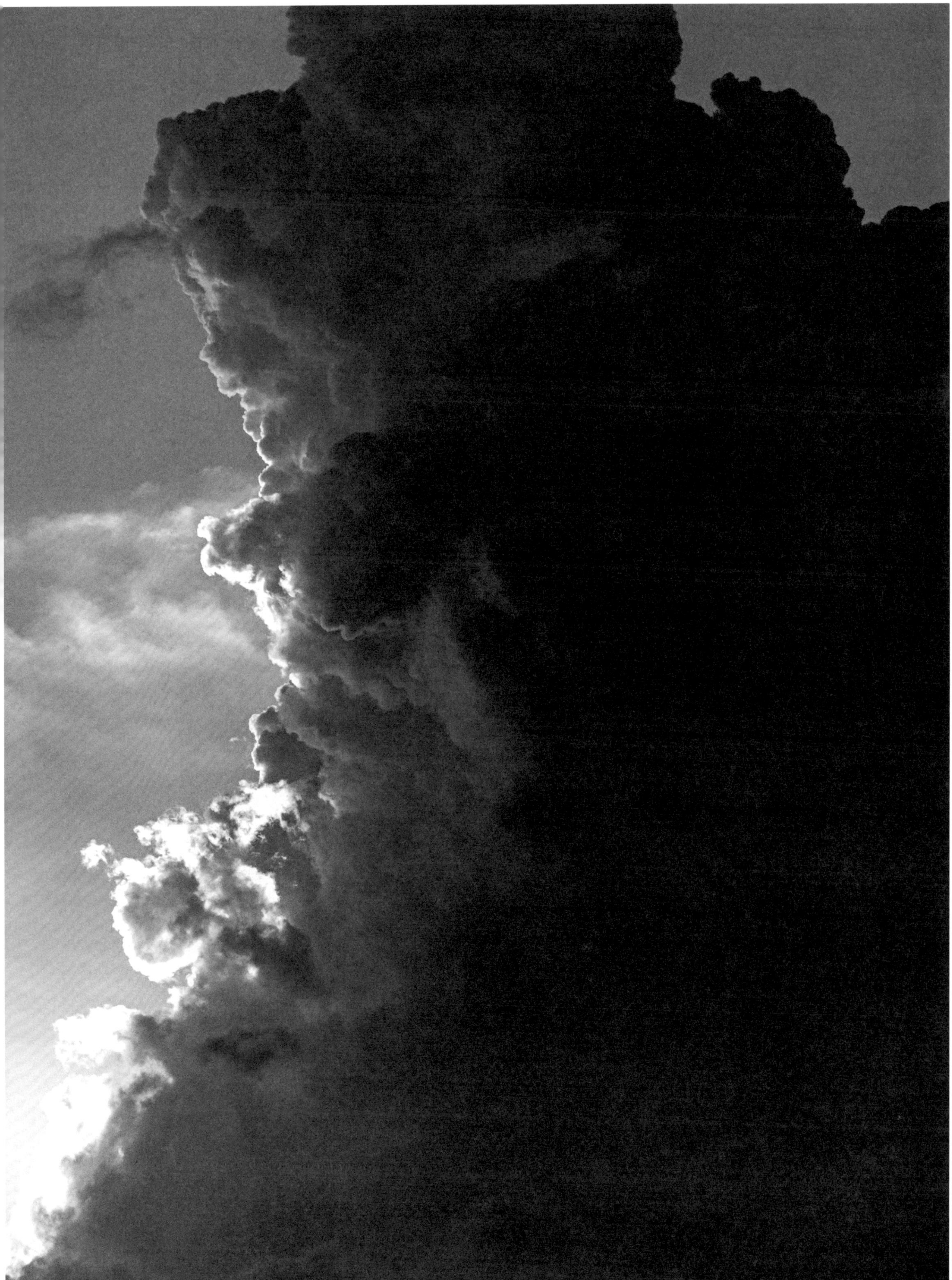

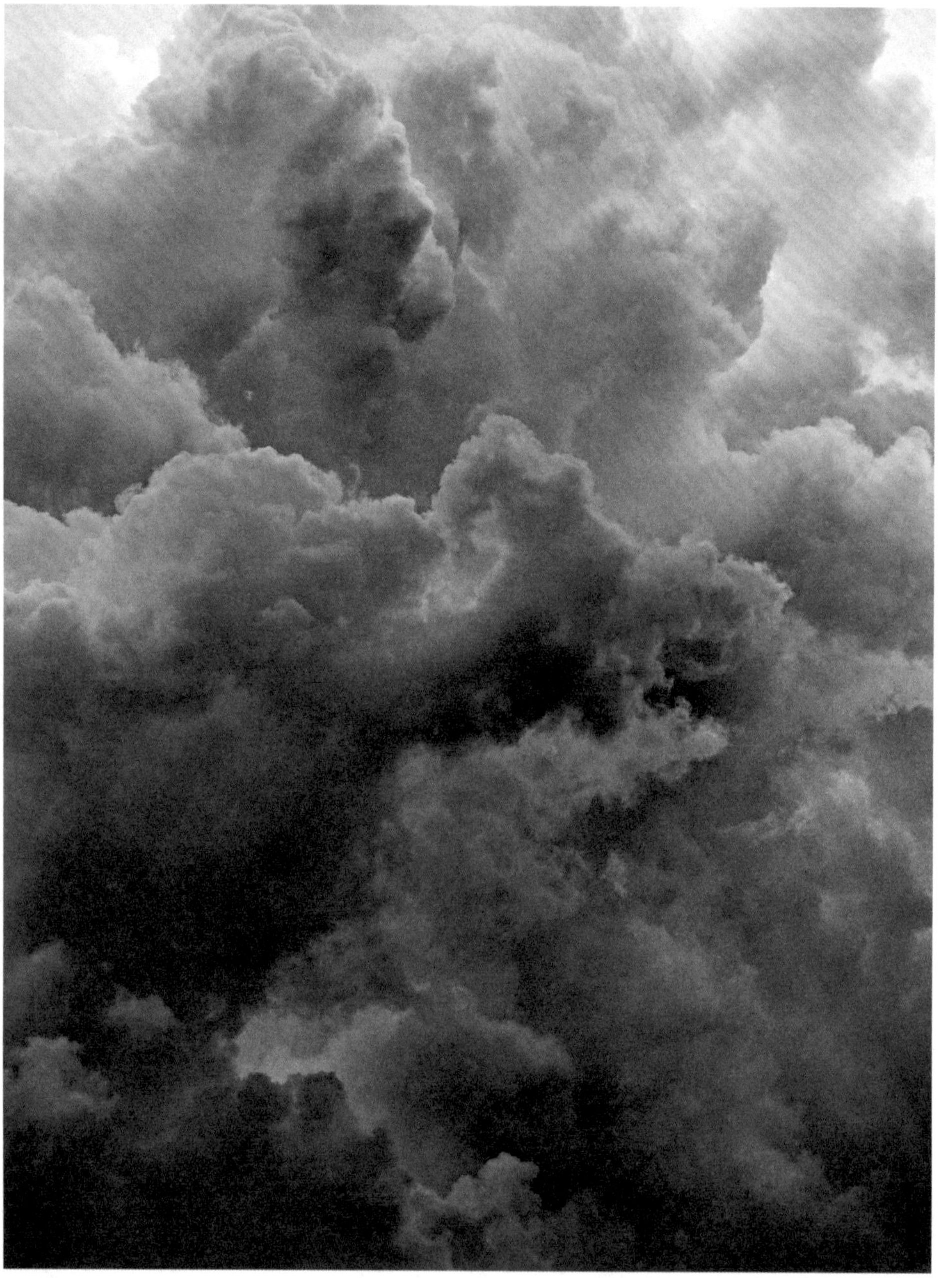

Photos by Bear Guerra

Requiem

Chapter 1

EARTH STORM AN ENDING I CAN ALMOST FEEL

LONGEST NIGHT . . .
TASMANIAN TIGERS PACE
THE UNDERWORLD

FIRESTORM
THE REDWOOD COFFIN
SAFE UNDERGROUND

CHARRED INTO BARK A GAZE OF FIRE

BLOODWOOD MOON
A STARVING DINGO PACES
THE RAIN SHADOW

BONEYARD
THE DRY RIVERBED
CRACKED OPEN

GHOST RAINBOW
SOMETHING WRITTEN
WITH FADED LIES

RISING FLOODWATER
HOUSE LIGHTS DIM AND FADE
ONE BY ONE

BROKEN STARFISH
WAVES POUND THE BEACH
WHILE CHILDREN SLEEP

MEMORIAL SERVICE
THE CHANT OF FOREST RAVENS
UNBORN AND UNDYING

1 Ron C. Moss, *Broken Starfish* (Launceston, Tasmania: Walleah Press, 2019).
2 Moss, *Cloud Hands* (Walleah Press, 2021). First published in *Presence* 67, July 2020.
3 Moss, *The Bone Carver* (Ormskirk, UK: Snapshot Press, 2014). First published in *Shiki Monthly Kukai*, August 2009.
4 Moss, *Cloud Hands*.
5 Moss, *Broken Starfish*. First published in Hedgerow 144, 2017.

Susan Murphy Roshi

ALIVE IN THE SKIN OF A RIVER'S FLOW

"Haiku cannot budge from its seat at home on the Earth, even when conditions grow inhospitable, and the mood of time turns dark and sorrowful."

"alive in the skin of a river's flow"
Ron C. Moss (1)

THE HAIKU FORM, long after having come to the West from Japan, continues to reflect and refract its Zen-inflected origins. Now, its radically open form of responding to the world must encounter the ravages of planetary climate crisis. How will it meet this inhospitable reality?

That original Japanese poetic impulse moves freely through the world in a natural sense of relaxed emptiness, inhabiting impermanence without opinion or resistance, the poet disappearing into what is being observed. Haiku deliver a sentient world undivided from the experience of it, the sense of self lying low. If an "I" should break the surface, it's in wryly self-aware and low-key form—firmly ordinary and decidedly *un*-self-important.

Living so close to just what is happening means opinions about it need not apply; instead, a plain kind of wonder—an engaged not-knowing—can come into play.

Any fully inhabited moment is timeless, lived close to the eternal. And yet—to tell it in haiku is to locate its resonance in a particular time and place, giving the reader access to something that lights up the wholeness of the world, through one of its infinite brief dreams. "Dream," as in merged in sufficient measure with the mysterious core of everyday reality.

Experience arises *in* time and place, but also *as* time and place conjoining with mind. Thus, haiku have traditionally let in and relied upon the emotional "color" a seasonal reference (*kigo*) provides. While these may be the universals of summer, autumn, winter, spring, kigo may equally spring from the limitless pool of utterly particular *local* seasonal markers (such as summer cuckoo, ripening persimmon, deafening cicadas, first droning mosquito, migrating humpbacks . . . and so on, ad infinitum).

In a plainly precarious world in which nothing is certain, we confide our hearts to the shared agreement of the predictable enough seasonal round, and rest in what feels

"Born of the tilt of a sacred planet, the seasons provide what has long been welcomed as Earth's sacred rhythm, celebrated in rituals that echo the cycle of mortal life—but in the mode of eternal renewal."

1 Moss, *Cloud Hands* (Launceston, Tasmania: Walleah Press, 2021). First published in *Presence* 67, July 2020.
2 Haiku by Issa, Bashō, and Buson, as well as passages from "Learn from the Pine," by Bashō, quoted from *The Essential Haiku: Versions of Bashō, Buson, and Issa*, trans. Robert Hass (New York: The Ecco Press, 1994). Italics are mine.

*un*changing within the eternal flux. Born of the tilt of a sacred planet, the seasons provide what has long been welcomed as Earth's sacred rhythm, celebrated in rituals that echo the cycle of mortal life—but in the mode of eternal renewal. Something in us dares trust in the timeless quality of the seasons as a relatively stable reference point of accord with ceaseless change, allowing a feeling of timelessness to surface in the fleeting moments of mortal life.

The blessed round of the seasons, that always seemed predictable *enough* . . .

Haiku poets intuit their way to this poise of the eternal within the momentary by relying on just what is happening as the home place within it. Even if offered with poignancy or wry resignation, haiku bend always towards evident reality, and find subject arising exactly on the ever-creative edge of uncertainty itself.

Meanwhile, along with the seasonal kigo, haiku embrace the contingency of endlessly fluctuating *weather*, letting it also color the immediate moment and exacting circumstance so keenly noticed. Sometimes with the gusto of fourteenth-century Zen master Daito Kokushi, for example:

No umbrella?
I'll use the rain as my raincoat!
Daito Kokushi

Write the word "Eternity" in sand and the eternal waves themselves will duly wash it away for you. Again and again, an act of unshielded *noticing* reconsecrates the moment or thing with an exacting acceptance of what is fleeting and ever-changing, and yet—*in* that sheer acceptance—finding it to be wet through to the skin with eternity.

Unqualified acceptance is what dissolves the one who keenly notices into the thing itself to the point of sharing one skin with it; and the one who hears or reads the haiku—they come through into that one skin, too. When you feel that slight shift or lift of heart and mind that "comes in" with the edge of discovery in the poem, then poet, reader, and some unrepeatable detail of the timeless universe all arrive together.

It works like that. And what appears in that intimately attentive space of haiku keeps opening, free of interpretation. The relief! Each thing allowed to be just what is, minus all opinions about it.

"The bones of haiku
are plainness and oddness"
Bashō

THIS QUALITY of already yielding to "just what is" appears directly or by implication, even when the poet's heart is fiercely protesting. Acceptance folds into the pain. Witness the great haiku master, Issa, for example, marking the tragic loss of his dearly beloved two-year-old daughter:

The world of dew
is the world of dew.
And yet, and *yet*—
Issa (2)

Here is a traditionally Buddhist consent to the unbending truth of impermanence, offered as inseparable from a father's resounding cry of protest . . . This is not resignation, but refusal to diminish what it is to be alive in the skin of an agonized flood of grief.

Issa also leaves in the air an unvoiced question about this mysterious life, that closes nothing off while leaning into the eternal—a rare accomplishment that characterizes the very best haiku. "When did anyone ever lose by crying out?" it seems to wonder. With this contemplation at its heart, Issa's "And yet!" opens to embrace all humanity.

Every fleeting moment in this way is *always* "seasonal" in character—round, and yet never repeating, lost to time, and yet ever-returning—reconsecrating the eternal flux that renders each thing unquestionably of value.

Robert Hass's fine translations of the three great early Japanese masters of haiku, Bashō, Buson, and Issa, reveal how widely this tiny incisive form can move freely in the world of experience—noticing, feeling, enjoying, and forbearing—while remaining uncoercive and light of touch in a generous range of tonal moods.

The poet can reach with curiosity right through transience, contingency, and suffering to register the poignant and timeless quality of these things—and land in fully-human fellow-feeling for a relative stranger, as for example in Bashō's famous . . .

Deep autumn—
my neighbor,
how does he live, I wonder?

Bashō

Tenderness like this, tinted with loneliness, can also be ruefully aware of how easily attachment makes fools of us. Bashō unearths in himself the endearing absurdity of human beings when memory and nostalgia for something we hold dear removes us from it even when we're *swimming* in it . . .

Even in Kyoto—
hearing the cuckoo's cry—
I long for Kyoto.

Bashō

Or . . .

First day of spring—
I keep thinking about
the end of autumn.

Bashō

Haiku can also draw us with its keen precision right to the strangeness of reality hiding in plain sight—as in Buson's glimpse of a waiting horse, tethered in snow. No feet in the stirrups. For now, just the formlessness of snow, riding the world . . . No need to point up any overtones of emptiness in those snow-filled stirrups, which so delicately also draw in the ghostly presence of the human who tethered that horse in freezing conditions . . .

Tethered horse;
snow
in both stirrups.

Buson

Or the poet can enter in person to play along with what is, and do so with the relaxed and smiling gaze of Issa, so wonderfully shorn of *attitude* while so freely admitting to human failing in his companionable willingness not to bother the spiders of the house . . .

Don't worry, spiders,
I keep house
casually.

Issa

In all three tonal modes, feel for the way that *no*-time brings forth this one-off intersection of time, place, things, and human mind in the brief completeness of a moment.

And humor is never out of place in tempering the space a haiku opens to let reality look back at our human ridiculousness. As when Ron Moss, ever so delicately, lets the dance of a territorial crow, attempting to jostle its own reflection, glance off also in our own direction . . .

asphalt shimmer
a crow stares down
the hubcap

Ron C. Moss (3)

But now, a climate that has been reliable enough for our flourishing is falling into chaos, threatening even the timeless procession of the seasons themselves to the point that they are beginning to signal inescapable impermanence—Issa's "The world of dew," that is born in the morning and has vanished by the afternoon. *And yet*, like Issa, we must let such indigestible change into our hearts to meet directly with the protest of *impossible!* That's where the *truth* of suffering can render us real and find us present.

While seasonal signals waver and blur from cultural alignment, other markers of the mood of time in haiku remain changeless: the diurnal round of sunrise and sunset rolls on, unperturbed; the equinoxes and solstices continue, impartially, to temper the length of days and nights; and the moon sails serenely through its cycles, indifferent to the tidal surges invading cities, as humans scramble for some foothold in the waters of rapid change.

Plainly, the florid evidence of unseasonal extremes will not be denied entry to a venerable poetic form born in an earlier moment so culturally aligned with the seasons. The ruptured state of the seasons is simply too apparent and present to slip past haiku's focused act of *noticing*.

And so, *climate* now breaks into haiku for the first time, disrupting the *saijiki*—the traditional compendia of hundreds of settled and easily recognized forms of kigo in haiku—and potentially wreaking havoc on the poetic form and its uniquely seasonal "feel" of time, as the seasons turn more feral.

3 Moss, *The Bone Carver* (Ormskirk, UK: Snapshot Press, 2014).

The Australian summer, starting ever earlier in spring, is losing its old friendly name to "the fire season." "Stalled highs" cause deadly "heat domes" and stagnated "deep freezes." "Stalled monsoons" become catastrophic flooding impossible to mitigate, as "rain rivers" drown actual rivers. "Pyrocumulonimbus" bursts its way into the naming of clouds, as the smoke of "megafires" rises into the stratosphere, generating ferocious fire-created wind and lightning, and even spattering futile drops of rain.

Such words have not yet broken into haiku as uncouth new kigo to draw us into the uncomfortable new moods of time, but, if you're even half alive, the facts of their impact can't be kept out. And given how intimately embedded and embodied are haiku in the physical fact of here and now, could it be that to bear witness to the ferocity of the changes becomes a kind of kigo in reverse—locating us keenly in the ongoing *shattering* of the seasonal round?

For haiku cannot budge from its seat at home on the Earth, even when conditions grow inhospitable, and the mood of time turns dark and sorrowful.

> "In this moment, is it still possible to face the gathering darkness, and say to the physical Earth, and to all its creatures, including ourselves, fiercely and without embarrassment, I love you, and to embrace fearlessly the burning world?"
>
> —*Barry Lopez,* "Love in a Time of Terror"

THE LOVE AT LARGE in haiku is too natural, implicit, and bone-deep to surface in sentimentality; and so intimately felt that it can't separate feeling *with* the Earth from feeling *about* it.

old horses
days of endless rain
in their eyes

Ron C. Moss (4)

Satish Kumar loosens the strictures and solipsism of *I think, therefore I am,* reverses the flow, and delivers us back home into the mutual relationship that sources haiku, with *You are, therefore I am*. Self and other on a path of finding each other in one skin. A fierce-enough love for the Earth starts in this confirmed mutuality.

To fiercely embrace a burning world . . . Is it becoming the job of twenty-first-century haiku to fiercely, and without embarrassment, follow closely with the sacred seasonal procession as it tilts, collides with, and collapses into the heated chaos of "the weather"? To mourn the derangement of the seasons, yes—but with the spirit of Issa's powerful cry of love, *And yet!*, that bows to ceaseless change and loss exactly while not shying from the grief it generates. Instead, by opening to both as inseparable, we find what can be invited into steady realization, and even riskily befriended as the wild exacting form taken by the life of the Earth in this moment. The sense of invitation lies in our willingness to bear with and to follow nature while not flinching from what is human—one body of not-knowing openness. All of which can open the way to celebrate at least the ability and necessity of remaining humanly alive in the skin of even the sharpest of moments.

For as we've seen, while it will not turn away, haiku firmly refuses to presume to *know*. Then, even when admitting in full the pain of bearing witness, a steady embrace of what is carries the day. This is the generous, capacious not-knowing found always at play in Bashō:

It's not like anything
they compare it to—
the summer moon.

Bashō

While the new and ever-shifting categories of weather now stalking our lives will likely prove too unstable to ever form established haiku kigo, their impact will always register in haiku, as it so intimately partners with the natural world, to which, despite our efforts and our doubts, we fully belong.

It's this accepting and participatory love for the physical Earth that makes natural the way haiku lives into what is happening, directing attention to some radiant fact while closely following it, never getting in front of it with "knowing." Just like the wind that doesn't know what month it's in, even as it may be showering sparks of fire on unhatched eggs in a far too-early-warm spring that has lost its moorings in time.

"Haiku is . . . [a] deep breath of life"
Santoka Taneda (5)

SOMEONE CALLED NATURE *the hole in the heart* of our human world, diagnosing the source of an elemental sadness and loneliness in a species so insistently standing apart from the entirety of life. Bashō's advice to haiku poets in his short treatise "Learn from the Pine" is utterly simple and unfussy: "Follow nature and return to nature." In explaining this strong poetic spirit he calls *fūrabo*, he advises us to "become a friend with things of the seasons . . . [For] those who do not see the flower are no different from barbarians, and those who do not imagine the moon are akin to beasts."

Instead, "Make the universe your companion," he urges. Then the homely loneliness carried by the Japanese feeling called *sabi* finds its way with ease into haiku, lightly and willingly borne because it is accompanied—by each thing so closely followed.

"Followed" as in moving in accord with what is as it flows, without manipulating it. At home in doing so. Celebrating the constancy of change that will also take away our very lives in time, Bashō says, "Cherry blossoms whirl, leaves fall, and the wind flits them both along the ground. We cannot arrest with our eyes or ears what lies in such things. *Were we to gain mastery over them, we would find that the life of each thing had vanished without a trace"* (my italics).

Haiku finds it natural to disappear into intimate companionship with the world.

close to the waterfall the sound
I become lost in

Ron C. Moss (6)

Even in the throes of climate stress, the relaxed gaze that lets us move with what is happening can be found, confident at least in a depth of belonging. With little or no "I" in front of things, a haiku becomes an open-pored moment of simply moving *with* . . .

walking with mountains our
voices in the stones

Ron C. Moss (7)

Not-knowing mind opens a true conversation with the Earth. Then the stones can find our voice, and our songs can find the Earth. In Australian terms, it's Country—the Dreaming, moving and thinking *along with* the place where you are. This is the intimacy and artistry of not-knowing mind—leaving no finger-marks on every glistening fact and knowing not the slightest wish to do so.

And always, less is so much more. "Is there any good in saying everything?" Bashō wonders, plainly answering his own question.

The haiku form carves words away as close as you can get to their natural vanishing point, and in unfussy language, close enough to ordinary speech that it lets us draw close. Then a haiku is not a glimpse or image of the universe—just the universe, plain and immediate, inhabiting the poet, the reader, the stone wet with rain by the side of the path, the autumn moon, the tremor in a hand, a leaf turning bright dark bright dark as it twirls to the ground . . .

In this way haiku are a kind of open dreaming—mind and reality homing in on each other enough to touch something of the mysterious core of reality in what is here in plain sight . . . and then just following it by heart.

ocean of stars
the ancient humpback
going home

Ron C. Moss (8)

4 Moss, *Broken Starfish* (Launceston, Tasmania: Walleah Press, 2019). First published in *The Heron's Nest*, December 2014.
5 *Mountain Tasting: Haiku and Journals of Santoka Taneda*, trans. John Stevens (Buffalo, NY: White Pine Press, 2009).
6 Moss, *Broken Starfish*. First published in *The Heron's Nest*, June 2013.
7 Moss, *Broken Starfish*. First published in *Presence* 42, June 2018.
8 Moss, *Broken Starfish*. First published in *The Heron's Nest*, June 2018.

CMarie Fuhrman
ECHOIC MEMORY

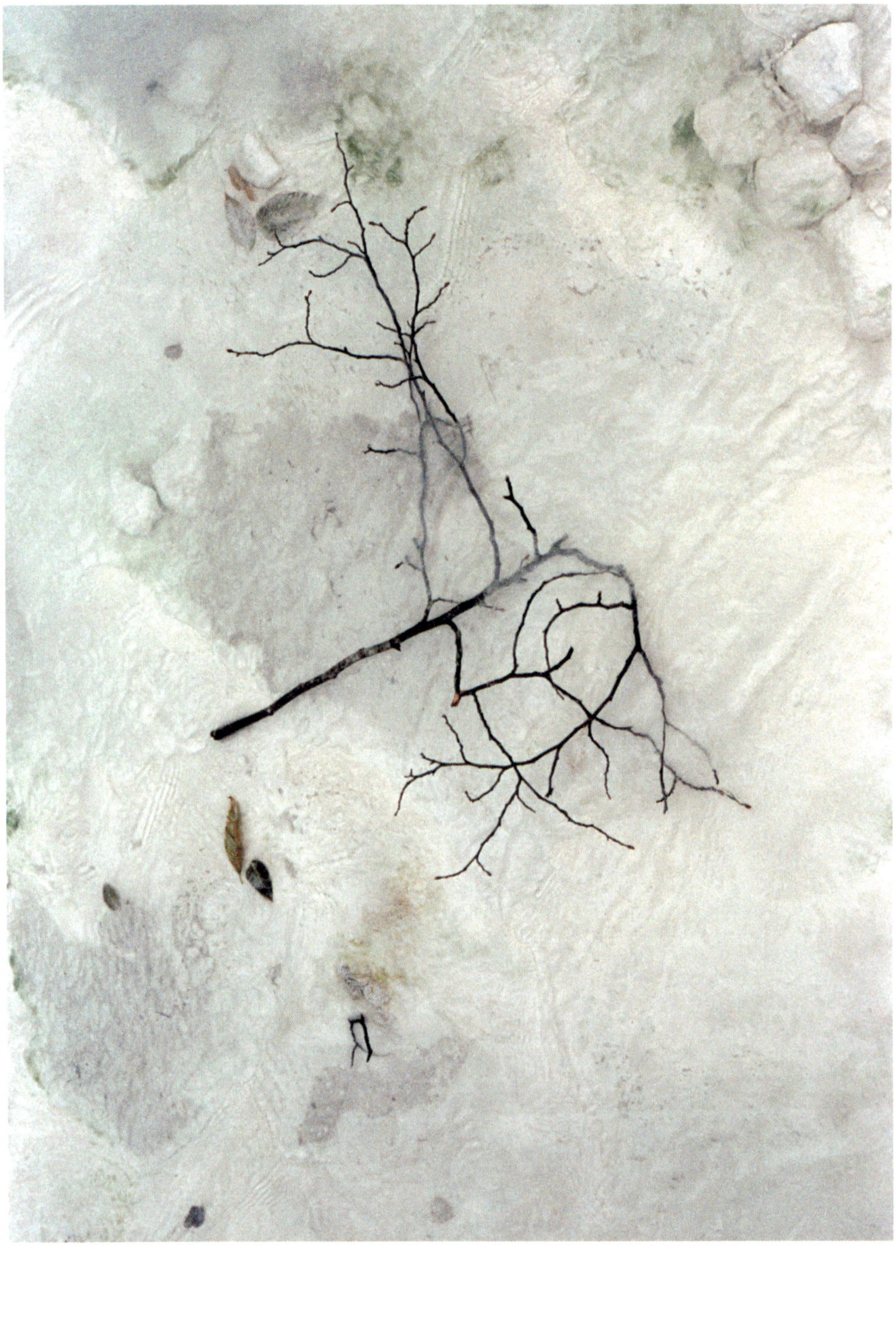

FIG. 1 Photo by Luca Werner (P. 46)

It was a rainy night, but not where we lay. We were curled on the ground in the Frank Church Wilderness. Our tent flaps were open because the rain was on the ridgelines south of us, but those ridgelines filled the frame of the open doors of our tent and so we lay in the dark, wide-eyed and more alive than we would normally be at night, or at all. Our old dog Cisco was between us, my partner and me. Our older dog, Carhartt, was fresh in her grave and I still held dents in my flesh from where I lay on the earth, two nights in a row, my ear to the ground, listening for a heartbeat or her breathing, not because I thought she was living, only because I wanted to know she was of the ground.

I am a person of ground. This is not to say grounded, but of earth, attached to the earth. I cannot even jump far from it. It is as if an invisible tether holds me close, closer to the earth. I am unwinged. I do not fly. I root. So it was, rooted on the ground, the ground of Tukudeka, of Sheepeater, of Nimiipuu and Shoshone-Bannock, of people who, too, knew ground, but also sky, that I stared at the place where ground met sky, the ridgeline, where lightning tapped and rain fell. The thunder was distant. Like a memory, or like the past calling. And the toes of the lightning reminded me of dancing. Of toes touching earth to the drum beat. And though my father's grandfather was born of thousands of years of this continent, so far as anyone knows, of people who knew a desert earth, it was land that connected us, this land, this island floating on a floating island in a sky that is a river that held the bodies of the dancers whose legs of lightning tapped the earth.

This is to say it was not a clear night and it was not the stars we sought. It was not even what could be seen that brought us here and my eyes blinked toward that horizon, grasping as they could toward the beauty of darkness inflected with shafts of dance, the same electricity we hold in our hearts, the light held behind my eyes, which finally closed, and where I fell was not so much into sleep as into a deeper understanding, as if my body grew roots, found mycelium and its memory, and other memories, which is where I believe memory goes, that opposite place from wishes and hopes and prayers. And perhaps that is why the latter is less reliable, because we can never lay our head on the wings of such unseeable things.

We had come to this high mountain meadow, this liminal place between alpine and not, to listen. To re-member. We are not content with borrowed starlight. We seek the illumination of our own experiences, the radiance of the first stories.

There, I recall another night, much like this one, and we were on the edge of Twin Lakes. We called the hike to get there *walking the High Lonely*, for there was only a ghost forest of Whitebark Pine. We walked a ridge that looked down into alpine lakes. There was silence until we reached the place where the trail dipped back into the forest. Caleb, my partner, stopped, unshouldered his pack and cupped his hands around his mouth. He was facing the trees, not a simple copse of them, but acres. And not simply a few, but thousands. Trees as far as we could see and behind us still the skeletons of trees. The white bark of the trees that fed Grizzly and *ispu'kux*, the name before the name Clark's Nutcracker, attributed to a feckless explorer whose name is everywhere, and about whom I care to know less and less, as if forgetting that abruptive history could make the one my partner was calling forth more present, as if time were layers we could unearth and in doing so return to. His cupped hands around his mouth, he drew a deep breath in and howled. We stood silent and listened, waiting, it seemed for the trees to do something. To look our way perhaps or maybe to grant us entry into a world that they protected beneath their understory. Perhaps, it was all understory. And we waited.

He howled again. It was midday so perhaps that explains the silence. Then again, perhaps it was because the past was not so easily uncovered and the present put a bounty on those that would howl back. I asked to try and Caleb nodded knowing that my attempts in the past had always sounded more like coyote or dog or someone who wanted to summon coyote or dog or summon coyote within them. There is a sound only we can make. Mine does not mimic well the Wolf. But I tried. I cupped my mouth, I drew the O, and what followed was more plea than howl. The trees, again, did nothing. But we waited, just in case pollen might rise. In case something like song would arise. Just in case we stirred memory.

We made our camp that night beside Twin Lakes.

We slept with our heads on the ground. I listened. It was quiet that night but weeks

"A day will come when we have flooded the earth with too much light of our making and we will only be able to see the stars we make."

later I heard the words to the story of the land where we had lain. The silence of that trail was a century old. Nearly to the date of our visit the last of the Tukudeka were captured, though the history writers used the word "surrender" to tell the end of a month's long plight of a handful of people who survived in the High Lonely, in the places where only Bighorn and seraphim succeeded. In the land of Whitebark, now gone ghost, too, the Tukudeka had, along or near the same trail we walked and gallantly howled from, slit the throats of their beloved dogs to silence them so the soldiers might not find them. They hung them along the trail, letting their pursuers know how far they would go to remain free, to be left unseen, but no matter. They were captured and chained together in heavy irons. Perhaps they were silent, as fate sometimes dictates in its arrival. Perhaps they whispered their histories into the earth. Words for earth and sky and enemy and end. Words for Wolf. Perhaps rather than lifting their eyes to a sky they only knew by sight they turned instead to an earth they knew by touch and emptied themselves of prayer. I might have heard this that night, had I known what to listen for, but the power of colonization lies in its insistence on recording story in a language only it can understand. What voice was left to howl the story of the Tukudeka did not and does not belong to colonizers.

The next morning when we woke, we walked around the shoreline and found bullet casings and bits of tack and one steel cigarette holder. As clouds sometimes cover the sky, history sometimes covers itself. I wondered what I might find if I scraped the earth until it bled. But this earth should not be disturbed. My elders have said that languages of the First People are sleeping. As we walked away, we walked into the pawprints of Wolves. Our dogs sniffed deep at their leavings and piss. What memory lit up the night of their minds' sky? We were careful as we placed our feet, walking to the side so as not to disturb what belonged. Leaving the trail to the silent Wolves. If they thought us pursuant, who might they kill for silence? Who might they sacrifice to show their determination to be free? To simply be?

And what about the Salmon? A single spawned-out carcass lay on the streambank alongside the trail we walked before coming to the meadow where we lay now with tent flaps open. A single spawned-out carcass. Single carcass. The run, I am told, was once so many as to keep those streamside awake at night. Imagine! Waking in the dark to the sound of Salmon. Just to peer into the water of late summer evening and see those flashes of silver, unbelievably large bodies who gave their lives to return home. I have often slept by streams and rivers and wondered what passed in the night when the earth turned her back on the sun. What had I missed that moved so close, what lives bisected my dreams, and what else had my feeble ears failed to translate? A single Salmon makes no sound. No, Salmon are even quieter.

I am a person of the earth, I carry it beneath my fingernails like ten black and waning moons. I have left my closest companions under a blanket of soil and I have buried dreams in cryptobiotic crust. My name, the one my parents gave me, means Bringer of Light. Means Star of the Sea. It carries connotations of celestial beauty and illumination. It says nothing of these roots I have formed, of my downward gaze. Of when I was a young girl and my father lay beside me on the grass of my childhood home and pointed to the stars. "That one," he said, pointing north, for it was summer, "is the North Star. Do you see how bright it is?" Stars all looked like stars to me, but I was a daughter seeking to please so I squinted hard in search for it and said, "Yes, I see," though honestly, I am not sure that I did. But he traced a trail with his finger which led to the Big Dipper and as he connected the dots, I did see it. He said, "The Little Dipper is pouring into the Big Dipper." I asked what it was pouring and he said that it was only a metaphor, nothing was being poured. I must have shrugged or seemed to lose interest. These were the days when the Milky Way was as obvious as the moon, and yet, it was not obvious to me that my father was not only connecting the dots to form a shape in the sky, he was re-shaping the sky to re-member it. My father, too, carried soil beneath his fingernails. "Sometimes, Bug," he said, placing his pointing hand on my knee, "it helps to stare at the place between the stars. Staring at the darkness makes the stars more visible." This, which I made metaphor, I carried, like the dirt, always with me.

When it is dark, you can hear your own beating heart. When it's this dark, you can hear the heartbeat of those beside you.

It was a rainy night, but not where we lay. We lay on the ground in the Frank Church

Wilderness. Our tent flaps were open because the rain was on the ridgelines south of us, but those ridgelines filled the frame of the open doors of our tent and so we lay in the dark, wide-eyed and more alive than we would normally be at night, or at all. This is to say it was not a clear night and it was not the stars we sought. It was not even what could be seen that brought us here and my eyes blinked toward that horizon, grasping as they could toward the beauty of darkness inflected with shafts of dance, the same electricity we hold in our hearts, the light held behind my eyes, which finally closed, and where I fell was not so much into sleep as into a deeper understanding, as if my body grew roots, found mycelium and its memory, and other memories, which is where I believe memory goes, that opposite place from wishes and hopes and prayers. And perhaps that is why the latter is less reliable, because we can never lay our head on the wings of such things.

We had come to this high mountain meadow, this liminal place between alpine and not, to listen. To re-member.

It was in that place, that river of silence that flowed after the thunder, that was carried by the blanket of earth, that lives quietly, like Salmon, like the place between the stars, that I had fallen finally into when the howling began. In the dark you can sometimes feel the joy that fills another. Caleb whispered, *Wolves*, as if he could not help it. As if saying the word made them so. They started in the north, below a star I had no name for. Then, from the south spawning. Finally to the east and the cries could have been Wolf or Dog or human seeking to raise something from its rest, but we did not move. We lay there one hand seeking another. Letting the sound rain onto us.

I am a person of ground. This is not to say grounded, but of earth, attached to the earth. I cannot even jump far from it, it is as if an invisible tether holds me close, closer to the earth. I am unwinged, I do not fly, I root. So it was, rooted on the ground, the ground of Tukudeka, of Sheepeater, of Nimiipuu and Shoshone-Bannock, of people who, too, knew ground, but also sky, that I stared at the place where pawprints were left in the soft earth around our tent. I looked deeper, wanting to scuff the earth with my foot and seek out other tracks, visitors quiet as ghosts, but knew that my passing had done enough damage.

A day will come when I stare into darkness and cannot see the stars, real or imagined. A day will come when we have flooded the earth with too much light of our making and we will only be able to see the stars we make. A day will come when darkness doesn't fall, doesn't sing with the howls or the lightning, bright as they both may be. It will all be new stories poured from one cup to another.

My name means Bringer of Light, means Star of the Sea. It does not mean eraser of dark. It does not mean that stars aren't shining even as we cannot see them. I am a person of the earth, rooted in the stories of my ancestors, and illuminated by the light of my own experiences. As I walk this path, I vow to honor the memories of those who came before me, to listen to the whispers of the wind and the earth, and to share my own light with the world, refusing to let the darkness erase what makes us unique, what makes us human.

Let us not be content with borrowed starlight.

Terry Tempest Williams
A HOLLOW BONE

“Be the hollow bone—
We can be a vessel that things move through.”

—Regina Lopez-Whiteskunk

Photos by
Christina Seely

"BE A HOLLOW BONE," Regina Lopez-Whiteskunk says as we look out toward Sleeping Ute Mountain on Nuche ancestral lands near her home in Towaoc, Colorado. "We can be a vessel that things move through."

Standing inside this era of uncertainty, where climate collapse is converging with real threats to our democracy—regardless of one's politics—we are in a season of change. Regina and I are both friends and neighbors in the Interior West. We have long devoted ourselves to the care of wild lands and wild lives, and the human communities that support land health, recognizing environmental justice is justice for all species, not just our own.

When seeking solace, I find my peace at home with the landscapes and people I live among in the hard times, especially in the hard times.

BE A HOLLOW BONE enters my mind in the season of winter at Great Salt Lake, where the palette on Antelope Island is not primary colors, but muted hues of salt-stained rocks and white alkaline flats, and a retreating saline lake whose color is a chameleon mirroring the sky from indigo blue to platinum to pink.

Walking the shores of this inland sea, I find a small bone bleached white —a hollow bone, a bird bone—bring it to my lips and blow. The sound is a haunting; once alive in the body of a bird in flight, it is now one chittering note.

My guess is this bone belonged to a grebe or a phalarope, eared grebe or red-necked or Wilson's phalarope, to be precise, seasonal birds who arrive in late fall at Great Salt Lake in the thousands, hundreds of thousands, to feed and rest before venturing south to Mexico and South America.

Flocks of grebes are arriving now, migrating at night. Constellations of phalaropes have largely left, winging their way to Argentina for warmer weather. These are threatened species whose sole diets of brine shrimp and brine flies are declining as Great Salt Lake declines to historic lows, with salinity rates rising, deadly to the shrimp and fly populations. There is no separation between a healthy grebe and phalarope population and a healthy human population along the Wasatch Front. All of our lives are threatened by a shrinking Great Salt Lake.

It is a perilous time for the Great Salt Lake ecosystem. Forrest Cuch, a Ute elder, spoke at a recent rally in front of the Utah State Capital. He spoke of how his ancestors depended on this ecosystem for deer and ducks to eat; for the adjacent stands of cottonwood, aspen, and willows to shelter and warm them; and for salt to cure meat. Salt was also used in ceremony. Facing west toward this imperiled water body, he said: "We must protect our Mother Lake—our *sacred* Mother Lake to whom we all belong." Forrest invited over a thousand citizens at the rally to face Great Salt Lake with him as we chanted together, "Our Sacred Mother Lake," "Our Sacred Mother Lake," "Our Sacred Mother Lake," "Our Sacred Mother Lake," toward the horizon, now a line of quicksilver in the last light of day.

WE CAN BE a vessel that things move through. This landscape of gentle grasses covering the rolling hills all the way up the flanks of Antelope Island's steep and rocky ridge, where Frary Peak presides twenty-five hundred feet above the lake, is restful. What appear to be black boulders dotting the blonde fields are bison breathing. They are the descendants of the plains bison, once numbering sixty million, who thundered through the prairies prior to the colonization of America.

The poet Eliza R. Snow, plural wife of the Mormon prophet Joseph Smith and after his death, a plural wife of prophet and colonizer Brigham Young, wrote in her palm-size leather journal in sepia ink while crossing the plains from Omaha, Nebraska, to the Great Salt Lake Valley, "June 30, 1847: . . . This is truly the land of the buffalo —They are in sight all the time an almost imnuberable herd and then came over the bluff—about to cross our camp—on their path to the river—our hunters met them and they changed their course much to our gratification." A few pages later: "Nothing remarkable except the multiplying of buffalo pattys which [is] bad from the bluff to the river. Saw buffalo and wolves." She goes on to write, "Capt. G brought me a buffalo skull on which was written by the Pioneers, 'All well, feed bad.' Was only 300 miles from SLC," dated May 9.

A small herd of twelve bison (four males, four females, and four calves) were introduced on Antelope Island in 1893 by private landowners who brought them by train to Utah and ferried them across Great Salt Lake by boat. The herd is now "owned" by the state of Utah. In 2025, there are roughly seven hundred bison roaming free on the forty-two square miles of Antelope Island State Park, now a peninsula because of the retreating saline waters.

Scientists tell us this particular herd is among the wildest genetic population remaining on the continent, as they were originally culled from the historic bison herds not yet marbled with the genes of cattle, so common in bison today. The wild bison on Antelope Island must hold in their DNA an ancestral memory and verisimilitude of their coexistence with Indigenous communities across much of North America. Do the bison also hold the memory of the genocide inflicted upon them? White settlers' dreams of western expansion were predicated on the deliberate wholesale slaughter of bison to "clear the land of Indians," knowing that if they killed all the buffalo, Native communities would be starved not only of their primary food source, but their cultures, which evolved alongside the buffalo, as well. The bison and the Plains Indian cultures were one.

Over 5.4 million bison were murdered by white men in three years. Colonizers had the power and intention to kill both buffalo and Indians, leaving mountains of bison bones and skulls as a monument to genocide. Two genocides.

The pathology of patriarchy leaves all of us scathed.

Over a century and a quarter later, bison are bringing us back to our own wild nature, our own gentle standing of authentic power and resiliency and how we evolve over time. In Utah's Great Basin, they are now the guardians of a retreating inland sea. Both are remnants of a much grander past, both testaments to their seasons of change.

Just as this bison herd is a remnant population of the Great Plains bison that numbered in the tens of millions across the prairies, Great Salt Lake is a remnant of a vast body of water known as Lake Bonneville that existed from thirty thousand to thirteen thousand years ago in the late-Pleistocene and contained Bonneville cutthroat trout. At its peak, Lake Bonneville's liquid hand spread twenty thousand square miles across northwestern Utah into Idaho and Nevada with a depth of over nine hundred feet and containing twenty-one different species of fish. In 2024, Great Salt Lake barely covers a thousand square miles, with a depth of twenty-five feet, averaging eleven feet deep. No fish are found in Great Salt Lake due to its salinity, but a remnant fish from Lake Bonneville, the Bonneville trout, thought to be extinct in the early twentieth century due to overfishing, loss of habitat, and toxic waters, is now making a comeback in Utah's rivers and streams after six tiny populations were discovered in the 1970s.

Again, seasons of change bring transformation—be it to a body of great weight like the American bison thriving in the desert; or to that of Great Salt Lake in another iteration that held other bodies of small hidden fish, once feared extinct then found in secret streams by wishful anglers who never stopped believing they were still here. These embodied stories of endurance, strength, and resiliency, instead of despair and demise, become our vessels of hope.

THE DEPTH OF a bison's gaze reflecting the landscape that surrounds them has become a marker for how I wish to see and be seen by my own loves and losses. Bison deepen my heart. I bow to bison whenever I am in their presence. It is my private embrace throughout the seasons: in the bucolic spring their sweet red babies are living proof of love; in summer, they roam and tarry in green mansions; in autumn, they snort and shine; they are boulders immovable in the blizzards of the Northern Rockies, breaking trail through the snow when the clouds clear.

The bodies of bison are a landscape unto themselves. This is what they gave to me, my own body becoming animal in relationship to other animal bodies. My erotic education began as a girl who wanted to be a bison. I stood at the edge of large herds of what we then called buffalo in Wyoming. These massive brown-on-black bodies with steam rising from the heat of their own hearts, beating in the chill of October mornings among the dew-drenched grasses, thrilled me. We were witnesses to their pleasure while they wallowed in the mud on their backs with their legs flailing before the sky. Upright, the curve of their shining horns on their massive heads created a crown of nobility, followed by the iconic hump on their shoulders, so thick with soft, curly hair, I wished to sink my fingers into their coats even as a child. My brother Steve and I settled for the found pieces of bison hair snatched by the fingers of sage.

The bison's muscularity is sculpted and accentuated by the narrowing of their hips down to their haunches. It is a shining topography against the monotony of the prairie. The swishing of tails and the sound of wind weaving grasses into a tapestry can hardly be differentiated.

In rutting season, the snorting among them quickened as they sparred and fought for their territories with blood-red eyes. A single bull circling a group of females mounted each of them within view. This is how I learned about sex. Their arousal became my own.

This is not bestiality, but a pansexual bonding of earthly bodies in an awakened state.

With age, my passion only intensified. My uncle gave me a buffalo hide from one he shot in Utah's Henry Mountains not far from where we live. I spent most of my adolescence wrapped in this buffalo robe holding my fantasies close, both human and wild. Informed by the pleasure of my own body, I saw myself lying next to a bison, any one of them, wet and ready. If we are gender-fluid, can we not be species-fluid, as well?

If our human connectedness to all beings and our evolving capacity to love who we wish and how we wish to be loved—beyond gender, race, and religion—why can't we extend our love and compassion forward in the name of an interspecies connectivity and telepathy toward all the many beings with whom we share this planet?

Our human exceptionalism has destroyed countless populations of species and peoples on this free-floating planet. We continue to pursue this relentless path of destruction in the places we know by name in our forever wars, abroad and at home. With our aggressive arrogance and ignorance, we place ourselves first, draped in greed and entitlement, as the world burns and floods within an ever-worsening climate. And at the same time, we are also trying to find some semblance of reconstruction, restoration, and adaptation to change by imagining a different way of being.

Honoring interspecies connectedness, the steady stillness of bison, the agility of flight among phalaropes and grebes who understand the necessity of return, allows us to acknowledge and celebrate our innate feelings of a cellular, cosmic love that pulses and throbs and awakens intimacy for all life. Our shared affection given freely and received openly from all the beings we live among is a deep, evolutionary genealogy that branches out in all directions.

Bison are formidable beings, it is best to keep one's distance, but I continue to witness and dream of them in rapturous moments of mutual recognition.

Both the lake and the bison herd are survivors within an ongoing narrative of change, what has disappeared in the past and what could disappear in our future by our repeated seasons of desire for more water, for more land, for more profit, for the taking—of everything. Both the lake and the bison are bodies of imperceptible stillness, except when provoked by storms or helicopters herding the animals into pens for annual health checks, or to be sold or slaughtered.

I remember last year being on the edge of Great Salt Lake on Antelope Island with a group of Harvard Divinity School students sitting in a circle around a fire with one of our local political leaders who'd been put in charge of the fate of this saline lake.

A student asked him about the recent petition sent to the U.S. Fish & Wildlife Service to place Wilson's phalarope on the Endangered Species list as a threatened species due to the decline of water in Great Salt Lake. He said, no species had been saved by this Act and began to pontificate his point of view to the students. Suddenly, a great thundering filled the air and the ground began to shake. We stood up to locate the commotion, when we saw hundreds of bison in a stampede running in our direction.

"I stand corrected," the public policy czar of Great Salt Lake humbly said, aware of the irony before us.

Be the hollow bone—We can be a vessel that things move through, says Regina Lopez-Whiteskunk.

The bison know. The native grasses they wander through know. The phalaropes and grebes know. The brine shrimp and brine flies know. The Bonneville cutthroat know. And Great Salt Lake is trying to show us, repeatedly, change can move through us.

Let us not squander our time when the opportunity to transform ourselves is upon us. Let us know when to be still and when to stampede when false statements and lies are delivered as truths. Let us learn how to migrate in the dark and return home to where we belong for nourishment. And let us move as one organism when we are called into a moment of flock consciousness.

LAST NIGHT, I dreamed of one bison who was approaching a crosswalk, white stripes painted across the asphalt road. The bison sat in repose and refused the directive when the sign on the other side of the road said *walk*.

WHEN I AWOKE, I wondered what it meant.

I WANT TO remain feral like the bison on Antelope Island with a genetic tie to the wild. I want to heed the actions of Great Salt Lake and retreat as she is instructing us to do until the truth of her absence brings us into a deeper understanding of her presence—

I write these words during the Black Moon, as an invitation to go inward and be still as bison breathing among boulders—until a stampede is warranted—and we make our motions on the ground match the flocks of twelve million migrating birds above, their hollow bones buoyant and mirrored in the clarity of our sacred Mother Lake.

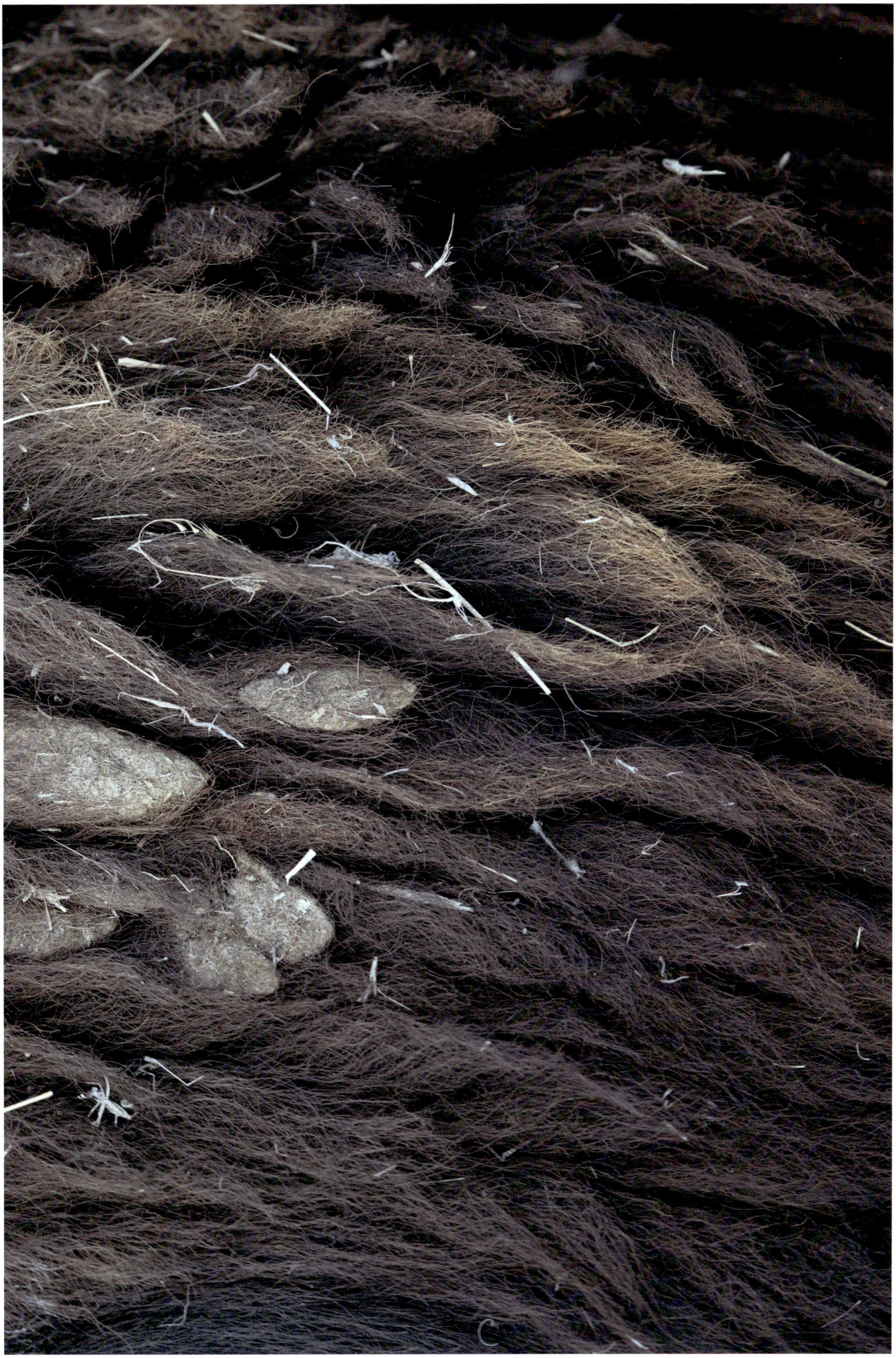

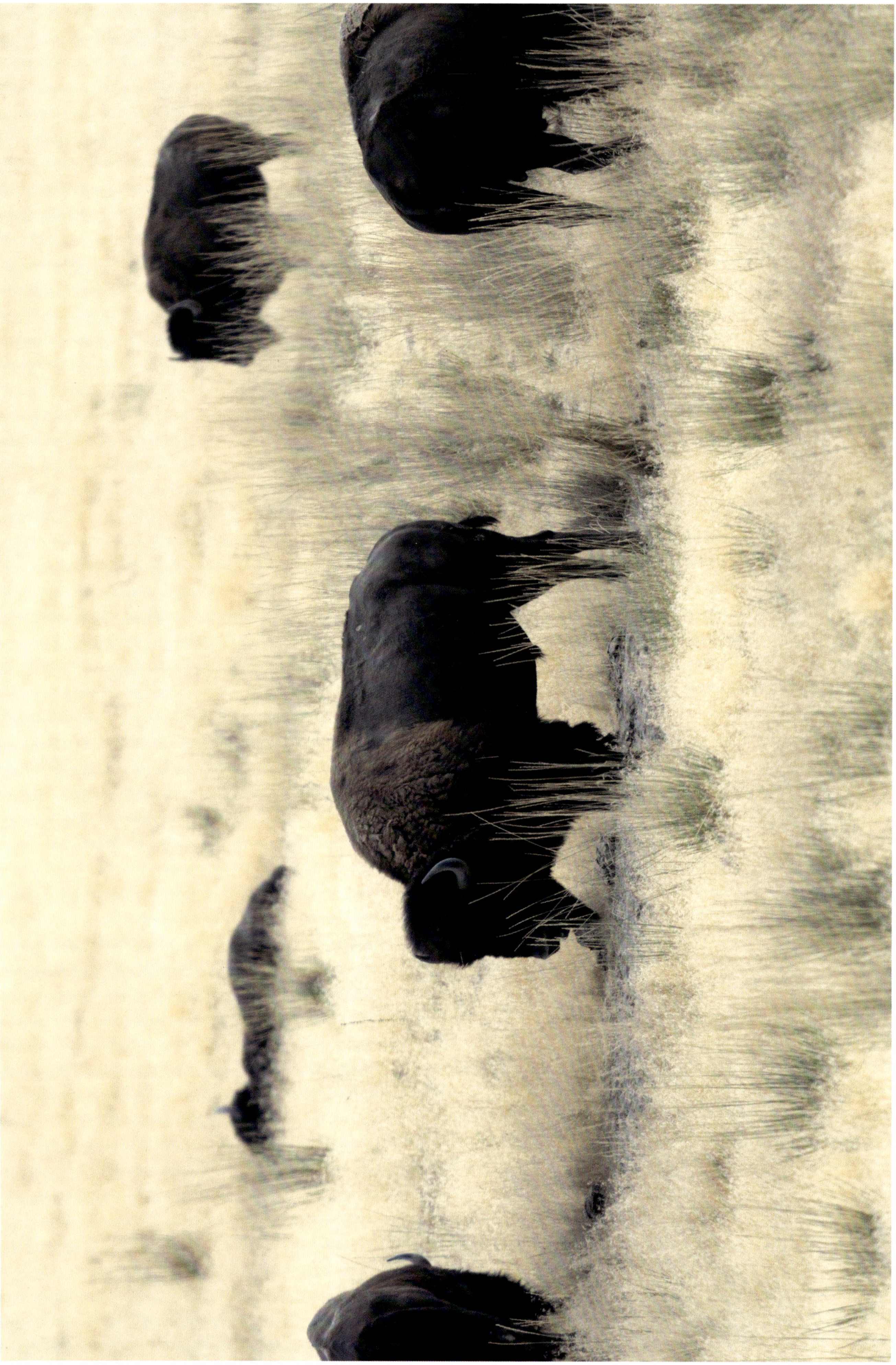

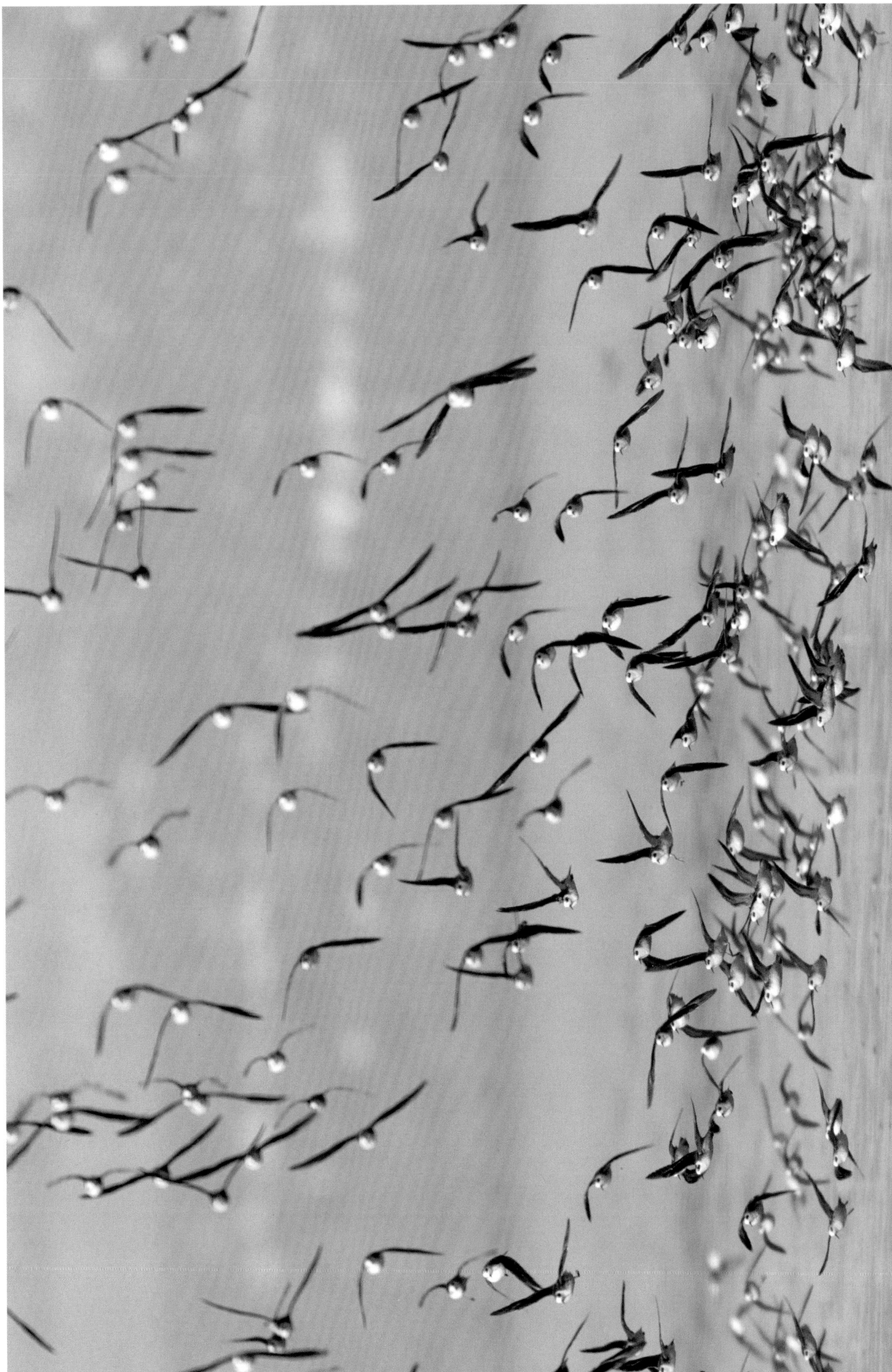

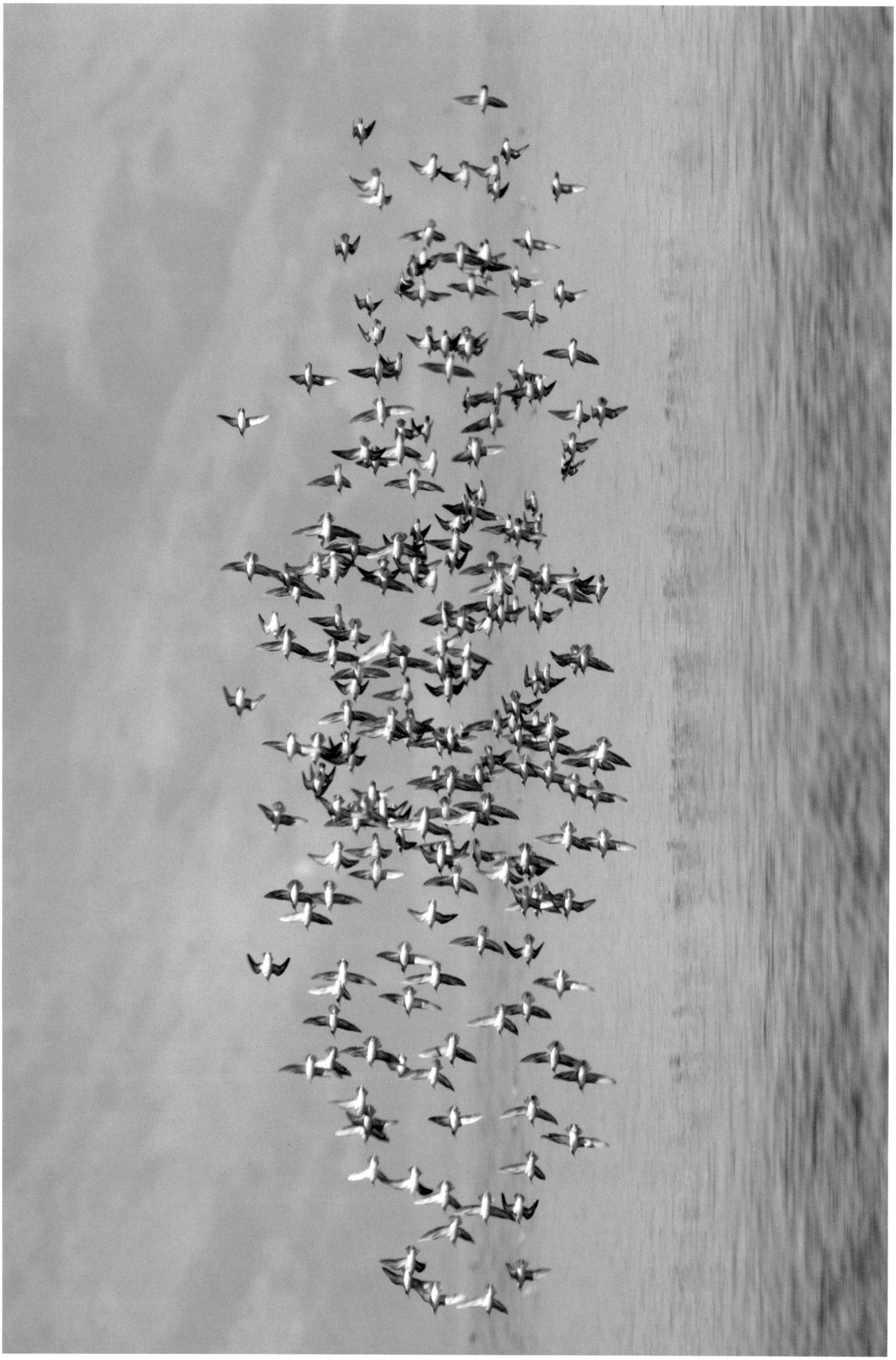

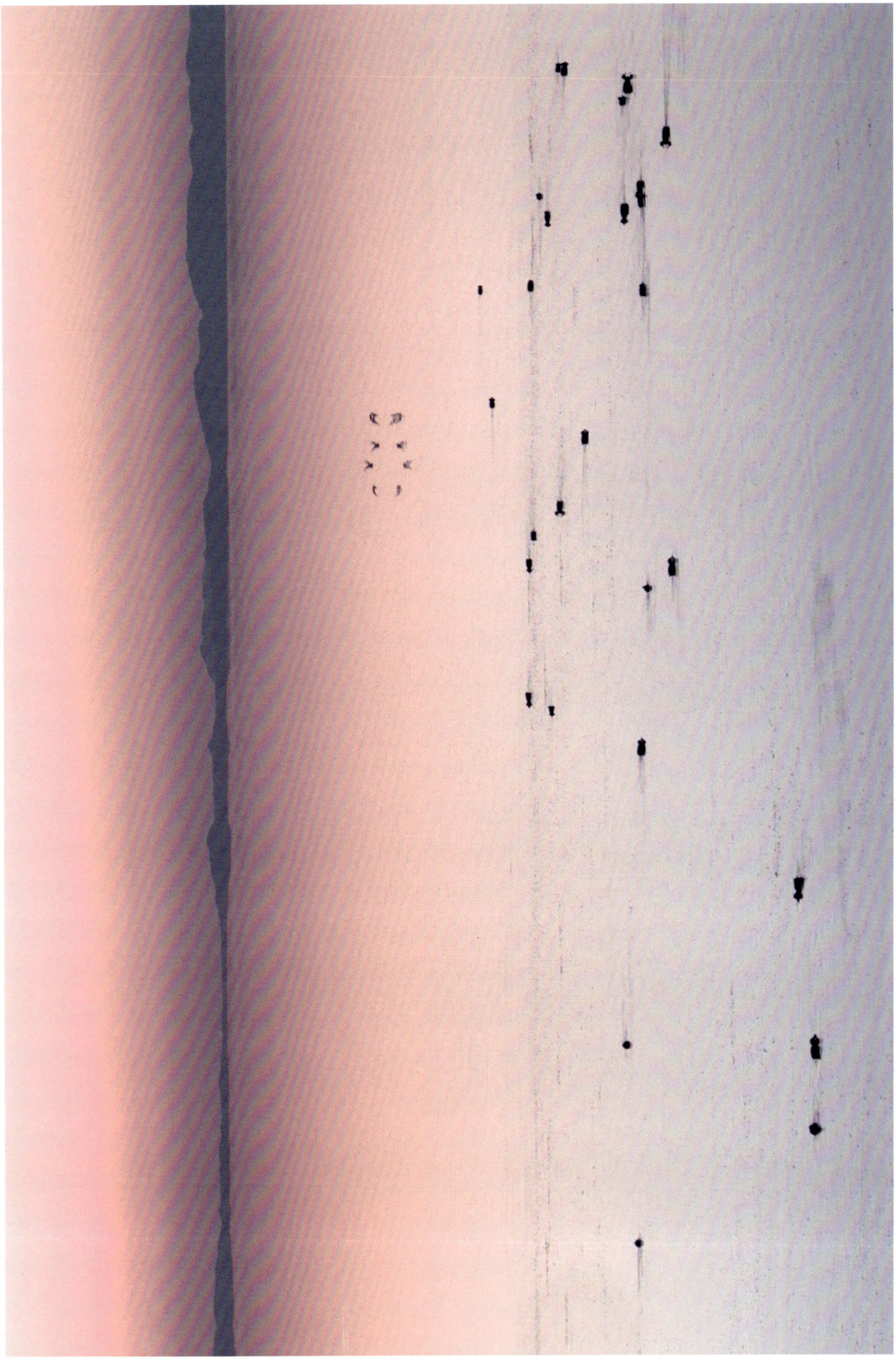

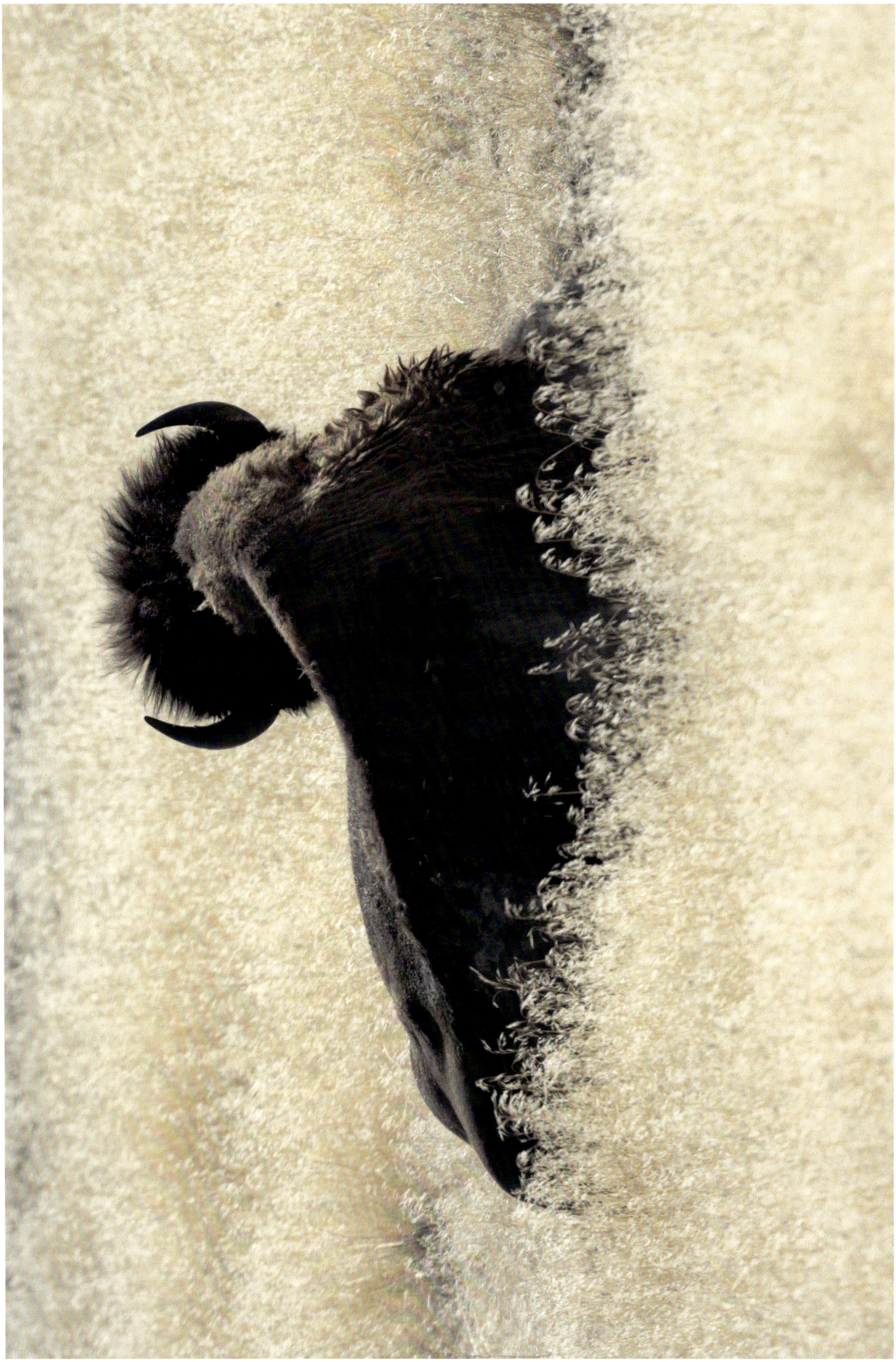

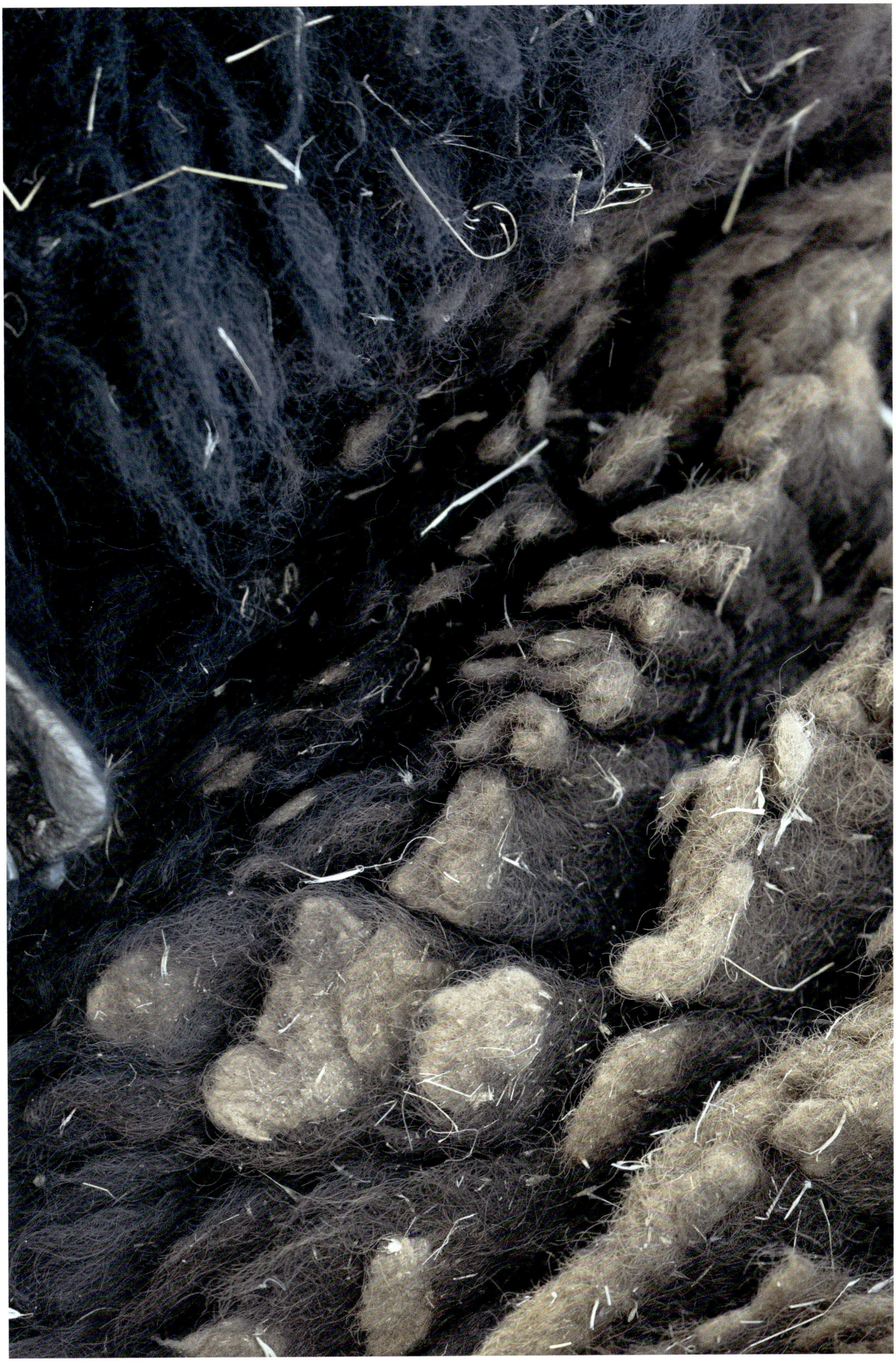

"Let us learn how to migrate in the dark and return home to where we belong for nourishment. And let us move as one organism when we are called into a moment of flock consciousness."

Zoë Schlanger

MEMORY OF WINTER

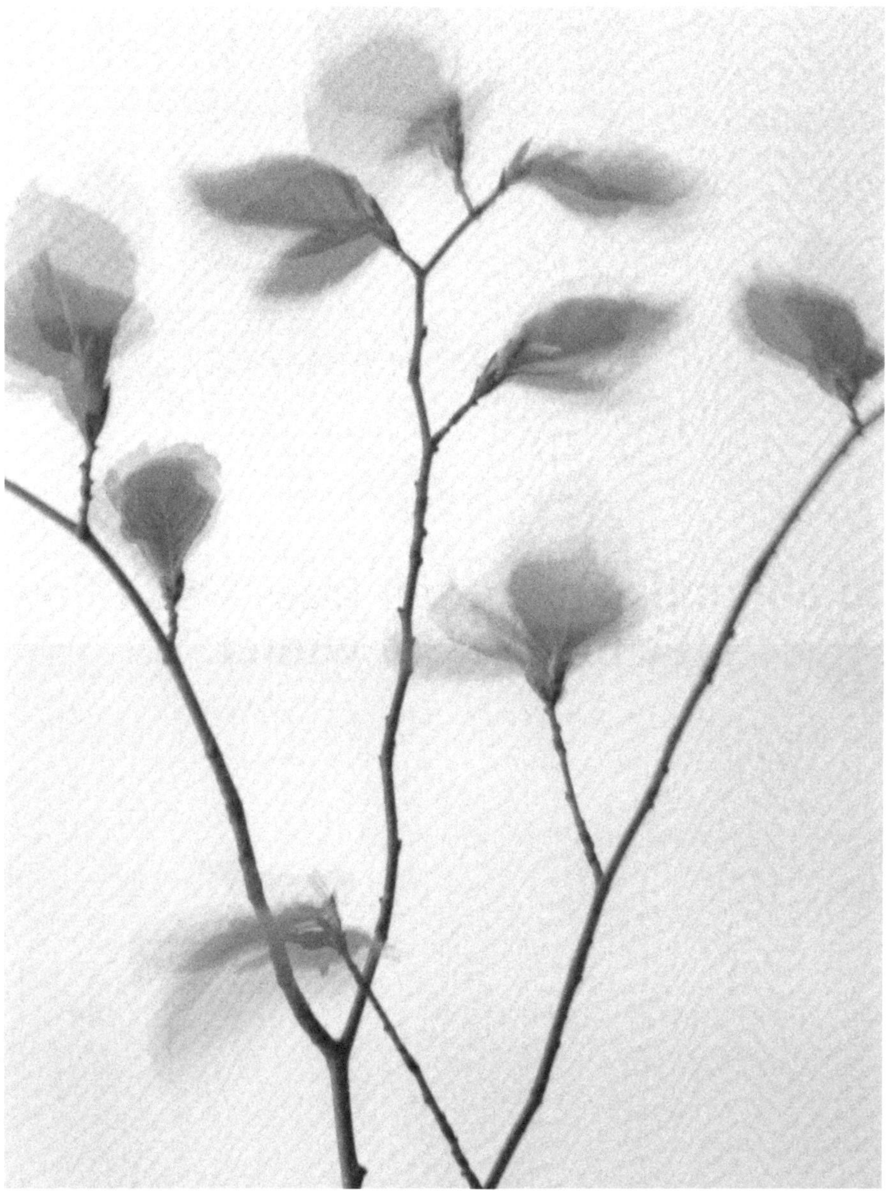

“Apples and almonds and peach trees won’t flower without the memory of winter.”

FIG. 2 Beech (*Fagus sylvatica*) long exposure over two days. (P. 65)
Photos by Sam Laughlin

My fiancée and I decided to try to have children. We are in our middle thirties, so this has now become a question of timing: How fast are we willing to do it? In a relationship of two wombs the biological clock is felt doubly. And both of us being people who write about the environment, the existential dread is doubled too. What world would we be bringing children into? But that conversation had turned a corner years ago; we had no right to foreclose hope in the future so totally. And foregoing children for climate reasons would be giving in to the corrosive myth that humanity is an ecological disease to be shed, rather than a steward in need of reminding of its role. There will be a future, and we could try, as a family, to be meaningful parts of it. So instead of the dread, we started to talk about how remarkable it would be to watch another human grow, to watch a life come into itself. To impart whatever we'd managed to learn so far, yes—but also to be a safe homeplace for another person to unfurl. By the time we reached it, the decision to have children was a joyful one: We took a hike, climbed a hill, looked at one another and decided yes, this is what we want. But *that* a conception does not make.

After the romance of our hilltop moment came the sort of research one might expect from a pair of reporters: the fertility forums, the journal studies, casting about for tidbits of advice from fellow queers who'd trod the road before us. Immediately I came upon shocking statistics. I'd had a hazy idea that waiting until forty might be a gamble, fertility-wise, but I'd naively thought that was a vague and malleable deadline. More like a suggestion. Soon I was looking at charts of precipitous fertility decline beginning around thirty-six, a line leading a body down the stairs, to the lower floors, away from the fecund penthouse of one's twenties. Forty was practically a subterranean dungeon. But! I protested. Everyone is different! I know a woman who had an easy and uncomplicated route to pregnancy at forty-six! And yet I also know about the false prophet of anomalies. Someone, I thought, should really have told me about this sooner.

That I now hold two senses of time in my body will be familiar, I expect, to anyone who has been at this crossroads before. There is now biological time and cultural time and they do not agree. Our bodies have not caught up with the demands of cultural time and are now out of sync. One's late thirties and early forties are a moment of personal and professional flourishing—the career that is finally taking off, the romantic relationships that are solidifying, the friendships that are growing more profound. By now I've dabbled in enough versions of myself to be clearer than ever about what worldly pursuits interest me—and I possess, at last, the clarity and authority to ardently pursue them. And yet, all the while, my reproductive system is running a different game. Whatever intellectual and social momentum I have must be set aside to have babies, or risk forever missing the opportunity. Parenthood is a walk through a one-way door; there is no going back. A chilling thought, to so permanently exit the excellent anteroom I'm in now. It really is great in here, have you seen it? But not stepping through the door at all is a forfeiture more dire, now that I've allowed myself to desire becoming a parent. And of course having children is its own wanted outcome. I feel the tug of them at the fringes of my vision now. I walk by the children's museum on my way to read in the park (a strongly anteroom activity) and think, I'd like to be the parent with the three-year-old stuffed in a snowsuit waddling toward the entrance. I do a spit take at myself. Where did that thought come from? Some deeply human place, probably, the mammalian voice in us all. But that children must come now still feels incongruous. At this point, the timeline of cultural adulthood and the timeline of human biology feel preposterously, maddeningly out of whack. The seasons simply do not align.

Spring is a time of furious becoming. The plants know what reproductive timing they should be on. The early signs are not subtle like the gentle sunset into fall but are rather declarative, ostentatious, befitting the furious life-making going on. Royal purple beaks of snow crocus puncture the frozen black earth. The gush of sap rises in the sugar maples. Forsythia spits splats of yellow onto brown sticks. The chartreuse of young leaves is garish with exuberance. What an absolute spectacle. Each haughty shoot and whorl of calyx pierces the veil; the long hard winter is ending. We've all made it to the other side. What comes next is nothing like what came before and that's pure relief.

The demonstrative nature of spring fluorescence matches its underlying biological truth: once a plant breaks out of dormancy, there is no going back. A molecular switch, or more accurately several, have been turned on and these cannot be turned the other way until next year. For all plants, this is the gamble of their lives, and timing is everything: Any error could prove fatal. Emerging during a warm spell in January is a disaster. And so they try their best to avoid this. Various proteins in a plant speak to each other, monitoring the fluctuations of temperatures between day and night, absorbing untold bits of data about the conditions of its world, and tallying the time. This is how plants spend the winter: waiting, sensing, counting.

I am not a winter creature. Despite all indications that I should be: I was born in Connecticut and have lived my whole life on the East Coast, the land of much of American winter mythos-making. But the four or five months of cold take their toll on my psyche as I hunch my shoulders to my ears on a walk in the wind. I want to attribute this lack of winter hardiness to Puerto Rican ancestors, but the reality is that they are out-batted three to one by the Eastern Europeans in my lineage, presumably winter-hardened, cellar-digging, root-vegetable-eating people. Either way there is nothing scientific about this analysis. Don't listen to me. I'm just looking for an excuse while my fellow New Englanders crave snow.

One year, I spent some months living on a farm in Connecticut. It was deep pandemic and I was writing a book about plant behavior, and it had all begun to feel like too much of an abstraction from the confines of my Brooklyn apartment, numerous houseplants notwithstanding (they are mostly tropical varieties, not winter creatures either). So my partner and I packed the houseplants into the car and drove some ninety miles north to the farm of close friends, one town over from where I grew up. We arrived for the winter months: November through January. I watched downy woodpeckers perforate the shaggy sugar maples and deer scavenge in the browning fields. I saw the kitchen garden behind the great farmhouse shut down: We walked out into the cold dark of evening to pull leek after leek for fritters and soups, we ate every last eggplant before the first frost. In the first week of December we planted the hardneck garlic in two neat rows, and woke the next morning to fresh snow blanketing everything; we'd done it just in time. I thought about the decline of snow in the Northeast in recent decades, and how, at a certain point, snowpack has a nonlinear

relationship to temperature, which means as the world warms New England may be destined to fall off a snow-loss cliff. I regarded the snow with nodding respect, as one might an elder statesman who has served his country well and might not be here next year.

For weeks after, as I waited through the cold, my thoughts drifted back to the garlic, each single clove silent in the ground, and each cell within them counting winter's passage. In June, spindly green scapes would emerge, and whole bulbs would develop where each clove was planted. But none of this would happen without a good long deep freeze. Indeed, what the garlic would need to send up its contribution to spring flamboyance in a few months' time is precisely this long period of cold. This requirement is called the "memory of winter," or, more scientifically, "vernalization." Apples and almonds and peach trees won't flower without the memory of winter either. The snow crocuses I waited for as a child in spring, and daffodils, hyacinth, tulips—these all need the memory of winter to bloom too.

While scientists are in the midst of discovering many forms of memory in plants, this sort of molecular memory—an elaborate and yet elegant calculation being made, continuously, inside each cell of the plant—has been known by farmers for centuries. Plants are time beings as much as we are. And time, as it relates to the natural world, is best thought of as passing in two ways: There is individual time, and then there is evolutionary time. Individual time is the turning of one's own circadian clock, the cycle of day and night, the experience of the seasons, the movement from youth to old age, even the passage of time between generations. It contains your memories, your mother's, your grandmother's. It reshuffles as necessary, adjusting for modern changes as best it can, even those not seen by your ancestors. Evolutionary time is much grander: The sweep of epochs. The rise and fall of species. The flow of the ancient into the now, by way of physiologies.

All of science, for the most part, concerns itself with one or another of these time-tracks. One field is concerned with plant evolution, for example, or one is concerned with novel processes happening in the shoots or roots or whole neighborhoods of plants today. But scientists know there are threads connecting the two timelines, because really, there is only one track. There are not two tracks running in separate rooms, but just one room, one track, stretching into infinity. This is the Earth, after all, and we are all contained on it, for all time. The threads connecting these two times, then, are the environment, the substrate of each life. We are, each of us, plant and person, porous to it. Our bodies are suffused by and mingled with the stuff of our environment. For plants, the weather, the wetness, the quality of sun, the soil its roots must probe, and whatever other biotic life is in the area—all of these together literally shape what the plant will become. The size and shape of each leaf is both the dictum of a plant's evolutionary lineage and the product of the environment that the plant had to encounter. All things in the environment are in constant flux, and a plant body's response to those changes quite literally shapes the direction of that body into the future. Every being is the product of biological time and the context of its moment.

Plants use both time-tracks to calibrate themselves to the seasons. Plants that require the memory of winter to bloom in the spring straddle both tracks at all times: Flowering in these plants is governed, we now know, by two sets of genetic switches. One is the vernalization switch, which is counting out a certain amount of elapsed cold, the length of which seems to depend on where the plant has evolved. When Dame Caroline Dean, a plant geneticist and world-renowned expert in vernalization, went to Sweden to investigate the vernalization of various varieties of thale cress—a weedy plant in the same family as cabbage—she found that the varieties native to the north of Sweden required twelve weeks of winter to fully vernalize, while those in middle Europe required only four. This makes evolutionary sense: Winter is longer up north; spring will arrive later too. A plant from farther north must have a sense for longer winters than its southern relations. Memories are meant to help a body make good choices in the future, after all.

Then, Dean tells me, when vernalization is satisfied, another set of switches takes over. These are monitoring every little variation in temperature and sunlight through the entire winter, even when the plant is in dormancy. They are attuned to the other time-track: the tumult of the immediate environment, how frigid nights give way to relatively warmer mornings, the changing length of a day. Yet all this data means nothing until the first switch—

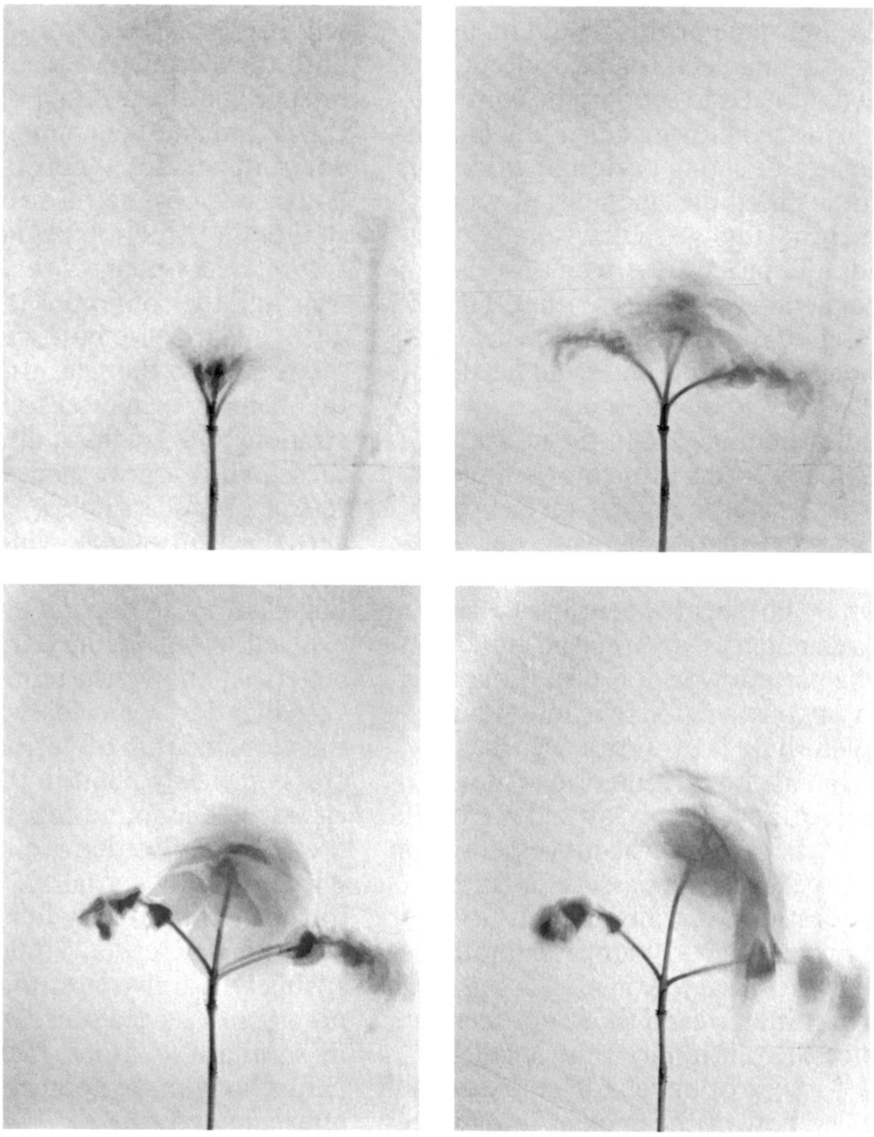

FIG. 3 Ash (*Fraxinus excelsior*) over ten days. (P. 72)

the one tied to evolutionary time, the deep conception of how long a winter should last—is turned off, having gotten its needed fill of cold. The first switch is like a gatekeeper, then, holding back the floodgates of information that the second switch is parsing. But now, winter requirements satisfied, the second switch is free to unleash a series of developmental changes according to how spring progresses. Now, a burst of warmth can change everything. Frondescence begins. A streak of warm days sends the crocuses bursting forth.

And yet this sublime marriage of the two ecological time-tracks is being destabilized by climate change. It is no longer enough to have an evolutionary memory of how long winter is meant to last, nor is it reliable to trust the fluctuating spring temperatures to make a solid choice to bloom. Deep biological clocks are no longer in sync with modern realities.

In my work as a climate reporter, I've written about how warming is producing more chaotic springs, leading, among many other outcomes, to fruit-related cataclysm. Spring, already the season of glorious chaos, of thunderstorms and wild temperature swings, is morphing into a caricature of itself. Freak spring cold streaks are obliterating fruit crops across the Northeast: In 2023, apple trees in New Hampshire that were fully vernalized—their memories of winter sated—burst into pink blooms only to have them browned and shriveled on the branch within a day thanks to a late-season frost. New York's Hudson Valley had a nearly peachless summer for the same reason. Connecticut lost between a half and three-quarters of its stone fruit that year, and another freeze in late May came for the strawberries and blueberries. In Georgia the year before, an unusually warm winter deprived the state's iconic peach trees of the period of cold they needed to bloom, and a cold snap in early spring finished off the ones that did manage to flower. Georgia lost some 90 percent of its peach crop that year.

Erratic springs are bringing other challenges too: stressed trees, strained by conditions they did not evolve to withstand, are more susceptible to pest infestations, which themselves are more frequent in a world with warmer winters. Stress accumulates over a tree's lifetime, weakening its constitution and changing its fruit. Record-warm winters can accelerate the life cycle of a fruiting plant, and unseasonable warmth early in the year can send fruit development progressing at warp speed, giving a peach or a plum less time to accumulate sugars. The very flavor of fruit could change as a result; a brutalized spring could mean a less-sweet summer. The tweak in timing distorts everything that comes after. The flourishing has gone subtly, horribly wrong.

When I asked Caroline Dean about this, it was the first of November. She was in the UK, and she said she'd just driven past a field of oilseed rape in full bloom, a whole field of blazing yellow flowers. That's not right at all, she said. "I don't quite know what's going on with that. We are seeing very erratic flowering behavior of our crops and our wild species now." Plants keep time in their bodies but it's not the same as what this new, warped version of spring allows them to keep. Things are changing too fast for plants' evolutionary time-memories to keep up.

Eventually the changes of the present will make their way into evolutionary time, because these pulsing changes to a seasonal cycle must, eventually, influence the future trajectory of a species. Those that withstand it will be the future of their species. Nothing is static, even if it may be cyclical—yearly, decadal, and centennial cycles alter in small and big ways, and so they push into the future at a new wobble. The great changes we are experiencing now—climate changes—will send some creatures' trajectories wobbling into new evolutionary directions, and for others the change will prove too great for that and it will extinguish them. Their absence from the tangled web—from the universal body of environment—will also alter the trajectory of everyone else. Nothing in a system happens without reverberation.

Climate change will shape our societies too in both dramatic and subtle ways we can't imagine now. I thought of the sugar maples at the farm, hundreds of them standing like yetis in the snow. In February, my friend, the farm owner, will tap them for their sap. I've eaten the maple syrup from this farm—from these same trees—over pancakes since I was a child. The changes they're experiencing now are unlike any they've seen before. Arnold Arboretum scientist Jake Grossman once put it like this:

> Maples have been evolving independently as a genus for about two million generations. This means that if you traced

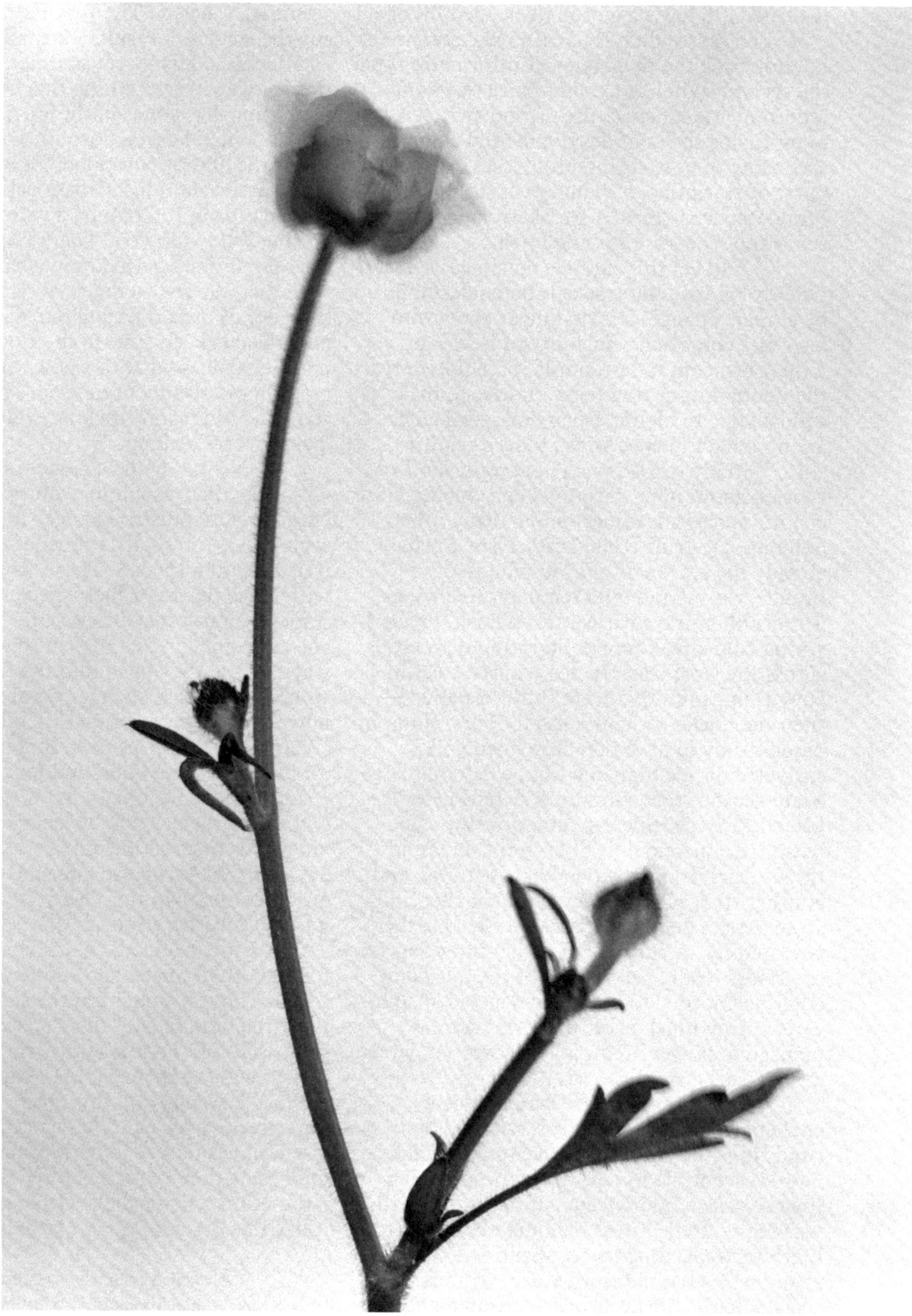

FIG. 4 Buttercup (*Ranunculus acris*) closing for the night. (P. 74)

75 MEMORY OF WINTER

> back any given maple tree two million generations, you would hit the grandmother of all maples. During that time, the climate changed a lot, going from periods in which there was no ice anywhere on earth through several ice ages, and maples evolved along with it. By 2200, in about seven maple generations, the climate could change so much that it resembles a past extremely hot climate that the world hasn't seen for roughly 1.5 million maple generations, or 50 million years. Maples will probably be able to survive somewhere on Earth in this new, hot climate, but they absolutely will not be able to evolve to be adapted to it in seven generations. For reference, our hominid ancestors began using tools only 1.8 million years—or 60,000 maple generations ago, so this future climate scenario will also be totally unlike anything we have ever seen.

Plants are much older, evolutionarily, than us. It is useful to remember that plants have been through a lot, long before us, and that we have been with them only through a fraction of their permutations. As a group they've been through ice ages and extinction events—but their lives and forms and distributions looked radically different then. In our short window of life alongside plants, we've grown fond of certain varieties, and of having those varieties where we have known them to be. We have cultural affinities—and they have lifestyles—that are in many cases unfit for the world we're handing them. That's not to say they're not doing their best. Plants are remarkably plastic; spring has always been chaotic, and for the most part they're able to withstand the extremes already usual in a growing season. But there's a limit to that plasticity. Our job now is to steward them into an uncertain future, one changing faster than their capacity to change with it, and in which we have been the primary force driving that profound and inhospitable change. This makes it all the more urgent for botanists to learn the ways plants respond to these time-changes, like which individuals or lineages manage the changes most deftly and should be grown in place of their less-well-adapted cousins, or which varieties from farther south should be transferred north to buy a species more time. Without that investment, the gulf between the timelines will grow wider, the threads more tenuous, subject to snapping entirely. With it, a road ahead might open, a future no longer foreclosed upon. Assisted reproduction, so to speak.

The next step, for my partner and I, will be to make our biological clocks fit the world we live in, to do our best to make them suit our modern timeline. We will use reproductive technologies my great-grandparents could not have dreamed of. Sperm cryogenics, then IUI, perhaps IVF, embryo freezing. I'm grateful for these innovations and what they mean for queer families—particularly those made in the context of a culture where doing this earlier than we are seems the only thing more impossible than doing it now. I carry the signature of my biological time in my body, but I'll adapt it to the present, pushing the plasticity of my reproductive system as far as it will go. The flourishing will happen, if we're lucky, at a very different time and in a very different way than how my ancestors did it.

But those future lives, and my own parenthood, will unfurl into a world that's very different too. Its seasons will have shifted far from those of a few generations ago, a ways even, perhaps, from the seasons of my own childhood. Ecological dangers may loom more frequently over what was once a region of temperate calm. The generational memories will no longer serve as guideposts for the future. Adapting to it will take reinvention, new ideas, a loosened grip on how things should be and an embrace of what they're becoming.

The garlic in the field sprouted beautifully in the spring, I am told. The peaches the following year were a different story; the chaos of a late-spring frost nipped much of the region's stone fruit in the bud. A changed spring will change plants, and so will change us. The changes will accrete. The reverberations will ebb and flow, stronger some years than others. But the result will be a new world. We don't know exactly what is next, but something will be. It will test the limits of our bodies to change, as it will theirs. The world, after all, has always been new.

Lydia Millet
TORTOISE STATION

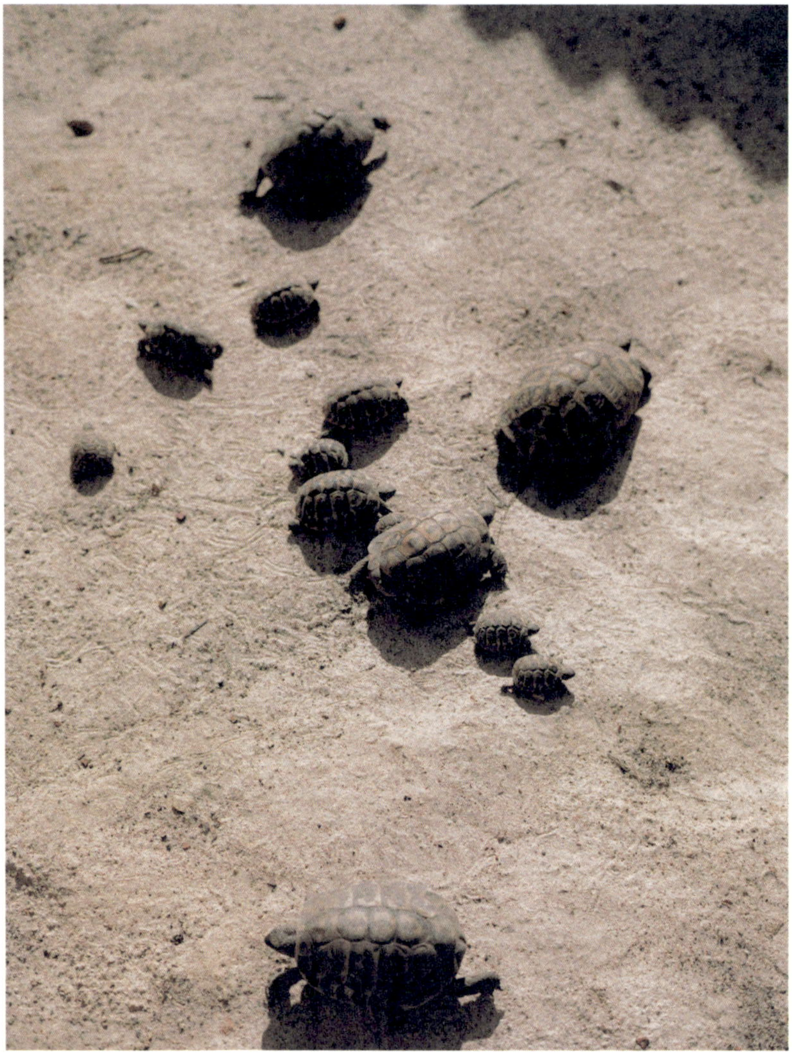

FIG. 5 Daniel Farò / Connected Archives (P. 78)

TORTOISE STATION

DURING THEIR LONG WALKS the females are dots on the map, slowly moving across a landscape of dry washes and desert vegetation. In my downtime I like to roll into the tech tent and park beside a watcher.

He might say, "Hey, you want to look in on Adah? Or how about Esther? Esther's *booking* it. Esther's on fire today."

He'll click on a dot and a scene will pop up.

The chips on their shells have microcameras programmed for a sequence of angles: close, medium, wide. We tend to see only bunchgrass or a bare stretch of dirt in a close angle, where a medium angle may show us a rusted-out stock tank or the concrete bank of a canal. Once, in a wide angle, we saw three condors feeding on a goat carcass. Watchers gathered around and sent the footage off to Condor Station.

Sometimes we see a dot that remains in place and an unchanging view of a brittlebush waving in the breeze, with its yellow flowers on their delicate but wiry stems. Or a stationary view of the gray skeleton of a fallen cholla, recognizable by its lacework of oblong holes.

This means the old one has died, and after an interval her dot will turn black and fade away.

In former times the female old ones didn't walk far—mostly it was the males who went to them. These days their walks can last for weeks. A female can walk for so long on her short, stocky legs that she perishes in the pursuit of love.

Scientists don't call it love when it pertains to other animals: they say mating or breeding, reproduction or propagation. They're afraid of imputing human emotions to other organisms. So in our funding requests and progress reports we use their words.

But here at the base we use our own. We see emotion as an animal attribute of which we, also animals, partake.

Even if their encounter is only brief, the old ones still wish for love.

Some of us follow the females, though not every female can be followed. Knowing they will starve if the journey stretches on too long, or their bodies will dry out and wither beneath their shells, some of us shadow them and recapture them before they can die. These followers call in a transport when their female becomes too weak and bring her back to the pens and burrows, here at the base, where she can lie low and gather strength.

To fatten them up for brumation we give them the fruits of prickly pear cactus, whose fuchsia flesh covers their brown faces in a bright stain. These fruits, the tunas, are their favorite food. We cook or pickle the pads for ourselves and save the raw tunas for them.

The old ones don't have chromosomes for sex—their sex is determined by temperature, and the eggs only hatch as males when the soil's not too hot. But the soil is always too hot, nowadays, so all the wild-born are females. The spread between genders is four degrees Fahrenheit, roughly: above 90.5, it's all females; between 87 and 90.5, a mix; and below 87, all males.

In former times it was against the law to bring about their union in captivity. It was also illegal to release the captives later, due to the risk of spreading disease. But we have no choice—we have to try. We ask the females to mate with the very few males, respected elders, who live in our enclosures. On the joyous occasion of a successful union we incubate the resulting clutch in our machines. Where the temperature is kept beneath 87.

Sadly such a union is extremely rare. The old ones seldom decide to mate in the spaces we offer them. They cling to the habits they remember, the lifeways they knew in their ancient home.

We keep the male elders, and care for them, in the hopes that one will be introduced to a female who will inspire him. The truth is that none of our male elders has mated in years. The youngest viable clutch hatched over a decade ago: four males, chipped and released at the correct moment, of whom one contracted an undetermined illness and another met with misadventure. In the form of a feral dog.

The dog who ate him was a labradoodle. So here at the base *labradoodle* has become our expression for dark doings and mayhem.

"Well, *that's* a labradoodle," someone will say, shaking their head at bad news.

Two of those males survive, green dots on the tracking map. Genetically unrelated females are regularly taken to their territories for sorties, and some matings have occurred, but so far no viable eggs have been produced.

Others among us are devoted to the prickly pears, working to keep them alive so that old ones on sorties can forage naturally. In former times four species of this *Opuntia* cactus were abundant in the wild, growing from the Chihuahuan and Sonoran to the Mojave with their clumps of oval paddles reaching for the sky.

Now, on sprawling farms from Mexico to Africa, they're raised as a human crop, adapted as they are to dryness and heat.

But in the desert, invasive cactus moths have descended to devour the prickly pears. They lay their eggs inside and the larvae destroy the whole plant. The moths first arrived on the continent far to the east, in what was then south Florida—a wonderland of cypress swamps and Spanish moss, mangroves and rivers of grass, and at the bottom tip a thin string of coral islands. Those were the days of the bonneted bats and salt marsh voles, Everglade snail kites and smalltooth sawfishes and numerous butterflies. Before all of it was covered by the sea.

They were the last days of the Florida panthers, too, whose endling died not from the rising ocean but a car.

From there the moths migrated west.

Some of us who aren't followers are finders instead. Mothmen, they're also called, though there are women among them. Moth traps appear as yellow dots on our maps, and when the moths begin to fill the traps mothmen are dispatched from base or redirected from another site. They go to the trap location and scour the cacti and remove all the moths and egg sticks they see, tossing them into crushers by the tens of thousands to halt their advance.

I know a finder who tried to eat the moths, believing it was a sin to let them go to waste. But they're not pleasant in the mouth, with their feathery, dusty bodies, and he quickly developed a strong gag reflex.

The followers are solitary folk. Some walk with a partner, if they're committed, but more choose a solo following. When a female sets out on her first mating sortie, usually at the age of about fifteen—either a captive, a found wild female, or one of the semi-wilds we discovered at birth and chipped—a follower will top off his or her pack and set out after her, armed with a wristband and a lightweight tablet for redundancy in case of a mishap or equipment failure. Both the devices show the red dot on the map and the camera view.

Most followers visit their females daily as the journey progresses, catching up with them to ensure they're all right or to investigate a scene the camera is relaying. This may be an accidental meetup with a person, such as a solar farmer patrolling his panel fields or a wind rancher tending to turbines. More frequently it'll be a coyote or fox or ravens. Ravens, in recent years, have begun to hunt together more regularly than in former times. They're highly intelligent and know the strength of numbers. This new group-hunting tactic enables them to attack even mature old ones with hardened shells, where before they only preyed on tender juveniles.

The followers call a raven flock an *unkindness*. "She met up with an unkindness," one will text back to us at base. "No harm was done. I dispersed them."

We have a directive never to hurt the other natives, but we can interrupt their predation.

If a female goes too near a road and appears to be on a course to intersect, a follower has to step in. This is risky because if he can't deter her by blocking, and has to pick her up, she may startle and release nearly all of her water. When that happens the follower has to bring her back to base. Near the beginning of her sortie she may be able to rehydrate and go out again, but near the end of the season she will have to wait.

The followers hate roads.

Mothmen travel in packs, and while the followers stay silent, the finder bands are noisy. They play music in their encampments and sing ballads about lonesome cowboys, engage in contests of strength and wrestling. Theirs is a warlike attitude—they consider themselves soldiers, mobilized in defense of the unmoving. They yell out strings of curses as they work, each trying to outdo the others in filthiness, and between sites march along to army cadences.

We see the videos they post of the moth purges or marches overlaid with the soundtrack of their chanting. *They say that in the army the chicken's mighty fine, one jumped off of the table and started marking time! Up in the morning, out of bed. Do some stretches, hit the head!*

Or they'll call out a foolish one they make up themselves, on the fly: *Another day another purge! Man oh man we feel the urge! We fight we fight the cactus blight! A plant can't walk so we talk and rock!*

Without these rituals—they do not say but the rest of us know—their job would be too depressing. For even the moths would prefer to live.

I'm a feeder, myself—I can't travel overland in my chair. It has rugged tires and my arms are muscular, but followers and finders have to navigate mountain passes, scree-covered slopes, and the loose sand of washes. And even if I didn't use a chair, I wouldn't be drawn to a hiking regimen. I enjoy the hominess of the base, its orange lights at nighttime, the comfort of shade and cool water to drink and the gravity showers. I rely on the steady rhythm of arrivals and departures and calm twilights over the familiar ridgeline. I know all the followers, even the newest ones on staff, and all the mothmen and their bands, their slogans and tattoos.

Sometimes the finder groups will shift, after a dispute or breakup, and one of them will confide in me. The warlike energy brings drama to the bands.

I have duties other than feeding the old ones, such as laundry and keeping track of food shipments and various other logistics, but feeding is why I'm here.

If a female old one finds a wild mate, her follower is celebrated on their return. Festivities are held. It may take weeks for a clutch to be laid, or no clutch may be laid at all, but after the union the follower either chips the wild male or, if his home territory is deemed high-risk, brings him back. At first, after the trauma of transport and newly captive, the wild males don't want to mate again. Male old ones are more frightened by relocation than females. Over time one may master his fear, but if he doesn't he's chipped and re-released. For that he needs to be taken back to his territory, and this second transport may traumatize him further.

It astonishes me how swiftly the old ones' pheromones seem to have adapted and grown more powerful. In former times they didn't range more than a mile or two from their birthplace. *Nonmigratory*, they were classed. And females didn't do the seeking.

Now almost every female is willing to travel. For dozens of miles in a season.

Last week a momentous event took place: a female named Bethel found a sequestered male in private captivity. He was living as the pet of an elderly woman, in a pen outside her rural trailer.

There was a fence between Bethel and the captive male, however, so her follower, Tomás, knocked on the trailer door.

The woman opened it holding a rifle.

Tomás stepped back with his arms raised and carefully described the situation.

"Huh," she said. "Well, I'm gonna need to get paid. If Sheldon's being used for stud."

"I am empowered to offer you significant compensation," said Tomás, reciting from his memorized script.

Inwardly he was sickened, as much by the crass word *stud* as by the demand for money. But he sat down with the woman on her front stoop—she did not invite him in—and showed her the map of hundreds of red dots, along with the six green ones that currently exist. He explained how painstakingly Bethel had traveled all those miles and appealed to the woman's sympathies, making his pitch for the monitoring of the male and the schedule for health checks and visitation.

To which she finally agreed.

Our protocols allow for involuntary seizure but the better alternative, by far, is to leave a rogue male in his preexisting habitat, avoiding the trauma of relocation and setting him up for return visits from multiple females.

Of course the old one is not the rogue: rather the rogue is his captor, keeping him separate from all others of his species and thus unable to help prolong their existence.

A previously sequestered male, if he can be chipped and kept safe, is a precious treasure.

That night Tomás bivouacked in the woman's yard while the old ones mated inside the enclosure.

But when the transport arrived in the morning to take him and Bethel back to base, the woman announced she wanted to revise the deal they'd settled on. Toward greater profitability for her.

"How about this," suggested Tomás. "A specialist will be in touch. To handle further negotiations. Heck, this contract stuff is way above my pay grade. You know—I'm just a lay biologist. A herpetologist. Herp guys, they call us. Or herp gals."

"Fine," said the woman. "But you better make it soon. I have a contact in Texas who'd *love* to buy Sheldon. She has some rare snakes, too. And she's willing to pay top dollar."

"I see," said Tomás. "Well, it does sound like you need a specialist."

He did not mention that the specialists, like the elderly woman, carry firearms. Though they rarely use them.

Still, she wouldn't enjoy her meeting with the specialist. Even I don't enjoy meeting with specialists. And I'm not harboring a sequestered male.

The specialists are given deference but avoided, socially. They move through base camp leaving a wake—followers, finders, and feeders fade into the background as they pass. They specialize in compliance, not disappearing life forms, and are in high demand. So they never stay put for more than a night or two. They'll get called away by a forest manager or a tribal river guardian. Or frequently they respond to calls from Condor Station, when a deer hunter is caught using illegal lead bullets. They travel to Wolf Station in New Mexico, Jaguarundi Station down in Hermosillo, Pronghorn Station or the large Multispecies Station outside San Diego that used to be a zoo.

Or Colorado River Toad Station, which has to contend with the licker market. Users of bufotoxin are known as "lickers" even though they don't lick toads directly—this can cause cardiac arrest. Rather they milk them for their poison and dry it out to be smoked. Lickers claim that the toads are sacred to them but refuse to accept synthetic substitutes. In their ceremonies, they say, they experience a sublime euphoria. They behold God and come away with calmer hearts.

Meanwhile the toads' population dwindles.

When Tomás and Bethel reached us, and he told us all the story in his celebration speech, no specialist was present, so one was alerted by text—we have to book specialists hastily when we need one. The potential buyer in Texas was a dubious claim, but empty threat or not, "Texas" isn't a word we like to hear. Texas is a synonym for death: once an animal goes to Texas, that animal does not return.

Texas is not a party to the Agreement.

It was as the celebration was starting to wind down, and the sky was turning a deep indigo, that the caravan arrived.

We hadn't been given any heads-up. The station chief, who was sitting at my and Tomás's table under the big tent taking sips from his festive glass of wine, got a voice call—from gate security, as it turned out.

He stood up, seeming flustered, and gestured impatiently for someone to turn off the music. Then he removed his hat.

The station chief isn't in the habit of removing his hat. His head is bald and pink and his wife, who lives with him in the management cabin, doesn't like him to expose it to the sun—after years of constant rebukes he's decided it's easier to keep the hat on all the time, more or less. Even when there's no sun around.

We all call him the Egg. It's a term of endearment and he considers it a compliment: eggs are our Holy Grail.

Over the door of the cabin he shares with his wife hangs a sign we made. "The Nest."

"Announcement!" he said. "An important visitor is arriving, I'm told. A dignitary. In from the capital."

"The capital of what?" asked Ron. He's a finder and had been dancing in a freewheeling, spinning style when the music stopped. Now he stood in the middle of the floor holding a beer bottle. He wore only a pair of baggy shorts, bearing a Hawaiian print, and flip-flops. Ron takes any opportunity to remove his shirt. He's proud of his torso ink, a jungle-like mass of colorful extinct plants. *In Memoriam*, proclaims his chest in a flowery script.

"The whole shebang," said the Egg.

He was distracted, craning his neck to see past Ron to the distant front gate. Where a line of headlights had become visible, wending its way toward us in the gloaming.

"What kind of shebang?" asked Ron. "There's a shit-ton of shebangs."

"You better put your shirt back on," said the Egg. "*That* kind of shebang. Anyone else around half-naked? If so, get fully dressed ASAP. For the love of Pete!"

Ron flip-flopped over to his table, put down his beer, and grudgingly lifted his T-shirt off the back of his chair.

By then the line of cars was parking, one beside the other, in a neat row along the leading edge of the parking zone. The Egg came around his table and walked in their direction, weaving along the paths between the cabins and enclosures and bathroom outbuildings with the rest of us behind him.

We don't get a lot of dignitaries here.

I took up the rear: my arms were sore from folding. It had been a laundry day. So all I could see, at first, were the legs and lower backs in front of me.

I heard a low murmur of surprise as—I assumed—the dignitary exited a vehicle.

"No way!" exclaimed a follower beside me.

"Who is it?" I hissed.

"No fucking *way*," muttered Ron on my other side.

That was irritating.

He was still bare-chested, with his T-shirt slung over his shoulder. His mouth hung slightly open.

People were talking up at the front of the crowd and maybe shaking hands. I heard someone laugh politely. Near me whispers rustled.

I grabbed his arm.

"Ron. Tell me who it *is*," I insisted.

"It's the chief."

"I meant, who's the dignitary?"

"The chief! The big chief. The chief of the whole Service."

"Director Douglass?"

She'd never made an appearance at our station. And the last time she'd showed up at the Multispecies it had been for a grief ceremony after an endling frog died.

My first feeling was fear. It made my stomach lurch. Maybe we were losing some of our funding. Or the water allocation had been cut.

"Looks older than I thought she would," mused Ron.

"Put your shirt on. Seriously. Before she sees you."

"Fine," he grumbled, and pulled it over his head. "Oh, hey. She's got her kid with her. The one with the syndrome! That synesthesia thing. She's introducing him to the Egg."

"He's her only kid. So you don't have to say 'the one with the syndrome.'"

"Whatever."

"Good people!" came the Egg's voice from up front. "As you can see, we have Director Douglass with us tonight. A great and unexpected honor. Let's give her a warm welcome. Mourning Dove Douglass, ladies and gentlemen."

Clapping.

"Thank you," said the director. "Thank you very much. It's an honor for me, too. This is my son, Bright Holding. He goes by Hold."

"Hi everyone," came a child's voice. "Can I see an old one now?"

"We're headed for Delta Station," said the director. "To meet with the Cocopah riverkeepers. It's been a long trip. But Hold is fond of the old ones. And he's only ever seen them in videos. I said, Why don't we make a quick stop? So it's just a personal visit. Say anything you like—I won't be using my scribe."

"Well, we better get to it, then," said the Egg. "You never know who'll be outside a burrow at this hour."

"Cre-pus-cu-lar," piped up the child's thin voice.

His voice was drowned out as the group started moving. I had an advantage, though—the back of the crowd had turned into the front. I spotted Bethel in the G enclosure, as a motion-sensitive light snapped on, and rolled up to the low wall.

In the center of the enclosure she was wolfing down tunas.

Behind me people cleared a path, and then Hold and the director were beside me, along with the Egg. And Tomás.

"This is Bethel," I told the boy. He was smiling. "Tomás brought her back to base today. We're very excited about her. Because she may lay eggs."

"Eggs!" said the director. "How wonderful. Then we'll have new old ones, Hold. Baby old ones that are boys."

"What it's all about," nodded the Egg.

"Her shell is so dusty," said Hold. "And she's so brown."

"She's really brown," I agreed. "I sometimes think the old ones are the brown of rocks and mesquite bark and desert willows. Like they all came out the same brown because they've lived together for so long. So it's the brown of time."

"The brown of time," repeated Hold.

"Sorry. That doesn't make much sense," I amended.

"Yeah it does," said Hold. He was still smiling. "Totally! There's the brown of time and the green of time. Those are the colors of time."

"What about blue?" asked the director, with a tender pat to his shoulder. "Like the ocean? Or the Earth from outer space?"

He shook his head. "Blue's an excellent color. But not the color of time."

The director winked at me.

"I'd let you touch her shell," Tomás said to Hold, "but when people touch her, it can be upsetting. And she was just relocated. So she's been touched a lot today. Already the maximum."

"She's already been touched the maximum," echoed Hold.

"But you can touch another old one, maybe."

"It's OK," said Hold. "I don't need to touch. I can hear the shape."

The syndrome, mouthed the director behind him.

"See?" said the boy. "Look!"

Suddenly he dropped to the ground and bent himself into a hump beside my right wheel. I had a close-up view, and it was strange:

I wouldn't have thought he could do it. Or that anyone could. I can't say what the contortion was, exactly—how he shaped his body in such a precise mimicry.

But damned if he didn't capture the essence of an old one. For a fleeting second.

Then he was up again, sand and pebbles on the knees of his pants.

He didn't bother to brush them off.

"I tell you what," said the director to the Egg. "Why don't you give me the tour. And Hold can stay here for a bit."

"Happy to."

She moved past her son, who was leaning against the low wall gazing at Bethel, and looked me in the eyes.

"Would you mind watching him? Say, half an hour?"

"Not at all."

I gave her my name and my job title, and we shook.

"OK," she said. "You're in good hands, Hold."

Then she and the Egg and Tomás moved off, drawing the crowd after them.

Hold and I stayed quiet for a while. He was patient, watching the old one—a patient, smiling boy.

Bethel had a fuchsia beak. And neck and front feet.

"She's a messy eater," I said.

"*I'm* a messy eater."

"As soon as she stops eating," I said, "try talking to her and see what happens."

The old ones have excellent hearing. We don't play loud music, even when we dance at celebrations, so as not to disturb them. This is one reason the finders get rowdy out on their moth runs.

I told him about the prickly pears and the finders and moths. And at last Bethel seemed satisfied. She ignored the last tunas in her pile and began to move sluggishly toward her burrow.

"Wait! Don't go in yet, Bethel," said Hold. "Stay out till I have to go back in the car. Pretty please."

She paused and turned herself in our direction.

"Whoa!" said Hold. "Magic! It's like she understood me!"

"They respond to the sound of voices," I said. "They're curious. Just keep talking. It doesn't matter what you say."

"Old ones don't stay with their eggs," he said as she neared us.

"No," I agreed. "But here at the base, that comes in handy. We can go in and collect the eggs and put them in an incubator and she won't mind at all. She may even lay another clutch."

"They work so hard to lay them and then they just go away," said Hold. "Anything could happen. They leave it up to the world."

Bethel had made it to the bottom of the low wall. She stood up on her back feet, scrabbling her front ones against the wall and reaching her head up toward us, and Hold bent over and stared at her face.

"In former days," I said, "they could trust the world. They lost plenty of eggs to skunks and snakes and birds, but enough survived. Because here they are."

"They could trust the world for a long time," said Hold.

"Their ancestors came here from Asia over thirty million years ago. And these particular animals, some paleoecologists say, may have existed for five million years. There might have been some tunas around then for them to eat. Prickly pears go back five million years too."

"That's long."

"Well, the oldest *Gopherus agassizii* fossils we've found are from the Pleistocene. But that's still a hundred and fifty thousand years."

"Now they can't trust the world anymore. So they have to trust us," said Hold.

"I guess they do."

"You can trust us," he told Bethel, and turned to me. "She can trust us, right?"

"We do our best."

"Is it enough?"

"Ah. Only time will tell."

"Brown and green will tell."

"There you go."

After Bethel ambled into her burrow, we had a few minutes left and I didn't think we should try moving to another enclosure. The director might not be able to find us right away. She might get nervous.

"Tell me this. How come green's a color of time but blue isn't?"

"It's hard to explain."

"I bet."

"It's like, brown smells old and green smells new, but they're both time."

"So what does blue smell like?"

"I love blue. Blue smells sweet. But not like time. Just life. Or wait. More like possibility. Wherever there's blue, there's possibility."

"Is it tough, sometimes? To be smelling colors? And hearing shapes? When most people don't?"

"It's just how it's always been. Only explaining it is hard."

"Sorry I asked. People must ask a lot."

"It's OK. I mean, you being in your chair—if someone else isn't *in* a chair they can't feel how it is. No matter what you say. Right?"

"That's true."

"The words mean different things. At least, the words for senses. The sense verbs, my mom says. And if words mean different things to other people, they don't get it when you say them."

"But isn't it frustrating?"

He shrugged. "Only if you worry too much. You have to let it go."

"I guess I do that too. With being in the chair."

"Or with the old ones. We can't *be* them. We can try to imagine. But we can never know. But it's OK. Because their world is still *there*. Outside and inside ours. It's a secret kingdom."

The director came striding back along the path, the Egg's wife by her side and two bodyguards in uniforms with guns and tasers in their belt holsters.

The Egg's wife held out a packet of cookies.

"For the road," she said to Hold. "I baked them myself. Chocolate chip."

"Excuse me. I'll take those," said one of the bodyguards, and intercepted the packet.

"Just a standard precaution," said the director apologetically.

"Oh," said the Egg's wife. "Of course."

They said their goodbyes and headed off toward the parking zone.

Hold turned and waved at me as they went, still smiling.

"Goodness," said the Egg's wife when they were out of earshot. She shook her head. "They have to screen *cookies*?"

"She does get threats," I said. Recalling the media reports.

"I suppose."

"And . . . *was* it just a personal visit?" I asked. "Or was there bad news? I heard there could be water cuts in the offing."

"No bad news," she said. "But get this. *I* heard, from a friend at Ocelot, that she brings the child with her as a litmus test."

"A litmus test?"

"If he likes the personnel, she's reassured. If he's on the fence, she finds a pretext, sticks around, and observes. And at that point, major staff reshuffles can come down."

"Oh!"

"So congratulations are in order. You must have done all right."

After the caravan had turned into taillights and been swallowed by the night, I stopped at an outbuilding to wash my face and brush my teeth. Back in my tent, on my cot, I took off my work smock and pulled on my nightgown. I smoothed an analgesic gel onto my aching arms and lay down on my back, gazing up into the dark.

Black, I wondered. How does black smell?

It smelled of my pillowcase, right then—the artificial lavender of our bulk detergent. It smelled like the aloe gel on my arms, the lotion on my face, and the minty residue of toothpaste in my mouth.

All smells are the smell of time, I thought, drifting off to sleep. Time flowing past me. Or me flowing through time.

And now is the time of waiting. We wait to see whether a clutch is laid. And if it is, wait again. To see whether the eggs are viable.

Wait, also, to hear whether the specialist is able to persuade the elderly woman to keep her old one where he is, healthy, stable of mood, secure in his routine, and available to females. Rather than ordering in a care team and commandeering both the pen and the property.

Or—if the woman tries to resist with force—falling back on the last resort of direct seizure, which would make our hearts sink. Since it would, almost surely, result in another relocated male too traumatized for love.

We watch and feed and follow. Meanwhile a new influx of moths has begun and mothmen are once again dispersing across the land. Yelling out their cadences as they march past derelict gas stations and mining shacks and through the ghost forests of Joshua trees.

Melanie Challenger
THE SPRINGING TIME

"Spring is not a season, a *time* per se: it is a form of knowledge."

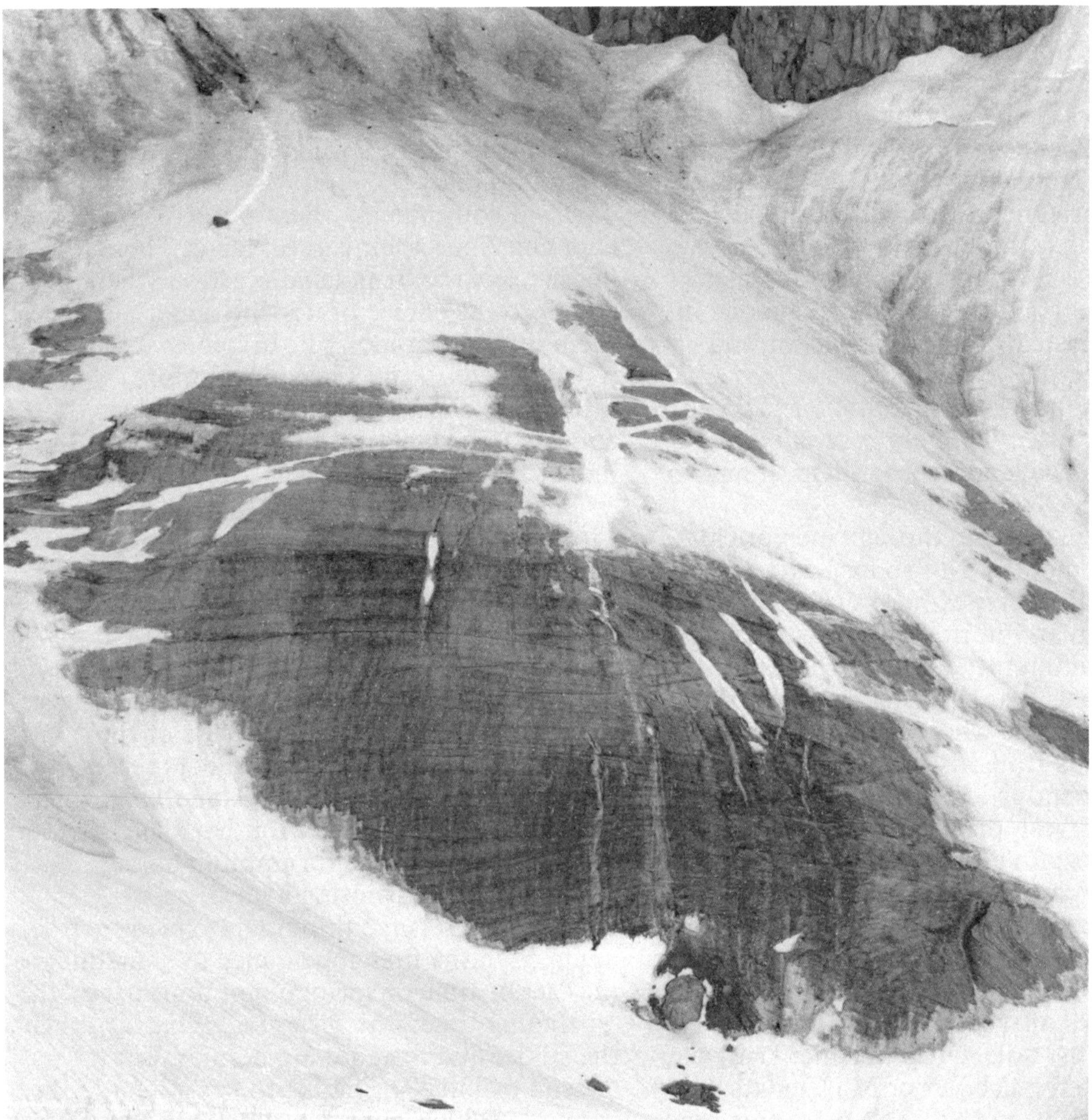

It is late February, several weeks from springtime, and my body is being rocked gently inside a narrowboat on the River Cam. The yellow curtains are drawn, thick and textured like layers of pressed pollen. I'm only half awake. My husband is sleeping fitfully beside me on the three-quarters bed built into one side of the boat. Instinctively, I rest my hand on my abdomen. Lodged deep in my womb, the cells of my first son are multiplying, drawing off nutrients and energy to support growth, intertwining the substance of our bodies.

On this late winter morning I am unused to the idea of being pregnant and uncertain what the future holds. Before long, worries draw me from the night's rest. Slowly and carefully, I slip from under the duvet and tiptoe into the sitting room. I take my quilted jacket from the peg, pull it over my pyjamas, and open the doors.

Once outside, my senses split open and the river's elements rush in. The air is sharp as vinegar. Wind froths the waters at the earth's edge. Nobody is about—or at least, no other humans. One of the neighborhood cats in our boating community is stalking. A swan sails distantly, mid-flow, with the muscular sheen of an egg. Otherwise, there's no one in view and I close my eyes, lift my chin, and savor the quiet.

Thoughts rise and fall. *Am I ready to be a mother? What will happen to my work, my freedom?* The landscape is silent. It has no answers.

I begin drifting through memories of the past few months. Not so long ago, I was standing on the Perspex-hard surface of a frozen lake in an interminable dusk. Joavie, one of the community elders of the Arctic town of Pangnirtung, was showing me how to fish in the ice near a place where he remembered summer camps from his boyhood. There was a polar bear, roaming alone, somewhere nearby. We had seen fresh prints. But she did not show herself, a ghost on already haunted grounds.

In my mind's eye, I see Joavie smiling at me, at my pathetic efforts to ice-fish. It is all so easy for him, as elemental as the swan's river glide. This is how he survives in a landscape at the very edges of what is possible for our species. Cut the hole. Drop the line. Trust the tug and whip the fish out of its elements into air so terrifyingly cold that the animal is dead and icestruck before it touches the ground. Gut it, throw it on the makeshift stove, and eat it fresh, the heat of the meal flowing like a summer river inside.

I am remembering all this and how the scene is ingrained with sadness, at the loss of his people's way of life, at the phantom of climate change that threatens to introduce an endless spring in the Arctic. At the epidemic of suicides in the town.

Then someone nudges into the real landscape before me, bringing me out of my thoughts, returning the memories to the ice-world where they belong. It is the clerical face of a common coot. I see their beak first, the chalk of their brow. What strikes me as I watch them is their diligence. Something in the directedness of the flow. They are up to something. I keep watching as they tug in and out of the vegetation along the riverbank. Before long, it is clear. They are building a nest. This shocks me. It is only February. According to my calendar, it is nearly a full month until the official start of spring, and my hands are braced by cold.

I continue my silent observation as the coot continues their careful labor. There doesn't seem to be much discretion when it comes to the choice of nesting materials. I see them carry what look like brambles. I see wilting reeds, some sticks that a more discerning dog would discard, and what appears to be a plastic straw. But who am I to judge?

After a while, the chill defeats me and I head inside to light the stove and make a cup of tea. It is lovely to be back in the warm interior of the boat. I open the curtains in the sitting room, the river pixelated by condensation on the panes. It is then that I notice another quiet messenger—a spider has spun her web on the lefthand side of the window. During winter, the spiders recede from view, tucked away, I presume, somewhere dark and neglected by us. But here she is, optimistically visible, thrumming on her glittering mesh, awaiting a meal.

This sets me thinking. If spring gets its name from the first appearance of something, the "act or time of springing or appearing," the "springing time," the *springing of the leaf*, then the spider and the coot are heralds. But it doesn't feel like spring yet to *me*. What do the coot and spider know that I don't?

FIGS. 6, 8, 9 Photos by Lena C. Emery (PP. 97, 104, 105)

Let's leap forward more than a decade from this moment to 2022. It is February. The child that was growing in my womb is now on the brink of becoming a teenager. I am only just managing to revive my professional and intellectual life after a beautiful extended winter raising two young sons. My days have now cracked open with the possibility of research and writing. One of the papers I have been reading is by a professor of environmental systems analysis at Cambridge University. His team have released a report on UK records of springtime. The headline is that spring now arrives on average a month earlier than it did in the 1980s.

The lead author of the report, Ulf Büntgen, and his team analyzed records and observations spanning 250 years of the first flowering plants after winter in the UK. They found that species' flowering times vary most according to fluctuations in temperature but that there's been a marked shift towards an earlier spring since 1986, as defined by the "springing time" of wildflowers.

A year or so earlier, a report from the UK's Woodland Trust had also highlighted a trend towards earlier springs, using a wider set of indicators from the spawning of frogs to sightings of birds nesting (like the Cambridge coot). And the effect hasn't been limited to the UK. Many countries and regions have been reporting signals of earlier springtimes, most often using the first leaf and blooms of certain plant species as measures, like lilac and honeysuckle. In these reports, then, spring is determined by "phenology," the life history strategies of plants and animals and their interactions with the environment.

Yet for many of us humans living in postindustrial countries, spring is marked on our calendars according to the equinox—when day and night are roughly the same length. This mismatch between spring as a feature of the living world and spring as a date that we timetable is, in part, a function of the severance of human societies from the natural rhythms of the environment on which we depend.

As most of us live within controlled interiors, where temperatures are kept at a season-free norm of around 20 degrees Celsius (or 68 Fahrenheit), and where artificial lighting and curtains extend or contract the hours of day and night, we rely on an ephemeris to tell us that spring has arrived rather than the direct interface of our skin cells with the environment beyond us. This muffling effect on our bodies is amplified by a growing distance between us and other living beings in our communities. A survey in 2016 found that one third of children spend less than thirty minutes playing outside a day. While the pandemic caused a hike in the number of hours that adults spent outside in nature, follow-up surveys suggest that this effect is already beginning to wane. Today, over fifty percent of all Americans put in less than an hour a day out of doors. This can only increase as we steadily turn over the real to the artificial, exchanging wilderness in the truest sense (which is to say, that which is its own, irreducible to utility) for the virtual and fabricated.

And so, most especially in modern, urban, hyperconnected environments, humans have become an indoor creature. This has been dubbed the "inside epidemic," but it has impacts beyond the obvious ones we might expect on our physical health and well-being. Spending most of our time in controlled, human-designed spaces also dramatically reduces our direct knowledge and experience of other living beings. And, increasingly, it leaves us vulnerable to knowledges of a dubious or unknown provenance: the hiss of disinformation, the commodification of unverified, uncontextualized ideas. The effects of this are harder to track but no less significant. On either side of the most vocal discussions around climate change, for example, is often a shocking narrowness of thought, and sometimes a willful distortion of knowledge.

And I think back to Joavie again. He had grown up close to nature, in constant communication with it. It is hard for someone who has never been to such places to properly appreciate how insulated many of us are in the postindustrial countries of the world from the environment and its realities. But in a place as fierce as the Arctic, there's no freedom to detach. Cold and hunger will come at you regardless. As such, Inuit in the Arctic were some of the first people to warn us about climate changes through their direct witness of a shifting world. Yet despite the opportunity offered by these sentinels in the North, their experiences didn't provoke us to respond in a timely way. While I was on the frozen lake with Joavie, in the pearly violet of the winter months, the UN climate change conference was taking place in Copenhagen in 2009. It felt like a big deal at the time, yet here we are fifteen years later and little has meaningfully changed. Our awareness of the scale of the situation has altered. But not our extractive or exploitative behaviors.

Another arbitrary marker of spring is Daylight Saving Time, the moment when the clocks in many of our countries "spring" forward or "fall" back. An artifact of the First World War, daylight saving has less to say about the biorhythms of spring and more to say about how our cultural institutions determine when it's time to spring. The clock change was implemented as a means to scrimp on the use of coal during wartime, a legacy of a world dependent on fossil fuels.

Meanwhile, among humans, a different kind of life history event is now happening earlier too. My child is going through puberty, a slow and somewhat bewildering phenomenon that unfolds in and across a child's body, sometimes to their own consternation. There are averages for the onset of puberty, just as there are averages for springing time, and we have known for some years that children, most especially girls, are undergoing puberty much earlier than in previous generations. To date, nobody knows for certain why this should be. One suggestion is that children are better fed, in some cases overweight, and that this is a contributing factor. Another hypothesis, for which there's also some evidence, relates back to the fact that children stay indoors more than they used to and are thereby chronically exposed to certain synthetic chemicals, from cleaning to beauty products, that act as endocrine disruptors, shifting hormonal patterns. Yet another possibility is that increased stress may be nudging young bodies into blooming early. And so, the so-called "spring awakening" is coming prematurely to the bodies of our children all around the world.

I think about all of this, and it sets my mind spinning. The plants and animals whose actions and priorities give shape to springtime sense the changes afoot, materially and substantially. But they don't know *why* things are changing. And so they adapt straightforwardly.

Meanwhile, we humans know the primary reasons climate change and pollution are happening, and that we are culpable for a disturbance in seasonal patterns that is unsettling what we take spring to mean now. And yet we are finding it enormously challenging to adapt. At the risk of being flippant, one might question the worth of our kind of knowledge then, our precious rationality. Good for counterfactuals, maybe. But for direct, positive action?—perhaps less so.

So what would it take to reattach our knowledge of the world to our ability to adapt our behaviors positively? Are there lessons to be found in the springing time?

One of the concerns of those studying variations in springing time in nature is that organisms that rely on synchronizing seasonal patterns could find themselves diverging from a critical food source or exposed to other, novel threats. In other words, so many species are interdependent that seasonal disruptions could threaten these relations, potentially causing sudden declines. This has been raised among scientists anticipating that plants and pollinators, for example, might become drastically uncoupled.

And yet, intriguingly, in many of the studies that have been done to date, there are signs of greater flexibility and resilience among species than might have been anticipated. Most research has focused on pollinators like honeybees. British entomologist Pat Willmer noted that "pollination mutualism is likely to be buffered against climate change" because most plants are generalists and pollinators are distributed across a wide enough area that the effects are more diffuse. She did warn, however, that for specialists or already vulnerable and declining groups of organisms, the added stress of adapting to an earlier springtime could be significant.

Another study found that "even relatively specialized pollinators were much more flexible in their use of plant species as floral resources than their local flower visitation suggested." Glimmers of hope? Well, yes. But, here again, the authors of the study called for some caution, not only because data can be poor for rarer species of pollinating insects but also because the effects may differ depending on whether the diversity of plants in a region remains intact.

But how does a plant or animal know that an important change has occurred in the environment? And how does information translate through the prism of their bodies into meaningful activities?

For most of human history, it has been impossible to look inside an organism and

FIG. 7 Alex Strohl / Verb Photo (P. 103)

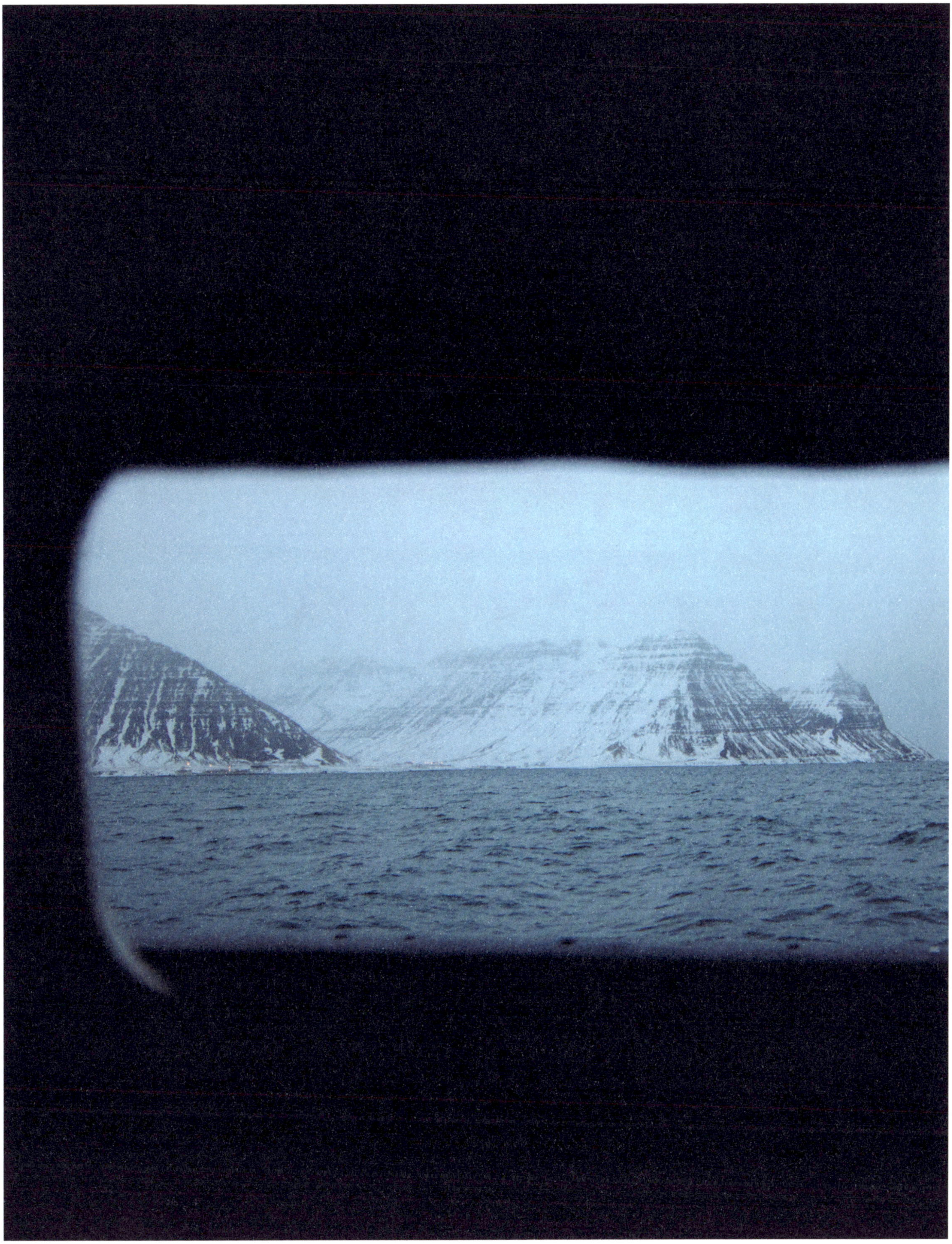

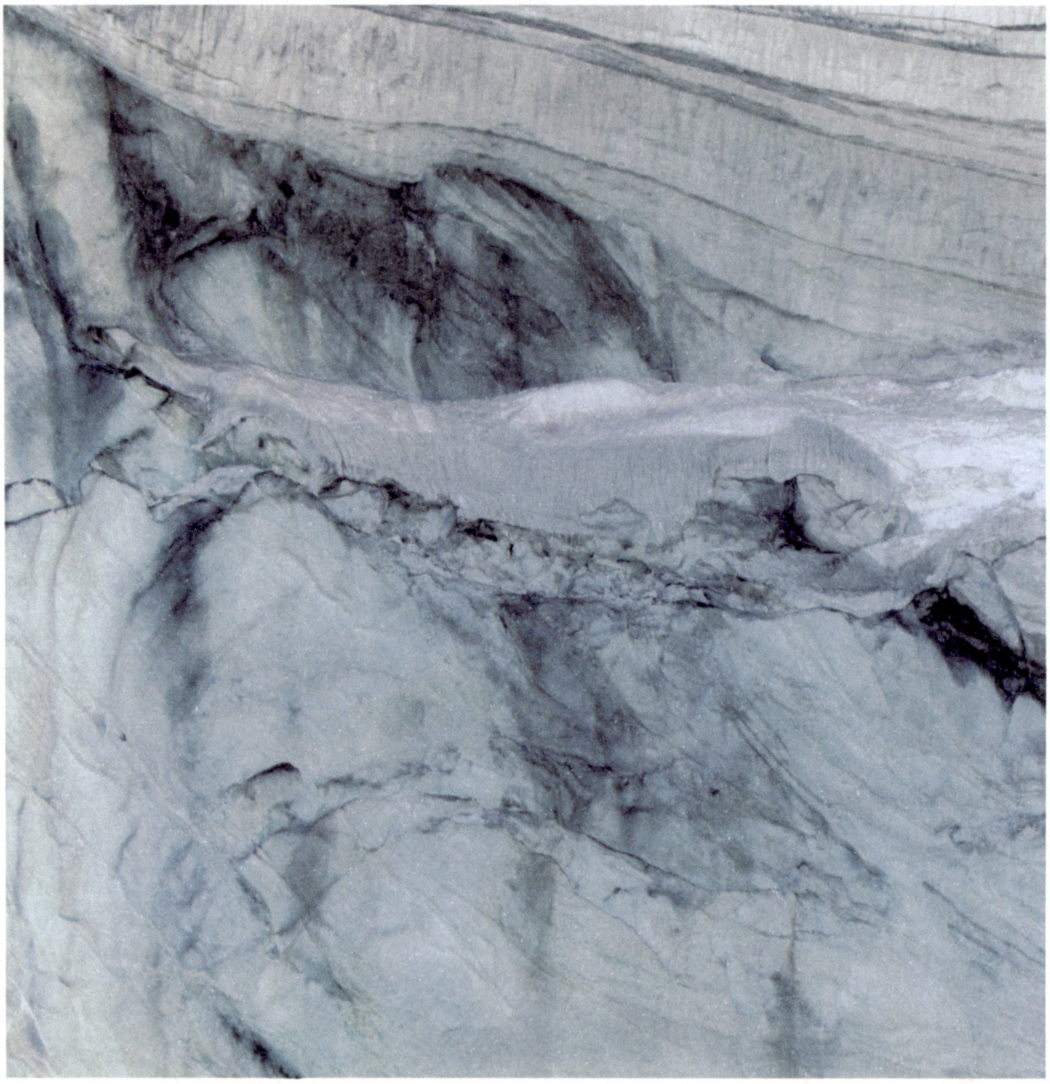

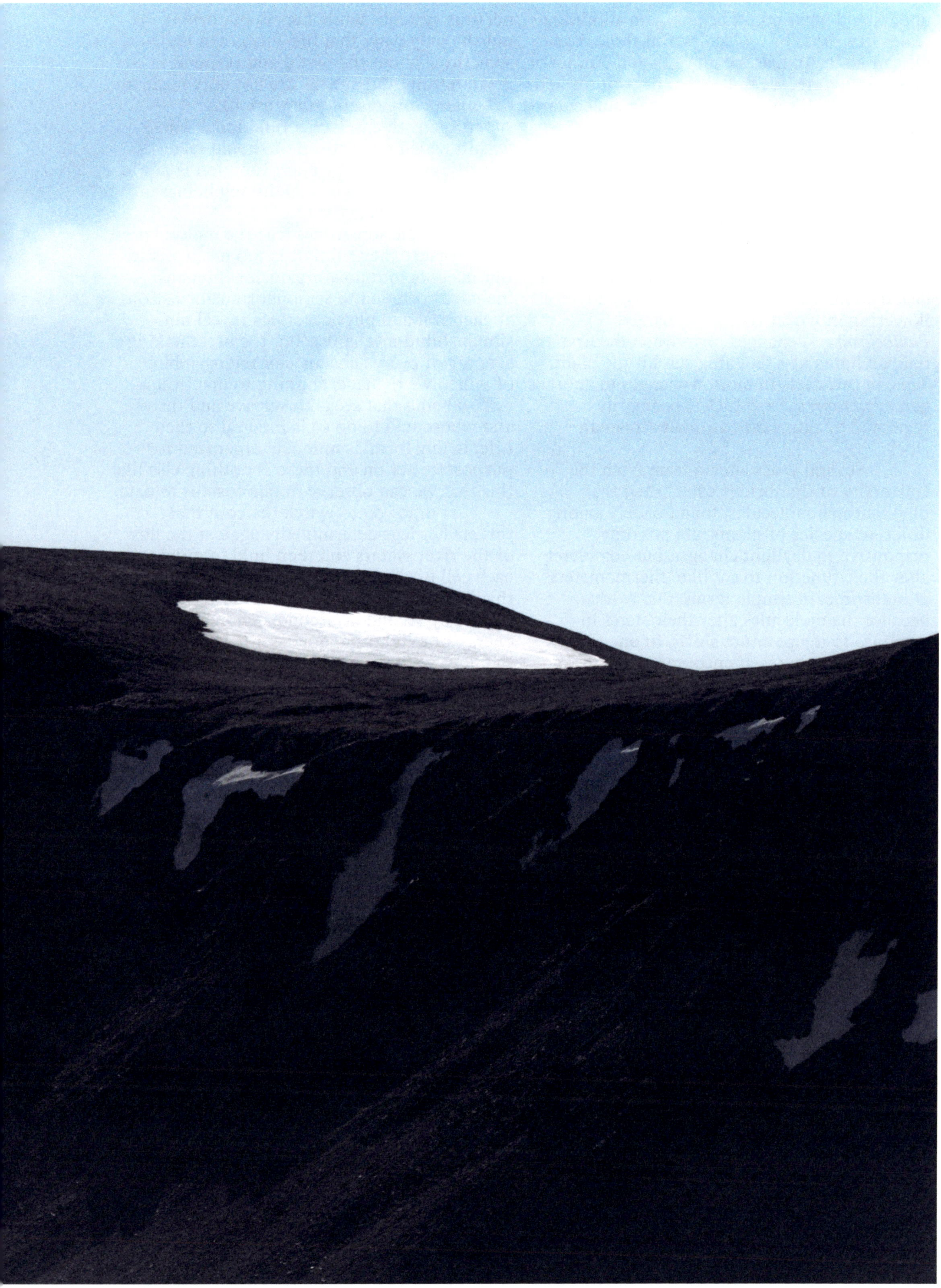

understand what might be going on at minute scales like those of molecules. But these days we can do it. And, as we move in and out, up or down, in nature, we find different patterns and new insights. It's heady stuff. At the molecular scale, we can discover some extraordinary capacities to accommodate change in the environment that are integral to a living being. Indeed, it is at the level of the molecules of life that we begin to catch sight of how life-forms "know" when spring is.

In 2013, scientists in California discovered a gene that, when "knocked out" or deactivated, led to considerable delays to flowering in wheat. The gene, named *Phytochrome C,* changes form when the first reddish lights of a dawning sun hit the plant. This, in turn, sets in motion changes to another gene, *Photoperiod 1,* which is ordinarily regulated by the plant's 24-hour circadian clock.

Several years later, a team from the University of Cambridge established that phytochrome molecules, found widely among different species of plants, are not only responsive to daylight changes, but completely alter their function to act like "thermometers" at nighttime. In simple terms, this works because the molecules alter their states in response to temperature shifts. In one state, they inhibit genes that encourage growth, and in another they "release" the genes, allowing growth to continue. The advantage this offers the plant is that the change in state of the molecules stimulates the growth, rather than simply a set of "instructions" within a gene for a particular seasonal pattern. This means that plant growth of this kind isn't "directed" by the gene in some rigid way, but rather the molecules within the plant work holistically and flexibly so that growth follows from what the season happens to be like, moment by moment. Springing time, then, begins through a direct interaction between the season and the dynamic body of the plant.

For the researchers, this discovery was hailed as an opportunity to "accelerate the breeding of crops resilient to thermal stress and climate change." But for many of us, what intrigues is the capabilities of the plants. When we consider how plants adjust to changes in their lifetimes, we might ask whether we humans would be as flexible and resilient in the face of climate change as the species around us. Contrary to widely held beliefs, brains and nervous systems, while hugely important, are not the only ways that life-forms can know something about the world and respond meaningfully. Organisms are not only made up of separate organs, but they are like superorgans themselves, a functional whole within which no part can or should take priority, and whose primary function is not to survive but *to know how to*. Living beings are like organs for *purpose*.

People sometimes fear the molecular scale because they think it is too mechanistic. But insights into how organisms (humans included) respond to seasonal transformations at chemical and physical scales reveal not simple, blind mechanics, but the breathtaking synergy of every substance or endosymbiont of which we're made, aligning to manifest a self—a being that seeks to survive and thrive and whose will to do so is integral to them. Life, in any form, is uniquely organized for purposeful action and there is nothing else like this that we can observe in our cosmos to date.

I urge you to watch the coot that thrusts her legs determinedly against the flow of the river waters and then hold in mind that each cell of the coot's being, and every part of that individual creature, is working ceaselessly, second by second by second, channeling the energy of a lightning bolt, swithering against the flow, with the goal of making her nest. This is mind-blowing. So why do we chronically underplay the significance of how living beings come to know the world?

One reason is that the metaphors we have used to understand biology undervalue the capacity of other beings. When we look at how plants flower or how a bird decides to build a nest, we've tended to tell a simple story that species respond to "the program" in their genes. By this view, there's no agent to whom anything really matters, just a biological machine following the goals that evolutionary process has left behind.

However, such metaphors are not only misleading scientifically, but also ethically. They can encourage objectifying distortions of a much more complicated and dynamic reality. Many harms towards other life-forms are committed and justified because we tell ourselves that other living beings, in the absence of our conscious and reasoning gifts, cannot really *know* or decide on anything. As such, we see them simply as material things in our world, as tools, backdrops, as a pretty mirage of autonomy. And because they are not "really" acting intentionally in the world, but merely reacting as a machine might, their lives can be reframed in terms of their function or utility.

But new insights within the science of cause in biology are transforming our understanding of the intelligence of living beings. Life-forms are profoundly interwoven with their environment and each other but are nonetheless locally distinct. This allows for a dynamic interior that senses the outside world and can react purposefully to survive the changes. A number of vital attributes are locked together for this to be possible—especially metabolism, the ability to bias energy towards a goal, and homeostasis, the ability to rebalance the body towards the optimal conditions for survival. Through these attributes, the whole body of the organism works ceaselessly to make sense of the world and respond in ways that support flourishing and survival. In this way, every micromillimeter of a bird or a plant (or you and me) is an instrument of meaning, harmonizing and changing state. And the amount of energy pushed around the body to make all this possible is quite extraordinary, like lightning storms within us, flashing and swirling until the day we die.

Most crucially, life-forms are structured to achieve goals that follow from whatever state they are in relative to their environment and what is happening to them. When we understand how life-forms create changes to themselves, we can begin to appreciate that spring is not a season, a *time* per se: it is a form of knowledge. The changes and activities of organisms are the literal embodiment of what we take spring to mean, radically determined by the organisms themselves. In the absence of living beings' responses to the world beyond them that they've come to know—putting out buds, bringing their bodies together, building the cradles for their young—spring is meaningless. It is only the undirected dance of electromagnetic radiation and the Earth on its axis.

Seasons are powerful opportunities to see how individual organisms, in the present moment of their life, make different or novel decisions, internally and externally, in response to changes. This isn't infinitely flexible—organisms each have essential needs that can't be compensated for amid huge disruptions to a season. Yet it is a mistake to see living beings as objects passively altered by variations in their world. Rather, life is active by its nature, and all living beings are wildly alive to the changes, opportunities, and perturbations that surround them and that have meaning for them. The state of being alive is all about sensitivity, flexibility, and attention to change. There is hope in this for the future.

Yet humans, despite being highly sensitive creatures capable of introspection and a phenomenal breadth of action, are changing for the worse. How have we become so disconnected? What has got in the way between our bodies and the world?

To answer this question fully would take more than an essay. But the simple reason is human culture. Whereas the kind of direct knowledge between our physical bodies and the environment is almost impossible to hack, the other way that animals can accumulate knowledge is through cultures—collective ideas and behaviors that are learned and shared. There are huge benefits to this kind of combined and cumulative knowledge, but there is always a very real danger that it can be coopted or distorted away from any fundamental goal of positive adjustment.

That is what we see today. There is ample evidence that the world is altering in ways that are detrimental to many of us. Pollution is perhaps the easiest of these to grasp. According to the World Health Organization, ninety-nine percent of the human population (and we can therefore deduce much of the rest of the biotic community) breathes air that has been polluted by human activities. Tracking the effects of this across such a colossal dataset is almost impossible, and so when we are told that this contributes to at least seven million deaths annually, we can assume that this is an almost meaningless figure. How much does pollution contribute significantly but indirectly to strokes, heart disease, and cancers, for instance?

We can see, taste, and smell pollution, and yet we struggle to make the necessary changes. This inertia is mostly down to the absorption of widespread cultural values, such as prioritizing economic growth, that drive us towards choices that disrupt the pathways between the identification of cause and a proportional response. And there are, perhaps, further obstructions. Many of us have formidable psychological barriers between the physical realities of the world and our beliefs about life. For example, spiritual beliefs about the superiority of humans over the rest of creation that convince us there is no limit to how we subordinate the Earth to our needs and wants. Or commitments to ideologies like neo-libertarianism that legitimate private impulses at the expense of collective measures towards change in the human sphere. One barrier comes in the form of good old-fashioned optimism that we will somehow manufacture a solution or, alternatively, good old-fashioned nihilism, appeasing us with the notion that we are screwed anyway.

Yet an acceptance that we are mortal beings who, first and foremost, need to understand our interdependence with the fabric of the world around us remains mightily powerful. Future cultures must recognize our biological reality again. That is a lesson that my time in the Arctic gave me. There, cultures emerged out of direct communication with the wider environment and other species. That is a sensibility we need to cultivate now. And I feel this as my last child stands on the threshold of puberty. As a more experienced mother now, I know how this stage of life will draw him out of the safety of our loving home and into a world of uncertainty and unsettling realities. I know that our time together in the richness of this intimacy is drawing to a close. Parenting is a long goodbye, seasoned with both joy and grief. All I can gift my youngest son is the knowledge that culture should always be sensitive to one's biological reality.

And so, today, as the summer is sinking into autumn, my son and I have come to say goodbye to the swallows to experience the changing of the seasons. Together we stand in the middle of the road, following the valley's line to the sea. The light, heavy and granular, draws down the sides of the dale like sands through an hourglass. The swallows chitter and swoop, restless as teenagers, conjuring new orbits, new physics, an orrery of birds.

Countless times I have seen swallows and house martins possessed by *zugenruhe*. It is one of the most poignant expressions of seasonal shift that a human can witness. Their readiness to migrate charges the air, almost bears down on those close by. It is vortical. Sublime. We watch them, mesmerized, for what feels like hours until the cold begins to catch us. "Shall we go back inside?" my son says to me, eyes like sun on a turning leaf. *Soon,* I say. *Just a little bit longer*.

Swirling between and around me and the slight body of my child, the swallows seem to gather up something of who we are as dust is embodied in the gyration of the storm, carrying us with them to other worlds. And I wonder who in Africa will greet them as signals of a new season, whether a mother and her son will look up to the skies in KwaZulu-Natal and know that I am thinking of them.

Jake Skeets
SUMMER LIGHT: A FAILED ESSAY IN FOUR PARTS

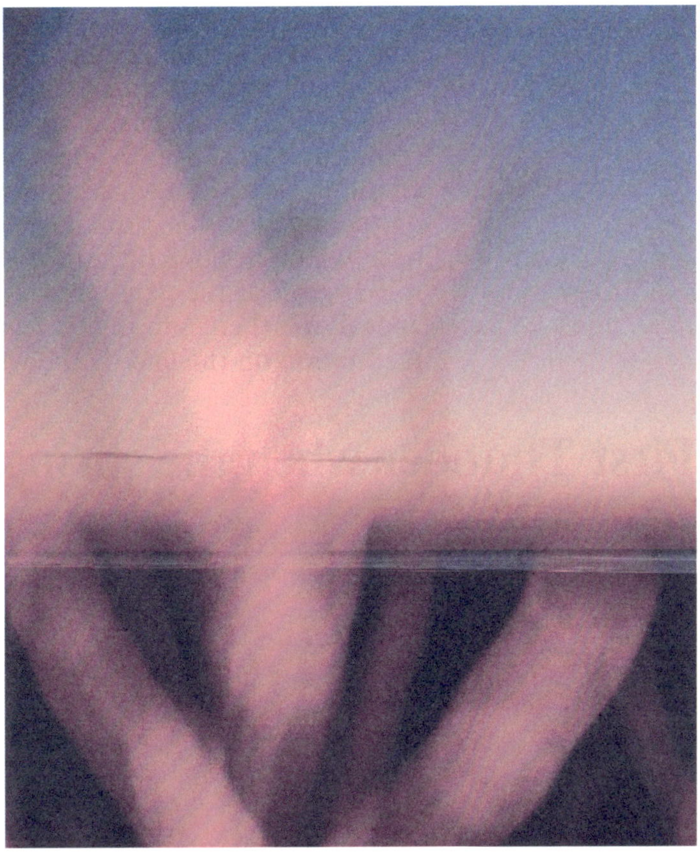

I. I'M WRITING THIS ESSAY DURING AN EXCESSIVE HEAT WARNING

I'M WRITING THIS essay during an excessive heat warning. For days, the skies have been singed a hazy pale blue. Just the other day I went for a walk in the evening and the sunlight was pink as if a wildfire was burning nearby. We can recognize a wildfire by the way it slants the light. I held my palm in the air and watched the light fall onto my skin in shades of rage and discontent. I'm writing this essay during an excessive heat warning, and I have never been shy to heat. I'm a boy born of desert. I'm a boy born of summer. I am also a boy born of drought.

Drought conditions created by a warming planet and years of resource extraction that stole water from Navajo communities to build cities like Las Vegas and Phoenix have been an ongoing issue across the Navajo Nation. Conditions tightened in the 1990s, and as a boy growing up at that time, I remember people gossiping, often, that we could run out of water. Fortunately, Navajo communities still have access to running water on the reservation—though strained access at best, which became illuminated during the initial peak of the pandemic. I wrote about apocalypse then, and in the years since, my meditation on the end of the world has shifted

"We call it the First Thunder when the spring storms come."

FIG. 10 Photo by Hans Borg (P. 111)

but the materiality of it has only heightened as we see more and more signs of climate catastrophe.

I'm writing this essay during an excessive heat warning, and I learned of apocalypse as a boy. I remember witnessing the way the land shifted around me as time moved on, how my brothers and sisters often talked about the end of the world, and how grief falls into a room like sunlight.

The earliest memory I have of wildfire involves the first season of *American Idol*. As Kelly Clarkson was singing on the television, I stood outside and watched the sun set in a stunning red and neon orange glow, different from other sunsets. The air smelled of smoke. I'm pretty sure the fire was the Rodeo-Chediski Fire that burned nearly a half million acres in 2002, though I can't be sure exactly which fire that year was big enough that I could see its smoke on the reservation. Later that year—as Laura Paskus wrote in a feature for a *High Country News* issue aptly titled "The Great Western Apocalypse"—Navajo Nation president Kelsey Begaye declared a drought emergency across the reservation and ranch owners were urged to cull their cattle: an action that has been deeply scarring for most Navajo people, who have had to battle livestock reduction for decades since the government's initial mandatory reduction program in the 1930s. It feels like every one of my summers on the reservation since 2002 has had elements of wildfire. Each memory holds the stench of smoke and singed sunset light. I'm writing this essay during an excessive heat warning.

When I was a boy, the heat was not an aggressive factor in how much time we spent outdoors. Even on the hottest days, we raced cloud shadows on the dirt road in front of my house as dry winds carried small clouds across the sky. To keep cool, we dug into the dark soil under tall trees. We drank water from the hose spigot and swam in the small stock ponds that were carrying on through the heat that even then felt excessive. When we were lucky, one of our aunts or uncles drove us into Gallup, New Mexico, so we could swim at the community pool. We always spent a week with our late aunt in Albuquerque because her apartment complex had a swimming pool. Each morning, we ran to the pool and only came back for lunch and after the pool was closed. Our skin darkened from the sun, and each August when we returned to school, we held our arms against each other to see how brown we had become over the wild days of summer.

And as I'm writing this essay during an excessive heat warning, I'm thinking about those summer days on the reservation and the way heat became a contour of my life. I always said summer was my favorite season. My best memories involve the evening time in July, sitting on the porch eating watermelon with my brothers and sisters. The past two years, however, have tested my appreciation for summer, as excessive heat warnings have begun plaguing most of the summer months. When we were boys, we looked to the west and the southwest during hot days to see whether dark clouds were growing. If we saw the clouds, it meant the monsoon storms were coming and the heat was about to break. It always began with the wind, sometimes gritty with sand. As the monsoons neared, sand twisters became more frequent. We were always told to keep a distance. We were given many reasons why we had to stay away from them: they were spirits, they make you confused, they take something from you if you're caught in one, they are a sign of bad things to come. As rez kids, though, we never really listened. The sand twisters were markers of the coming storms, so we welcomed them as they grew, sometimes several feet into the air. We often ran straight into them, feeling the sand scatter across our bodies. What I did not know then was that the sand these twisters and the winds carried was a sign of climate change.

As boys, we would walk barefoot over the sand dunes that grew in the deeper parts of old, abandoned cornfields. Today, when I return home, I see sand dunes taking up even more space. Sand dune migration across the Navajo Nation is eating entire roads and homes as drought conditions worsen. So those reasons to stay away from sand twisters might have some weight, because they did start to take things from us in the end. I mean, I am writing this essay during an excessive heat warning after all.

"Triple-digit heat index" was not a phrase I thought I would ever use, despite writing this essay during an excessive heat warning. I've always had an affinity for the weather. The 1996 film *Twister*, with Bill Paxton and Helen Hunt, was a staple of my boyhood. Back then, we only ever owned a few VHS tapes and *Twister* was one of them. I pretended my laundry basket was a tornado as I chased my toy trucks across my house and in the dirt outside. I often recreated the first tornado scene in the movie, when Bill (Bill Paxton) and Jo (Helen Hunt) have a close call with a tornado as they are driving in a ditch. I remember picking up any VHS tape from Blockbuster that dealt with tornadoes, often watching documentaries about the weather. I remember I wanted to be a fireman because "fire twisters" were something I could potentially see in person. Then, I wanted to be a weatherman after hearing about meteorology and the study of weather. I somehow shifted and became a poet instead, but my career as a writer brought me to the University of Oklahoma, where I teach now. I can safely say that close calls with tornadoes are as scary as I thought they would be and just as exhilarating. During severe weather days, I often monitor all the weather channels in Oklahoma just to listen to the language they employ to talk about the weather: mesocyclone, dry line, wind shear. I now realize that tornadoes in Oklahoma mark the season the way weather marked the season back home on the reservation.

Seasons, then, are deeply interior. They rest in an instinct that is both deeply human and deeply temporal. They represent a relationship humans have had with deep time for generations. And as I'm writing this essay during an excessive heat warning, I'm wondering how the climate crisis will impact our relationship with the weather and the way we have mapped seasons for ourselves. I'm writing this essay during an excessive heat warning, and this might be a new kind of calendar for me; a new way to mark the summer. The way sunsets fall into my palm in a singed light, the color of rage.

I'm writing this essay during an excessive heat warning, and it has made all the difference. Go outside and see if you can smell smoke. I know I can.

II. SEASONS ARE TO THE BODY

SEASONS ARE TO the body what memory is to time. Back home, we have unique ways of measuring time. As kids we are taught how to tell what season it is not by using a calendar but by looking to the weather. It all begins in October. "Ghą́ą́jįʼ" is the Diné word for October, and it can mean "half" or a kind of summit but can also mean "the separation of the seasons." It also marks the Navajo New Year. The moon is important here too. "Cold air is coming," my partner says whenever the moon looks like a bowl turned over. Cold air is spilling from the moon.

The Navajo dictionary I often use to help me with translation and working with Diné language lists "Ghą́ą́jįʼ" as "October," but it also gives "back-to-back" as a literal translation—as in, "summer and winter are back-to-back." The word "Ghą́ą́jįʼ" then is a sibling to the words for the various parts of the upper back, including "ʼíígháán" (backbone), "ʼagąąstiin" (shoulder blade), and "ʼagąągah" (area of the shoulder blades). If we layer this new orientation to seasons and the body with the word "kʼos," a word that means both "cloud" and "the neck," we come to understand the way the body is uniquely tethered to the land and its weather. We see parts of our body as parts of the world around us: our necks are the clouds, our shoulders then become the mountaintops that touch the clouds. Our upper bodies are tied to processes of transition: breathing, pumping blood in and out, swallowing food, and talking. They are systems tied to each other.

Seasons are to the body what clouds are to the mountains. We honor this relationship by leaping into time as an actual practice. The annual snow bath is the way we mark the start of the winter. When the first snows come, we are told to jump into the snow to let it cleanse our bodies. It's a kind of renewal. In the summer, we use the weather again to mark the seasons shifting.

We call it the First Thunder when the spring storms come. As kids, we were often home alone during the early storms of the year because our parents worked all the time. As I grew older and took on the role of babysitter for my younger siblings, my brothers and I grew quite familiar with thunderstorms in the spring. They felt different from monsoon storms, which are often dense and windy. Spring storms looked taller. I could often see through the curtains of rain to the other side of them, whereas monsoon storms were thick, choked by rain and rising dust. Whenever we heard the First Thunder, we were always told to stretch to shake winter off our bodies. Just like First Snows, First Thunder was an insistence of the body. The first thunderstorms were always the loudest.

Once, my brother busted his head open when a storm started outside and he rushed to open the door. The wind was so strong, the door swung open and pushed his body into a dining room chair. Another time, a storm caught us as we got off the bus after school. We only lived a few yards from the main highway where the bus drop was, but it meant having to run in the mud as the rain came down in harsh and sudden ribbons. The lightning was fast, and the thunder was loud. We ran toward home to find we had left our keys behind. We were stranded. So, we broke into my uncle's truck through his back window and rode out the storm inside his truck—the thunderstorm outside reminding us of its strength. I remember the act of looking: witnessing its immensity. It felt like I was watching the body of eternity walk through the trees. A wide swath of pressure and moisture. A body of physics ancient to the earth beneath us.

These early storms marked the spark of summer and mirrored the monsoon storms that would mark its waning. Interestingly enough, the Diné word for summer is "Shį́," which bears a striking resemblance to "shí," or "me." The meaning is changed depending on the sound we employ. If we add an additional "i" to the word, it then becomes new words that are conditional upon time. For example, the word "shíí'" means "mine" but a "mine" conditional with time, as "became mine [over a period of time]." The word is only possible with temporality. The word "shįį́" is another word evocative of time, which can mean "maybe" or "perhaps." Of course, I can't make a connection between "Shį́" and "shí" as I did between "Ghą́ąjí'" and other related words, but I like to theorize that the "sh" consonant sound here is referring to the sun or a kind of interior energy that brings life and energy. The word for sun—when not referring to the holy deity but a general reference, as in "sunlight"—can be "shá," as in "shá bitł'óól" or "sunbeam." (When translated literally, "shá bitł'óól" means "the sun's string.") For me, the linkages between "Shį́" and "shí" are too prominent to ignore, especially when thinking through the meaning of "shá." But though we don't fully understand, we can still react to the texture of these linkages—what becomes an instinctive sinew between seasons and the body. I don't know why I need to stretch at First Thunder or bathe in the First Snows, but I can engage with their premise and gestures. The thrums of my ancestry sing when I practice these kinds of ritual because of the way it "feels." It's a kind of poetry that probably bridged my interest in the weather and my career as a writer. Weather after all is a kind of poetry. But if I'd been a weatherman, I might have only learned to make meaning of the weather. Whereas poetry taught me the way to take things we cannot understand as a kind of meaning-making. Seasons are to the body what First Thunder is to me.

As I write the phrase "seasons are to the body," I'm thinking through the somatic nature of our daily experiences. We experience the world through our bodies. We measure pressures and physics using the processes of our various organs and nerve endings. It's almost as if our body is acting like a spider web. The other day in my family group chat, my brother sent a picture of an Orb-weaver Spider that made a home near some oil canisters in my parents' back porch. He told my sister to touch the spider's web, because if she did, she would learn how to weave. The gesture of simply touching a spider's web as an act of faith, to me, is like jumping into First Snows and stretching at First Thunder. It's a way to honor the life we have in relation to the life around us.

I think of the late Native philosopher Viola Cordova's theories of the air around us as a kind of yolk and that we should consider our lives as not existing in open air but in a closed, contained system. Air is a pressure, after all. It's composed of elements. It's a life force with an "invisible architecture," to borrow a term from the poet Barbara Guest. I also think of the late Carol Edelman Warrior's essay "Indigenous Collectives: A Meditation on Fixity and Flexibility." She meditates on the non-structures of slime molds as a kind of metaphor for organizing societies around collectivity and flexibility and posits that Indigenous people had often followed these ideas before contact. In the essay, she wrote, "Controlled by humans, the slime mold's purpose shifts and becomes foreign and antagonistic to the slime mold's natural relationships, environment, and self-determination. It seems to me that this definitional process is both analogous to the work of a gaffer on a blob of glass and the effect of external definitions of identity and boundaries in treaty language. Transformational capabilities are slowed, relationships between people and peoples are constrained by formal (codified) language, and relationships

“Seasons are to the body what clouds are to the mountains. We honor this relationship by leaping into time as an actual practice.”

FIG. 11 Evelyn Dragan / Connected Archives (P. 117)

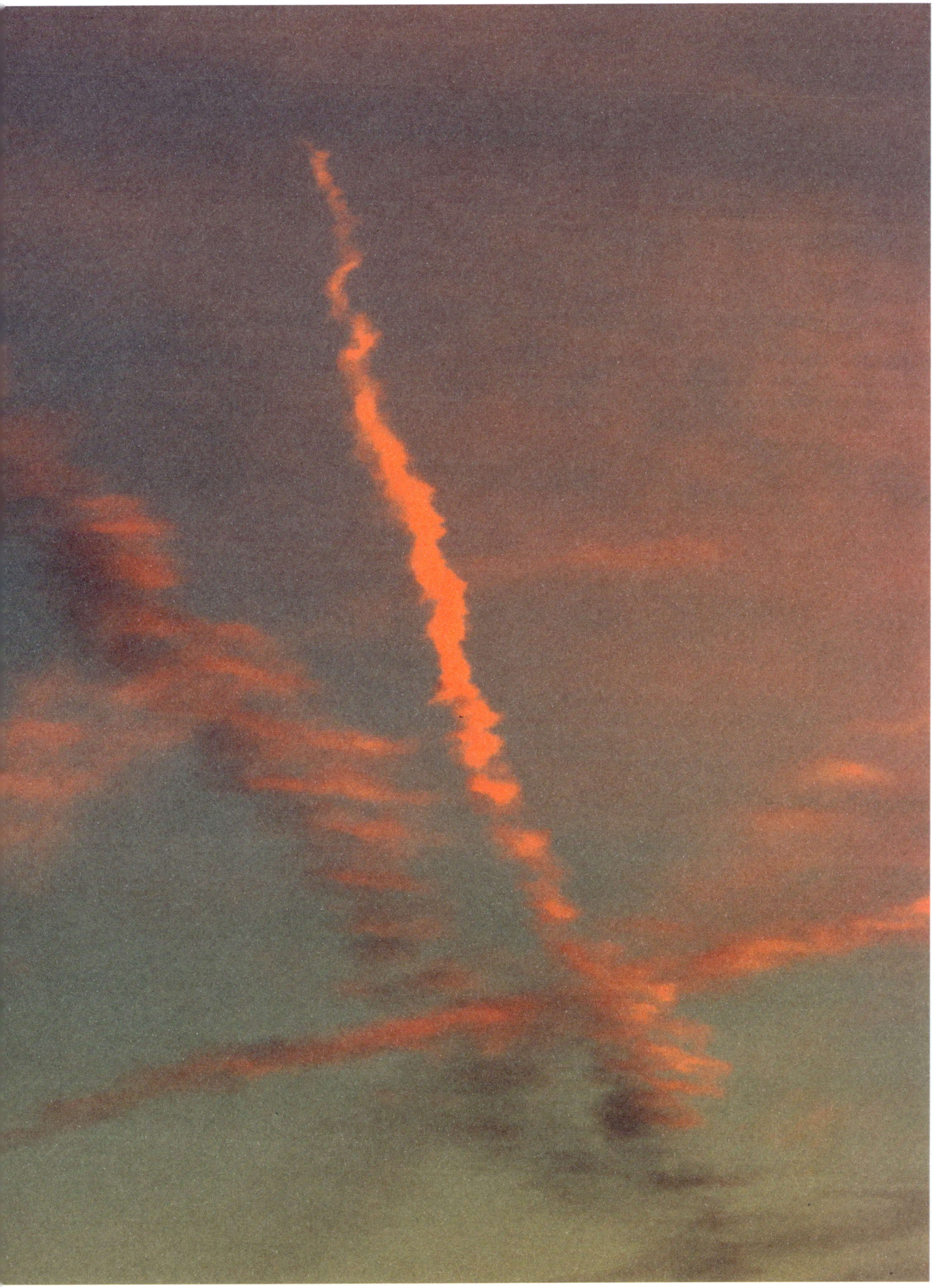

in places suffer under the pressure to commodify and control." She continued, "I am excited by any life or existence that defies the rationalist bent to impose a language of authoritative definitions onto life forms: the unilinear, cartographical, bordered, and hierarchical structures that constrain the meaning of identities, self-determination, places, and the exercise of sovereignty."

If seasons are to the body, then calendars are to seasons what walls are to people. We use language to restrict the very movement of our bodies and energies across time and space. We contain the intricate, innate, and instinctive nature of our relationality with the world around us. We employ punitive systems that oppose corporeality, emotion, and flux social orientations. The very nature of our language becomes a cage. And we look to what poet Joyelle McSweeney calls "the necropastoral," as in slime molds, to see the ways in which life continues to subvert, resist, and reclaim a kind of sovereignty on and below the ground beneath us. If seasons are to the body, then seasons are to the body.

III. IN THE EVENING'S LAST LICK OF SUMMER LIGHT

In the evening's last lick of summer light, I catch a glimpse of dragonflies stuck to the gesture of two spans of time connected by the sun's ribbon. On the road along the long evening, I stand in the current of another memory. I'm in deep; the scope of singed light carrying with it an elegy to January cold. Calling me into the deepest part of the ditch where my brothers broke their bones more times than I can count, boys of late night holding cheap cigarettes between their teeth, a long night of drinking tucked somewhere behind their ear. They taught me how to glide my hands through my hair so I could be like the men in the movies, to woo some poor girl into loving another broken Navajo man with a crooked smile. I look through the constellation of our howls in the summer's hottest day to find each one of them shivering in January, waiting for the bus to take us to a school built on the broken bones of our uncles, who still sweat into the brim of their trucker hats and cowboy hats. I'm sorry to say I lost some of them and others don't look the same.

We're older now, our bones solid in the grooves of where they were once broken. I mend the broken seam of the memory with a long gaze upon this never-ending evening, lasting another eleven hours it seems. Summer has always been my favorite season and somewhere in the distance I am still making snow cones with my brothers along the 602, and we are bright with anticipation and potential and intellect, not yet stolen from us. My arms are still making imaginary waves outside the passenger window. From this, I look with regret at finding myself here all over again, the pond water at my feet, a low bird lurking just above the still water, and suddenly, a rock slides across the pink horizon. There is tremendous time in the evening. I savor every moment during the summer, when the evenings last a lifetime and I'm holding onto the night's breath with just the promise of another morning. In the evening's last lick of light, I'm thinking of summer as an orientation to the world.

Summers back home are a window. With all the trucks and trailers driving along the dirt road by my house, the dust would float above the ground like fog does in Mississippi. Sometimes, all the Navajo cowboys and cowgirls with their cowboy hats and boots would drink and drive, throwing their beer cans and bottles all along the road. Sometimes, all the Navajo cowboys and cowgirls would drink way too much. And sometimes, they would roll their trucks clean off the road.

IV. I'VE BECOME A WRITER OF MEMORY

I've become a writer of memory and it's terrifying, because memory is the one thing I'm afraid to write. The first physical manifestation of memory is scarring. During the summer, my body would become a museum of scars. How else are we to be one with the land if we are not subject to its violences? As kids, we made dirt ramps along the road and jumped our bikes into the sage brush. We would sit on our porch in the evening, sweating in the heat, but fully alive. There is tremendous time in the evening. I often return to the sunset: the colors dancing from behind the clouds. Lightning blooming in the south inside a pink-gray storm cloud. The wind speaking in small sentences as I sit in the

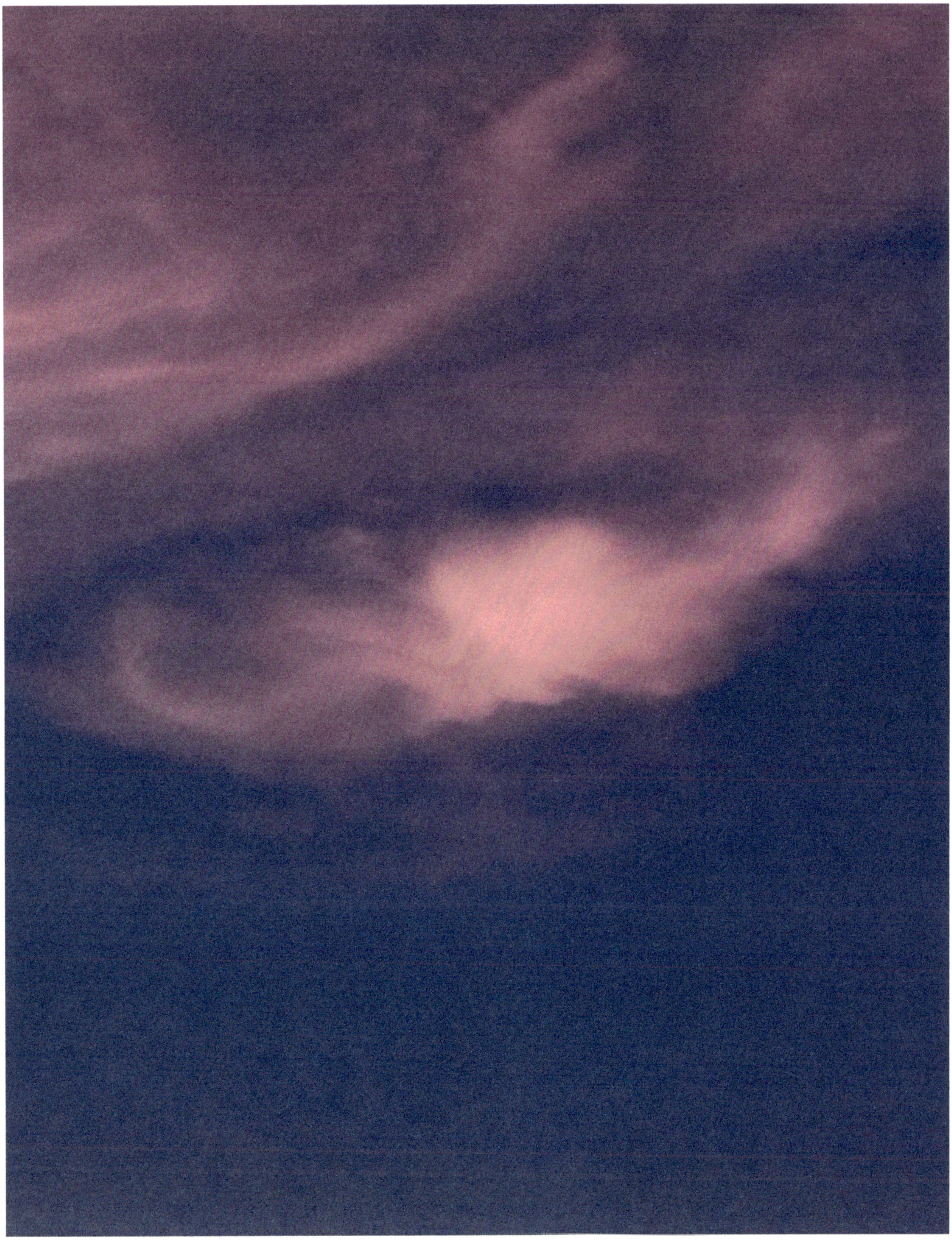

“The end of the world is the bent light we get as the sun sets through the haze of a wildfire or city smog, but even something ending can be a gesture toward something else.”

FIG. 12 Kristin Bethge / Connected Archives (P. 121)
FIG. 13 Photo by Franz Grünewald (P. 122)
FIG. 14 Evelyn Dragan / Connected Archives (P. 123)

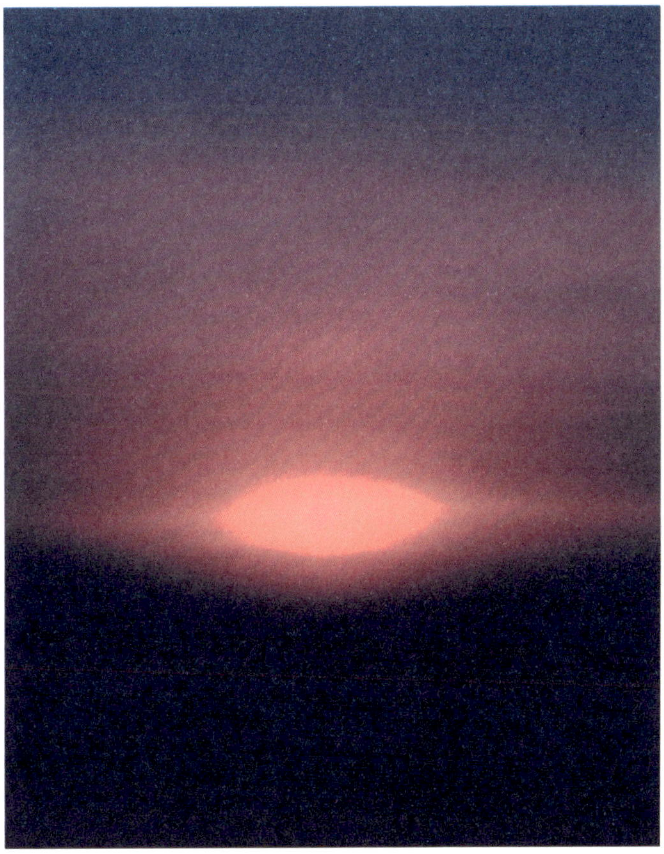

sky's time. It's gold, then pink, then deep aqua: the kind of blue that only exists in the evening. This blue, unlike any other, halos around the brain.

I heard that the stripe design in a Diné Chief Blanket could represent many things, but the one I carry with me is the stripe that represents an embrace of the sky and horizon. I look to the west in summer's late evening when the sun has set and there is an aura of calm as the night sinks in. Sky and horizon. The two dance and river for miles across the reservation, caught in cosmic touch and only for a moment. Imagine being so inspired by that sight, that dance, that you push to mirror it. We tend to seek out the things that compel us, hurt us, move us, love us. The evening time becomes a kind of love story, the sun reminding us that all things are temporary, and I have to write about this because I've become a writer of memory.

I would live my life only through the summer evening if I could, because I've become a writer of memory. A sudden burst of everything, all at once, and it moves on, away from me, and I must learn to be on my own again. The winter's evening comes too soon sometimes. I'm never ready for it. I close the curtains as if to forget about it all. Sometimes, I don't want to be reminded of things the evening has to tell me. Sometimes, it's okay to turn away from things we love if we need to relearn how to love ourselves. Sometimes, the evening is too much all at once and lasts forever.

It's an orientation to the world that I don't mind much. From a Diné worldview, summertime represents farming. It's the season of movement and big sky. We witness the weather act like a mirror during the summer, because it's moving, too. What is our weather telling us now? Excessive heat warnings. Floods intensifying in areas flattened by wildfires. Extraordinary hurricanes. The end of the world is the bent light we get as the sun sets through the haze of a wildfire or city smog, but even something ending can be a gesture toward something else. Shį́į́. Only time will tell.

For now, I invite you to sit with me during the long and wide evenings during the summer in open light. Hear the bugs sing in the bushes. See the cars on the highways move like geese walking along a pond's edge. Maybe a neighbor waves or a deer catches your scent and gallops off into the tree line. Or maybe you're sitting on your apartment balcony and the evening is being reflected by a thousand windows and the lights from the city beneath you are the bugs that are singing in the bushes. Because I've become a writer of memory, I must wonder what stories they are telling. We often look to writers to tell us the future. To tell us why we're hurting or help us contain our joy. But what writers won't tell you is, we are human, too. We experience the same evenings. We feel the heat of summer and we fail to write about it. I consider this essay a failure in four parts, but only because it happens to be about time. Any essay about time is meant to fail. My body is the essay about time. It's the essay about summer. I hope we can read it at some point in the future. Maybe at the evening's last lick of summer light.

SOUTH OF HOLLYWOOD / IN THE OC: A BROWN GIRL REMEMBERS

leaves did not fall there in fall because there was not really
fall there sometimes rain slicked hightrafficked roads
and they called the rain season winter and sometimes
parching dust blew in on hot wind though they didn't think
of that time as a season they called it always summer there
always spring called it always could be sunshine bright
grave markers they laid flat like steppingstones
on greengreengreengreen lawns so we drove by
graveyards we weren't supposed to notice because
they needed to believe everything always stayed alive
there flowersflowersflowers always open on stalks so many
bushes burning with pinkyellowwhite blooms all those
trees festooned with red and purple paperthin petals I lived
there from two and never saw a hearse until I was a childwoman
with my first small breasts and monthly blood didn't
know how a body could go when a body went nothing
for reference no upright headstones not even trees
showed me what letting go of the dying looked like no
one around looking old even no everyone sosososo
beautifully young in that place with no fall no real
winter where berries swelled all year olives ripened stone
fruit sometimes dripped from even burst on the trees

An Interview with Sam Lee
THE NIGHTINGALE'S SONG

Interviewed by
Emmanuel Vaughan-Lee

EVL I spent the last week immersed in your work, reading your book *The Nightingale*, listening to your albums and some of the remarkable recordings you've done singing with nightingales. And I was really struck by the relationship and parallels between folk music and birdsong, both in your work and also more broadly in the deep connection to place and landscapes they both embody. So I was curious to start our conversation today by asking how you first came to experience this relationship between folk music and birdsong, one that ultimately led you into such a unique relationship with the nightingale.

SL I come from a nature study background, having grown up at a wonderful [summer camp] similar to what you'd have out in the States, a very alternative, left-wing radical organization called Forest School Camps, that enabled a unique way for children—and then me as an adult, as a staff member—to grow up in a playful, very community-orientated but also ecologically minded relationship with nature. That allowed me to grow a confidence in being there, but also a confidence in myself. And it went hand in hand with song, because the campfire singing tradition there was prolific like nowhere else I've ever come across: hundreds of songs, many folk songs, including many of the American classic folk songs, but also a large proportion from a traditional repertoire that spoke from that point of view of our elders, our ancestors, in the way that folk songs do so beautifully, which is to speak quite openheartedly about adoration of nature. And that recitation and the repetition of melody over and over again, verse after verse, allowed me as a child and growing up to see the natural world through many eyes and many stories, story being the most important part of our being in this world and in nature. So it was sort of distilled in me from an early age.

And in those songs, birds seem to appear everywhere, almost more prolifically than maybe one would have been aware of just listening to the sound out in the world around. I befriended them, maybe before I'd even heard them. I heard the nightingale through folk song long before I got the opportunity to hear one in nature. And the same with trees, and what those trees and what those birds meant to those characters in those songs and how they gave a sense of an older wisdom that I had an inclination towards.

EVL You said that after your first encounter with a nightingale you were reduced, childlike, "to a state of wonderment, grinning inanely and transported through deep time, deep song, and deep earth." That sounds like quite a transformative experience. Could you share your first encounter with a nightingale, what that was like for you?

SL There is a beautiful story around it. I was taken down with friends of mine and a pregnant mother who was full-term. We heard the bird sing, and yes, I went through this kind of giddy . . . like my first kiss. [*laughs*] I think of it like that sense of: *Wow, I want this again*. But at the same time, what it revealed to me was that, all the while I'd been singing these folk songs—with a nightingale here and a nightingale there, or a lark here or a turtledove there—what I was doing by hearing that bird—really in such a ceremonial way that it was a marked journey, to go and meet the bird and be in his presence—was experiencing the voice heard by every one of the folk singers, who for hundreds of years had sung that song and whose shoulders I stand on. I was experiencing that quality of excitement that they had felt when they heard their nightingale sing, three hundred years ago, a thousand years ago, however old these songs are, and some of them go back a very long time. And I was suddenly able to inhabit the place of those ancestral singers in a way that I hadn't before. And I realized that the more I stepped into those stories in nature, the more I understood the songs; and the more I understood the songs, the more I understood what my human relationship with nature was, that they were my vocabulary and they were my entry point into the natural world in a way that made sense to me—as a part of the natural world, but also as a human teller of story and of nature's song.

EVL Hearing you describe that sounds spiritual in a certain way. It really captured you on multiple levels. And that's something I really felt when you were describing some of these experiences in your book. And there's a wonderful line that has stayed with me and describes the nightingale in this way and its influence on you: "This tiny bird led me across a threshold and introduced me to a way of being in nature that I had never reckoned with. The experience was both a meditation on stillness yet also a provocation to dance with abandon." That's very beautiful.

SL [*laughs*] I think maybe some context is really important here, because the bird doesn't exist in America. There are birds called nightingales, but it's very much a European and Eurasian bird. He sings his courtship song—it's a night song, the *nachtigall*, "the night wind," "the night voice"—and he'll sing in that silence all night, from 11 p.m. through till dawn, unrelenting. It's a persistent, extraordinary, improvised, constantly new song but constantly pulling from his repertoire of 1500 different sounds and 250 phrases, always cycling a new combination. And within that musicality and ecstaticness and the energetic explosions, often in the coldness of the night and in the stillness of the night, I recognized another artist who dared into this space in a way that energized me; like I had permission to be an expressive person, because the nightingale's response to that pure innate call, the call of nature, gave me the opportunity to express. [*laughter*]

EVL Your ongoing project of singing with nightingales, as far as I understand, started with your desire to honor an encounter between a very famous British cellist, Beatrice Harrison, and a nightingale in 1924, early in the history of recorded music and radio. I wonder if you could share that story and talk a little bit about Beatrice and what she did.

SL Mmm, absolutely. She was a very incredible woman. I should contextualize that by saying she was around in the 1920s, which is relatively recent in the history of where music and nightingales have existed. Her story is our kind of British apocryphal tale of where the nightingale came into popular consciousness. And it happened because, as a darling society character, she was the muse of Edward Elgar, she played the premier of Elgar's Cello Concerto, she was friends with royalty, she was real out there on the scene and a real pioneer of women's rights as well. And she convinced the BBC, much against their judgment, to try out some new broadcasting equipment that would allow microphones to be small enough to take outside of the studio.

And so on the 19th of May, 1924, the BBC—brand new at that point and broadcasting internationally—interrupted one of their concerts to say, "We have a broadcast from the thicket of Beatrice Harrison's back garden down south of London," where a mile of cable linking up to the telephone exchange brought the song of the nightingale that night with her improvising on cello and playing some pieces. And it was a viral sensation, the ultimate first in that kind of media experience that traveled around the world. Millions of people listened to it; fifty thousand people wrote letters to the BBC to say, "Please, can we have more?" And she became this figure—the lady of the nightingales. Every year she did this broadcast, and she sold millions of records. She traveled the world and would play the Carnegie Hall several times a year, inviting all the Americans to come to her home in Oxted to have tea with her and listen to her nightingale, which they did in the thousands. Literally tankers of humans came over across the sea to hear her nightingale. She really sparked that kind of popular appreciation and did a lot in terms of the preservation of birds and the popularization of the Royal Society for the Protection of Birds, our big charity. So she's a formidable figure, but what she did was bring art and the nightingale together.

EVL And is that what inspired you, the confluence of your love of birds and nature and then hearing somebody who had found a way to be in relationship with them as a musician?

SL I wish it was as obvious as that. No, not at all. I'd been listening to nightingales every year as a kind of pilgrimage, and I got this lucky commission. The BBC had completely missed their ninetieth anniversary of this seminal event, and I wrote an email to the man at the BBC, as one does, going, "Uh . . . can I uh . . . can I make a little documentary about this?" And they were like, "Heck, yeah!" I had forty hours' notice to go and make it. It was the fastest turnaround in BBC history, I think. And I did; I made this little documentary.

And it was in going out there to sing a song with the birds in homage to her that I discovered the birds actually sang back. And that was the big threshold for me. Really, the most important one: not just the discovery, but realizing the birds and I and other musicians could collaborate, that the birds changed their key and their frequencies and their decoration to adapt to your music. And that blew me away, because I'd only ever been a silent participant—a listener. Never would I sing with the great master, you know, interrupt. But lo and behold, he invited me in. That led to this kind of, "well, if I can do this on my own, maybe I could get an audience to come and experience this too." This is nature connection. The elixir. A kind of shot up the arm. The adrenaline hit of hearing musicians and birds in collaboration is a sensation like no other, and it's quite a transformative experience. So I've created this sort of concert, but I think of it as a ceremony for the birds that allows people to have an experience with nature that we in England don't often have the permission to have because of the country we live in and the laws and the way we are and our relationship to land. It opens up all those boundaries and other people's thresholds and comfort zones in a very powerful way.

EVL One thing that you wrote about was that you feel that nightingales have sung with humans for millennia and that you're convinced this ability for musical kinship evolved between nightingales and humans singing side by side, and that there is an epigenetic imprint of their song upon our ancestors that is undeniable.

SL If there was ever a teacher of what trance is, the nightingale has been the one to reveal that. The footprints I'm walking in, in hearing that bird, strip away that sense of time. That bird is exactly the same as the bird that sang at the time of the Lascaux or Chauvet Caves. In fact, those nightingales would have been singing outside those caves for the whole of spring and summer. And likewise, the song that I'm singing is able to bring those ancestors into my circle, into our circle; I feel I'm part of something very ancient. And in my research, I've met many different communities,

"Your eardrums thrum and throb to their sound, and you feel it inside your heart. It's a quivering sensation as the frequencies pass through you. That's a gift."

traditional song communities and master musicians who've learnt from the nightingales as their teaching has dictated. And in many ways, living in England with a very strange secularity within our folk repertoire has allowed me to explore what a sacred spiritual form of practice might be with these birds and how they might enable a re-enchantment. I feel like nature is my spiritual leader in this respect and the nightingale is my imam at the top of that tower calling the prayer out.

EVL You've spoken about their relationship to you personally as kind of a gateway to reconnecting on a much deeper level to the natural world and, specifically, to the healing power of nature. And I loved how you described the nightingales as the head surgeon in this practice of healing—for you, but I think you're also speaking more broadly for us collectively.

SL Mmm. They have a particular way of opening you up, and there are few creatures that can do that. And they're not the only ones. I found an agency with them that allows me to do that work and to bring that work to others. But healing is different for every person, because we all bring our own sickness, our own pathologies, and, yeah, our own problems. And we see that in the legacy of poetry and prose and folk song how the nightingale has appeared always in this place of wisdom keeper, of unlocker. They unlock you and they rinse through you, because that's their power. They sing at ninety decibels. They are so loud. It's like being next to the speaker in a nightclub. Your eardrums thrum and throb to their sound, and you feel it inside your heart. It's a quivering sensation as the frequencies pass through you. That's a gift. Sometimes you have to work very hard to have those palpable experiences of cleansing, of communion with nature. And then you bring the nightingale in, and it's just like womp! [*laughs*] They knock you out.

EVL You describe something about the way the nightingale sings, which is about silence: that there is as much power in the silence of the nightingale's song as there is in the notes that it sings; and that it taught you about the great art of decorating silence, a phrase I like very much. I wonder if you could talk about that a little bit.

SL Yeah, absolutely. It's a kind of unspoken rule of unaccompanied singing. And British tradition (and very much the American Scots-Anglo-Irish traditions of folk song that went over to the Americas) was very much about singing solo unaccompanied. The Americans put a bit of instrumentation—fiddle and banjo—to it, but in Great Britain it was one singer, one song. And the space you held as a singer was all about the gaps you left, because that was the orchestration, that was the arrangement, that was where the listener could enter in. That was the invitation. And I learned a lot in that art from those old singers, you know, and here was the nightingale doing exactly the same thing, even better, with such grace. And the timing that he leaves between expressions is formidably brave. And in that space, so much is happening. Although it's silence, it's a very rich and fertile place for the imagination, for listening deeper into the places that one never knew they could hear, inside and outside. And the nightingales are doing it with great intention. This is not just because that's the way it is; there is a reason why they're leaving those spaces. And I can conjecture what they are, but there's a lot more than we'll ever know about why they are singing the way they do.

EVL When I was younger, before I got involved in filmmaking, I was a jazz musician. And one of the great lessons I learned—or tried to learn—was that it's not the notes that matter, it's the space around the notes that you leave. That's what creates a deeper relationship with what you're trying to express.

SL Just to know when to shut up, really [*laughs*]. But also, another thing—and it's an old adage—that you have two ears and one mouth, and you should use them in those proportions. And I like how in that space of silence there's the opportunity for listening, and you receive so much more than when you're just broadcasting. That's a very sacred ratio, that.

EVL That there's a space for communion in the silence more so than there is necessarily in the notes themselves.

SL Yeah.

EVL There's a question you ask in the book. It's a big question and one that obviously haunts you a great deal, and that is, will the next generation be able to hear the nightingales?

SL This is in our hands. One can be scientific about this and look at models of decline. And when I say "next generation," I'm speaking specifically about people in England, because the nightingales only live in the very southeast part of England, and they're declining there at a rate of like eighty-seven percent a year. So we're expecting in thirty-five years they might be gone. They may not, because maybe they'll cling on; but actually the wider issue for them, which concerns me more than anything, is that although we have the highest rate of nature depletion in the UK, in Europe, we're one of the worst countries in the world for deforestation relative to the amount of ancient woodland we have. We are criminal in what we're doing to our land. We have so little left, yet we're destroying it so viciously and uncaringly. And that's a big problem for the birds. But actually, I think the greatest issue is their wintering grounds in sub-Saharan Africa, the intensification of agriculture and also the rising heat there and what that's going to do to their winter life. And if they don't fatten up to make that journey back, they can't return; and that worries me more than anything, because that's a global issue. It's not just about, you know, allowing more scrub to develop and creating nightingale habitats—which is a wonderful thing, because it's good for all birds—but actually, what we're looking at is a situation where they simply don't have a home. It's a migrant crisis. It's going to be replicated in human existence. So in some ways, of course, I'm devastated at the prospect that my children and my children's children won't get to experience what I have. But I also know the other side of that: there are worse things they're going to face. The ways that we practice our adoration of this bird today and the art that can emerge from that will be a way for that generation to experience as much as possible what the power of the nightingale *was*, if there ever becomes a "was."

EVL Towards the end of the book, you speak about living in an age of extinction and you use the term "solastalgia," which is a term I guess you could say I painfully resonate with. Maybe that's what we all do. That's what it kind of embodies. And also the term "endlings," which is what you use to describe the last of a species that is going extinct. And singing with nightingales knowing that they may not be singing in England in thirty years changes perhaps the way you see extinction. Although there is obviously the tremendous loss that we're going to be facing individually and collectively as we embrace this apocalyptic time of climate breakdown, there is also the ever present need to fill our hearts with the richness our lands offer. So I wonder if you could speak to that a bit.

SL Yeah. What we're dealing with here—and we're all dealing with it, and I know your listenership and you are commonly encountering this—is the concept of grief. How do we celebrate grief and learn to dance with it and nature and these practices? My singing with nightingales is one of many ways that we can practice an entwinement with the natural world that can help us identify where that grief is. I feel the grief with the nightingale all the time: not just about his extinction, but knowing that at the end of May, he'll stop singing and then fly off, leaving me like a forlorn lover. There's grief all throughout, but also that grief comes with a great joy, because that is what nature does. The exuberance is there as a way of supporting us and allowing the sentimentality to be shared and consoled. And it makes me sound like a very morose person, [*laughs*] because I'm not. But actually, you know, I remember this from a wonderful account written in the Vancouver Museum of Anthropology. A Nuu-chah-nulth elder was asked this question in an interview referring to the potlach: "What would they say if the ancestors came back today (in, like, the 1990s) and saw the potlaches today?" And he said, "Well, I think they would see that it's all changed a little bit. But, they'd say, you're still celebrating the good times and making the best of what you have." I'm misquoting here. And I kind of feel like nature is saying, "You know, just be joyful. Be playful. Be here, be present in us. Take what you will respectfully and give back, and that's the best thing you can do."

Invitation

Chapter 2

OUR UNTOLD STORIES ARE THE DARKNESS IN A RIVER'S FLOW

RECORD HEAT
A SOON-TO-BE-MUM
BACKS INTO THE WAVES

BUSHFIRE SPARKS
ON A SHEARWATER'S EGG
READY TO HATCH

FIRST DAY OF AUTUMN
BURNT GUM LEAVES
IN A RAIN SHOWER

DROWNED TREES
THEIR BONES TEAR OPEN
THE MIST

COLD WATER SWIM
THE TINGLE OF GOOSE BUMPS
ON MY SUNSPOTS

THE LAUGHTER
OF A KOOKABURRA
ON THE WEATHER VANE

PASSING CAR
A TINY HAND OPENS
TO THE RAIN

AFTER THE FATAL FLOOD
THE JACARANDA'S PURPLE
SATURATED IN BIRDSONG

THE DEPTH OF HEAT
IN THE YELLOW SONG
OF A SUNFLOWER

6 Moss, *Bone Carver*.
7 Moss, *Bone Carver*. First published in *Notes from the Gean*, December 2011.
8 Moss, first published in *Blue Giraffe*, 2010.
9 Moss, *Bone Carver*. First published in *Frogpond* 30, no. 3, 2007.
10 Moss, *Cloud Hands*.
11 Moss, *Broken Starfish*. First published in *Upstate Dim Sum*, Autumn 2014.

Kerri ní Dochartaigh
MAKING LIGHT, AN INVITATION...

"The earth is always speaking to us, and I have begun to understand light as one of her most loving whispers."

I grew up in a place that took things —ideas, concepts, fears, griefs, joys— and made them into stories.

I grew up in a place
where the eyes of horses were never
just the eyes of horses;
where a rainbow was never
just a rainbow;
where snow meant so much more
than the sum of its glistening,
planet-bright parts.

I grew up in Derry, in the northwest of Ireland, a handful of miles from a man-made border that tried to cut that green, dancing island of mine into two separate parts.

I began my growing there, in that oak-fringed, river-mapped city, right in the very middle of the Troubles. In their exact center. A time which proved to be a thin time; a harrowing time; a liminal time; an unthinkably *bright* time.

The brightness of that time was its own story—became a tale that took many of us who had grown in those times—and showed us the way through. It feels unimaginable, unspeakable even, to write of brightness when writing of those times.

Those days of bloodshed, of terror, of loss, of fear.

Those nights of violence, of cacophony, of horror, of darkness.

So many of us, in the northwest of Ireland; so many of us in the north, south, west, and east of so many other bodies of land on this, our planetary home, did—and continue to do—our growing through days and nights like those.

Violent times leave us, so very often and so very deeply, with a sense that all light is gone.

That all light has left us; the most traumatic abandonment.

Violent times can make us feel that we are living, for reasons outwith our control, in terrifyingly dark times. The very nature of violence—of the brutality that is such a core part of the story of our time—is such that it tries to leave us feeling helpless. The cruelty that ties our days together with its fierce, bloodstained rope is trying—in myriad ways—to bond us to hopelessness.

It feels, does it not, no longer possible to imagine a life lived outside of the ropes of brutality.

The thing is—the thing that those of us from Derry, those of us from every place that has known violence and the attempt to separate—we are more interconnected, more finely and exquisitely woven one to the other, human and more-than-human, than we might ever find the words for.

I am *you*.

You are *me*.

You & *me* are *we*.

And we are moss; we are lichen;
we are acorn; we are oak.

We are eel; we are starfish;
we are coral; we are whale.

We are clay; we are mud;
we are sand; we are rock.

We are sky; we are sea;
we are earth; we are fire.

We are perpetrator; we are victim;
we are them; we are us.

We are starlight; we are moonlight;
we are planet bright;
we are hidden light.

(How does light work in a
world held in place by darkness?)

(How do celestial bodies move on a
planet kept in orbit by violence?)

May I take your hand—lead you back in time & place & myth—to that city built of tall walls, crimson blood & tiny acorns?

Let me hold your gaze here, a wee bit longer.

(Yes, it is dark, here, dear child:
but draw closer.)

But look!
But linger here a little longer.
Look here, look now.
Look deeper, look wider.
Look like your heart & your body
& my heart & my body—
look like *all* of the hearts
& all of the bodies
depend on it.
Like it all depends on your looking . . .

And what do you see?

Yes, it is bright and brightening still.
Yes, despite the darkness: a soft, tender glimmer.
Yes, even in the darkness, it is light.

It is light, it is light: *it is light*.

* * *

I grew up amidst a kind of darkness that took the world and made it stranger, wilder.

That took the heart and made it stranger, wilder, too.

A kind of darkness that took the heart and made it widen.

Wider, wider still: a strangely, wildly inversed pinhole camera.

Instead of light dripping in slowly: a rush; a flood; a brightening.

We are living through a time in which many people would have us frame the story of light as one of scarcity.

Like violence, ideas of scarcity would have you as simply *you*, me as simply *me*.

There is no *we* with a
scarcity mindset.

Scarcity, like violence, lives closely with fear.

Scarcity, like violence, lives closely with separation.

We are living through a time in which many people would have us frame the story of light as one of separation.

Us here, alone, in darkness.
Us here, abandoned, in helplessness.
Us here, adrift, in hopelessness.

Many of us, so, so many of us, are beginning to think, feel, and dream into other ways.

Other stories.
Other truths.

Other invitations.

This year, at Bealtaine, the Celtic festival of fire, I stepped into a relationship with light that changed my life.

Bealtaine is a *cross-quarter day*, one that marks the beginning of summer.

At Bealtaine, we are closer to the fires of our being than at perhaps any other moment in the circle of the year.

My ancestors lit great bonfires to herald in the season of hope, of harvest, of the heart, at Bealtaine.

Bealtaine: *Bright Fire*.

White.
Bright.
Shining.

The rituals held in the arms of this festival remind us that for our ancestors, this was a time of pyres; a time of purging; a time of protection; a time of merry making; of fertility; of moving from darkness into light.

This has always felt clear-cut, deeply illuminated truths leaving no room for any in-between-ness.

At Bealtaine, we finally enter the mouth of May. We bid farewell to the month of the cuckoo, the month of storms, the month of loss. April can be a fierce, butchering month in Ireland.

In May we cross a threshold.
In May we dance with a
gossamer-thin veil.

We are unshackling ourselves from the darkness!

We are promising ourselves to the light!

(But, child, draw closer,
once more. Look . . .)

Bealtaine may be held as
the season of light,
but what does light really mean?

And how do we make it?

What exactly does it take to make light?

* * *

I have said this shift in my relationship with light began last summer, but truth be told I know it was not as simple as all that. Things—especially those of a celestial, magical, ethereal nature—are very rarely simple. But, somehow, they are also much simpler than we might ever fully grasp.

It began, if I really must pin it down, with pinky-grey Irish midland skies.

Pandemic skies.
Geese skies.
Pregnancy skies.

It began with a story, as it always does;
as everything must.

It began with a story,
and with a sky,
and with a small seed,
as it always does;
as everything must.

I first began to understand light
as invitation the year
I first fell pregnant.

I first began to understand invitation
as love the year
I first made light.

Those pinky-grey pandemic skies—
emptied as they were of metal birds,
full as they were of singing birds—
changed life as I knew it.

Those skies above an Irish bogland—
emptied as they were of normal life,
full as they were of new life—changed
light as I knew it.

(What does it mean to be making life as
loss ripples around the world?)

(What does it mean to be making light as
darkness dances around the circle?)

The year I fell pregnant with my first child, the world as we knew it had changed beyond all measure.

It was the first year of a global pandemic.

The world had, in many ways, grown darker.

The world had, in many ways, grown brighter.

It was hard, was it not, to hold both these things in our shaky, scared hands.

The darkness.
The light.

To be cracked wide open, wider still, to the ways in which these two things—darkness and light—are much more alike than we might, before that year, have accepted them as being.

It was wild, somehow, to observe the ways they danced together, back then, that darkness and that light: seed and tree, in aching harmony.

Growing, at that scared, sacred time, towards deeper understanding of the ways darkness and light coil around each other's beings—we grew, did we not?—towards deeper understanding of our place in it all, too.

Who and what we coil around.
Where and who we braid ourselves to.

How we slot in.
Who we fit with.

The ways our loops and spirals, our lines and circles, meet with all the other shapes of this exquisite, ever-shifting earth.

Does darkness have a shape?

Does light?

And what about when they are so close together, in our shaking, human hands, that they become one being?

What is the shape of darkness and light, held tenderly, held knowingly, in these human, human hands of ours?

I have grown, these last years, since 2020, to understand the story of *being human* as being a story of *holding*.

To have human hands is to
hold human hands.
To have a human heart is to
hold human hearts.

To be human is to hold.

How do we hold everything at once through this grief?

How do we hold anything at all
in this dark?

I am taking you back, now, to Bealtaine.

I am taking you back to the first morning of May, in the year 2024.

I am taking you to Ireland, a land many of you will be more intimately connected to than you might even fully understand.

I am taking you, not to the north of that island, but to the West.

To County Clare.

A land of lakes and sea; fields and valleys; folklore and community. As the first light reaches a rented garden, in the east of that western stretch of land, a wren is making her way over a bed of soft moss.

A mother, just as the light was leaving the sky a few hours before, laid a garland of wildflowers on the doorstep of her home for us.

Bluebells.
Plantain.
Daisies.
Herb Robert.
Common vetch.

She placed it there for protection.

At Bealtaine, the Sídhe, the fairy people, are especially active. The Cailleach, a divine elder woman, a hag as we would have her, wanders too, often disguised as a beautiful young hare.

The mother placed these bright, fresh blooms on the threshold of her home to ward off these evil spirits for the year ahead.

The mother did not manage much sleep on this thin, bright night.

In the night, wakeful and weary, she drew her small light in close.

A blue one, one that holds the whole world inside it.

She watched, as the light filled the morning sky, a toddler—a wee girl around the age of her son—die on a table in a field hospital in Rafah. The wee girl had only half her face left, but still her wee features shone up to the mother from the device in her shaky hand. She had, only recently the mother guessed, just reached that stage where she was beginning to look, not like a baby any longer, not like her mama's baby, but like a little girl.

A small person.
A little human, shining brightly.

The mother watches as her own small human wakens in the newly May sunlight; watches as he stretches, cat-like. Watches as his sleepy, golden face leaves the land of sleep and returns to this land of the living. Outside, the dawn chorus greets the morning. Light, that never quite disappeared in that short, liminal night, fills the whole earth as the mother knows it.

Bealtaine.
Bright Fire.
Ancient protection.

Later that morning, her young son, who she loves more on that day than she ever has in her whole life, will ask her, as she photographs the green shoots of the poppies they have grown together—

"Mama, are you making light?"

—and she will hold back tears, ancient, harrowing, hallowed tears, as she tells him—

"Yes, wee one, yes, wee one.
Look at all this light that we
have made."

I am taking you back further, now, back to that most early, that most ancient, of all pink mornings.

I am carrying you, in these human arms of mine, back to your first morning in this aching, amazing-beyond-all-words, world.

I am cradling your newly formed human body, on my human body, the whole way back to your first day on this exquisite, ethereal-in-every-way, earth.

Let me hold you.

Let me mother you.

Let the human in me make room in my arms; my hands; my heart, for that small, pink human body you once were.

All those years back.

When all you had known, for months upon months, was darkness.

The darkness of the womb.

The darkness that was all and everything for you.

The darkness that was your safety.

The darkness that protected you.

The darkness that was your home.

The story of *light* is a
story of *holding*.

The story of *making* is a
story of *holding*.

When we make—amidst unimaginable brutality—room in our own hands for other hands, we hold the whole world in those hands.

When we make—in times of incomparable cruelty—room in our hearts for other hearts, we hold all of the dark, every single particle, and the light, too—all of the light.

We hold all of it; every human experience we've got; every delicate dancing dot.

The thing with holding, though, is that from that very first pink-skied morning, we are being shown how.

The thing with light, though, is that we are being invited in; from that very first moment we arrived here.

The earth, our mother, is always holding us, and I have begun to understand the sky as one of her most tender embraces.

The earth is always speaking to us, and I have begun to understand light as one of her most loving whispers.

* * *

We are journeying now, quite some way, back from that day that you first joined this incredible, breathtaking planet—to the early autumn of 2024.

In my Virtual Village—a WhatsApp group of local mamas who support one another in the raising of our babes—an American friend sends us three images: pink and green lights, right above the government-planted forest, right beside her home. That same week, this same friend watches from afar as the Appalachian Mountains of her home flood in ways she has never known in her lifetime. We try to hold her, us mamas, as she goes days without being able to contact her own mama. I cry for that friend, for that mama, for those blue mountains, in ways I might never fully understand.

Slowly, drowsily, many of us make our way out of our own front doors. Onto laneways, into fields, out to the main street, up the boreen, up a bit further, up to the trees, over to the clearing: out into the proper, planetary, dark. No one says this, none of us mamas, but I have the deep-rooted sense that each of us journeys alone. We leave our bábógs asleep in the warmth of our homes, their dadas or their grandparents, their older siblings or their trusty hounds, there to keep watch over them as we trace our way back to the beginning.

I find out, just that morning, that I am in the very early days, once again, of making light inside of me.

Of holding space, inside of my human body, for another human body.

Just now, they are the size of a poppy seed; a pinprick of light; a dot shining brightly, in darkness.

It is early, so early, in the journey of this newly forming human, that only three of us know of this wee cluster of swiftly multiplying cells.

I stand, alone, beneath a sky darker
than I ever imagined I could
withstand.

I stand, alone, beneath a sky darker
than I ever imagined any of us
could withstand.

I stand, not alone, but in beating,
breathing, beautiful one-anotherness.

I am *you*.

You are *me*.

You & *me* are *we*.

I waken, the following morning, to a host of images of dancing light, on all of my feeds—the pinks and the greens; the reds and the soft greys of the once-dark skies—but of the perhaps thousands of images that my phone offers me, it is, as often is the way, words, not an image, that rattle my bones most deeply.

A friend, a very new one who already feels like one I will hold close for all times, writes—

"I went out into the dark to
look at the light."

And I am floored by it all, by the darkness and the light; by the tender, breaking, beating hearts of us all—by our *humanness*.

By the shapes light takes as she
lingers in our periphery.

By the shapes light takes in the dark.

Those ropes that try to keep us apart;
that try to make us forget what it
means to be a human—with human
hands and a human heart—those
ropes are looking increasingly frayed,
much less powerful—on such a
phenomenal, phosphorescent planet.

(How does light work in a world
held in place by darkness?)

(How do celestial bodies move
on a planet kept in orbit by violence?)

The world is dark, so dark,
and the world is light, so light, and
this is our invitation.

The world is dark, so dark,
the world is light, so light, and
this is our love.

Waking bright.
Taking flight.
Doing right.
Making light.

In memory of wee Gabrielle.

Brian Isett
THEIA

**"What was it like to see stars?
What was it like to see the Moon? Tides that kept a familiar rhythm will surge past the sand."**

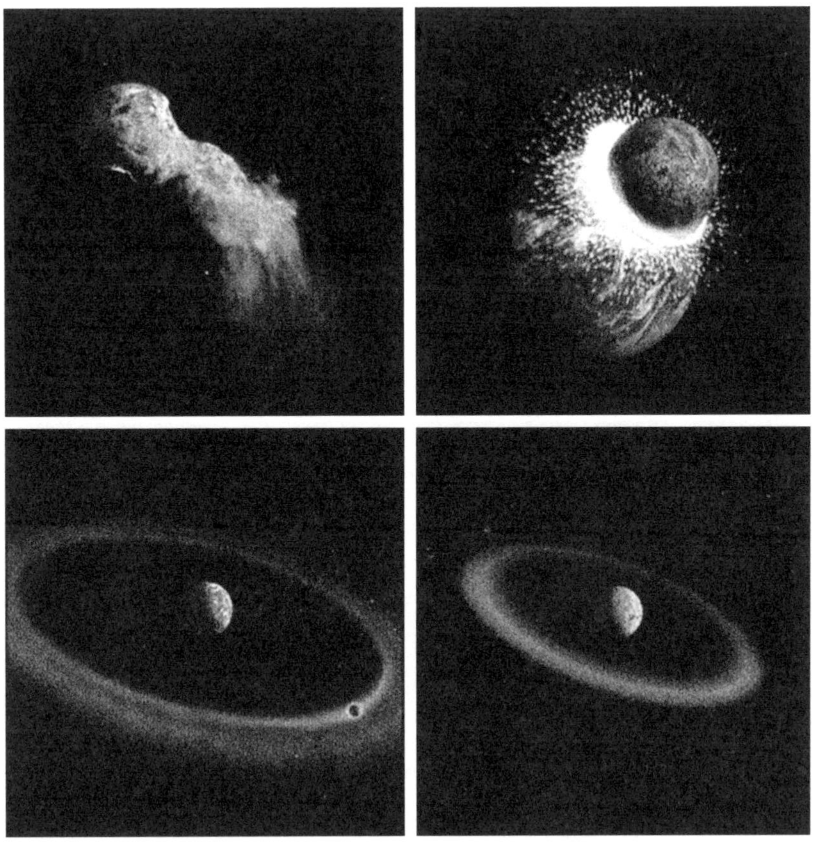

There was one star bigger than the rest in the night sky. Almost a moon. And one day it loosened from its fixture in that black expanse, overcome with an urge to wander. Over successive nights it grew larger and larger as it traveled close. It wobbled as it approached, appearing to stumble through unfamiliar constellations. On the final night, a glowing red planet filled the sky. A wall of molten rock lifted on the horizon, as the Earth itself reached out to embrace this traveler. The old Earth was splashing, lifting up, letting go, spinning and tilting.

FIG. 15 How the Moon was formed. (P. 159)

I TAKE A TURN through the low Appalachian ridges of central Pennsylvania and the Moon drifts back to the left side of the car. It is low on the southern horizon and exactly high enough for my three-year-old daughter to see from her rear-facing car seat. Most things are not. I wait with anticipation for it to enter her view, a possible highlight on a long monotonous drive. A few seconds later she shouts, "I can see the Moon!" It's hard to miss, nearly full and with few clouds to hide it. It shines alone above black hills, the sole source of light in a stretch of highway distant from any city. And a little later, my daughter asks, more quietly, "Is the Moon following us to Pittsburgh?" And so it appears to be. The Moon as Earth's acolyte, the Moon as timeless companion. "Yes, it is following us," I say, knowing the feeling.

But as a scientist, my second thought is, well, no. That's not how the Moon works—the distance to the Moon being so vast, and our six hours of traveling, though an eternity to a three-year-old, being in fact quite short—the Moon's companionship along the dark highways is a simple trick of perspective. Among those tricks, the sense of following chiefly arises from the phenomenon of motion parallax, where objects closer to us appear to move faster than objects farther away. This gives the Moon an oddly serene sense of floating along. It appears effortless for the Moon to keep up with our travel. Yet despite this appearance, I think, the Moon doesn't follow us any more than a distant mountain or tower.

The drive goes on and the Moon creeps back out from a ridge to stare at me head-on. In that moment I realize I am only partly right. The Earth is traveling through space at a blistering speed—without a deep gravitational embrace, wouldn't we leave the Moon far behind? Aren't these embraces a celestial manifestation of "following"? Back home, and with the girls in bed, I search online for the speeds and distances involved. Indeed, without the mutual pull of gravity, the Earth would have continued on at 65,000 miles per hour, doubling its distance from the Moon on our six-hour trip. The Moon would have barely made it to Pittsburgh.

Instead, the Moon followed us. And its steady presence on the horizon began to create a local rhythm: cycles of appearing and disappearing caused by our drive into valleys and around the edge of ridges. Because it was so close to the horizon, it rose and fell to the shape of the Appalachian Plateau. Over short stretches the Moon follows, but over longer periods it phases in and out of fullness, dividing our year into twelve lunar months.

The words "moon" and "month" are ancient, stretching back in similar form for thousands of years to the proto-Indo-European word "*mḗh$_1$n̥s*." It is thought that *mḗh$_1$n̥s* would have meant both "moon" and "month," suggesting that the Moon and the ways it measured time were tightly intertwined in human thought. And because the proto-Indo-European root "*meh-*" meant "to measure," this might be interpreted as capturing both the Moon and what it does across a month: the Moon that measures time by filling and emptying, like a cup of flour. In Latin, the word for month was "*mēnsis*," also descending from "*mḗh$_1$n̥s*" and leading to the modern word "menses." Anything could measure time like the Moon or follow the Moon's cycle, including people. This etymology of "moon" and "month" reveals a dual nature, both static and always changing. It feels difficult to fully appreciate a single word filled with so much meaning and action, but I am reminded of how modern physics describes light. Four thousand years ago, people already understood the Moon to be both a particle and a wave.

The rhythmic companionship of the Moon has given it profound cultural clout. In China, for example, the phases of the Moon have been used to describe a lunisolar calendar that dates back to at least the Shang dynasty three thousand years ago, when it was described on fragments of ox bone, called "oracle bones." The Chinese Lunar New Year usually begins on the second new Moon after the winter solstice, marking a period of welcoming spring and preparing for a new beginning. On a dark night past the shortest days of the year, even the Moon starts over. But the Moon's rhythms and companionship can sometimes become unsettling. Behind clouds, or outside our notice, the Moon's phases can march on without us. Encountering an unexpected full Moon is exciting, jarring, and, in my case, expletive-inducing. People can see a face on its rocky surface, visiting and leaving: the "Man in the Moon." When this companion again "follows" a traveler, but the weather is bad and thick clouds pull the Moon in and out of darkness, sometimes the companionship feels closer to stalking. These tendencies of the Moon to shift and change, to hide, stalk, and unexpectedly reappear, all contribute to our darker cultural associations with the Moon: the mental state of "lunacy," the transformation of werewolves, the persistent fear of overflowing emergency rooms when the full Moon arrives. Even the phrase "the dark side of the Moon" captures more about our reservations than facts about the Moon itself: there is not a side of the Moon perpetually in darkness, there is only a side that we never see.

Soon after our long drive, I find myself pulling a birding telescope out of the basement and onto a cushion in my daughter's bedroom. I point it out her window above the streetlamp, and the Moon is almost blindingly bright. She jumps up and down with excitement, jostling the Moon out of frame and focus. With a closer look, a surprisingly rugged texture normally blurred away by the naked eye comes into view. Dark patches explode into craters and mesas. It is vast and multihued, cold and alluring. I have the same sensation even pointing a pair of binoculars at the Moon: it has so much more going on than I expect. When we are done, I ask my daughter what she liked best about seeing the Moon. "The rocks," she says, by which I think she means "the craters."

She does not ask that night, but inevitably she will ask—as so many of us do—"Where did the Moon come from?" And inside that question there are more. And despite all of the relevant science, we still end up with some version of, "Because it was so." But short of that ultimate intractability, waiting for us at the dawn of time, what is the best story we can tell about the Moon today? And the answer surprises me. Because within that answer, there are more answers, explaining the origin of nearly every rhythm on modern Earth. The beginning is Theia.

Theia is a hypothesized planet, named after the ancient Greek Titan who birthed the Moon and the Dawn. When Theia arrived, Earth was still hot and new, circling the Sun with oceans of molten rock glowing under a cloudless sky. Days and nights might have flickered past in hours or churned slowly over months, yielding sunsets like a match going out or sunsets that blazed red and orange for a week. We don't know. The sun might have set in the east and risen in the west. Days might have even been exactly like they are now, or there might have been almost no day at all, only a dark half of the Earth and a light half. After Theia's destructive arrival it is difficult to know something so delicate as the timing and location of Earth's original dawn.

What is more certain is that before Theia, there was no Moon. The early molten Earth would have experienced faint tides caused by the Sun alone, not dramatic high and low tides like our ocean experiences today. And on calm nights, a hot Earth rippled under a dark sky of unfamiliar constellations. Earth's seasons would have been equally unrecognizable. Seasons emerge from a planet's axis of rotation: if it is tilted towards or away from the Sun, there are seasons; if the axis is parallel or perpendicular to the Sun, there will be none. Like Earth's spin, the precise tilt of the early Earth is difficult to know. By some estimates it could have been similar to how it is today. By others it could have been tilted ninety degrees, so far that the North or South Pole would be facing the Sun, meaning the year would pass without the arrival of spring, summer, fall, and winter. Without the familiar rhythms of months, tides, seasons, and days, Earth traveled with an unrecognizable relationship to time.

After millions of years orbiting in Earth's gravitational wake, Theia was jostled by the gravitational pull of another planet, sending it on a collision course with Earth. Theia approached with a wobbling impact that spun Earth into an endless pirouette around the Sun, creating days with sunrise in the east and sunset in the west. The same collision knocked Earth onto a tilt of about 23 degrees. Rock ejected by the collision soon coalesced into the Moon, which pulled high and low tides on the molten surface of the new Earth, dazed and glowing. Earth spun with four-hour days while the first new Moon smoldered in the night sky. A taciturn planet had been given a song.

When my first daughter was born, I remember a fall storm that passed by the hospital windows without us feeling its force. Somehow the glass was too thick, and the sounds we expected were all missing. Night and day were muted by overhead lights, and then almost entirely replaced with new rhythms of crying, diapering, feeding, holding. Our daughter was very healthy, but she required a

“A taciturn planet had been given a song.”

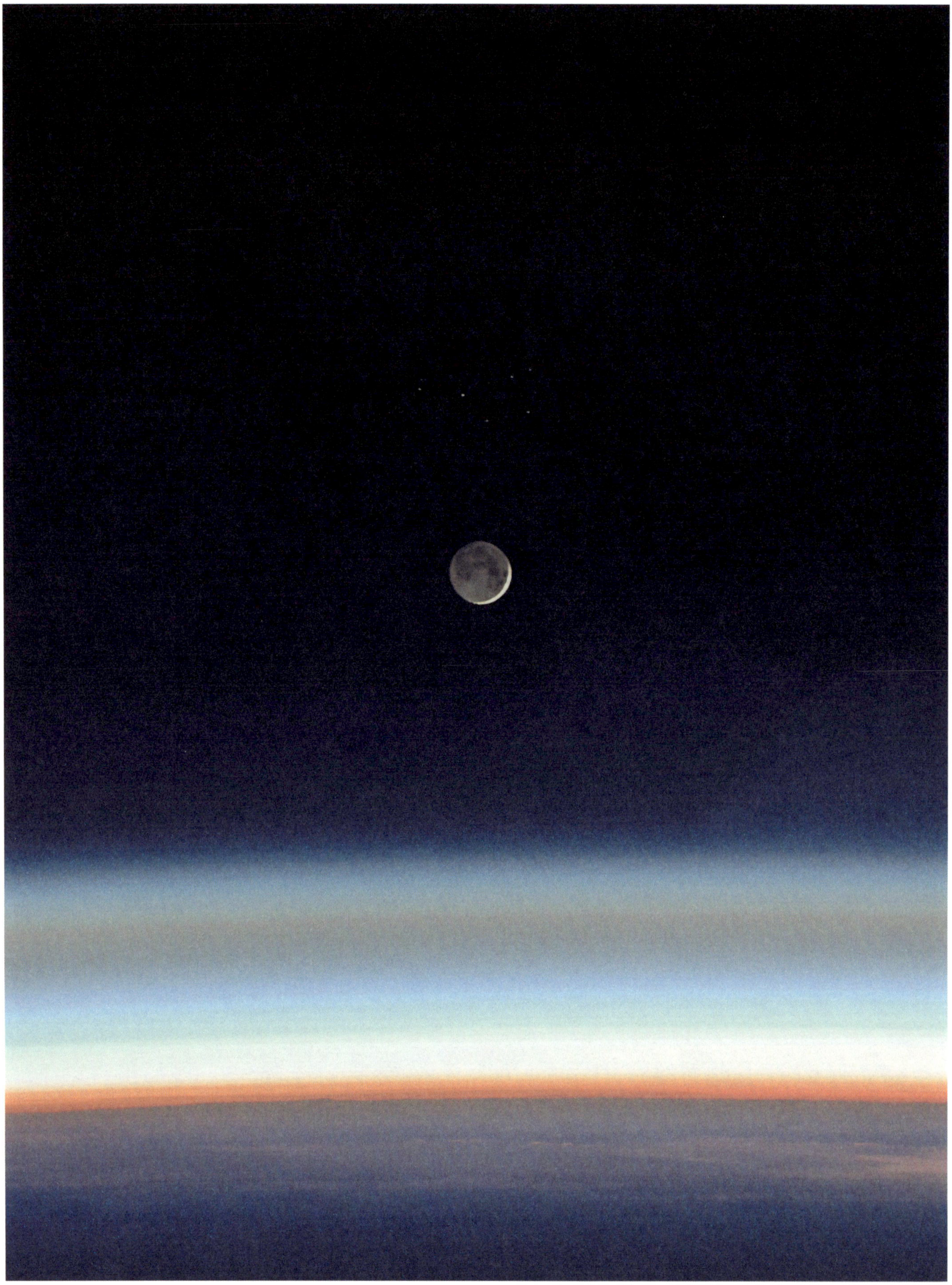

FIG. 16 Earth's reflection on the Moon / NASA. (P. 166)

lot of bouncing to feel calm. I started to wonder if we had given her some unrealistic expectations in utero about bouncing during our frequent hikes. Leaving the hospital, my wife held my daughter and I held a vase of flowers. When I looked down, I noticed I was bouncing the vase as vigorously as I had been bouncing my daughter the night before, the water now spilling out. Rocking and bouncing would be the first of many new synergies, tacit dialogs of movement, sadness, hunger, calm, and sleep as we passed through shifting cycles of need. Like reborn planets, infants cycle through shortened days, and we did our best to keep up.

The Earth's new rhythms also synergized and syncopated over the ensuing millennia. The Moon, for example, slowed the spin of Earth from its original four-hour days—which nearly flashed by—towards our familiar twenty-four-hour day. The cost of that slowing pushed the Moon farther away from Earth, and both processes continue today, with days slowing and the Moon distancing. As my daughter began sleeping through a longer night without a single bounce, I had to remind myself that children are not moons, that we are not bound in these same laws of slowing and distancing. That as our rhythms mature, we are not destined to drift apart, we can still come together, our rhythms shifting and churning, in perpetual cycles of change.

BEFORE I LIVED in western Pennsylvania, I attended graduate school in Northern California, which is where I met my wife. In December of 2015, news began to circulate in our lab that a group of thirteen hundred monarch butterflies had been observed overwintering nearby for the first time in a tree in Berkeley's Aquatic Park, instead of their more popular overwintering sites in Santa Cruz, eighty miles to the south. It seemed like a once-in-a-lifetime opportunity. My excitement was not shared, however: there was only one postdoc who agreed to make the trip down to the park early one morning.

She and I walked through a foggy winter day, both with binoculars around our necks. It turned out both of our moms had tried to get us into bird watching, and up to that point, the effort was largely unsuccessful (on both accounts). But as we walked through the small park, binoculars felt like little advantage. Muted light turned every canopy into a shadowy gray-green mass. After poring over every hint of orange or black we could see, we still hadn't found a single butterfly. In colder weather, monarchs cluster even more tightly, rarely opening their wings to reveal their bright orange-and-black coloration. Instead, only the underside is exposed, and this is, as we learned, the exact dull color of tree leaves on a foggy day in California. Eventually we searched the park instead for someone—anyone really—who could help us. Somehow, we did eventually find a hiker who knew what we were talking about, and they pointed to a clump of dead leaves about a hundred feet away that we had entirely overlooked. With the help of binoculars, we could verify that this clump of dead leaves was in fact a gray-green drop of several hundred butterflies. They looked incredibly fragile there, like a strong wind could scatter them to the grass and dark waters of the bay.

The migratory travel of the monarch butterfly continues to defy human interpretation, best described by David Abram's phenomenological questions in the article "Creaturely Migrations on a Breathing Planet":

> What rolling sequence or succession of blossomings helps summon these millions of butterflies across the belly of the land? What alterations in the olfactory medium, what bursts of solar exuberance through the magnetosphere, what attractions and repulsions . . . ? For surely, really and truly, these migratory creatures are [. . .] riding waves of sensation, responding attentively to allurements and gestures in the topographical manifold, reverberating subtle expressions that reach them from afar.

Among migrating animals, the monarchs are just one of thousands who slide up and down the ecotones of our planet, riding a climatic impulse in search of a familiar life; a life they can live well. Due to the tilt Theia imbued to Earth, staying still anywhere outside the thin margin of Earth's equator means that change comes to you. Seasons in the northern and southern hemispheres are inevitable, as one half leans deeper into sunlight than the other, with this light shifting through the year as Earth's tilt stays steady in its yearly orbit of the Sun. Days and nights grow shorter or longer. It is a rainy season or fields turn to husks in dry heat. To reduce that change, you must migrate.

This is what it felt like I was doing when I fell in love with that monarch co-explorer in California and, after a long-distance engagement, left to follow her to a new job in Pittsburgh. Staying in place would have meant an unbearable season of loss.

THE WINTER OF 2023 my daughter, now four, asked a new question. "Why don't we ever use the sled Santa brought last year?" I understood why she was asking. That year it did not snow enough in our neighborhood to use it; nor the year before. I grew up in Pennsylvania, and as a child, a sled was always a good investment. Somehow that has already changed. I tried to explain to my daughter that it is getting too warm for snow, but this seemed confusing. She can only remember three winters, all mild, so what is winter supposed to mean?

Climate change threatens everyone with unending seasons of loss. Inside buildings with thick windows, the storm of that change has felt deceptively quiet to far too many. Children born now will be insulated from Earth's past in a way we've never known, and today's parents must grow to expect devastating questions. What was it like to have winter? On an increasingly frequent basis, straight-faced geoengineers suggest our best solution might be to block out the sky with a chemical smoke. What was it like to see stars? What was it like to see the Moon? Tides that kept a familiar rhythm will surge past the sand. What was a beach? What is a month? And possibly much sooner than that: What was a monarch butterfly?

After I left California, I remember talking to a collaborator and friend, Claudia Biçen, who still lived there. I excitedly told her that she had to go and see the hibernating monarchs in Santa Cruz—after seeing that clump in Berkeley in 2015, I had gone to Santa Cruz the following year and the lazily fluttering mass was as memorable as my first encounter. But by the time we talked in 2020, there were almost none. The western population of monarchs had completely collapsed into fewer than two thousand hibernating individuals. There were talks of extirpation, pesticides, loss. Since then, the western population has made a temporary recovery, yet the numbers are still down 95 percent from the millions observed in the 1980s. I now wonder if the wayward clump of monarchs I saw in 2015 were making a last-ditch attempt to hibernate somewhere a bit cooler, farther north. Some desperate effort to undo the interaction of Earth's tilt and the mess we've made of the heating world.

The existence of Theia, the old reason for our climate and its careful rhythms, has just now come into view. Even in this perilous time of forgetting, we are discovering chunks of Theia buried under our feet, deep in Earth's mantle, under Africa and parts of the Pacific, generating a large portion of Earth's ongoing tug of gravity. These discoveries feel like our own last-ditch attempt to remember, collectively, our connection to Earth's ancient rhythms and how they hold us, both literally, through gravitational pull, and more figuratively, by holding us to account. Without appreciating these connections, we too will be clinging to the low branch of an unfamiliar tree, in a winter we can't recognize.

TWO WAYS

Someone just powered up a weed whacker outside.
The two-stroke motor growls and curses. The motor, amplified,

screams. Now is the season for weed whackers.
For push or riding mowers running over and over

neat lawns. Inside my house, inside my body, the noise is so loud
the crowns on my molars vibrate. The vibrations hurt

the backs of my eyes. Goodbye spring and hello summer.
Hello migraine. Hello allergies. In the middle, or maybe

the beginning of the American Century, nurseries began, almost
exclusively, to breed male trees. Females bear fruit, leave stains

on sidewalks. City planners have no time for messy females.
Now the air is puffed thick with male trees' pollen.

Hello allergies. One machine stops and another begins. Still,
all those fruitless trees drop their leaves in the fall.

They slick up walkways. Dangerous heaps of brown
many hate. Fall is the season for leaf blowers. Where I live

there's never a quiet season. In winter, while plants regain strength
to grow into their own cycles of desire, snowblowers kick on.

One machine stops and another begins. Trim season. Mow
season. Blow season. Push season. Then start each motor

all over again. The machines take my body. It hurts.
The body thirsts and it hungers. It forgets there is another way.

Let grass grow into a soft rustle. Let weeds flower
into a gentle array. Let fruit grow and let plants go

to seed. Let leaves fall. Let them fall. Let them stay. Let them soften,
in slow time. Before and under and after the silencing snow.

Camille T. Dungy

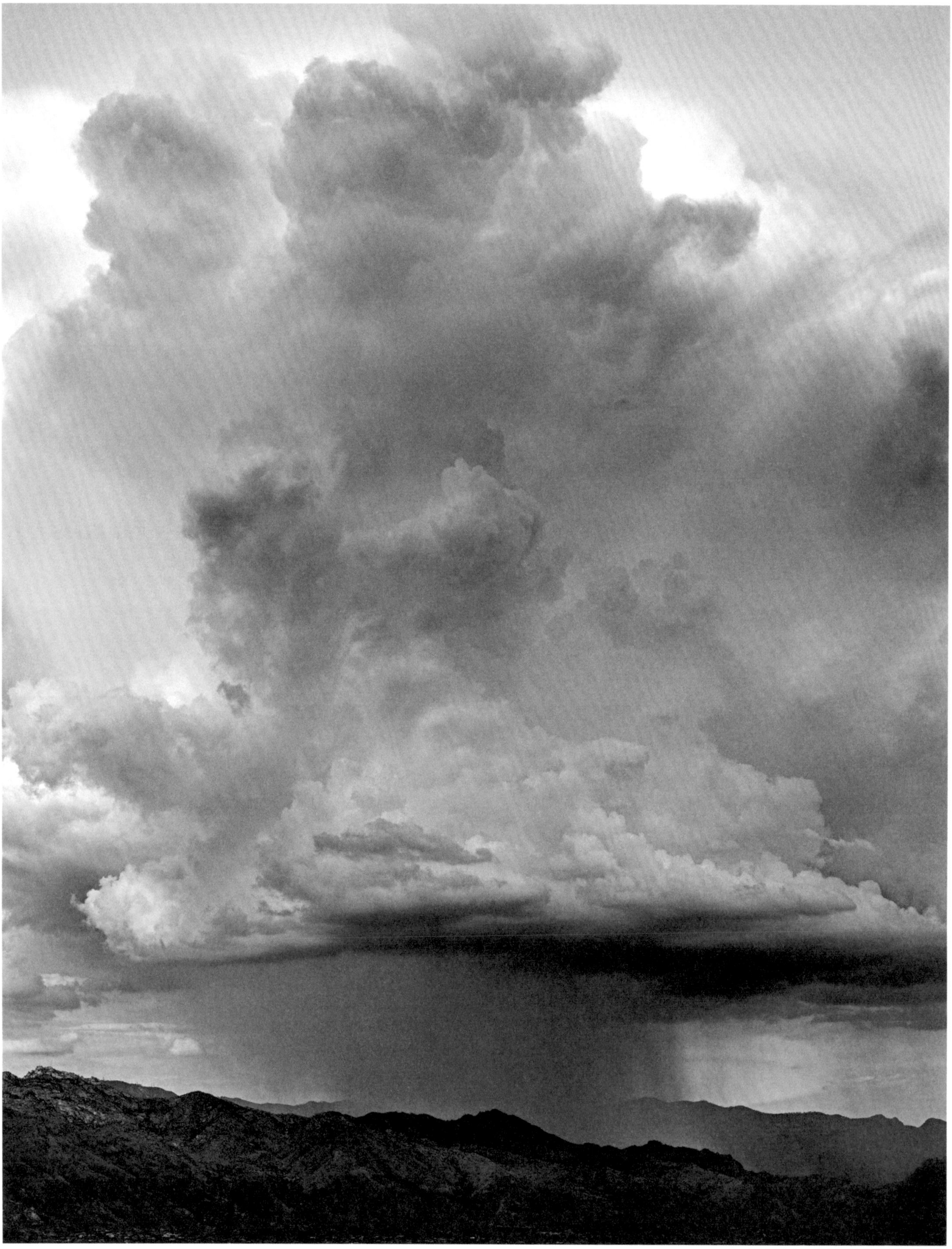

 Invitation Bear Guerra

Bear Guerra
MONSOON

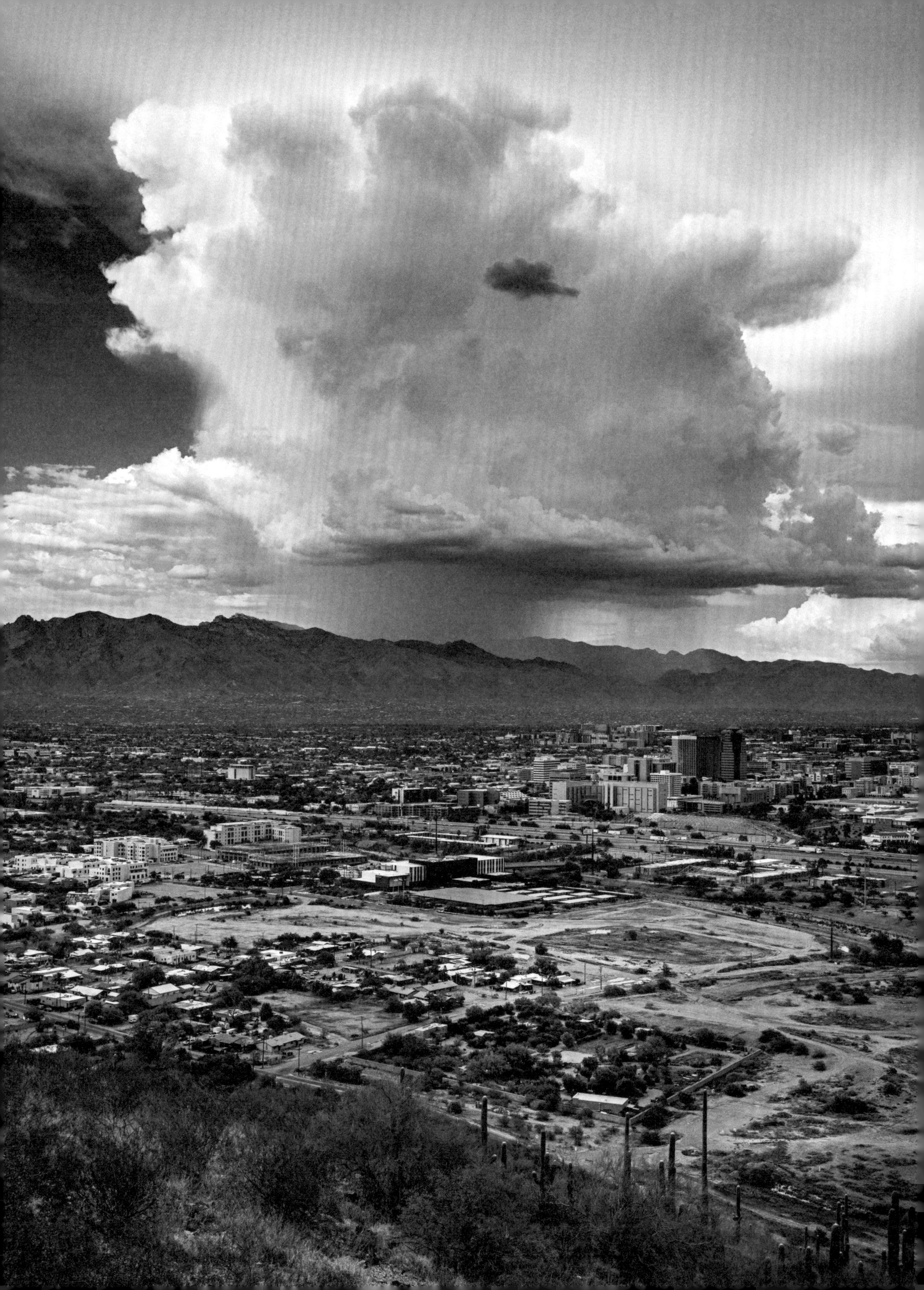

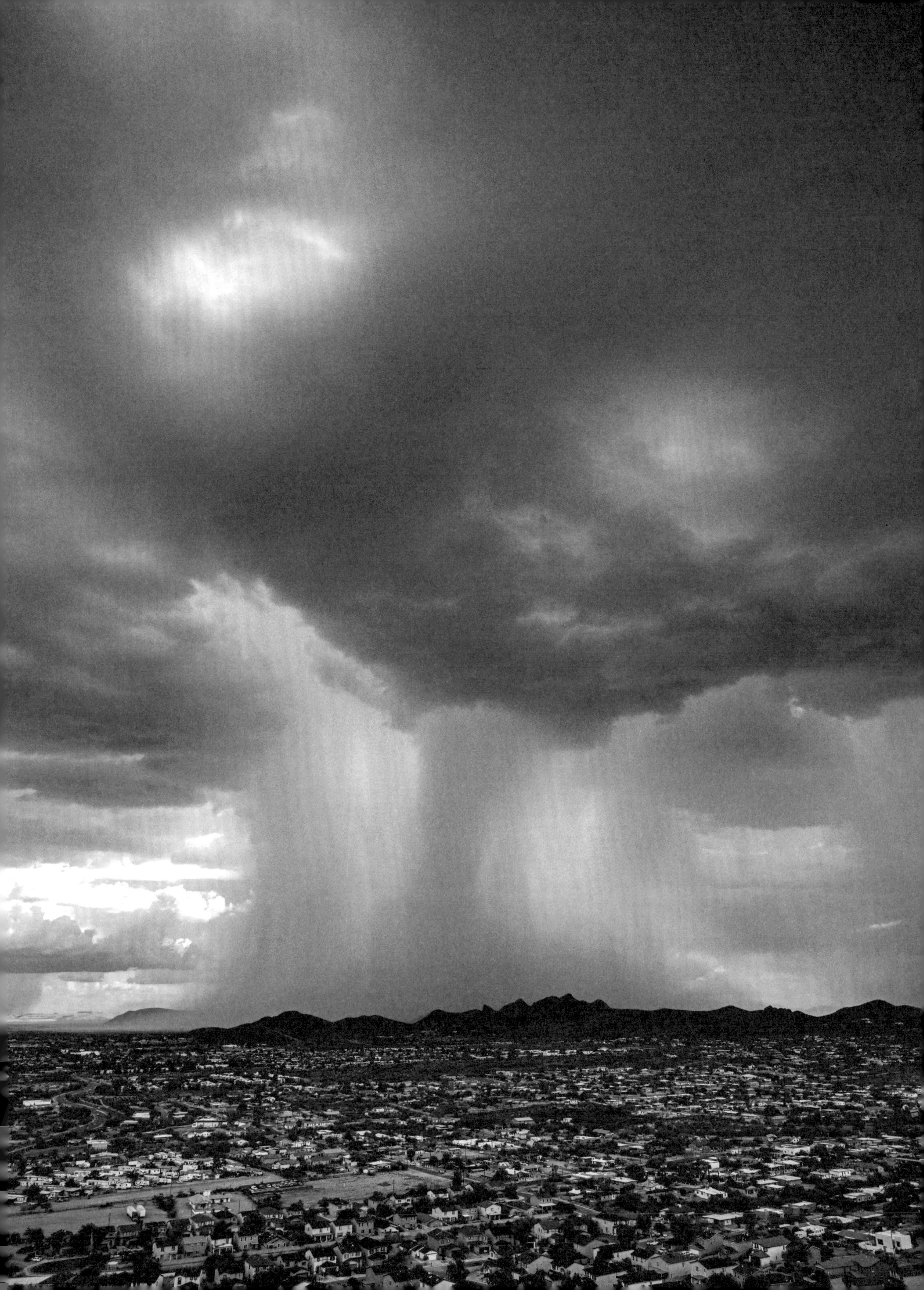

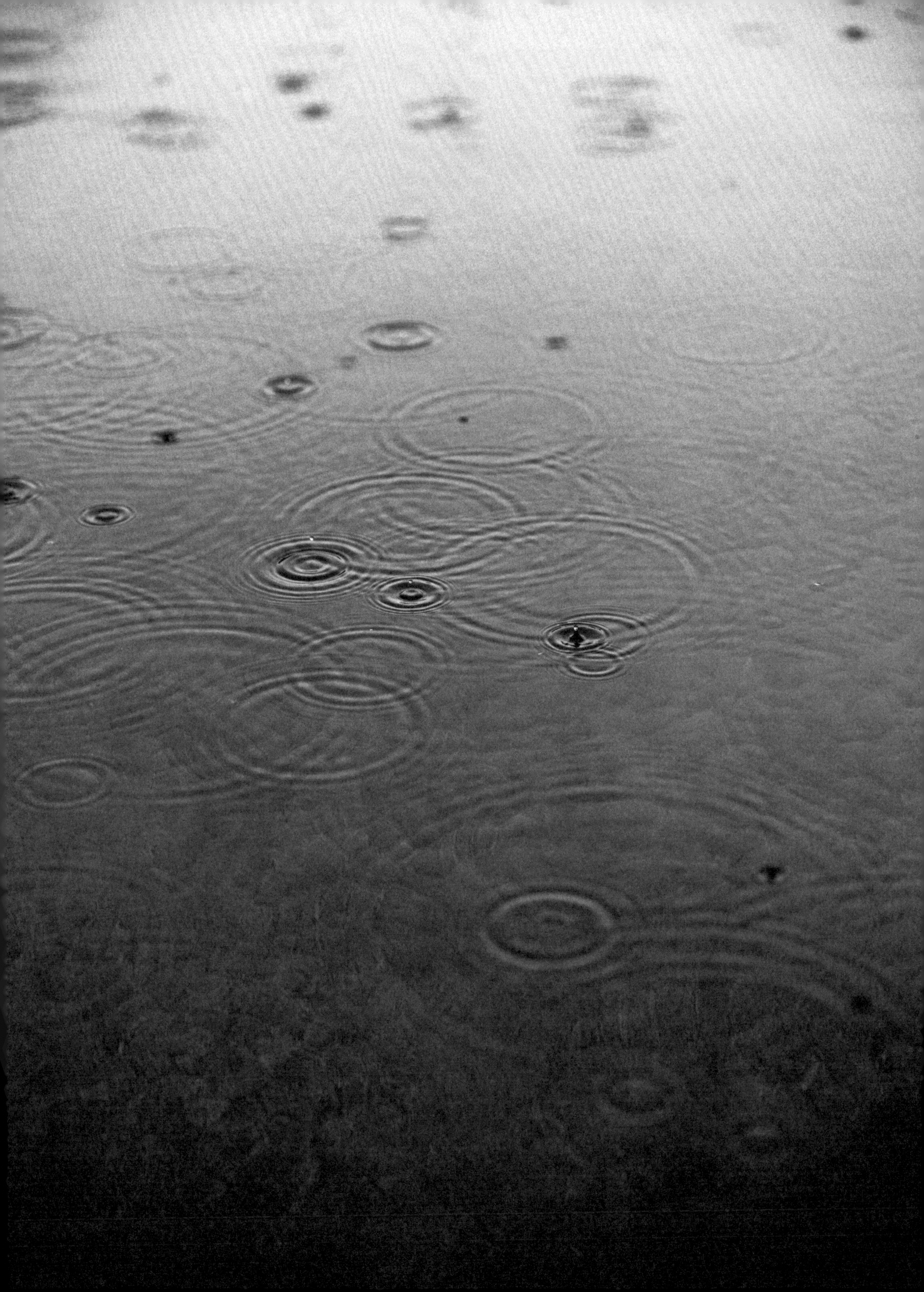

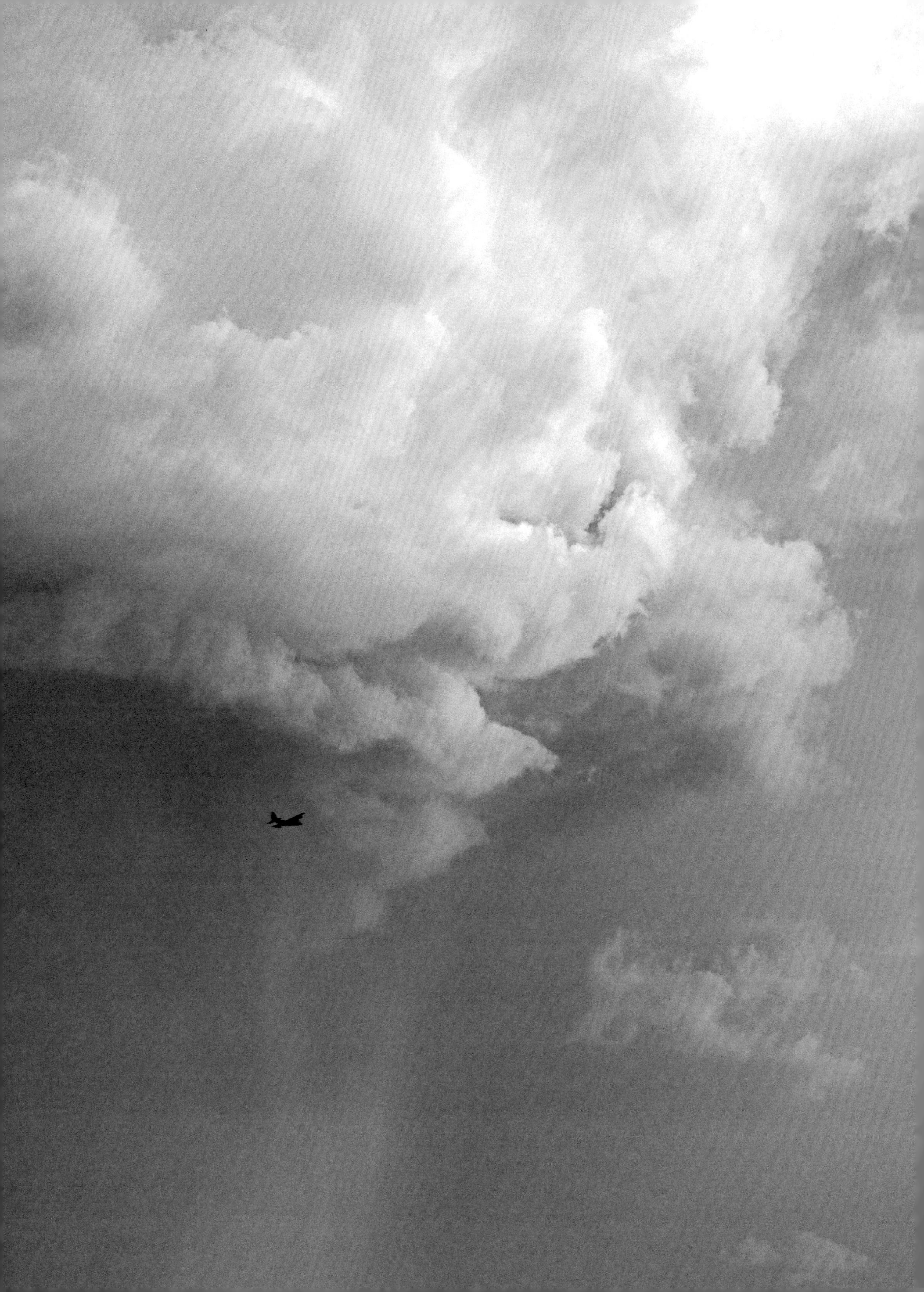

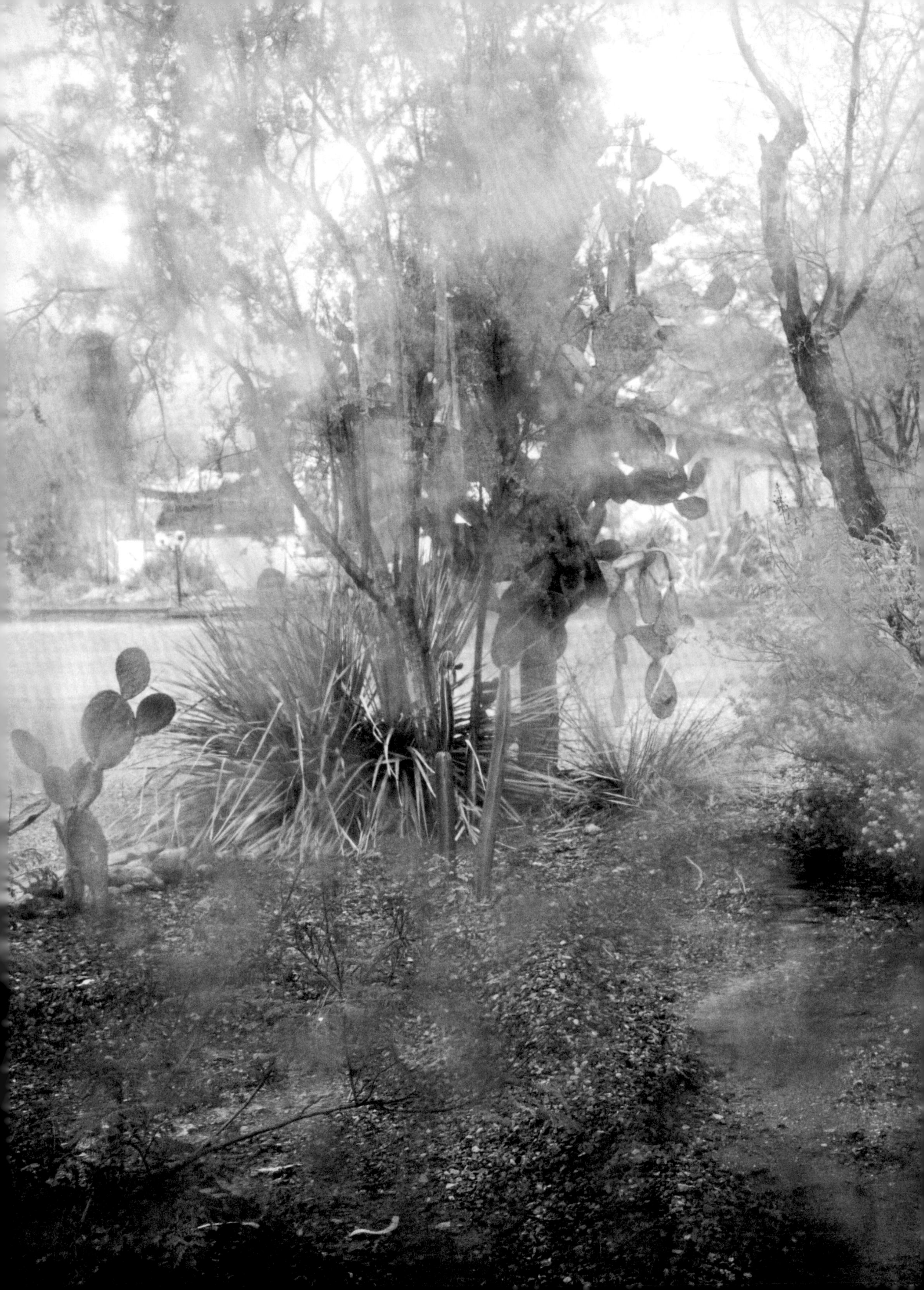

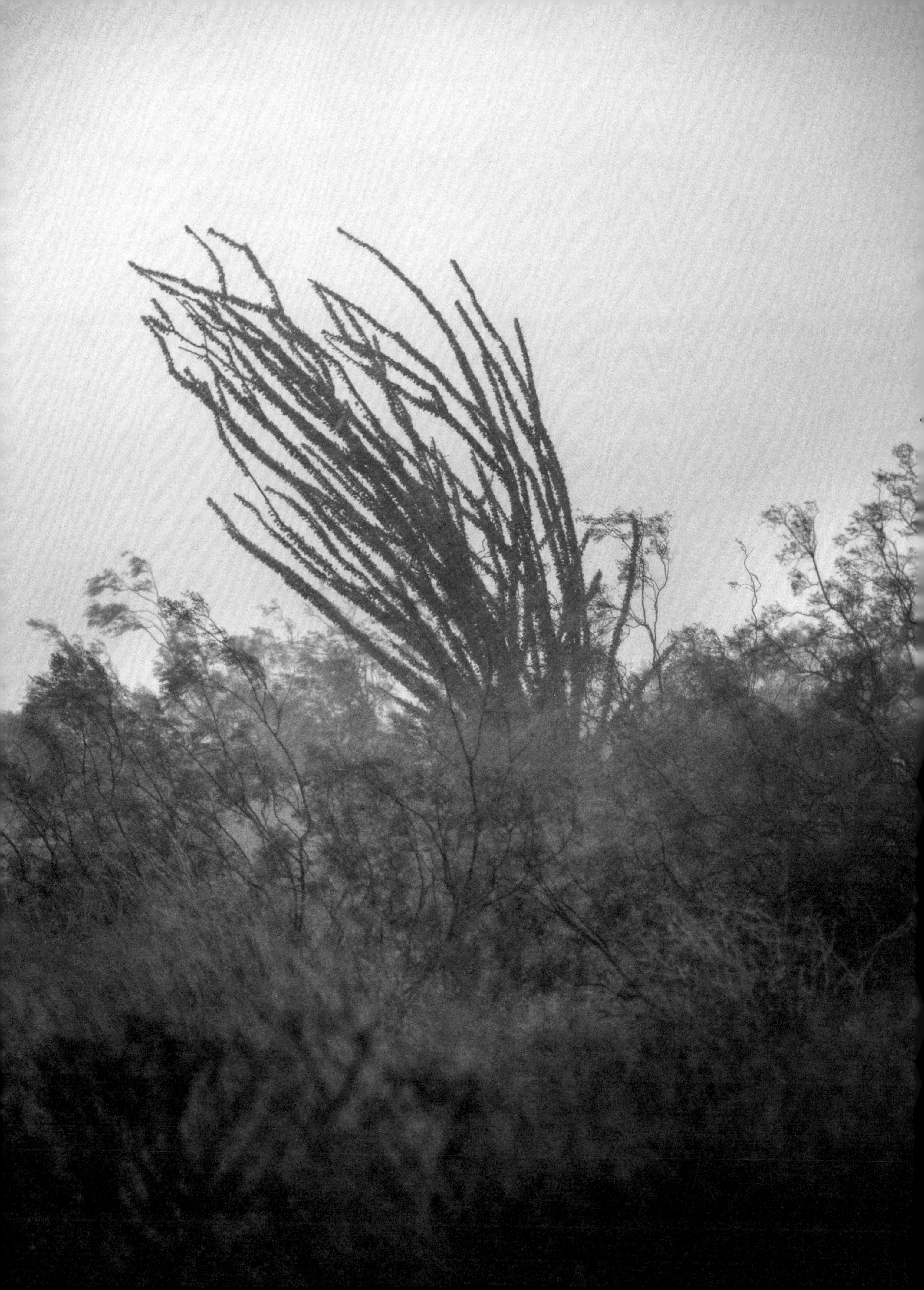

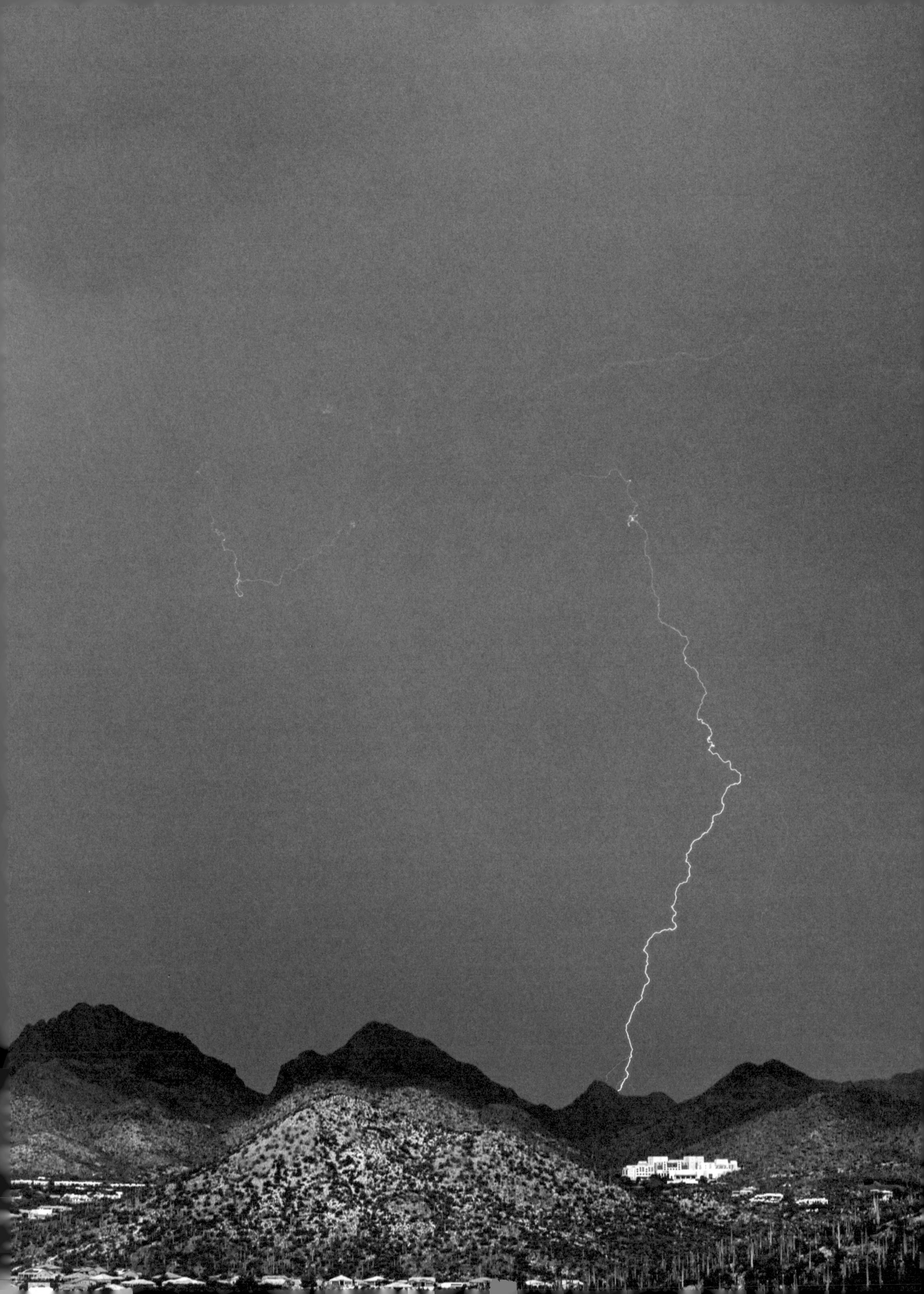

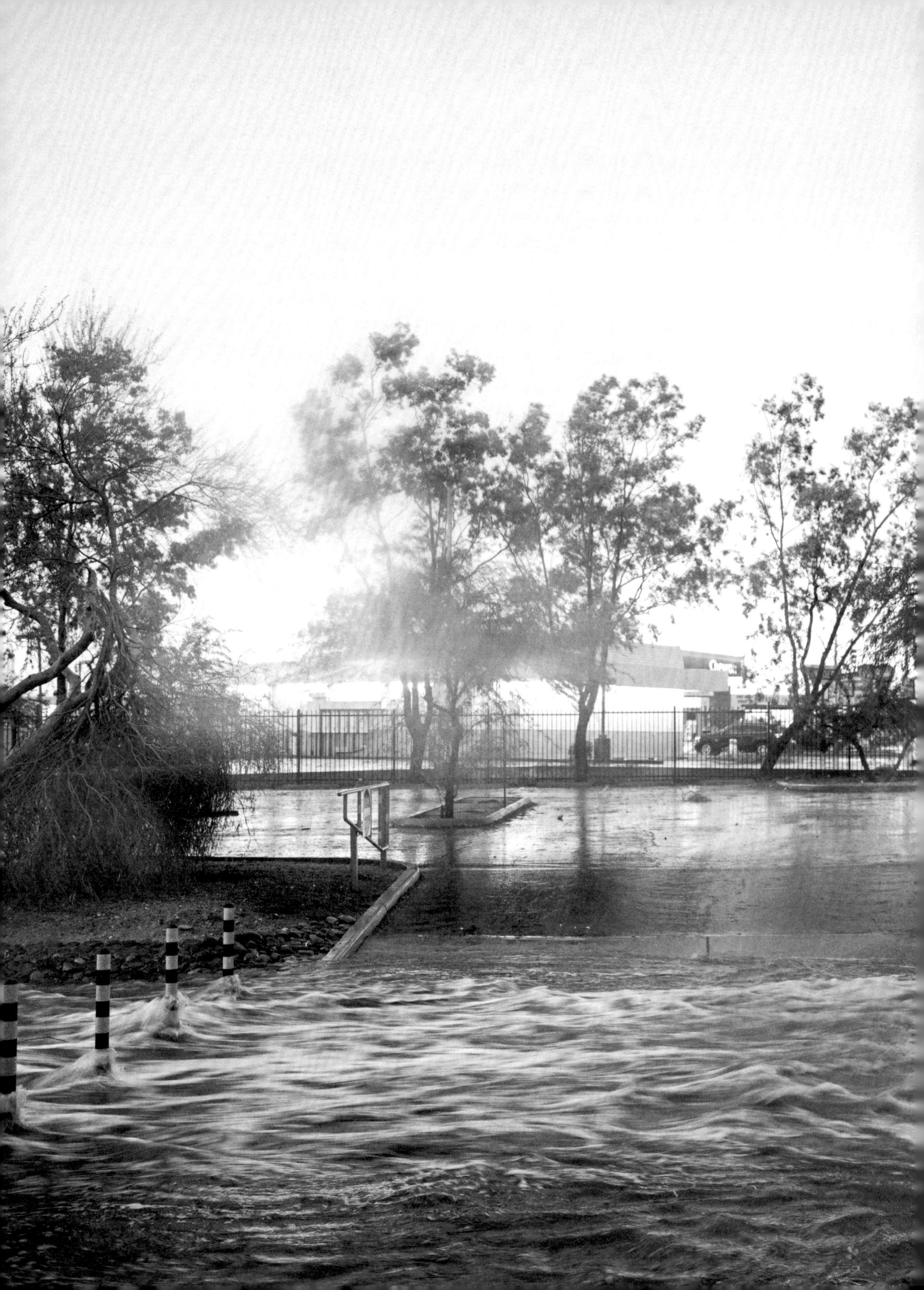

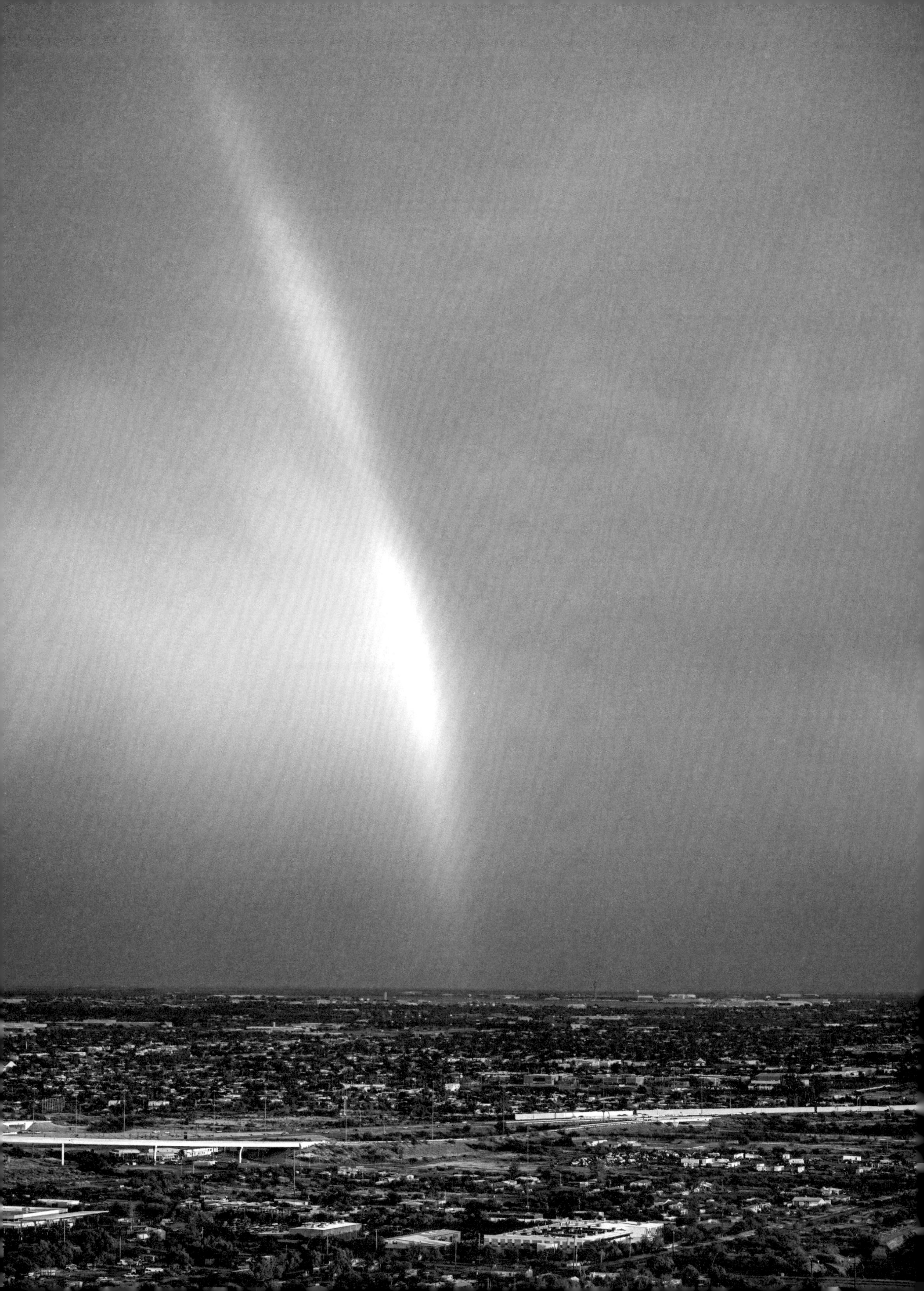

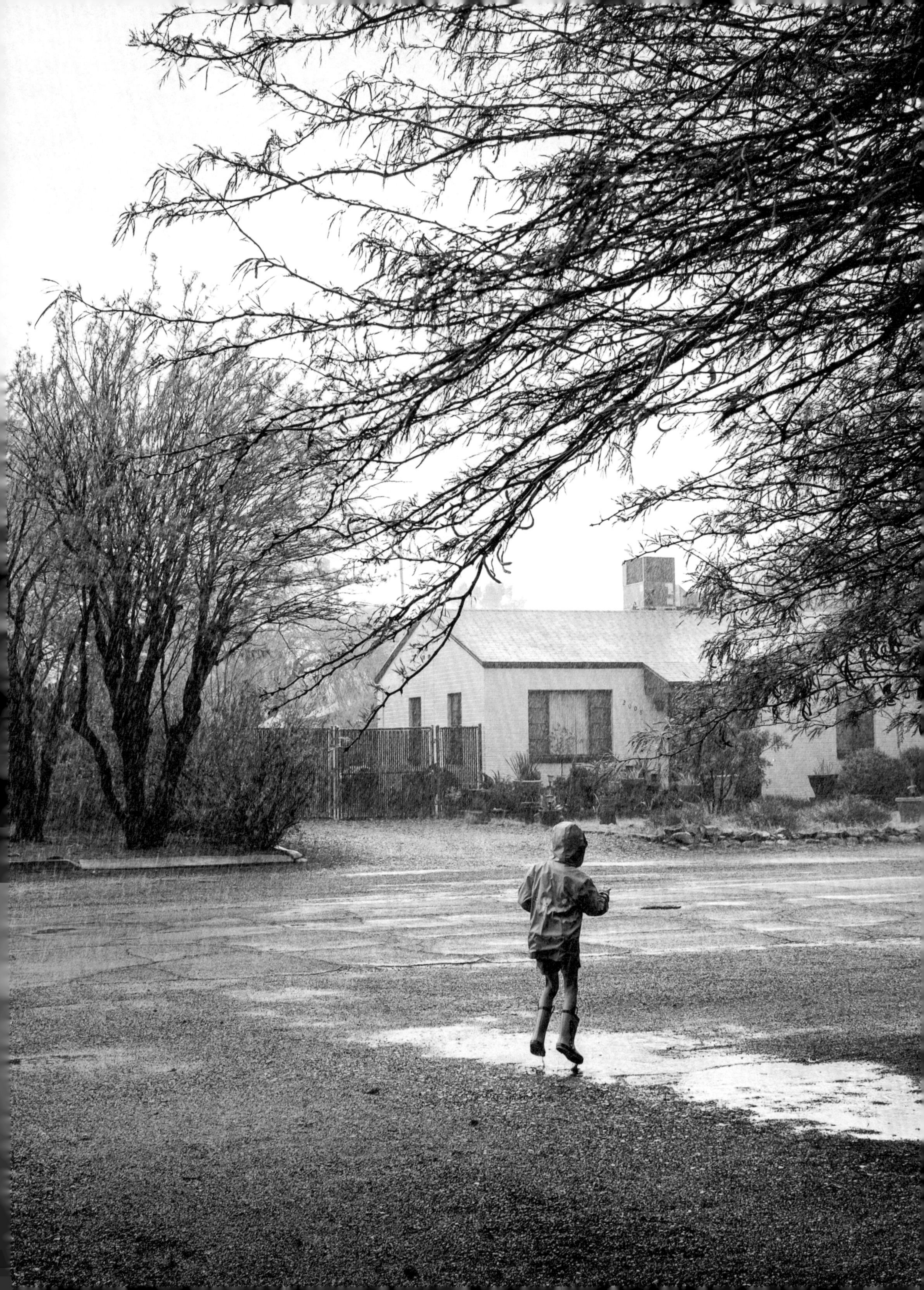

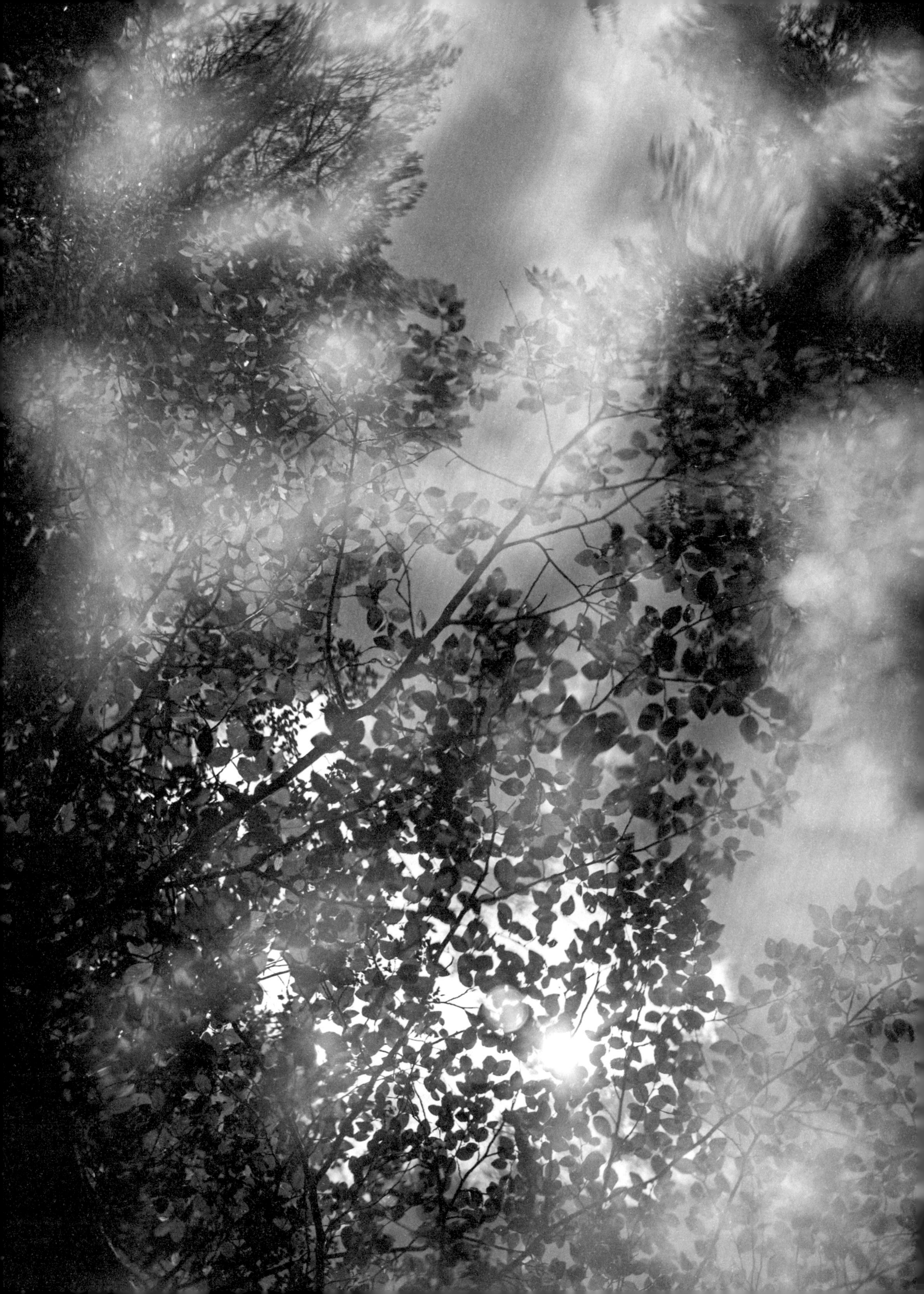

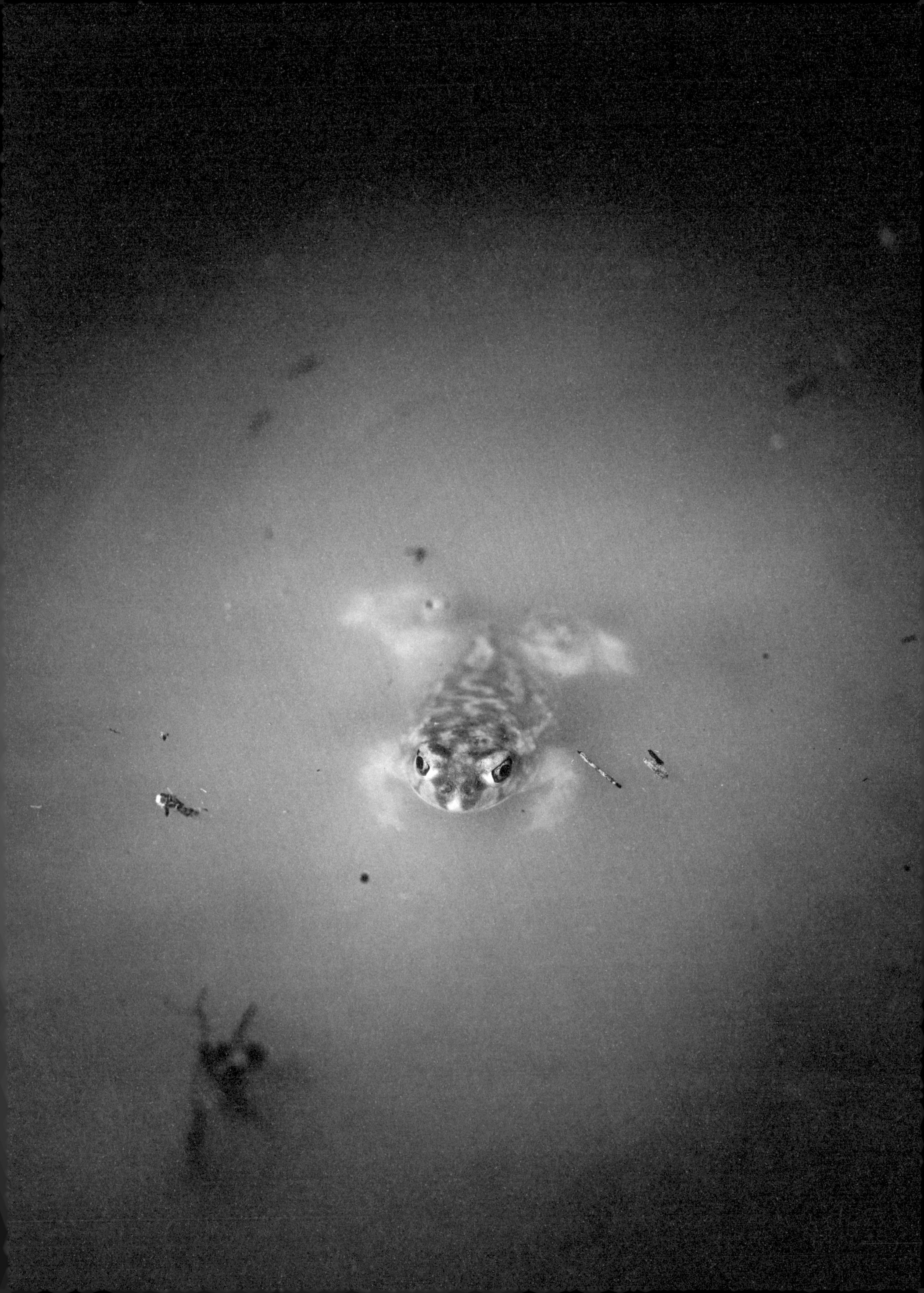

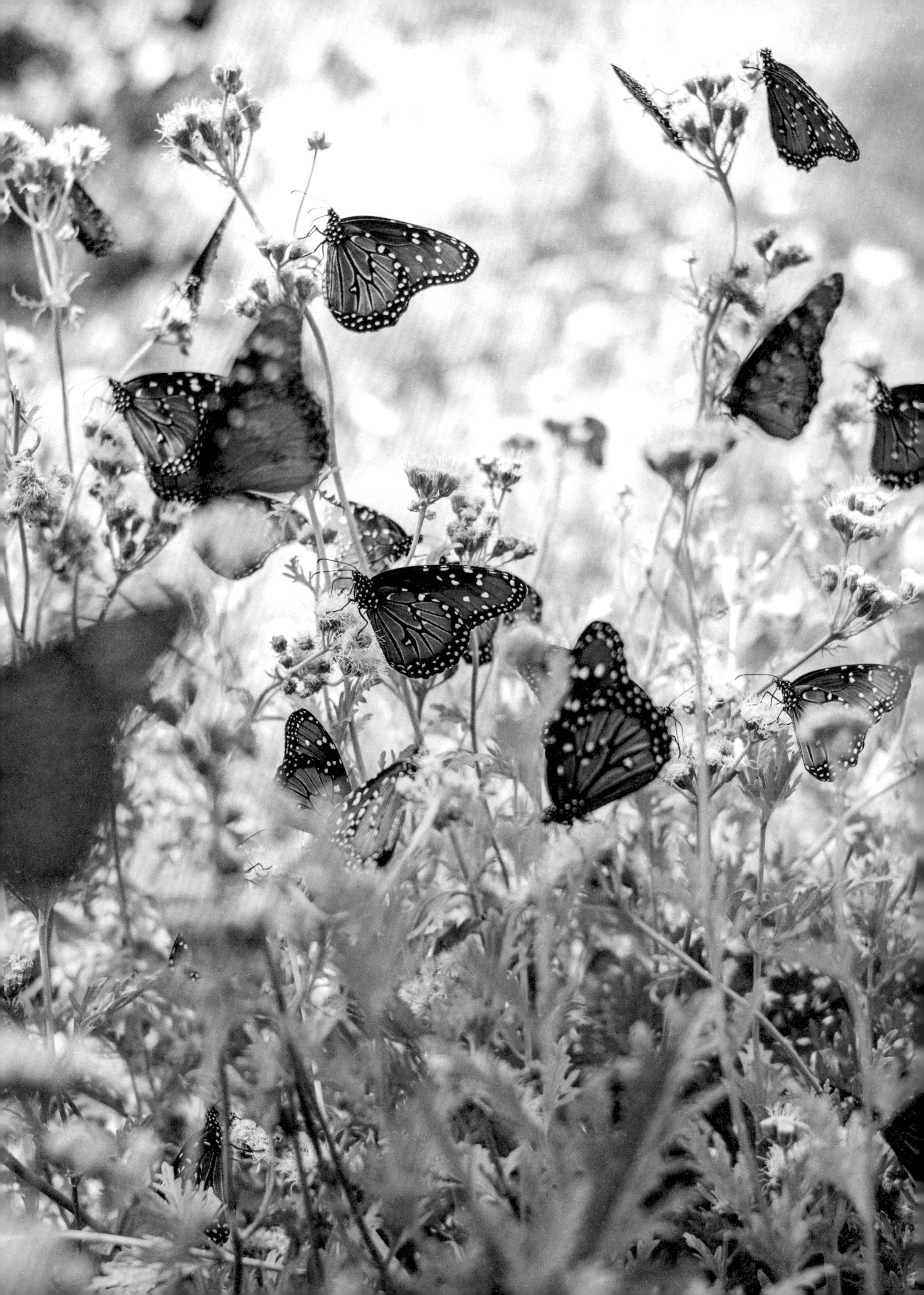

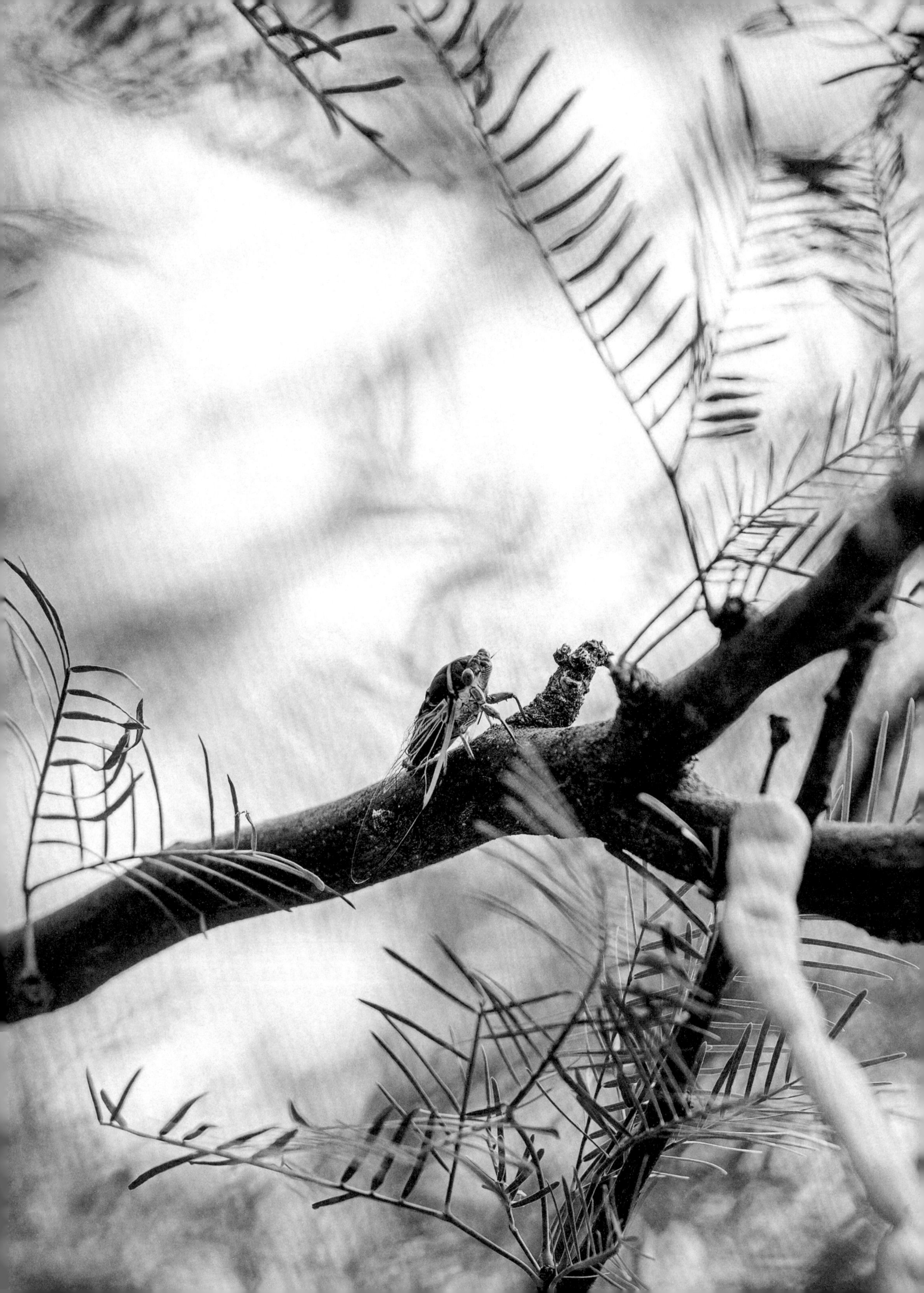

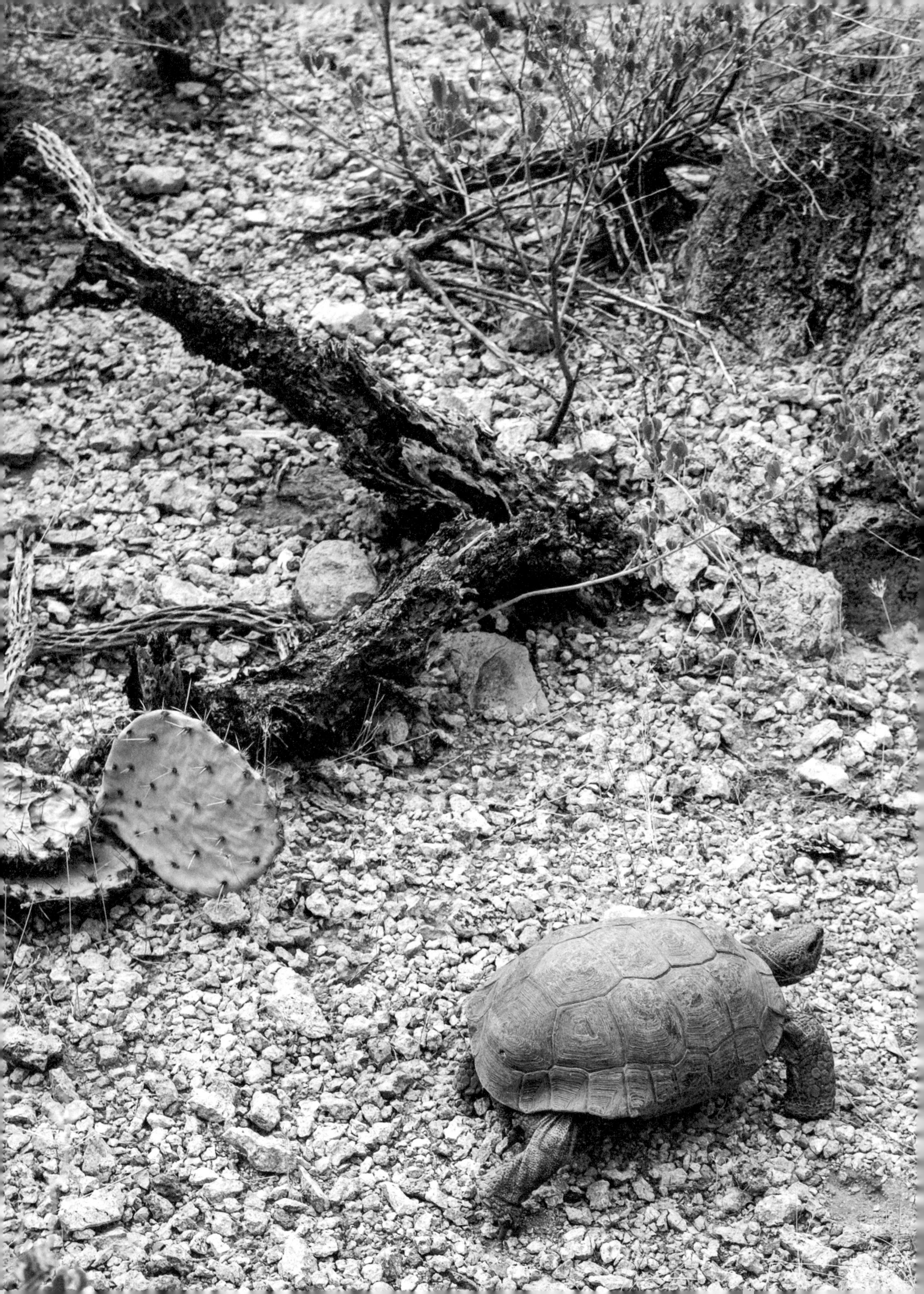

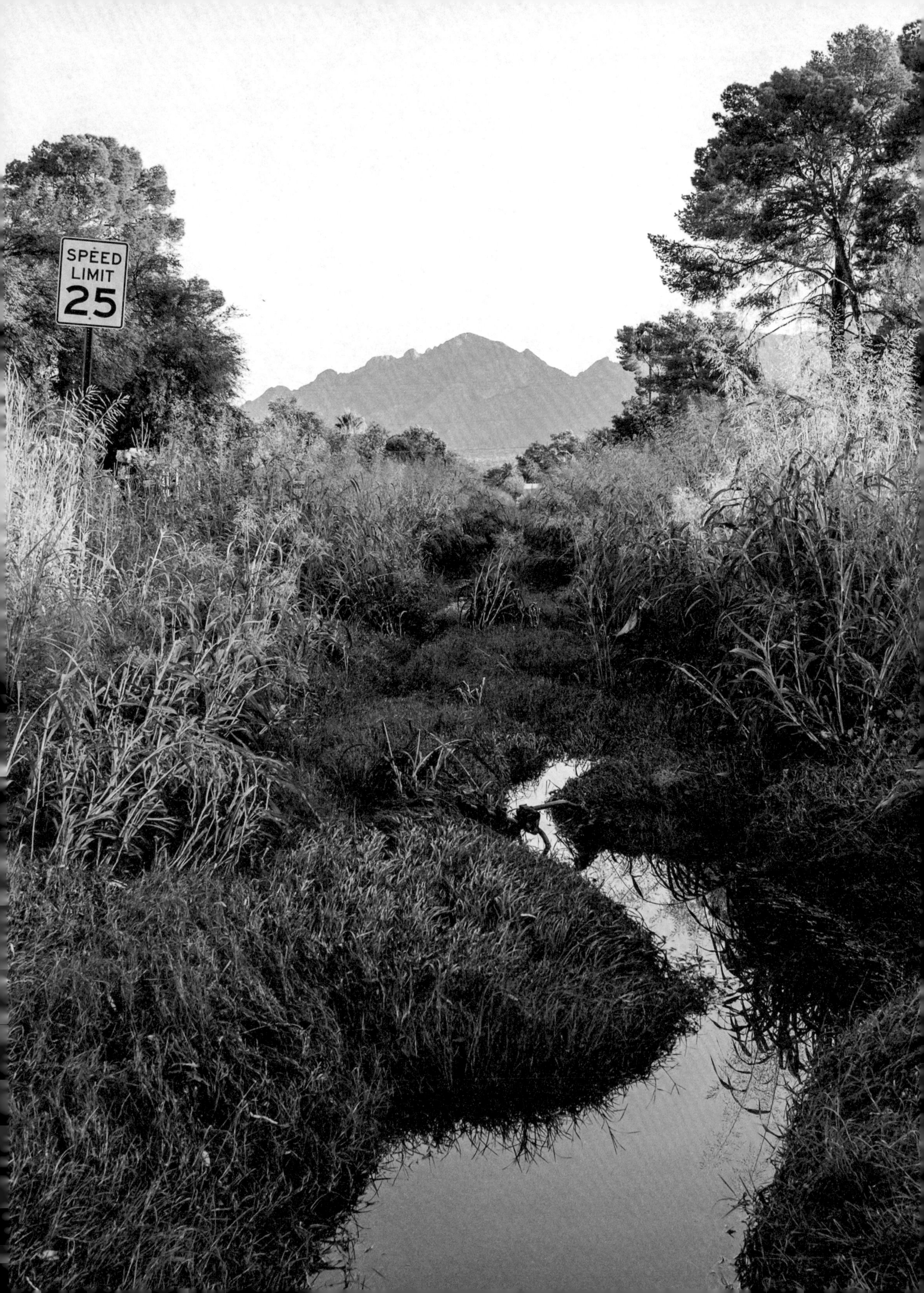
SPEED
LIMIT
25

In the Upland Arizona region, we have five seasons: autumn, winter, spring, foresummer, and summer monsoon. Traditionally, for the Tohono O'odham, the arrival of the summer rains marks the beginning of the new year, while according to the western calendar, monsoon season starts in early July and lasts through mid-September. The months preceding the onset of the season are hot and dry, leading to increasing humidity as winds moving in a clockwise pattern bring moisture from the Pacific Ocean and the Gulf of California across northern Mexico and into southeastern Arizona. The atmospheric pressure builds for weeks before, hopefully, the first dramatic storm of the season brings relief, and when the rains come the desert ecosystem seems to almost instantaneously teem with life once again.

How many plant species might one write off as dead during the dry months, when in fact they are simply lying dormant, conserving resources while waiting for that first storm? How many plants sprout leaves or flowers in response to the torrential downpours that come only at this time of year? Here there are insects that only appear right after a monsoon season rain—their life cycles tied completely to it. The spadefoot toad, too, emerges from underground only after the first rain to lay its eggs in puddles left behind, the tadpoles growing in a race against time before the water disappears in the desert sun.

Like seasons everywhere, the monsoon is becoming more erratic. We all can't help but wonder what will happen to the desert if at some point the monsoon no longer arrives.

J. Drew Lanham
THE SLOW SEDUCTION OF A FLEETING AUTUMN

"The goldenrod's gilded flowers flag the change, and I feel it heart-wise more than the other three divisions of the calendar that we humans count by days and weeks in square numbered blocks."

I AM SEDUCED to wanderlust chasing autumn's fleeting blush. The possibility of cooler air refreshing humid days and colors emerging other than summer's tired green domination is a finger-curling, "come hither" invitation to settle a little deeper in. The birds moving south feel this before I do and know the time coming by cues we can't see. Shifts in dark sky constellations and a more oblique slant to the sun's rays guide them to lower latitudes. Even as the dawn chorus goes silent, there's a different pulse coming that treads quietly, but powerfully. It is in this season that I pay attention to the subtle declaration of a new chip note in the old field's dog fennel or a half-hearted sub-song that's whispered in the weeds. It isn't the drama of a May morning's claim to nesting territory or securing of a partner to make more, egg by egg, but rather a note to notice the subtle; to see what lies beneath the obvious. The shorebirds lead the way, showing up before the end of July on Southern Piedmont pond margins all the way from Arctic breeding grounds. A spotted sandpiper's brief respite at my farm puddle means it finds something good enough to stop for in the broken landscape I'm trying to recover by letting it rest from prior abuse. A flycatcher whose identity vacillates between yellow-bellied and other *Empidonax* finds the topmost fence line suitable enough to sally forth and back to earn a buggy living from. A palm warbler appears, maybe from a boreal region where it may have kept company with grizzlies, wolves, and Sandhill cranes. It flips its tail in the meadow lane as if to say, "I'm here!" and October is yet to arrive. The goldenrod's gilded flowers flag the change, and I feel it heart-wise more than the other three divisions of the calendar that we humans count by days and weeks in square numbered blocks.

Birder demigod Roger Tory Peterson's hallmark "confusing fall warblers" shouldn't just be about the frustration of identifying brightly plumaged birds gone to look-alike olive drab, it should also offer lessons in looking more carefully for slight differences in quaint cues. I call these "feel marks." Then, the heart arcs with the head, and the urge to prioritize objectifying counts and x's on a list loses ground. "Wandering" is an autumnal watchword. *Zugunruhe* is the wondrous German word that defines our (yes OUR) restless migratory mood to be somewhere other than where we are. It arises in me with spring but swells to full-on longing when fall arises. The seasonal shift from growth to dormancy as summer retires is a full-moon tidal pull that has pushed me to an extreme tension between impatience and wanting more. I know autumn is an ephemeral season, as all seasons are, but because it is defined by falling leaves and departing souls, its inability to stay is most desirable. I feel this when the first white-throated sparrow's song drifts out of the overgrown brush pile. There are words about "Poor Sam Peabody" and "Oh sweet Canada" offered by texts and experts to help us know the whistled tune, but I wonder what the sparrow means beyond what we glibly think? I envy it for the secrets it keeps. Whatever its intent, I know when I hear it that fall is full-on and winter's monochrome cannot be far behind.

Pay attention to what flies or skulks away from your typical center-focused perception in this season. Slow down. Take your binoculars down too and gain a wider field of view in the periphery. Then, let your vision blur a bit to see more clearly. The loss in magnification will bring a differently deeper appreciation. A chance to identify with the birds, instead of just identifying them, will emerge. And don't forget your "feel guide." It is the most essential reference tool.

An Interview with David Hinton
AN ETHICS OF WILD MIND

Interviewed by
Emmanuel Vaughan-Lee

EVL David, I want to start our conversation today by asking you to read a poem. It's a poem that underpins much of what you explore in your book *Wild Mind, Wild Earth*—an ancient Chinese poem that you suggest holds within it an ethics that we so desperately need at this time of great ecological crisis. Could you read that poem for us?

DH Sure. It's called *Egrets*.

> Robes of snow, crests of snow, and beaks of azure jade,
> they fish in shadowy streams. Then startling away into
>
> flight, they leave emerald mountains for lit distances.
> Pear blossoms, a tree-full, tumble in the evening wind.

EVL So, tell me about this poem.

DH It's a pretty typical classical Chinese poem that's short—four lines, five words per line—written in the ninth century. And what's interesting about it is that it's all images. There's sort of no abstract, isolated self looking out on the world thinking about it; it's all the immediacy of crystalline images. The interesting thing about this is that after we see the egrets leave, suddenly in the last line there's something completely different that has nothing to do with the egrets. There's this big leap from the egrets leaving emerald mountains to suddenly *pear blossoms, a tree-full, tumble in the evening wind*. There's no kind of logical connection between those. There's a kind of imagistic connection, because the egrets are small, fluttering white things going up, and pear blossoms are small, white things fluttering down. But why did we go from one to the other? That's part of the magic. Because images have no kind of abstract intellectual content. And then that leap between the two has no content. They're empty.

Part One of the book is called "How a Little Poem from Ancient China Could Save the Planet," which is meant to be in part serious and in part facetious. At bottom, what's driving the ecological crisis is our sense of being centers of identity—in the West we call it the soul or the spirit—that are radically separate from, distant from, detached from, what we call nature. And you notice the word "nature"—and also the word "wild"—by definition it incorporates these assumptions about identity in the world. And those assumptions are that nature is everything other than us—that is, we're not part of nature and the wild is everything other than us. We're not part of the wild—we're something else. And that I think is what's driving the ecological crisis at its deepest level, because that distance, that separation, enables a kind of instrumental and exploitative relation to "nature."

In the moment of pure perception, like this poem is presenting, that self, that detached self, disappears. There's just you. If you can have an empty mind and you're looking at the world, you're mirroring the world—that is, there's no identity. There's no sort of spirit center separating you from the world. In that moment there's just the world mirrored: it's the content of consciousness. I mean, we all experience this. You don't have to be a Zen monk to do this. Anytime you see something that surprises you—you come around the corner and see, whatever, a fire truck racing down the street—there's the first moment of surprise when you're all eyes and you just see the fire truck. Then you step back and start thinking about it: "I wonder what's going on," et cetera, et cetera. But that first moment—that's the mirroring moment.

EVL In the book you use the term "wild mind, wild earth" repeatedly. You return to it again and again. And although it may be self-explanatory—and it's a simple term—it also holds a great deal. And I wonder if you could unpack the term for us and what it means and how you're using it and how you're expanding and exploring it.

DH Well, there's what I mentioned just a moment ago—the idea that we normally think of the wild as everything other than human. This is the idea of *wild mind*: consciousness as wild, just like Earth is wild. We think of Earth as nature or wild, but wild mind is incorporating consciousness into that. It's easy for us to say, well, we're animals, we're bodies like any other animal, any other body. To that extent it's easy to think of us as part of the Earth. It's much more difficult to see, to *experience*, mind or self or identity as wild, as no different from everything else. And that's what the book is trying to work through: how do we rewild mind?

EVL You describe how foundational stories of our Western, Christian paradigm are based on this idea of "a self-enclosed human realm separate from everything else," and that this paradigm is a wound—one "so complete we can't see it anymore, for it defines the very nature of what we assume ourselves to be." And yet at the same time, you say, "however deeply we have forgotten it, we must still be wild in our original Paleolithic nature—wild and kindred to wild earth." And that our "kinship is itself a truly primordial ethics, an ethics before question and argument." Can you explain that?

DH To start that answer, I'll read the first paragraph of the book:

> Before intention and choice, before ideas and understanding and everything we think we know about ourselves—we love this world around us. How can that be? How can we *love* all this when our cultural assumptions tell us in so many ways that we "humans" are fundamentally other than "nature," and that "nature's" only real value is how it supports our well-being? There's no love in that. Doesn't love require kindred natures? And what is kinship with wild earth but wild mind?

EVL Well, that does a really wonderful job of simply explaining wild earth and wild mind, as well as linking it to kinship.

DH And that kinship—to sort of circle back to your question—that kinship I think was there in the Paleolithic. For Paleolithic hunter-gatherers, like the Paleo-Indians in North America, there was no sense that they were radically different from anything else. All the animals had the same status as humans. It was assumed that they all had sort of rich interior lives, that they had social lives.

I mean, in the West there is this broad assumption that the world is really here for us: humans are what it's all about. And that's that radical separation. In the Christian myth we're spirits here on Earth sort of working out our divine fate. And so we're kind of here as aliens from somewhere else, and it's a proving ground where we're tested and then we go back to our real home, which is this spirit realm called Heaven where God lives. That kind of idea was completely absent for the Paleolithic.

Identity was completely woven into what we would now call the "ecosystem." And I think that changed.

The consciousness we have now began when Paleolithic hunter-gatherers started settling into Neolithic agricultural villages. And then at that point there was a separate human space—the village and the cultivated fields around it. Hunter-gatherers didn't have that. They were just wandering through the "wild," the "wilderness." Of course, that idea would make no sense to them, because there was no separation. So they would—if they could understand that—just say, "It's all wilderness. I'm wilderness. Everything is wilderness."

In the Neolithic, people started sort of manipulating or exploiting nature in the form of domestic animals and plants. So, as opposed to just moving through the ecosystem, they were setting up these separate human realms within the ecosystem. And then next came writing. Because for preliterate peoples, the mind worked like anything else: like weather or like a stream flowing. It was just this constant flowing of thinking—thinking appearing and disappearing. But once you can write things down, then that mental realm suddenly starts looking timeless and radically different from the world around us. And I think that's what really created this sense of an interior—what became with the Greeks and the Christians a kind of soul. This thing that's actually made of different stuff. It's made of spirit stuff instead of matter, different stuff from the earth. That came, I think, from writing.

These giant transformations in the structure of consciousness, and the structure of what it is to be human, happen not because of ideas changing and developing, but because of material changes: that is, the change from hunter-gatherer to agrarian; the change from wandering to a village; the change from oral tradition to written—those are technological changes, material changes. And that's what transformed consciousness. The Greeks took that material change and they mythologized it into the soul. And then, of course, Genesis—the creation story in Christianity—says that the world is here for humans. It was created for humans to use, to dominate, to exploit in their trial here to see if they're righteous or not. So at the end of that you've got the formula. The sixth extinction was already built into that structure thousands of years ago. It just took thousands of years to build up the capabilities through which that instrumental exploitative relation to landscape and Earth and the ten thousand things became so catastrophically powerful.

EVL You write about how over the last few centuries here in the West there's been a simmering revolution of sorts unfolding: a revolution that has been challenging this dominant human-centric paradigm that emerged from that Christian model in Genesis and that has been seeking to return to a more ancient paradigm of kinship with the Earth, which was so central to so many ancient and Indigenous cultures, as well as to our original Paleolithic nature. And that this revolution—one that's grown dramatically in the last few decades as the impacts of climate change, colonialism, and capitalism have pushed people to examine the root causes of these crises—is not the first such revolution to take place. It has a precedent in ancient China that we can look to. Can you talk about this?

DH So, to start, I sort of trace out these parallel developments. The development in China was about three thousand years before the one in the West, which began with the Enlightenment but really took hold at the end of the eighteenth century. Europe was largely in the thrall of that whole Christian worldview and—this is just amazing to me—what happened was that people in North America were talking with Native American elders and writing books about traveling among Native people in North America. Well, these books and these accounts became very popular in Europe, especially among intellectuals. And one of the things that they took from these accounts was this whole different idea of the relation of humans and nature: that is, prior to this, nature was considered sort of evil, something that had to be tamed and brought into God's order, and this Native American view was a view of kinship, of belonging to the landscape and the ecosystem. So this had a huge impact on a lot of major thinkers, like the German Romantics and Alexander von Humboldt, who was a gigantic superstar / naturalist / scientist whose books were on the desk of Thoreau, Whitman, and Rousseau.

But I talk more about the impact on the British Romantic poets, because their poems are sort of articulating this newly found kinship and wonder at the natural world as a kind of antidote to the industrial age alienation of urban life, with all of its commercialism and sort of the whole industrial realm. So this is Wordsworth and Shelly and Coleridge. They start discovering this wonder at nature. What we take for granted now—this sense that nature is this wonderful, sustaining place—was really not known in the West until the British Romantics and the German Romantics of the late eighteenth century. So then that idea, again, which came largely from Native Americans, went to Europe, transformed Wordsworth, for instance, and then came back to America through those writers when Thoreau and Emerson read them. So it comes back to Thoreau, and it influences the intellectual history of the nineteenth century in the US: Whitman and John Muir, who helped found the Sierra Club, and on to the modern environmental movement. And this thing we take for granted, this sense of love for the natural world, kinship with the natural world—that's where it came from. It was this transformation that was catalyzed, generated, by Native American "philosophy."

Now, in ancient China the same kind of thing happened: there was a monotheistic system, very similar in its basic outlines to Christianity, that fell apart, and then the philosophers we know of as the seminal Chinese philosophers tried to rebuild a philosophical system out of the ashes of that monotheism. And they were very empirically minded like we are. And so what they built was Taoism. The *Tao Te Ching* is the earliest book in Taoism, and it dates from around 600 BCE. But it's mostly made out of fragments of ancient—maybe even Paleolithic or what descended from Paleolithic—wisdom traditions: that is, it was compiled by gathering fragments from this wisdom tradition—an oral wisdom tradition—and editing them, translating them into classical Chinese, and building them into a book. And then Taoism becomes Ch'an Buddhism, which in America you'll know as Zen Buddhism. So Taoism and Zen Buddhism are sort of China's eco-centric philosophical system: that is, in the *Tao Te Ching*, in the early Taoist tradition, they speak always of the "Tao," which is this sort of generative tissue of reality, of the Earth—that's what Tao is. It's a very empirical idea. And that's referred to over and over as female, as a mother. So it goes back to a time when cultures were built around this sense that the sacred is a generative force of the Earth, of transformation. That's the connection.

And then the book in the end says, well, the Paleolithic model isn't that useful for us now, even though everything came from it: that is, the Chinese transformation and the Western transformation really grew out of the Paleolithic way of seeing the world. In both cases, that Paleolithic consciousness went underground for a century or two or three, and then reemerged: as the *Tao Te Ching* (Taoism) or as Romanticism, and then on into the modern environmental movement. But the Paleolithic worldview is a little less useful for us because that was a material culture that's just completely gone. We're not ever going to be hunter-gatherers again; we're not going to wander the wilderness.

However, ancient China's version of the Paleolithic paradigm is useful because ancient Chinese culture is virtually the same structurally as our culture. It was a diversified market economy. They had money. They were bureaucrats working in offices. They were intensely textual, highly, highly educated, et cetera, et cetera. So that's why in *Wild Mind, Wild Earth* I spend time trying to build out and explain how the Chinese system works, so that we can see how it might be useful for us here in the West today.

EVL And how do you feel it's different—this ethics that emerged out of the Paleolithic era that influenced the ancient Chinese cultures and led to the *Tao Te Ching* and to Ch'an Buddhism and Zen Buddhism? How does it need to be different now if

"Winter is a kind of pregnant emptiness. Spring emerges out of that—it flourishes. And life flourishes in summer and then dies back into that emptiness of winter."

we're going to embrace these ancient ways of being in relationship and kinship with the Earth as we deal with the complex issues of a modern society, with the sixth extinction?

DH I don't think it needs to be very different. There are a lot of Zen Buddhists around—it seems to work here and now. No, it doesn't have to be much different. This book is arguing that the real driver of the sixth extinction is a bundle of philosophical assumptions: unthought, unquestioned assumptions, all operating in the mental realm. And the Taoists, Ch'an Buddhists—I use "Ch'an," the Chinese word for "Zen"—they're all about self-cultivation. And that's where these assumptions operate: they operate in consciousness, in our minds. And that's where you have to examine them, or a culture has to examine them, and start thinking about changing them—like ancient China did. And like I said, a lot of this work has been done over the last two hundred years in the West. So no, I don't think it has to be different. I think it has to be a decision that we're going to cultivate this other different way of seeing the world—and it's a kind of self-cultivation in the end.

Most environmental books now are about practical technological innovation or social changes that have to happen. My argument is that's not going to work, that's not going to happen. It requires a transformation in our assumptions about the nature of what we are and what the world is. Otherwise, that instrumental and exploitative relation will remain. Even if some people want to preserve a piece of land, that's how they want to use it; other people want to frack natural gas out of it, that's how they want to use it. Because you're sharing the assumption that the piece of land is something to use, then it's just a disagreement. But if there were an assumption that that land, the animals on it—their self-realization—is equally important to ours, then the whole conversation changes dramatically.

EVL Yeah, one of the things I found very interesting is that you talk about how, despite the widespread ecological advocacy that can be attributed to the modern environmental movement, the Western philosophical tradition it's based on is ungrounded; and that the current environmental movement's sense of kinship lacks the depths of a Taoist/Ch'an cosmology or a Paleolithic nature at its heart. And yes, it may be on the verge of integrating that, and there are a lot of efforts to support that, but it still lacks that grounded sense that Ch'an and Taoist philosophies offered.

DH Yeah, and that might be the whole reason for this book: to say, oh, here's where you ground it. It's not that hard and it's not that foreign—it's not foreign, really. This transformation in the West has already gotten us almost there. A lot of people are there. But government leaders aren't there. Industry leaders aren't there. They're still operating in the old mode. So yeah, it's there. We just need to ground it, right?

EVL You say you don't offer solutions to tackling the sixth extinction and the environmental crisis, but you did put a lot of emphasis on the practices that emerged from Taoism and Ch'an Buddhism and how they can help heal wounds—the "wound of consciousness" that was "torn from wild earth," you say. And today we might call these practices that emerged in the Taoist and Ch'an Buddhist schools a deep ecological practice.

DH Yeah. Just for instance, meditation, which you don't have to go to a Zen monastery to do. If you just sit quietly and watch what's going on in your head—that's how Ch'an meditation starts—you realize very quickly: Oh, I am watching the thoughts go through my head. I am not those thoughts—which is what we assume we are. We assume the soul, spirit, whatever you call identity center, is the center of rational thought, of thinking. That's Descartes's bedrock: after he strips everything you can't know for absolute certain, he comes down to, "I think therefore I am." *I think*. So thinking is his bedrock. But here you are after five seconds of Ch'an meditation and you see, oh, not so. I am this kind of quiet awareness watching thoughts come and go, come and go, come and go.

So already we have taken a big step toward integrating consciousness with Earth. Because it's that thought process, it's that whole sort of interior realm of thinking and feeling and memory that we assume is us—that's what separates us out from the rest of the world, right? So you sit for five or ten seconds, and you see that you're not that. You are just this awareness. Then you sit for a little bit longer, and maybe your thoughts slow down a little and you can sort of watch how they're working. And you see that what's happening in your head is that thoughts appear out of nowhere. They evolve through their transformations, and then they disappear and new thoughts appear. So there's this appearance, evolution, disappearance. That's what goes on in the natural world—things appear, they go through their lives, and they disappear. You can think of it like the seasons. Winter is a kind of pregnant emptiness. Spring emerges out of that—it flourishes. And life flourishes in summer and then dies back into that emptiness of winter. And you realize, oh, my thoughts are doing the same thing that the ten thousand things do, the ten thousand things in empirical reality. And then you realize, oh, well they're part of the same tissue. Things emerge out of emptiness, live their lives, and disappear into emptiness. That happens in the head. And so that's another radical reweaving of consciousness and wildness. There you're starting to see what I mean by "wild mind."

EVL You explain in the book—it's peppered throughout—that this Taoist, this Zen/Ch'an meditation practice which leads to empty mind, leads to a deep mirroring of the cosmos and in turn a celebration of the cosmos. And so there's a "deep seeing," as you describe it, or an experience that can come from this space that you could also say is a practice that can heal the wounds of consciousness.

DH If you keep meditating beyond where I was describing, pretty soon your thoughts will start falling silent. And then you are just inhabiting that pregnant emptiness. And that's sort of the end place for Ch'an Buddhism. I mean, not that that's all it's about—getting there—it's not. But that's what the Zen people call "empty mind." If, at that moment of empty mind, you open your eyes and your mind is emptied of thought, empty of content, whatever you look at is mirrored directly and immediately inside of you—that's what's going on. It's just this mirroring. And at that point, whatever you are looking at, whether it's a subway car or a wild peak someplace—that is the content of consciousness; that is identity. And that's another radical reweaving of consciousness and landscape and the world. That's why that poem is so important—it's a poem of that mirrored seeing that comes at the end of a certain amount of Ch'an practice and that reweaves consciousness with the world around it. And that was the fundamental pursuit for the Taoists and for the Ch'an/Zen Buddhists: reweaving consciousness with landscape, with the Tao, with the generative tissue of things—exactly what I'm saying is necessary to really deal with the sixth extinction that's going on now. It's not going to happen until we are rewoven with the Earth and its creatures.

So I'll read the poem again, and maybe you can hear it differently, because now you'll be hearing it as this mirroring. Is that okay?

EVL Yeah, please read it.

DH *Egrets*

Robes of snow, crests of snow, and beaks of azure jade,
they fish in shadowy streams. Then startling away into

flight, they leave emerald mountains for lit distances.
Pear blossoms, a tree-full, tumble in the evening wind.

So you see, that's why that leap from the egrets to the pear blossoms is so interesting or profound, because there is no thought process going on. There is no thought process driving this poem. It's just the whole egret/mountain thing, and then suddenly the next image, which is completely different—no real relation to what had come before. It's just perception, perception, perception. No logic. No reason. No thought process. Hence, it's a kind of meditative practice.

EVL Another thing that you explore is how in this space of deep seeing there is an emergence of love that comes forth—that kinship, that connection. When what you are seeing is a mirror of what is unfolding inside of you, that creates a certain bond: this weaving, as you describe it. And that is one of love, which seems to be so central if we are going to find a path forward individually or collectively that is different from the philosophical framework of the West's modern experiment, which was not grounded on love for the Earth. Do you feel that it's possible to move beyond an individual experience of love into something that is more societal as we grapple with these challenges?

DH Yeah, well, it really is societal only if it's all the individuals. But yeah, that love is there if you're not separate from something, if it's total kinship. Or even like those egrets—in that moment of seeing the egrets and the pear blossoms—that's the content of consciousness; that's the content of identity. So the ethics becomes kind of radical: whatever you do to one of those egrets—if you take your shotgun out and you shoot it—you're doing it to yourself, because there's no real difference between you and the egret. Mencius, one of the old Chinese philosophers, even says that whatever you do to the world, you do to yourself in a very real way. And maybe that's part of that wound that you've mentioned a couple of times: we're constantly tearing ourselves apart, but we don't quite realize it.

EVL So, what is this wild ethics? Obviously, we've been speaking about it maybe more indirectly, but if you had to distill it down, what is the ethical framework that we can live our lives within?

DH Well, I think the hunter-gatherers—having no separation between themselves, no radical distinction between human and nonhuman—thought everything else was kindred. Literally, they thought if you went out to hunt and you're hunting a deer, the deer is your sister or your brother, or maybe your ancestor, or maybe, more precisely, past/future forms of yourself. Because I think the ethic was that you hunted with prayers and sacrifice and humility. You're asking a deer—a brother or a sister or an ancestor—to give its life for you. But you know that the next time around it's going to be asking you to give your life for it. So, it's this beautiful web of life that they're participating in, and it has an ethics. You'd never go out and kill your sister just for sport, just to prove you're a man. I think that's a pretty radical ethics that we come to once we start unraveling that very detached Western self with its instrumental and exploitative relation.

I'm here in Vermont, where Native Americans have lived for over ten thousand years. The ecosystem was basically intact before Europeans arrived, and that's because they had that ethical system built into their fundamental cultural assumptions—the assumptions that guided their lives. They didn't think about them. They didn't question them. They were simply assumptions, unthought assumptions. When the Europeans got here with their unthought assumptions, they clear-cut the whole state within a century. And those two outcomes—one, an intact ecosystem after ten thousand years, and the other, a completely devastated ecosystem after a century or less—those are philosophical differences. Those are differences in cultural assumptions. That's what drove those two things. It's not technology.

Like now, we're talking about how technology could save us or how we need to change our behavior to save ourselves. That's what all of the climate change discussion is about: avoiding disruptions to the human project. And that's what I'm afraid of. As long as the human project is the center, the be-all and end-all of planet Earth, I don't think we're going to get very far.

EVL You spoke about how, as relevant as Chinese Taoist and Ch'an teachings are today and as much as the practices that came from those traditions can be gateways to rekindling that sense of kinship with the living Earth, the greatest teacher at this time might be the sixth extinction that is unfolding around us, which you described as a great vanishing—and *this* might be the teacher that helps rekindle this relationship that Taoism and Ch'an was trying to do.

DH Like what I wrote at the beginning of the book: We somehow love this world, and we feel kinship with it, but how can that be, because of our Western assumptions? And then, well, actually there is this cultural movement that began with the Romantics that is changing our cultural assumptions. But not enough. Then think about how the sixth extinction is really teaching us how much we *do* love this world. Because a lot of us find it unthinkable; it's so painful. And if we're feeling all that grief—the destruction is so massive, and we feel it so deeply—that's teaching us. That's saying, look how kindred you are. Look how much you love this. You didn't know this two hundred years ago. You don't know it enough now. But every day more species are lost, more individuals are lost. So that's where I start with the idea that the sixth extinction is now a great teacher. And I hope that's thick with irony, I guess. You don't really want to pay that kind of price for a teacher, but we don't have a choice.

EVL You also talk about how this process of experiencing this grief, and trying to learn what this experience is teaching us, is also revealing to us our most profound and beautiful selves at the same time.

DH We're so much more than we think we are. We are so much more than just this little bundle of obsessions going on in our head. And that's a beautiful thing to discover. And the sixth extinction is helping teach us that, because it's teaching us that we are profoundly kindred with the ecosystem, with the wild, with the ten thousand things. That's the whole point of Taoist and Ch'an Buddhist practices: to discover that vast self that we are.

To put ancient Taoist and Ch'an and even Paleolithic insight into modern scientific terms: We think of ourselves as this little bubble of obsessions and memories going on in our head that's detached from everything else. That's the wound. That sounds pretty isolated and bleak to me. But the scientific account of the universe is that the cosmos evolved generation after generation of suns, and in the third generation *our* sun and *our* planet. And on our planet, the cosmos evolved life-forms—like us. And some of those life-forms developed eyes—like us. And so when we look out at the world, we are quite literally the cosmos looking out at itself. That's consciousness totally woven into the cosmos, into Earth, into landscape. And even when we think about the cosmos, when we think about the sixth extinction, we're the cosmos thinking about itself. And when we feel it, when we feel love and grief—that's the cosmos feeling itself. That's our greatest, that's our biggest self. And it's kind of been hidden from us by Western intellectual history and the assumptions we've inherited.

A SINGLE WOOL BLANKET

In the summer,
I took the wool blanket off the bedding.

In winter, I put it back on.

A single wool blanket,
plaid, of blue wool, red wool,
and black, with a little yellow.

In a world of summer and winter grasses,
of sheep, of wool, of weavers.

In a world where cries
of a goshawk in June, of crows in December.

What world was it.
Tell me.

What world,
in which some could so easily
do this—
add a blanket, subtract one—
and some could not do this.

We slept in it, math-less,
ate as we could of its berries and meats.
Wanting to live.

Betrothed, bewildered mammals,
beheld & beholding, bequeathed of existence.

Jane Hirshfield

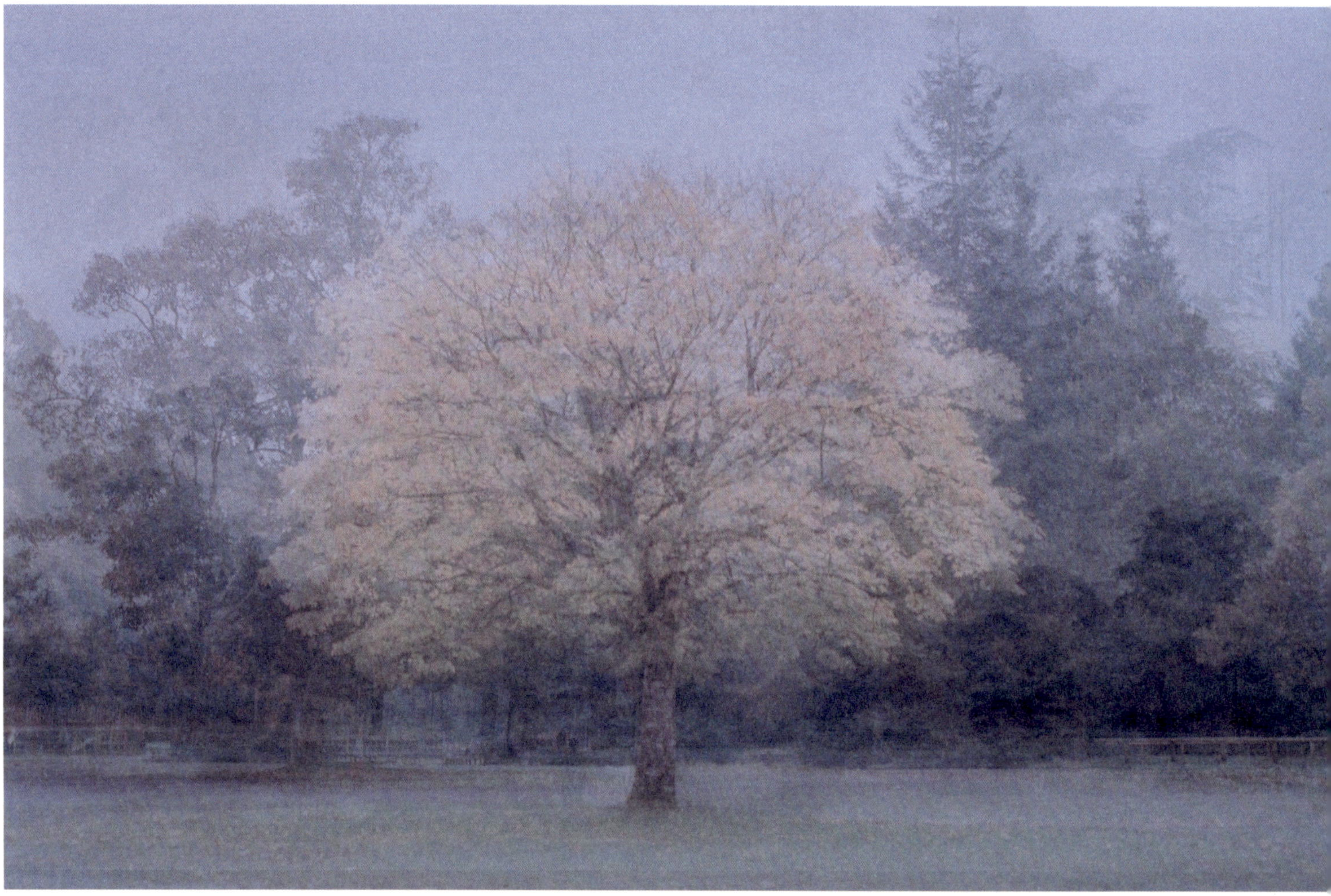

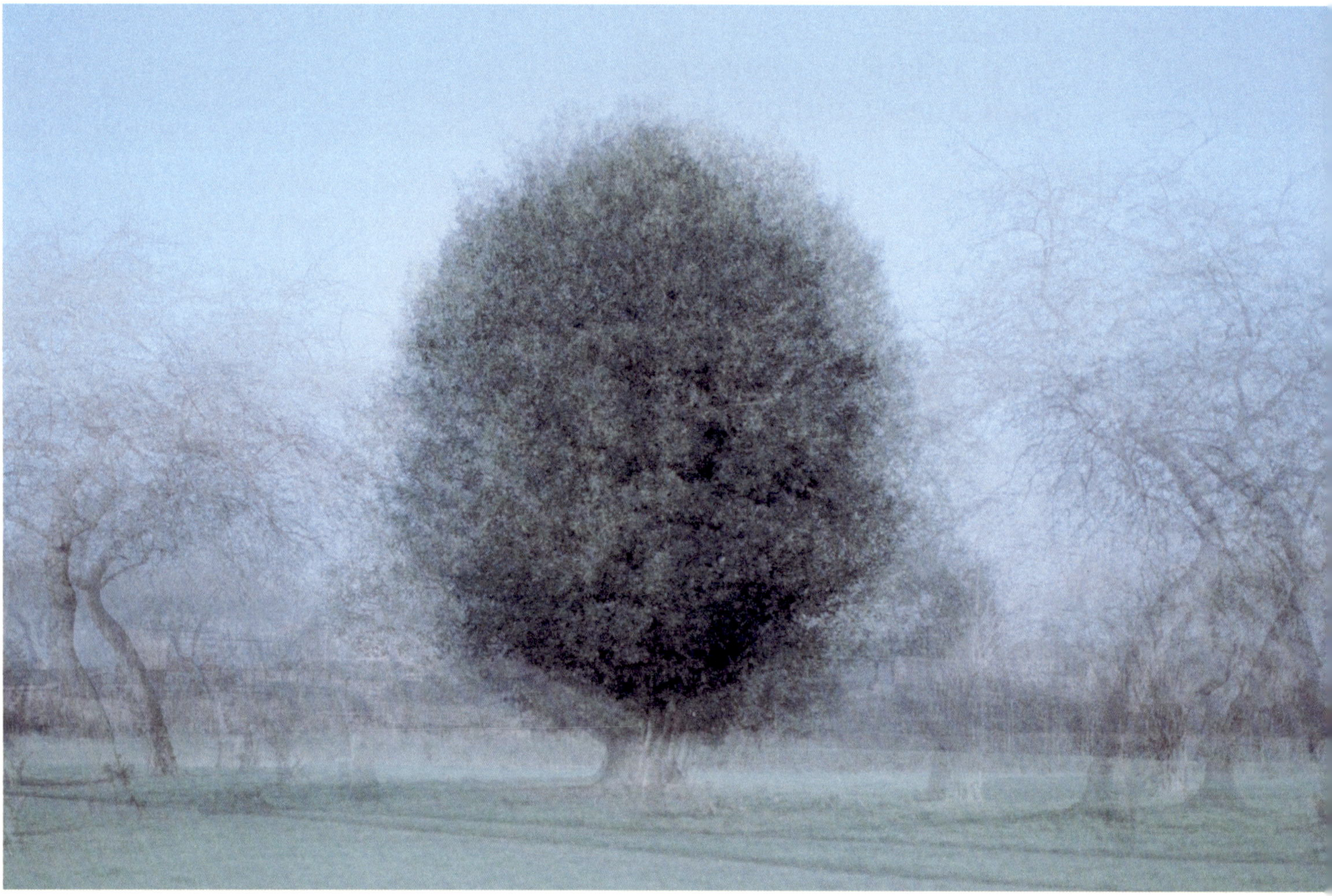

FIG. 17 Millennium Images / Gallery Stock (P. 224)

Celebration

Chapter 3

WILDFLOWERS BLOOM IN WHAT'S LEFT OF HOPE

DRIFTING TO SLEEP
WHAT OF MY FELLOW TRAVELERS
FACES IN THE SNOW

STORM CLOUDS
ALL THE COLORS
IN A RAVEN'S CALL

WARM SAND THROUGH MY FINGERS THE COLOR OF JOY

GREEN PERSIMMONS . . .
A FINGERPRINT GLISTENS
WITH MORNING DEW

RIVER OF STARS
A LITTLE BOY WIGGLES
HIS MILK TOOTH

DUCKS DIVE
THE OVERCAST SKY
ROLLS OFF THEIR BACKS

CHARRED CEDARS
HOW COLD THE WHITE
OF EARLY SNOW

END OF SUMMER
FIREFIGHTERS HUG
IN THE LIGHTNESS OF RAIN

UNBROKEN HORIZON
A LONE SWIMMER
ENTERS THE SEA

12 Moss, *Cloud Hands*. First published in *Presence* 42, 2019.
13 Moss, first published in *World Haiku Review*, 2012.
14 Moss, *Bone Carver*. First published in *South by Southeast* 15, no. 3.
15 Moss, first published in *Yah Words, Sea Bandits*, September 2012.
16 Moss, *Bone Carver*.
17 Moss, *Cloud Hands*. First published in *Autumn Moon Haiku Journal* 3, no. 1, 2019.
18 Moss, *Bone Carver*. First published in *Yellow Moon* 11, winter 2002.
19 Moss, *Bone Carver*.
20 Moss, *Bone Carver*. First published in *FreeXpressSion*, January 2007.
21 Moss, *Cloud Hands*. First published in Acorn, summer 2015.

Dara McAnulty
THE THREAD OF BELONGING

"This is summer!
The meadow. The hunting barn owl.
The way the light slants through the heavy leaves of the oaks.
The singing blackbird.
The skylarks!"

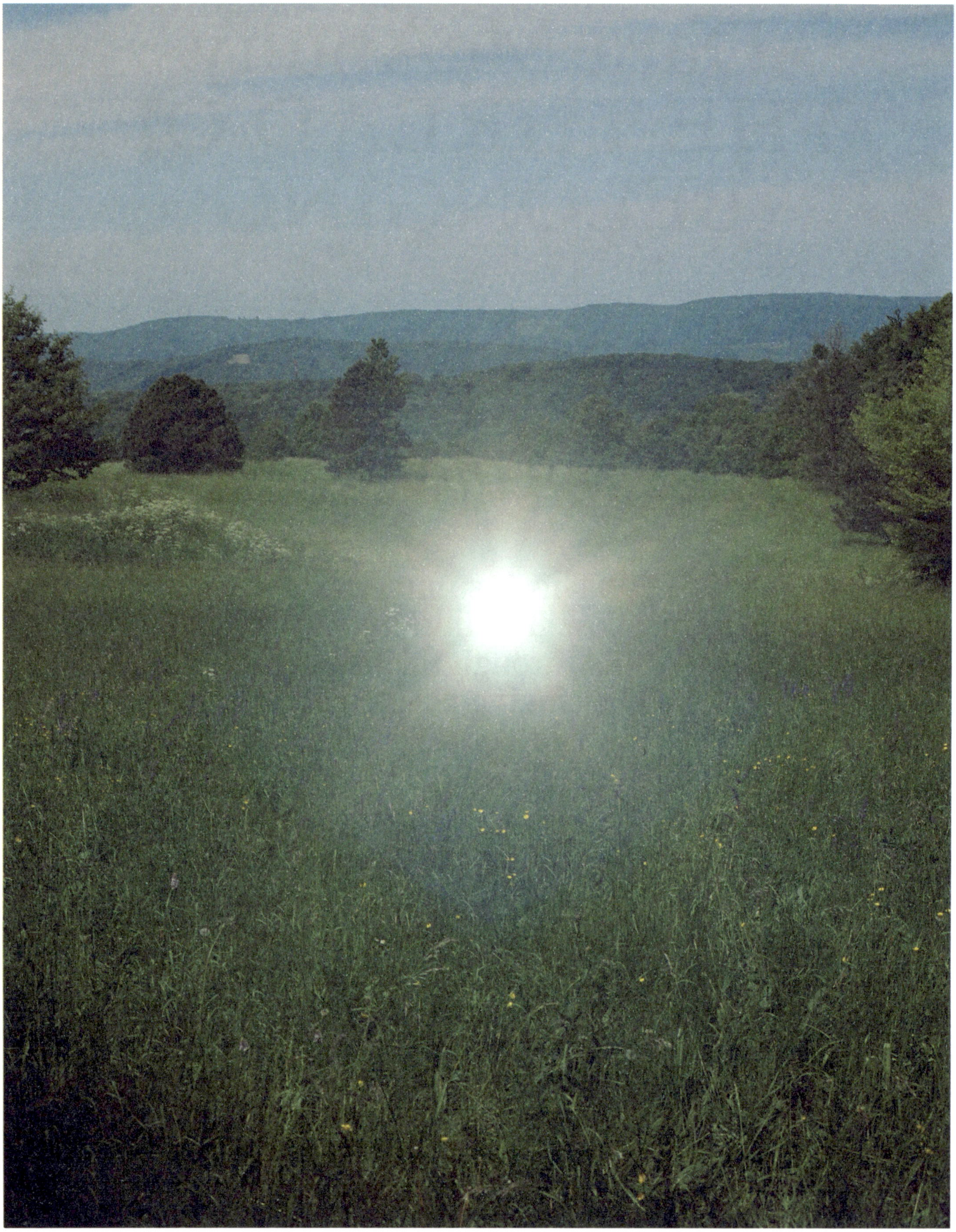

FIG. 18 David Avazzadeh / Connected Archives (P. 242)

We were saying goodbye to another year of the hardest and most intense work, making a celebratory circle on the fast-becoming-brittle June grass. Cambridge, even in early summer, is too hot for my temperate Irish bones. The meadow flowers were still long and luscious, though, tickling our cheeks and tipping fragrant notes into our already bubbling chorus of excited chatter. Exams were over and we would all soon be blowing like dandelion seeds to our foundation corners, to feel the clucking and fussing of those who had missed us.

Summer shone in without my realizing, a novel experience as I, from a precociously early age, had categorized and chronicled each week and every month of my cognizant childhood. Notebooks filled with dated pressed flowers, weather reports, birds and animals sighted, festivals celebrated. Descriptions and feelings. A young naturalist alongside a young writer. Reliving every moment to ease the overwhelming noise of the other world: that of people and the unnatural soundscape of hustle and bustle.

I had then become a "seen" chronicler of that same "other world." In front of it for all to critique, to disseminate and form opinions, not just on my words, but on my appearance, my autism, and the confusing notion that I was who I am. And who I am—so synchronized with the seasonal happenings of nature—had fast become lost as the requests and requirements rushed in; what had once been a natural flowing of my being became, admittedly, a false introspection. My joy and wonder formed into a public simulacrum rather than an authentically lived experience. So, I became untethered, frighteningly so. I cut all ties with my pen and channeled my vision toward just becoming an essence in the world.

University life was beckoning, and wiping the slate clean became irresistible. Arriving in Cambridge I began to seek out sensory adventures, much as I had in my younger years. I sought out places where wildlife existed, from the intimate activity outside my window to the horizontal expanse of the fens, which breathtakingly, dizzyingly, gave me roots to grow into myself, away from all I knew. I then became surrounded by friends I never thought I would have; and although my brain considered each intricate detail of life amidst the living of it, my spirit did not itch to fill a page. It did not last, though, for writing to me is like breathing. Deep breaths which when easily forgotten leave us breath-less, but not for long. Inhaling all and letting it once again fill thought crevices. My body, as nature does in each turn of the season, sent out signals that it was time, and so (to use a favorite Seamus Heaney analogy), I dug once more with my pen, and (like in Heaney's peat bog) I have been reaching new depths with it. Equilibrium once more. As small tremors happen above and below ground, innate propulsion, the desire to scratch the surface with ink or the tapping of keys, writing, once more, becomes uncontrollably natural.

The barn owl came silently, and we silenced our revelry, as outstretched spectral wings caught our breath in its wake. Glowing against the arches of oak. Traversing low and capturing unspoken reverence. The light! Summer had at last descended upon the dull ache where homesickness lingered, and with quickening pulse, so did the realization of coming home. Of leaving the horizontal land of the fens for the contours of the mountainous coast, for waterfalls and waves. Oystercatchers and redshanks, their luminous calls ricocheting against my bedroom window. The starlings, coating next door's field with their pulsed shapeshifting. The wonder of seeing how our Brigid's cross had gone from green to wheat.

Although seasons in Cambridge are more clear-cut, marked by distinct weather, they are clouded by deadlines, lectures, supervisions, and a moody anxiety. No family rituals of walking down the Holloway to Ballynoe Stone Circle to welcome each paragraph of our yearly story. The only respite: early morning rowing. Stillness as the sun rises. My walk to the boathouse is the anchor, a window of heeding. My feet crunching on just-fallen autumn leaves. The glistening of kingfisher on winter mornings, my patterned breath catching dunnock song as its first spring notes hit the bare branches. The first primroses on the riverbank. The ever-present mallards, quacking rasps of melody, keeping me company as I walk across the Mathematical Bridge to my lectures; energy fizzing in my arms and legs, muscles purring from the stretch of the morning's action. Back and forth. Swerving the river surface. Small happenings seeping between the cracks, making me whole. Noticing. Nature and the cyclical turnings—

they complete me; satiate my inner hunger for depth. Knowledge can only partially fill the soul. It can excite, thrill ... transform it. But not weight it with the satisfaction of sensation.

During moments of intense home heartache, when going to the ceilidh house for the songs of home is just not enough, I recall from my inner curiosity cabinet of memories the seasonal chimes marking Earth's cadence and rhythm: Hanging the washing out with Mum in March as three whooper swans bugled vernal honks. We smiled knowingly. The first time I saw an otter as the river felt the straining branches, laden with late winter snow. Scrabbling amongst the fields and peering over cliffs on Rathlin Island to find hints that all was well with its nature—the pyramidal bugle flowering, the puffins arrived. The constant need to know that all is as it should be. The swallows that come—during my last week of homely rest before another April drive to the ferry—and nest in the woodshed. Tucked tightly within their astonishingly robust architecture. The joyous relief of beholding is as intense as the reluctant oncoming suitcase packing. Walking as a family through Murlough Woods to welcome the cuckoo's steadying two-beat harbinger, my exit call to exam term. Returning home exhausted in June to find fragile fledglings; we have much in common. And the pond! No longer stagnant but brimming with life. Emerging emperor dragonflies, red darters, pond skaters, water beetles. Daphnia. All whizzing and scrambling. A frog! Camouflaged on the grass. Just one, but one can become more than "just one." Water forget-me-nots and marigolds attracting hoverflies. Continued blossoming. I stare for hours. Thinking time. We all need a lot more thinking time, to observe not just our atmosphere but our inner workings and how they charge together.

These are the moments which bind and bond. Nature's pulsating, stamping imprints on memory, love, and fellowship. Connection to all living things enlivens spaces into ecosystems. Everyday places into wonderlands. When the aperture is expanded to panoramic or narrowed to proximate, everything becomes a living painting. Claude Monet painted his *Water Lilies* series: two hundred and fifty paintings of his beloved flower garden, from all angles, in all seasons. Each work shows the subtle changes of a space in time. I find them tender and yet, stirring. An act of quiet, delicate presence and patience. Patience seems to have been overtaken by instant gratification, a frenzied need for increasingly more. Now, now! Tempered observance brings awareness of the intimacy and intricacy of change, enabling us to withstand change within ourselves and our lives.

As an autistic young adult, I have embraced change—an intense and difficult journey—by becoming more than an onlooker. Entwining myself with the knowing that change is a gift of renewal and growth, an invitation to feel truly alive. Nature and seasonal change have thrust me towards emerging wisdom and self-acceptance. As I move from teenager to young man, seasons are no longer about marking the points of time, but its passing: leaving and coming home. The thread of belonging separating into a trinity of home, friendships, and college life. Gone are the one-dimensional, juvenile note-takings, replaced now by a cornucopia of feeling in my entire being, propelling every sinew and muscle into action. A need to keep moving through the world with eyes wide open. I find now that my mind photographs and catalogues all by itself, without hints, prompts or evidence. Over time nature has become a role model for living and it has taught me all the lessons I need to know. Reciprocity. Patience. Resilience. Understanding connection, and limitations.

Of course, there is one blaring roar not to be ignored. A seismic shift precipitated by capitalism, greed, and the carousel of ideologies which threaten to pull the wool over our ever-necessary discerning eye. That of our changing world, where the seasons are no longer particular folds in the Earth's map of existence. Where extremes are causing immeasurable damage and distress. Death and destruction. I cannot go there very often, though; it paralyzes my capacity to be of use. Powerlessness and despair are just feelings, though; they are nothing more. We can acknowledge them and still go through the world doing the best we can.

As I write, in late August, I am preparing for a field trip to Borneo. I have never left Europe, and although I see destruction on a small level—a few felled trees, the mowing down of a wildflower verge—and on a bigger scale—the blue-green algae in our beloved Lough Neagh—I need to prepare myself for vast

“When the aperture is expanded to panoramic or narrowed to proximate, everything becomes a living painting.”

swathes of deforestation. And displaced animals. Indigenous lives forever altered. I know, too, that I will experience such colossal difference in air and nature. That anticipation also excites me. I can still feel wondrous feelings, despite the background noise of desperation. Suffering and beauty can coexist; albeit uncomfortably. Occasionally, the heaviness does become too much, and then translating the beauty, illuminating it for myself and others, feels like a band-aid on the suffering, writing, at best a momentary whoosh of pain relief for a terminal condition. I must stop myself before the dark propellers that power the negative thoughts have won. When harsh winds and storms darken my own weathering, I must breathe my own light into the shadows. Dispersing, even lightly, some veined webs of possibility. I reach for the flow of life and allow rivulets to spring into cascades, to force me back into movement, to keep me connected. As a mycelium network connects a forest, I must do so with all that I touch, feel, see, and hear within nature. I am not whole without it.

Thinking now about how I will be on the other side of the world as the willow tree outside our sitting room window goes auburn, as the swallows scythe the sky in gluttonous swoops—a nourishing preparation for their long flight home—already floats nostalgia. My early years crashing through leaf piles, lying on my back, looking up at scudding clouds, signaling change. Comforting the pain of going back to school, the arrival of the first brent geese to the wetlands and shores, the safety net of visiting them at weekends, inspiring me to calm, to look slightly ahead. A balm to cover wounds of difference and loneliness. Punctuations of soothing respite.

The curlews will come down to the coast from the uplands, their remembered song ambushing melancholy, and fluttering within me an inescapable assurance that nature keeps striving. That we are striving, too much. They will come and I will not be there to pick the blackberries and laugh with Lorcan and Bláthnaid as they meander down the lane to the beach, mouths full and dribbling burgundy juices. No blackberry crumble in the jungle! I will miss it all.

I wonder if my own internal clock will be suspended, returning to so much change without moving myself along the lived surface of it. For immersing myself in the worlds of the creatures and phenomena we share the Earth with is how I regulate my nervous system. How I view the seasons is inextricably connected with all living things and matter. When we moved house three times during my childhood, I saw them as a beat I could march to that aligned with the wonder of the natural world and how it swayed, danced, larked; that bound me to something bigger than my own smallness—and to be reminded of our own smallness is a lesson in much needed humility.

THE BARN OWL DISAPPEARED and left in its slipstream a tremendous rippling. Of feeling, friendship, and our oncoming fragmented lives. I explained aloud, "This is summer! The meadow. The hunting barn owl. The way the light slants through the heavy leaves of the oaks. The singing blackbird. The skylarks! Not the heat, not the end of exams, not a date, not the obvious." They laughed with fondness, looked around, and wholeheartedly agreed. As darkness finally descended, we had embossed the emblematic on our collective remembering.

Afterwards I returned to my family, the fledglings, the greenhouse full of tomatoes, and the broccoli, green bean, and carrot seedlings, all lined up, ready to bloom, grow, and feed us. To the long, light evenings full of laughter, love, the pond, and the life happening all around us, with us, in us.

Forrest Gander

FIFTY-EIGHT FACES OF CALIFORNIA SPRING

COLUSA
And over there, a rough keyhole punched through the concrete block in an irrigation channel running through Pleistocene alluvium. The frizz of small twigs and early grasses—like pencil scribble. Here at the San Joaquin Fault Zone. The soft D-flat gurgle of swirling water.

SUTTER
Non-marine sedimentary sand. The mottled road yields to a *glorieta* of tire tracks shooting off across the plain. How many months more before the packed ground loosens and wind begins to lift away winter's scars? Sutter Buttes Fault Zone.

MENDOCINO
Along the coastal belt, sandstone and Cretaceous shale. Fallen birch branches sprawl over their counter-branch reflections on the stream's surface. Here near the Mendocino Triple Junction.

MONO
Near the Owens Valley Fault, a frost-crusted slope of volcanic mudflow. It bottoms out onto Holocene playa hardly settled enough to underprop the frequently flooded and patched road. In the end, the river will have its say.

DEL NORTE
Smooth contours of white Jurassic limestone bubble up along a creek bed punctuated by pyroclastic boulders. Salts, water-stowed into tiny fissures, crystalize at night, fracturing the rock. A birch seedling directs its root into the edge of the fracture. Cascadia Subduction Zone.

MARIPOSA
Edged against the Melones Fault Zone, fog-softened yellow poplar trees. The dirt road winds along Merced River Canyon through Paleozoic hills. Under the pale green deergrass, sandstones. Beneath the blue oaks, schist.

SAN FRANCISCO
Do we recognize ourselves in what we see? From beds of infectious marine sand below the interchange, a few thin, branching shoots go scrabbling toward an abutment blazed with exotic graffiti. The San Andreas Fault.

ALAMEDA
Loose lake terrace deposits underlie islands of sawgrass linked by a zigzag boardwalk. Wild bees nest in soil along scissures of the Hayward Fault. Who can say? Are we *in* or only *of* this world?

SACRAMENTO
How long will it last, the vestige of the human? A tranquil shadow-scrim of trees and brush gestures from the stream's pearly surface. Loosely consolidated Pliocene gravel. At high risk for earthquakes. The San Andreas Fault running the whole length of the county's western edge.

NEVADA
Adjacent to the Sierra Nevada Fault, a litter of broken limbs and twigs remain of what had been forest. As the deep roots die, subterranean water rises, drawing salt with it. Termites, with fungi in their guts, are beginning to digest the wood. A soil expressed from quartzite and sandstone.

AMADOR
There are tongues of volcanic mudflows to the north. To the west, the Bear Mountains Fault Zone. Here, sedimentary beds are run-through with schist and phyllite. Dead oak leaves catch in skeins of weeds just starting up through cracks in the abandoned parking lot.

SOLANO
In estuarine marsh above Suisun Slough, north of Grizzly Bay, a torrent furrows its way through alluvium and Holocene lake deposits close to the San Andreas Fault Zone. Not tilth, but waterlogged sod, last year's grasses. The litter layer is unhurriedly carried away in runoff. Your ear catches a musical trickling, percolating.

SANTA CLARA
East of the serpentine pluton running along Silver Creek, two massive redwoods grew into each other and shared a body. Now the afternoon sun articulates medullary rays between the rings of that double tree's amputated base. Along the San Andreas fault line. Where is there a landscape without an observer?

MARIN
Plugs of volcanic rhyolite jut up from Cretaceous sandstone north of the visitor center. From the beach, children drag lengths of bullwhip kelp to a sandy boardwalk and leave them for the (imagined) marvel of those to come. The San Andreas.

GLENN
East of the northwest-trending Coast Range Thrust Fault, Elk Creek runs wild along striated bedding planes of shale and sandstone into Stony Creek. A wide rock beach. Nothing breaks the water's surface but an intangible expression of collateral relations.

LOS ANGELES
A burnt foundation. Bounding the wet concrete slab, naked trees push up through syenite and pre-Cambrian gabbros of the San Gabriel Mountains. Their root secretions, attracting mites and springtails, begin to renew the soil. The San Andreas and a hundred smaller active faults.

TRINITY
Near the steeply uplifted and folded southern Klamath range, metamorphosed sedimentaries are riven with igneous intrusions. Timber in the mountains, irrigated crops in the valleys. Two sets of bike tracks temporarily scar the slope to a construction site. At the center of each forsaken footer, a stump of upright rebar. The La Grange Fault and the North Fork terrane.

VENTURA
Broken sea wall, patched road, railroad tracks on a crushed ballast bed. The sharp-edged stones interlock under pressure from the ties, stabilizing the rails. Sand and gravel quarries in Fillmore. Shales and conglomerates in Ventura. The San Andreas and over a hundred smaller active faults.

INYO
An alluvial fan below hillocks of eroding feldspar-gneiss. Gravel and small rocks cluster in the interzone between roads streaked with salt and gypsum. This spot: the lowest point in North America. What of the world arises from our minds? Owens Valley Fault Zone.

MERCED
Here are interrelations no map can contain. Beyond a crazed road and oaks swarming the smectitic riverbank, a sequence of naked hills extends to the limits of our looking. Ortigalita and Bear Mountains Fault Zones.

SAN BENITO
Landslides blot away the road. Upper Cretaceous sandstones, shales, and conglomerates eroding from the Coast Range. The serpentine-heavy soil supports Jeffrey pine, incense cedar, and a few rare species: the San Benito evening primrose (which will bloom next month) and a millipede (with more legs than any other). Nearby, the imperceptibly quivering San Andreas and Calaveras Faults.

SAN LUIS OBISPO
These wave-cut conglomerates, cross-bedded with shales, embrace granite and quartzite pebbles beside lenses of erosion-resistant jasper. A stark littoral zone near the San Andreas, Hosgri, and Los Osos Fault Zones. The tide going out.

STANISLAUS
Susceptible to landslides, the eroding slopes of the Coast Range expose sedimentary rocks close to the valley margins. The hills slide slowly down into faulted crevices where an ephemeral creek runs, giving rise to quick hallelujahs of grass. Here, near the Ortigalita Fault, we might ask ourselves: When did the land stop belonging to the land?

KERN
More than fifty thousand active wells—drilled four hundred to four thousand feet down through layers of Pleistocene lignite and sandstones rich with plant imprints and fossil bird bones—suck up the oil that migrated from old marine beds into discrete sand lentils. At the tamped, barren surface, the dirt fails to hold air or water or micronutrients. Not even an ant walks over it. The San Andreas and Garlock Faults.

YUBA
Upwelling magma conveyed gold deposits into fractures in the folded Sierra Nevada. With aggressive mining, sedimentation whelmed the floodplains with gravel, annihilating trees, altering the river's course. Now needlegrass, blue wildrye, and broomsedge undulate in an old stream bed. Swain Ravine Fault and Big Ben-Wolf Creek Fault Zone. The road relinquishing itself one chink at a time.

PLACER
Silt plumes into the lake's shallows where river-rounded stones of monzonite and Mesozoic granite hold their breath underwater. Foothills Fault System. We don't start a conversation with a stone. And yet we find ourselves in conversation.

CALAVERAS
Along strands of the San Andreas Fault Zone, vortices of dry, minnow-shaped leaves float on subtle currents in a stream reflecting dark, bare trees. Paleozoic schist and hornfels mixed with shale and chert underlie the stream. We say beauty. We say beauty exists. That beauty exists for us.

TUOLUMNE
Unsettled earth. Eye to the ground. It's as though the rocks self-evacuated from the crumbling wall and fire pit. Tertiary volcanics east of the Foothills Fault System. The hill's grading has obliterated brush that protected the soil, exposing weathered, rounded cobbles.

SHASTA
Franciscan Complex basalts. Uplifted terraces punctuated by an incised stream canyon give rise to this tarn. Which overlooks a secret salmon spawning ground. Poor soil with low permeability, clay in the shallow subsurface. Battle Creek Fault Zone. The grin of a crack in the megalith.

LAKE
The rift starts at Hwy. 29 and runs north across a plain furry with weeds toward ash-turbid Thurston Lake. Though within the Konocti Bay Fault Zone, this fissure, jokingly dubbed "Guy's Fault," follows the trace of a collapsed channel built to drain Manning Flat. Marine sedimentary layers of sandstone and limestone wink with local Lake County "diamonds" that locals call moon tears.

FRESNO
When did concrete enter our lives? Less than eighty years old, these busted pipelines are being excavated from a rubbled trench where gray, alkaline clay overlies lime-silica hardpan. The Nunez and Ortigalita Faults. In 6,500 BC, traders in the Levant stored water in buried cisterns. Cisterns made from concrete.

MONTEREY
Look closely and you'll see a measured series of terrestrial horizons from which the land's sutures have been plucked. To till soil is to gut it, to rip apart its microbial and fungal networks, to lift away the protective crop residue and lay earth bare to wind, runoff, and rain damage. Just adjacent to the San Andreas Fault Zone.

SIERRA
How many linked dimensions? Clouds mounding on the surface of the water merge with pale glacial detritus at the Foothills Fault System. Why do we say the landscape is over there if we are always a part of it?

NAPA
There are more than a hundred soil variations in the alluvial fans emerging from near hillsides onto the valley floor. Here, a marsh tributary, its dark surface banded with flotsam and chalky slicks. The West Napa Fault. Cretaceous and Jurassic sandstone bedded with limestone.

ALPINE
On the creek's surface, crystals bind to residual ice that has melted and refrozen. As night temperatures drop, an expanding glaze begins to shrink the dark haloes of water. Like skin healing around a wound. Nearby, on the forest floor, a black soil of till and colluvium. The Sierra Nevada Fault Zone.

PLUMAS
Under any place we stand, the archaic depths of persistent memory. On this ancient lake bed strewn with wet dirt, straw and twigs, we come across the ruined foundation of someone's house. An insistence of right angles. Almanor Fault Zone.

EL DORADO
Along the western edge of the Bear Mountains Fault Zone, a snow-packed, glacier-carved lake with

thick trees popping up from lacustrine sediment around the lake's apron. But on the further hill, scraggly pines struggle to thrive on thin soil beds underlain by rocky granodiorite.

BUTTE
Strongly metamorphosed white andesite slabs, pillow lavas, and flow rocks surround the lake's houseboats. Cleveland Hill and Sierra Nevada Faults. A gravelly soil with mixed cobbles.

CONTRA COSTA
It's gone now, whatever once brought people here with a need for direction and an exit sign. The cracked macadam—fenced, blockaded, and arrowed—erupts with April weeds. As they bury the fecal pellets of white-tailed deer, dung beetles scurry across a slope soil derived from exfoliating shale and sandstone. The Calaveras Fault and the Mount Diablo Thrust Fault.

SAN JOAQUIN
In lowlands north of the Stockton Fault, a wide valley filled with six-mile sequences of interbedded clays, silt, sand, and gravel. Little else. A dissolving rectangular slab of sand, a toss of pine twigs. Vehicle tracks. Leached sand. But in the act of looking, your body is there too.

ORANGE
Poor soil, little ground cover, tufts of sage, scoured runnels through pebbled Miocene sandstone. Sediment accumulating in channels. A lately denuded hillside. The San Andreas and more than a hundred smaller active faults. Life is elsewhere.

SANTA BARBARA
Coastal marine sand and silt drain from the bluffs of the Santa Ynez. Closer to shore, Miocene shales are chocked with fossils of mollusks and clamshells. The ocean here is plagued with fecal bacteria. With pollutants from runoff and from underwater oil field seepage fifty meters down. Santa Maria River and Santa Ynez Faults.

KINGS
Desiccated stalks from last year's sorghum silage cloak fields of gray-brown alluvium. Bioturbating worms thread underground channels with acids that, come June, will stimulate new plant growth. Four inches below the worms, a layer of chalk holds moisture for the roots. San Andreas Fault Zone.

MADERA
Tufts of grass knotted in disagreement. And everything is charged: grass positive and pollen negative. So while wind whips the grass in circles, grass sweeps the air for pollen. Undulating hills overlie basement monzonite. To the southwest, near the border with Fresno County, the Coalinga Anticline.

RIVERSIDE
Marked by the wide Santa Ana River watershed, the alluvial soil is coarse-textured and well-drained, the pH high. Two PVC pipes, glowing like tusks, curve out from the dull riverbank and over-cross the mud-colored flailings of exposed tree roots. San Andreas and San Jacinto Faults.

TEHAMA
With its linear trajectory, the fence can only approximate the arroyo's soft bend. Battle Creek Fault Zone. Dry-farmed pastureland, a stratified and acidic silty loam riven with tunnels excavated by gophers, and with gopher snakes just now waking and blindly trailing behind them.

IMPERIAL
Gathering its windblown materials from prehistoric Lake Cahuilla, a little transverse dune perches at the edge of the largest mass of sand dunes in California. The Imperial Fault. We comb the sand with our looking.

LASSEN
A snow-brushed, dehydrated lake lined by lava flow and scant brush adjacent to the Davis Creek Fault Zone. Local soil, the gravelly residuum of volcanic rocks. In the near distance, dwarf trees squiggle up from thin layers of dirt covering a bone-white strata of insoluble quartzes.

SAN BERNARDINO
Like road excrement, upwellings of crumbled tar and gravel cover the desiccated, skid-marked blacktop. Overlapping rings of tire rubber, squiggly fissures. Alluvial deposits and dune sands. The San Andreas and San Jacinto Faults. Where I was born.

SISKIYOU
The surrounding mountains are rich in pre-Cenozoic gneisses and hornfels. At a valley stream confluence, granitic rocks rounded by glaciation settle themselves into moist, sandy loam. An orange lichen secretes acids into the grains of its supporting boulder. Cedar Mountain Fault System.

TULARE
Splashes of leached salt and alkaline minerals dust the path of a dry, dendritic creek spooling through tangles of dead weeds and bracken. The slow-moving Foothills Fault System. Poorly packed plutonic granites underlie those hills.

MODOC
At the center of the intermittent flow zone, bunch grasses lie flat, rinsed with a coffee-brown residue of nitrogen-rich humus. The Surprise Valley Fault Zone. A volcanic ash veneer covers lacustrine deposits of crumbled basalt and andesite. On the 42nd parallel north, this is the northernmost edge of California where the earth's rotational speed roughly equals the speed of sound.

SAN DIEGO
Between the Rose Canyon and Elsinore Faults, directly across from the border wall, bootprints disturb silty clay interfingered with slope wash and a radiant spew of coarse granules, the weathered rind of rocks. Along a north-south axis, anonymous tracks on the damp ground lead in both directions.

SAN MATEO
The inherent overcomes the constructed. Concrete slabs and galvanized plates yield the rigor of their authority to tension cracks and sprouting weeds. An idea of order fractures in slow motion. Flood plain alluvium from hillside drainage. The San Andreas and San Gregorio Fault Systems.

SONOMA
On a trace of the San Andreas Fault, who has assembled these witchy stick teepees? Behind them, strange, glistering emanations of light play over the sand. An iconic monolith presides over two smaller rocks in the inlet—like a black bear eyeing her cubs. Some of the jasper and blueschist boulders along the beach have been polished to a high sheen by the rubbing of Pleistocene mammoths. Nothing moves but the onshore breeze crinkling the skin of the water.

SANTA CRUZ
Marine sands and gravels, twenty to fifty feet thick. Pretty sea glass on the beach from years of garbage-dumping at the coastline. A tide pool draining below cliffs fenestrated with eroded tunnels. Eerily, the old concrete pier foundation seems to step away through the fog into ceaselessly approaching waves. The San Andreas and Zayante-Vergeles Fault Zones.

YOLO
It's as though a cloud had transported swarms of gleaming grunion from California's southern beaches onto this swale along Putah Creek. Were we to pass through that cloud in a plane, we'd look down and see that the faults and folds across the valley are aligned northwest in concordance with the San Andreas. The Putah hauls alluvium to the Sacramento River. Fallen eucalyptus leaves sprawl along this narrow path through brushy weeds. With their hundred thousand teeth, slugs are chewing down the leaf matter.

HUMBOLDT
Flecked with foam and floating bands of silt, the tidal sloughs and estuarine channels fill in with erosional sediment from an upslope degraded by industrial logging. Once home to the southern torrent salamander. Mendocino Triple Junction. Representing nothing, what we're given to see is only what presents itself.

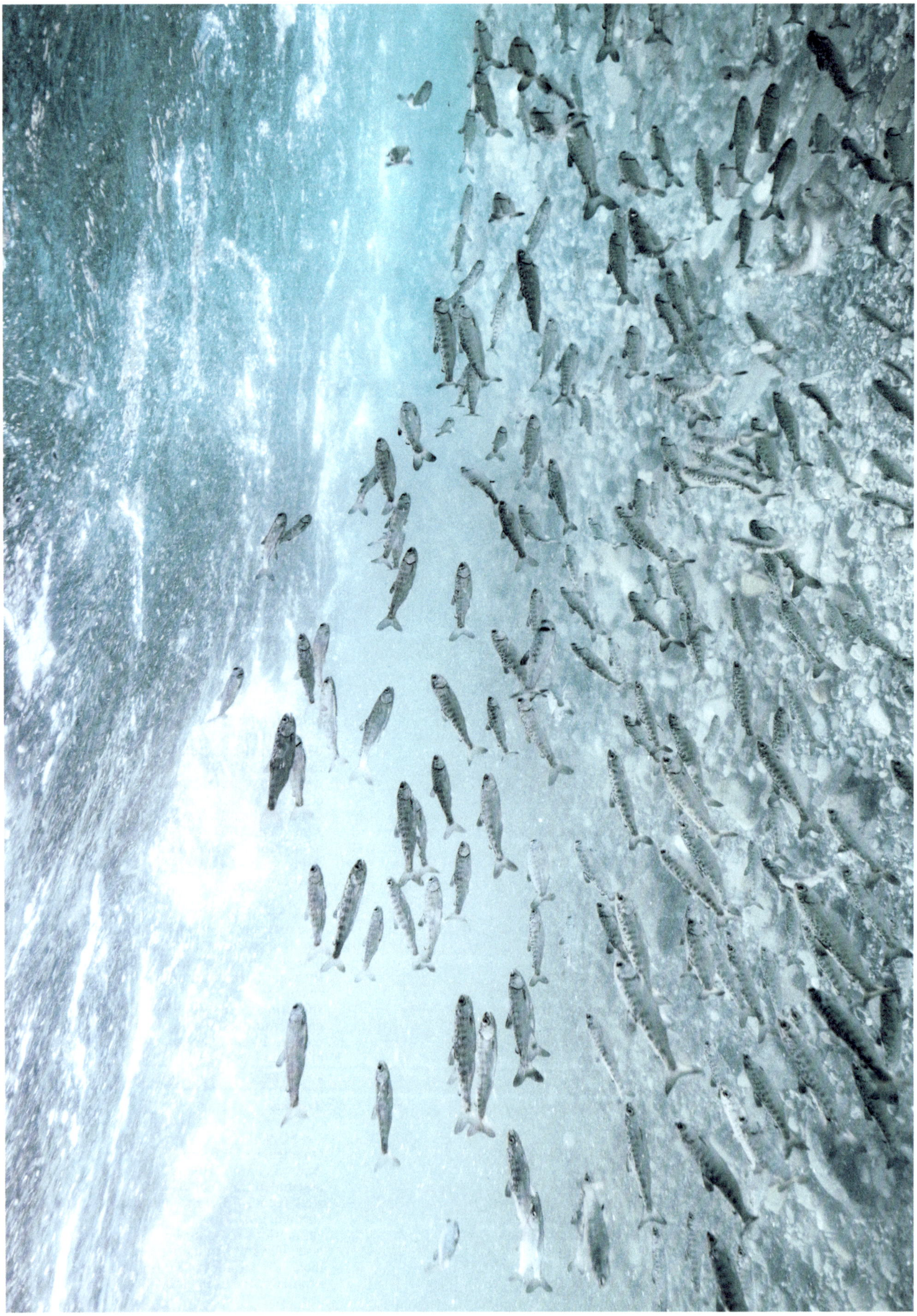

FIG. 19 Salmon smolts headed for the ocean will return to spawn along previously unreachable areas of the river, completing an ancient cycle. (P. 252)

Ben Goldfarb

A RIVER REBORN: ECO-CULTURAL REVITALIZATION ON THE KLAMATH

Photos by
Kiliii Yüyan

“Fish had begun to renew the world.”

EVERY SPRING, up a vast circulatory system of rivers in the northern hemisphere—in Alaska and Norway, Maine and Oregon, Labrador and Japan—salmon begin to run. When they enter fresh water, they are creatures of the sea, chrome-plated and plump; by the time they reach their spawning grounds, they are ragged and dying, having exhausted their life force in the course of their arduous journeys and in the production of eggs and milt. Their nutrient-dense bodies, upon being scattered by bears and eagles, nourish riparian forests as thoroughly as sacks of fertilizer; their gravel nests recontour the streams in which they spawn. Their arrival occasions human celebration, too, in places as far-flung as Kamchatka, Iceland, and Seattle. Salmon season is one of ecological nourishment and cultural jubilation, wrought by a fish that renews the world.

Salmon season was once especially profuse on the Klamath River, which winds more than 250 miles from Oregon's mountains to the California coast, splashing through high desert, chiseled canyons, and foggy redwood forest. The Klamath hosts two annual runs of Chinook salmon—one that arrives in late spring, one in early fall—as well as coho salmon, steelhead, and other aquatic bounty. As many as a million salmon once coursed up the Klamath annually, a surge of sustenance that fed Native peoples including the Yurok, Hoopa, Karuk, and Shasta. Thanks largely to salmon, one researcher wrote, the Klamath's Indigenous residents were "the wealthiest people in what is now known as California." To the Tribes, though, salmon were more than material riches: They were spiritual guides and sacred kin, the revered subjects of First Fish ceremonies that commenced each spring and ensured the fish would endure through the generations. Salmon, the Yurok and Karuk scholar and artist Brook Thompson once wrote, "are a direct tie to my ancestors—the physical representation of their love for me."

White settlement, alas, impoverished the Klamath and the Native peoples who relied upon it. Beginning in the nineteenth century, logging and mining battered the watershed's forests, and irrigation diversions sapped its flows. Most injurious, from a salmon's perspective, were the dams that impeded upriver migrations and sickened the river with toxic algae. Spring-run Chinook, the river's most toothsome and prolific fish, crashed to less than two percent of historic levels, to the profound detriment of Tribes who, as Yurok chairman Joe James once put it, consider the Klamath the "lifeline of our people." The destruction of Klamath salmon, some observers have claimed, is "the most significant human rights violation resulting from any dam construction in the United States."

The Klamath's collapse is archetypal: Per one 2020 report, many of the Northwest's salmon runs are today "on the brink of extinction." Salmon in numerous Pacific rivers—the Sacramento, the Snake, the Yukon—have suffered cataclysmic declines, and many Atlantic rivers have lost their runs altogether. Like most streams, the current of salmon populations tends to flow in only one direction. "The cry of 'Salmon in Danger!' is now resounding throughout the length and breadth of the land," Charles Dickens declared in 1861. "A few years . . . and the salmon will be gone—he will become extinct."

On the Klamath, however, salmon are now running in an unfamiliar direction—toward recuperation. In 2022, the federal government authorized a half-billion-dollar plan to obliterate the river's four most egregious dams and reopen more than four hundred miles of spawning habitat: the largest fish restoration effort, and among the most significant rectifications of environmental injustice, in American history. Eager to see this reborn river, I traveled much of the Klamath Basin in the summer of 2024, just before the last of the dams came down. I wanted to know how the long suspension of salmon season had changed the Klamath and its people—and what it meant that the fish would soon come home.

THE DAMS

In 1910, a twenty-three-year-old engineer named John C. Boyle arrived on the Klamath River and almost immediately set about transforming it. The river's tight canyons, Boyle realized, lent themselves to hydroelectric dams, which would impound the Klamath and funnel it through power-generating turbines. Over the decades that followed, Boyle and his ilk built six dams, including four on the lower river that came to power a relatively modest seventy thousand homes. "If properly conserved and utilized, there was enough water to supply every need which might locate in the Klamath Basin," Boyle later claimed cheerily—though he said little about fish.

Other observers were less sanguine. "It is feared that unless a fish ladder is provided, there will be a notable falling off in the number of fish," one newspaper reporter cautioned in 1913, with the completion of Boyle's first dam in sight—a warning that went unheeded. And the dams didn't merely block salmon from their spawning grounds, they fatally disrupted the river's natural hydrology. The Klamath, whose swift, chilly flows once swept juvenile salmon to the Pacific, transformed into a concatenation of sluggish reservoirs baked by the California sun. These slack and tepid lakes became cauldrons for toxic algae blooms that often dyed the river a nauseous green. Irrigation withdrawals for upstream farms and ranches further diminished the river. In 2002, an outbreak of gill rot fomented by low, warm flows killed more than thirty thousand salmon. "Our worst nightmare has come true," then-Yurok chairwoman Susan Masten lamented.

As salmon suffered, the dams twisted in the wind. Ownership of PacifiCorp, the power company responsible for the structures, bounced first to ScottishPower and then to Berkshire Hathaway, Warren Buffett's voracious conglomerate. The lower Klamath's four dams were hardly mouthwatering assets: They stored no irrigation water, produced less than two percent of PacifiCorp's power, and were reviled by protestors. PacifiCorp calculated that retrofitting the dams with fish ladders, as modern legal standards required, would cost more than decommissioning them. Finally, after years of negotiation between regulators, company officials, and Tribes, the government made its announcement. The dams would come down.

One morning, I went to observe the destruction with Ren Brownell, public information officer with the Klamath River Renewal Corporation, the nonprofit tasked with removing the dams. We climbed to a bluff overlooking Iron Gate Dam, the structure furthest downriver, end of the line for salmon since 1962. The scale of the operation below us confounded my mind. A colossal crater, wide as two city blocks, yawned where the pyramidal dam once stood. Construction equipment, yellow and tiny as rubber ducks, scraped at the

dam's foundation. Because Iron Gate had been a simple earthen dam, Brownell explained, the process of dismantling it was straightforward: the Renewal Corporation was returning the dirt, a million cubic yards of it, from whence it came. We watched bulldozers shove the earth into piles, which were scooped up by excavators and deposited into dump trucks, which rolled in caravans to the quarry where it had been extracted in the first place. It reminded me of watching a film played in reverse.

Behind what remained of the dam, the river nibbled impatiently at the built-up mud before flowing through a diversion tunnel and downhill, biding its time until freedom. Releasing the Klamath was a delicate operation, Brownell explained: If the Renewal Corporation had instantaneously blown up Iron Gate, the flood, however cathartic, would have endangered downstream communities. Instead, the group had gradually drained the reservoir via the tunnel in January, when adult salmon were at sea. Some five million cubic yards of liberated sediment had briefly turned the Klamath into a chocolate shake, but the river had since thinned to the color of milky tea—hardly the Caribbean, but plenty clear enough for salmon. "The more sediment we can move now, the better it will be for fish coming up this fall," Brownell said.

From Iron Gate, we visited two other former dams, called Copco 1 and Copco 2. (The fourth demolished dam, dubbed J.C. Boyle in honor of the river's hubristic tamer, lay miles upriver, across the Oregon border.) Most poignant of the pair was Copco 2, the first to come out, which had routed the Klamath through gargantuan steel pipes to a hydroelectric turbine. For decades the dam had completely dried up the river canyon below, nearly two miles of majestic basalt columns and boulders sacred to the Shasta people. Now the Klamath raced again through the gorge, roiling down its timeless course. I imagined the now-silent pipes rumbling and rattling with the river's trapped ferocity, and felt a vertiginous awe—both at the technological savvy that enabled humankind to bottle a river, and the shortsighted bravado that compelled us to try.

By late August 2024, a month after my visit, the dams were rubble, and the Klamath now flows free once more. Yet some of the project's greatest challenges still lie ahead. As the reservoirs receded, they exposed thousands of destitute, algae-clotted acres that, absent intervention, would become overrun by invasive vegetation. The task of rehabilitating these barren lake bottoms had fallen to a company called Resource Environmental Solutions, which, starting in 2019, had partnered with the Yurok Tribe to collect billions of seeds from nearly one hundred species of native plants. The firm and the Tribe began to sow their harvest as soon as the reservoirs drained, and also intend to plant a quarter million trees and shrubs. During my time on the river, the newly exposed flats behind Iron Gate were already carpeted with a vibrant sweep of emerald: an ecosystem both ancient and new, awaiting the salmon that would nourish it afresh.

The Tribes had good reason to believe that the fish would respond in droves. On Washington's Elwha River, where two dams were demolished between 2011 and 2014, coho salmon have sufficiently bounced back to permit the Lower Elwha Klallam Tribe to resume ceremonial subsistence harvests—and to restitch the river's tattered ecosystem. Vanessa Castle, formerly a natural resource technician with the Lower Elwha Klallam, has documented bears, cougars, and bobcats feasting on salmon and dragging their carcasses into the forest, where they donate nitrogen and phosphorus to maples and cedars. "These large predators have access to salmon where they haven't for over a hundred years," Castle told me. "That's connecting the aquatic world with the terrestrial world."

The Klamath, too, would surely experience rejuvenation. My tour with Brownell took us to Jenny Creek, one of the first tributaries that returning salmon would encounter, which now carved through the exposed floor of the Iron Gate reservoir. At first glance, the scene was desolate: our feet sank into black mats of dead algae, a fetid goo that reeked of tidal wrack. Yet the stream gurgled merrily along, as content in its rediscovered channel as a gloved hand. A few spindly willows had naturally taken root on the banks, and dragonflies zipped past our ears. "I will bet you money there will be fish spawning in Jenny Creek this fall," Brownell said. Nearby lay a jumble of logs that crews would soon install in the stream, forming pools and runs in which salmon would eventually shelter and spawn—an infusion of red blood cells, circulating afresh in the body of the Earth.

THE FALLS

The Klamath, like virtually every North American watercourse, flows through land long occupied and sculpted by humans. Near its mouth live the Yurok and Hoopa; closer to the headwaters dwell the Shasta, the Modoc, the Klamath, and the Yahooskin-Paiute. Between them lie canyonlands so rough-hewn and densely timbered that their inhabitants, the Karuk, were among the last Indigenous groups to be contacted by white people. The Karuk hunt deer, elk, and squirrel, and gather acorns, mushrooms, and manzanita berries; but salmon has traditionally sustained them. The typical Karuk person once filled his belly with 450 pounds of salmon per year—more than a pound each day. These days, the salmon that the average Karuk eats in a year could fit in a handbag.

Around a hundred Karuk villages once lined the river, known as Ishkêesh, the largest at a rapid called Ishi Pishi Falls, where Tribal members fish for much-diminished salmon today. "This is the center of the world," Ron Reed, a Karuk fisherman and ceremonial leader, told me at Ishi Pishi one hot morning. Just downriver, out of sight beyond a bend, the Masúhsav—the Salmon River—crashed into the Ishkêesh in a whirl of foam. Reed, who wore a braid down his back and a thin mustache, led me through dense brush to the river, blackberry vines plucking at his board shorts. Bear scat and otter spraints littered the gravel; overhead, a bald eagle tangled with a pair of ospreys. "That means salmon are in there," Reed called over the roar of water.

We entered the stretch of river that Reed called the "fishery," a jumble of truck-sized boulders, etched by water, that loomed precariously over tumultuous whitecaps. "This is my world. This is my sanctuary," said Reed, tranquil amidst hydrologic chaos. Between immense rocks, the river gentled into pools, eddies, and side channels where migrating salmon pause to marshal their strength. Reed and other Tribal fishermen ply these pockets with dip nets traditionally made of fir poles and iris fibers, swinging the nets through slow water to corral lingering Chinook. Reed kills his fish with a club and smokes them, barbecues them, or pierces the steaks with redwood sticks and roasts them over open flame. "I'll be catching the first fish here, and probably the last fish," Reed said.

We proceeded upriver, tracing a route that Karuk fishermen have followed for hundreds of years. The Klamath, normally azure in summer, was cloudy with dam sediment, but Reed was unbothered; if anything, he said, the opacity would afford shade for cold-loving fish. Reed pointed out his favorite pockets: "There's our first hole. The second hole. The meat hole." Though he was sixty-two years old, he bounded between boulders with casual grace, his Adidas sneakers fitting snugly into notches that his own feet had worn smooth. "When I can't make this jump anymore, I'm an elder," he said with a grin—then vaulted across a chasm, the Klamath raging beneath him.

Reed may not call himself an elder, but few Karuk hold deeper knowledge. He'd grown up in Happy Camp, a nearby mining and logging village, where white kids persecuted him for being Native. He sought refuge in basketball and the river, fishing with his mother and uncles at a time when Karuk fishermen would catch hundreds of salmon before noon. After high school he moved away—"I wanted to get the fuck off this river, because I associated being Karuk with poverty and hate," he said—and wandered for years in the spiritual wilderness before moving home to survey salmon for the Tribe and the federal government. During his first season, he was irked to see non-tribal biologists cavalierly punching temperature probes into the fishes' nests. "When there's fish spawning, you're supposed to totally respect that," he said. He complained to his supervisors, and Tribal officials eventually elevated him to a position as a cultural biologist. "They looked at me and said, well, we need this guy, because he questions everything," Reed said.

Reed also began to question his own youthful antipathy toward his upbringing. As he dug into the Karuk's history, he learned about how his people had been pressed into boarding schools and robbed of the ability to practice traditional ceremonies. "I grew up in that shit: intergenerational trauma, historical trauma, oppression," he said. The Karuk, once some of North America's richest people, had become some of its poorest and least healthy, as modern processed fare replaced salmon and other traditional foods, exacerbating maladies such as diabetes and hypertension. At the heart of it all were the dams, imperial monuments that had deprived the Karuk of salmon and transformed the river that was their cultural heart.

Reed threw himself into battling the dams. He flew twice to Scotland with a Tribal delegation to protest ScottishPower, to Nebraska to register his displeasure with Warren Buffett. He wrote articles, gave presentations, granted interviews to countless reporters. No single person was responsible for dam removal—the campaign had been diffuse and multipronged, incorporating a panoply of Indigenous leaders, environmental activists, and white commercial fishermen. Yet Reed had undeniably been a key player, the movement's moral and insistently vocal conscience. "The fish don't have a voice—that's my job as a medicine man," he told me.

Though Reed had never been more optimistic about the future of his river, the fight seemed to have cost him much. He struck me as a man pressed by the weight of history; a few times during our conversation his eyes turned liquid with tears. Though he no longer worked full-time for the Tribe, he'd spent years in its employ, trying to preserve and revive relationships between people and land. The Atlas-like task he'd assigned himself was nothing less than lifting the crushing legacy of colonialism—for his six children, eleven grandchildren, and the Karuk people. "I've got a pretty full schedule in terms of trying to fix the world," Reed said.

THE TRIBUTARIES

After meeting Reed, I needed to see some sacred salmon for myself. Although sediment had rendered the mainstem Klamath too murky for fish viewing, its tributaries were clear—particularly the aptly named Salmon River, which plunges through precipitous gorges to meet the Klamath below Ishi Pishi Falls. The Salmon still hosts a viable spring Chinook run, and, in theory, the mighty fish would be in the river.

The next morning I followed a tortuous road up the Salmon River, inching along cliff faces and nearly trading paint with oncoming cars, to Forks of Salmon, the minuscule town where the river's threads twine. I'd come to participate in the thirtieth annual spring Chinook dive, a salmon census, conducted by snorkel, put on by the Salmon River Restoration Council. Years of surveys had revealed a troubling trend: As recently as 2012, more than a thousand spring Chinook had returned, but by 2021, the run numbered fewer than ninety. Climate change had contributed, by depleting the snowpack whose frigid melt fed the Salmon and warming the watershed's flows; but the dams had undoubtedly hurt, too, by degrading the mainstem river that Chinook rode to the Pacific. A revitalized Klamath would thus help resuscitate the Salmon River, some of whose fish would, in turn, stray upstream to spawn above the former dams. The watershed was as entangled as mycelium, the health of its hyphae inextricable.

"Having better conditions on their way up through the system will help our fish quite a bit," Andy Ayers, the survey's coordinator, told me. "We might look back at this one day as a turning point."

I was assigned to a squad of four volunteers tasked with scoping an icy headwater known, in typically perplexing riverine nomenclature, as the East Fork of the South Fork of the Salmon River. We parked beside a bridge and donned wetsuits and snorkels. Below us, the East Fork was so narrow that a fly rod laid on one bank would nearly have touched the other. Perhaps Chinook had spawned here once, skinning up rapids and leaping waterfalls to reach this stronghold; but now, with so few salmon in the Salmon, it seemed unlikely they'd bother coming this high. Still, the stream was crystalline and lush, shaded by maple and fringed by umbrella plants with hubcap-sized leaves. If nothing else, it would be a lovely spot for a swim.

And swim we did—sort of. Much of the East Fork was too shallow to permit floating, so we stumbled along on foot. When we reached deeper pools, we lowered ourselves to our bellies, thrust our faces into the stream, and drifted, scanning for salmon. Fruitless hours passed. The stone cases of caddisfly larvae carbuncled the rocks, abrading my legs like the pores of a cheese grater. The sun was hot, the water cold. On a previous census, I'd heard, a volunteer had gotten hypothermia. Another, surveying the same river, had suffered heatstroke.

Snorkeling with massive Chinook, I'd been told, was a near-spiritual experience. "You and the fish surprise each other a little bit," Ayers had said—two megafaunal species, separated by several hundred million years of evolution, reconverging in water clear as gin. I wouldn't know: we didn't see a single adult salmon in the East Fork of the South Fork of the Salmon River. Nor were we the only ones to get skunked. Later, I'd learn that the other crews had seen, in total, 106 springers—among the worst years on record. Dam removal couldn't come soon enough.

Still, the river held life. Rainbow trout, Chinook's diminutive cousins, swirled in every hole, pink flanks blushing. Their fry flitted like motes of sunlight, snapping at caddisflies. Darting among them, I also saw the occasional baby Chinook, identifiable by the oval parr marks that striped their flanks—or at least I *thought* I saw them; hope may be the thing with feathers, but it also possesses fins. The quicksilver salmon, descendants of last year's spawners, seemed almost playful. They approached my fingers to peer at the strange protuberances, then danced away into the rocks. Most, I knew, were short for this world, future prey to kingfishers and herons. But a few would survive, trade their dappled stripes for silver scales, and wash down to the Klamath and thence the Pacific—the first generation in decades to ride the cold current of a free river.

THE MOUTH

The removal of the Klamath's dams may be the most consequential development in the checkered history of salmon recovery, but it's far from the only restoration project within the watershed. Up and down the Klamath, I learned, Tribes and agencies and nonprofits were busily reversing more than a century of degradation. Near the river's headwaters, Trout Unlimited and other groups were busy constructing artificial beaver dams to furnish habitat for fish that would soon flood back into the upper basin; further downriver, the Mid Klamath Watershed Council was excavating off-channel ponds to shelter baby coho. The river called to mind a relay, each partner passing the baton of restoration to the next.

If the Klamath is a relay, the anchor leg is run by the Yurok Tribe, whose reservation encompasses forty-four miles of river near the ocean. During my time on the Klamath, the Yurok's holdings were on the cusp of substantially growing. In 2008, Green Diamond, a timber company, had begun the process of returning nearly fifty thousand acres to the Tribe—among the largest land-back projects in American history. Around two-thirds of those lands, which should officially transfer back to the Yurok in 2025, will become a community forest, where sustainable logging will generate Tribal jobs, income, and timber. The rest will be a sanctuary surrounding Blue Creek, a cold-water refuge for the Klamath's salmon. "In a particularly hot, nasty year, this might be the most important tributary on the Klamath for fall Chinook," Mik McKee, stewardship director at the Western Rivers Conservancy, the group that brokered and raised funds for the complex transfer, told me.

McKee showed me the soon-to-be transferred land one morning. We drove up near-vertical logging roads, through redwood, Douglas fir, alder, and oak; below us, a white mattress of fog shrouded the Pacific. Although McKee, a forester by training, noticed that the trees were too homogenous in age, a hallmark of industrial logging, we were struck by the land's apparent good health and wildness. Trail cameras had picked up rare martens cavorting in these woods, and McKee often felt the eyes of mountain lions boring into his neck.

"It has so much potential," he said admiringly. "It's like a blank canvas with tons of opportunity."

Although the Tribe didn't yet hold title during my visit, it had already begun the process of healing the land. McKee took me to a ridgeline atop which Yurok crewmen in excavators and bulldozers were ripping out scraggly, overgrown trees. The Tribe was in the midst of restoring this seventy-acre site to prairie, which the Yurok had historically kept open as a travel corridor, firebreak, and game meadow. "The elk and the deer are gonna come thrive in here," Roger Boulby, a heavy equipment operator for the Yurok's construction company, told me after he'd hopped down from his massive Caterpillar. "It's going to be an oasis of food." The ungulates would, in turn, lure predators such as mountain lions, whose kills would feed condors, which the Yurok, who know the great vultures as *prey-go-neesh*, had recently reintroduced to the area. Many of the saplings and root wads that Boulby's crew extracted, he added, would go to the Tribe's fisheries department, which would install them in streams to enhance salmon habitat. "Saving fish is my jam," Boulby said with a grin.

The reclamation of their historic lands wasn't merely an opportunity for the Yurok, though; it was also a challenge. Although the forest was in decent health, it was veined by derelict logging roads, which bled silt into creeks with every storm and threatened to smother fish eggs. The Tribe, with the support of the Conservancy and other partners, had upgraded many roads, but dozens of miles more remained dilapidated. During our tour, McKee and I ran into Richard Nelson, director of the Yurok's watershed program, sweat-drenched and attempting to fix a dump truck's flat tire. "We got a lifetime's worth of work to do out here—my *children's* lifetime," Nelson said, lifting his baseball cap to wipe his brow. I was reminded of Ron Reed's vow to fix the broken world he'd inherited, and how heavily that responsibility sat on his shoulders.

McKee and I went down to Blue Creek, whose waters sparkled in the afternoon. In Yurok cosmology, this was a sacred place of healing sometimes described as a "golden stairway" into the restorative high country. It was also a haven for Chinook, who detoured into Blue Creek to seek thermal refuge when the Klamath got dangerously warm; McKee showed me one limpid, turquoise pool where he'd once snorkeled with hundreds of resting fish, stacked like cordwood. We trudged along gravel banks and bushwhacked through willows to the stream's confluence with the mainstem Klamath. The convergence stopped my breath: Blue Creek, clear and musical as a wind instrument, pushed into the muddy muscle of the Klamath, still turbid with the liquefied matter of the demolished dams. McKee and I stood on a bar in silence, watching the two rivers swirl like watercolors, abask in the power of a place sacred to humans and salmon alike.

Speaking of convergence: The previous evening, I'd visited the Klamath's mouth proper, where fog-veiled redwood forest abruptly turns to beach and the river punches through a sand spit to greet the crashing Pacific. I arrived at sunset to find the estuary teeming: seals bobbed in the waves, pelicans hurled themselves into the surf, and a pair of gray whales, astonishingly close to shore, exhaled mist into the orange evening.

A pair of Yurok fishermen plied the mouth with a gill net, holding fast to one end and permitting the Klamath's flow to carry the net into the ocean and pull it taut. Seals monitored their work in hopes of extracting an easy meal. "You gotta watch out, those seals are greedy," said one of the fishermen, who introduced himself as Sly. They hauled the net in, hand over hand, to reveal a waterlogged slab of driftwood. "Caught a log," Sly sighed. "Big-ass log," his friend muttered.

Still, the day had been productive. With their bare hands, they'd captured a lamprey, an ancient, eel-like migratory fish that once crept up the Klamath in near-uncountable legions, and which, like salmon, should be revitalized by dam removal. And though it was early for salmon, they'd caught a pair that morning. "They weren't that big, probably twenty pounds, twenty-five pounds," he said, holding his arms apart. "Still a nice size."

THE GIFT

Salmon season is an ancient phenomenon: The spike-tooth salmon, an eight-foot-long behemoth armored with protruding dentition, swam the Northwest more than five million years ago, long before *Homo sapiens* bestrode the Earth. Yet salmon migration is also a human-cultivated process. Nearly every Pacific Tribe has long engaged in "stream caretaking," practices to support salmon movement and habitat, as Kirsten Bradford noted in a 2024 master's thesis at Simon Fraser University. The Tlingit build crescent rock structures to create pools; the Heiltsuk spawn sockeye in baskets and transplant eggs to create new runs; the Ahousaht remove debris that could damage nests. The Klamath River Tribes likewise have a culture of stream caretaking, a practice that revolves around fire. The Karuk and other Native Californians traditionally burned forests to stimulate hazel and other useful plants, to maintain meadows for game, and to aid salmon, as the pall of smoke shaded rivers and kept fish cool. In a 2018 study, researchers including Frank Lake, an ecologist of Karuk and Yurok descent, analyzed wildfire smoke density on satellite imagery to corroborate the virtues of that custom. In the lower Klamath Basin, they found, smoke cooled water temperatures by around 1 degree Celsius, "conceivably benefiting cold-water adapted species such as Pacific salmon."

That result would hardly surprise Ron Reed, who is as passionate about fire as he is fish. Just as dams suppressed salmon in the twentieth century, fire was quelled, too: California officials jailed Native people for setting customary fires, as their ancestors had done, and the U.S. Forest Service fanatically stamped out lightning-sparked blazes. Lacking regenerative fire, the Klamath watershed's forests became as unhealthy as the river. Today, Indigenous firelighters are once more setting California aflame, though federal and state policies inhibit the widespread return of cultural burning. "Ecocultural revitalization is a connection that can only be created by fire application," Ron Reed told me at Ishi Pishi Falls. The resuscitation of salmon and fire alike are integral to what Reed describes as "world renewal," the grand project of restitching ancestral ties between land, fish, and humanity.

In late August, about a month after my visit to California, machinery scraped away the final river-blocking vestiges of the dams, and the lower Klamath flowed freely once more—"one of the highlights of my entire life," Brook Thompson told a reporter. There was little doubt that salmon would take advantage of the new opportunity, but *when* they'd do it was anyone's guess: Would fish that famously home to their birth streams swiftly find a stretch of river that had been foreclosed for more than a century? The answer, decisively, was yes. By October, fall-run Chinook had already passed the former site of the Iron Gate Dam; by November, scientists reported that dozens of fish had migrated as far upriver as Oregon. More than two hundred went into Jenny Creek, the first prime spawning tributary above Iron Gate, just as Ren Brownell had predicted they would. When winter arrived, the creek's bed was pocked with gravel nests incubating globular orange eggs, which would hatch into fry that would imprint on their natal waters and someday return as adults themselves, the ancient circular economy revived. Fish had begun to renew the world.

By then, I was back home in Colorado, though I'd brought a bit of the Klamath with me. Before Reed and I had parted, he'd bestowed a gift: a mason jar packed with strips of Chinook flesh, carved from a fish he'd caught himself. The meat, the rich ruby of a summer sunset, glowed through the glass, as though internally lit. In late summer, I unscrewed the jar and partook. The strips were tough and flaky, closer in texture to jerky than to lox, bristly with fine bones. The meat was peppery and redolent of the madrone with which Reed fuels his smokehouse; it tasted of beach campfires and fishing villages and waterfalls and river rocks, the timeless universe that is salmon season embodied in this savory cut of myomeres and skin. I chewed for a long time, the smoked fish turning fibrous and dissolving on my tongue, and ate.

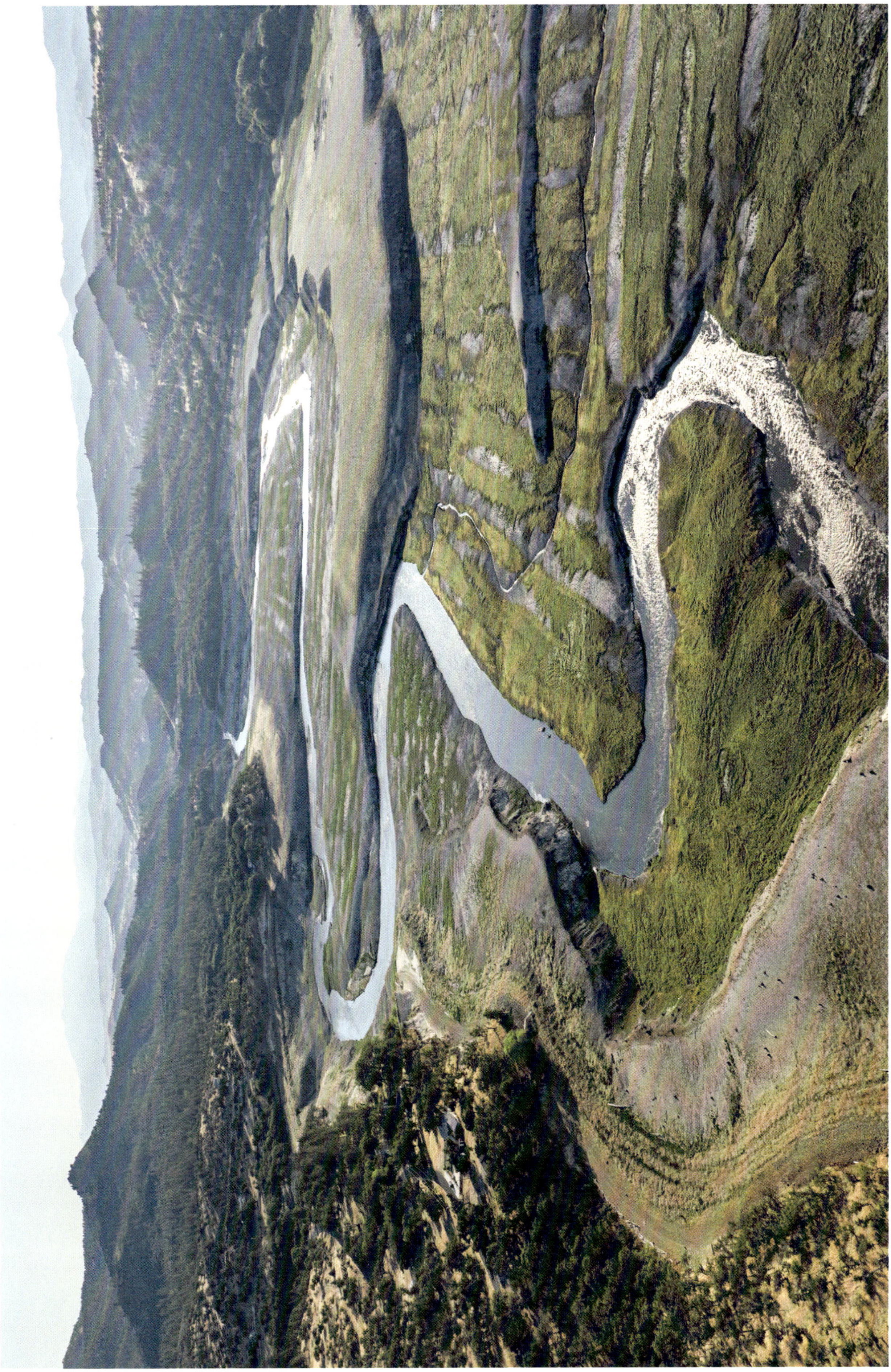

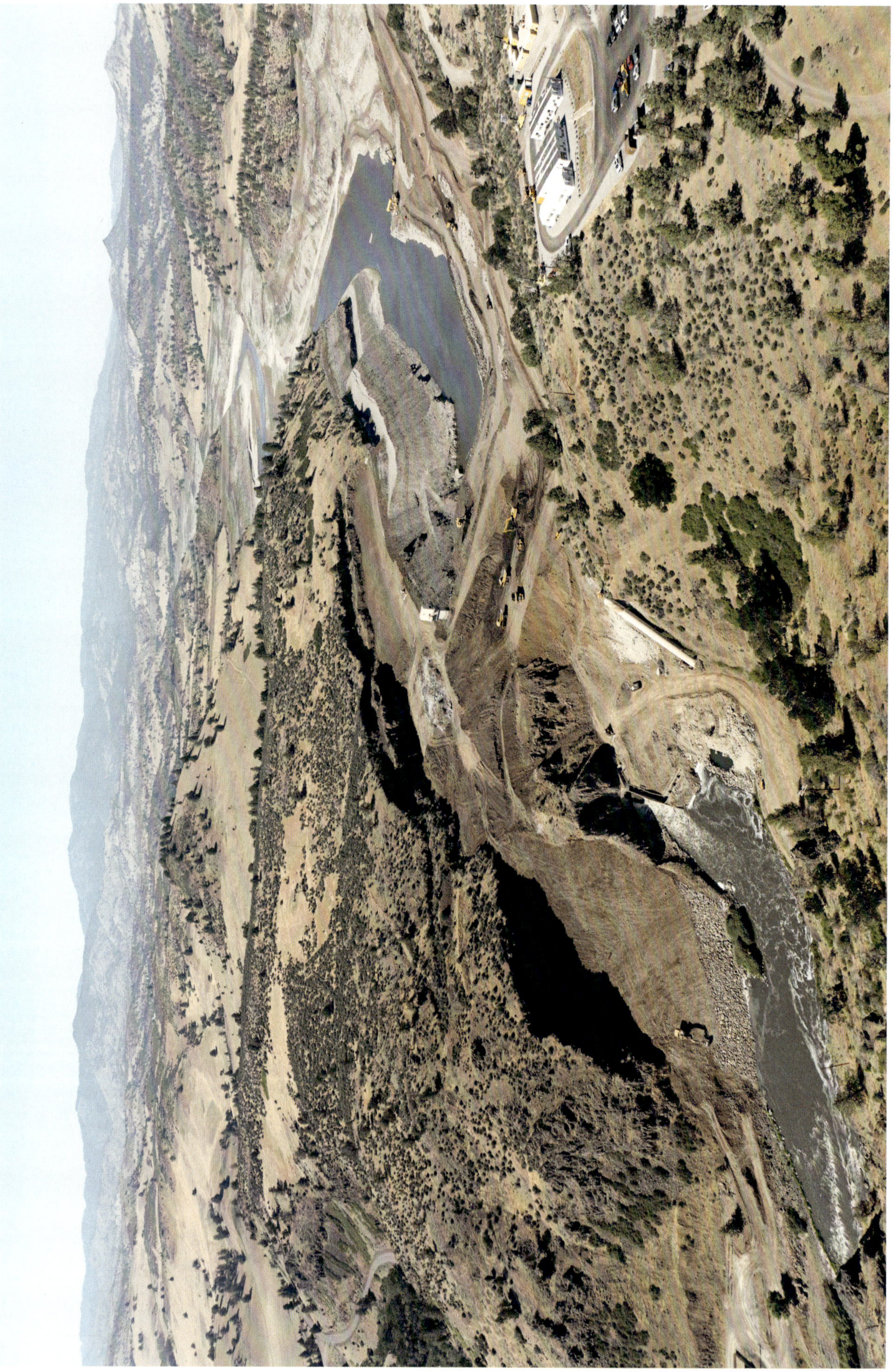

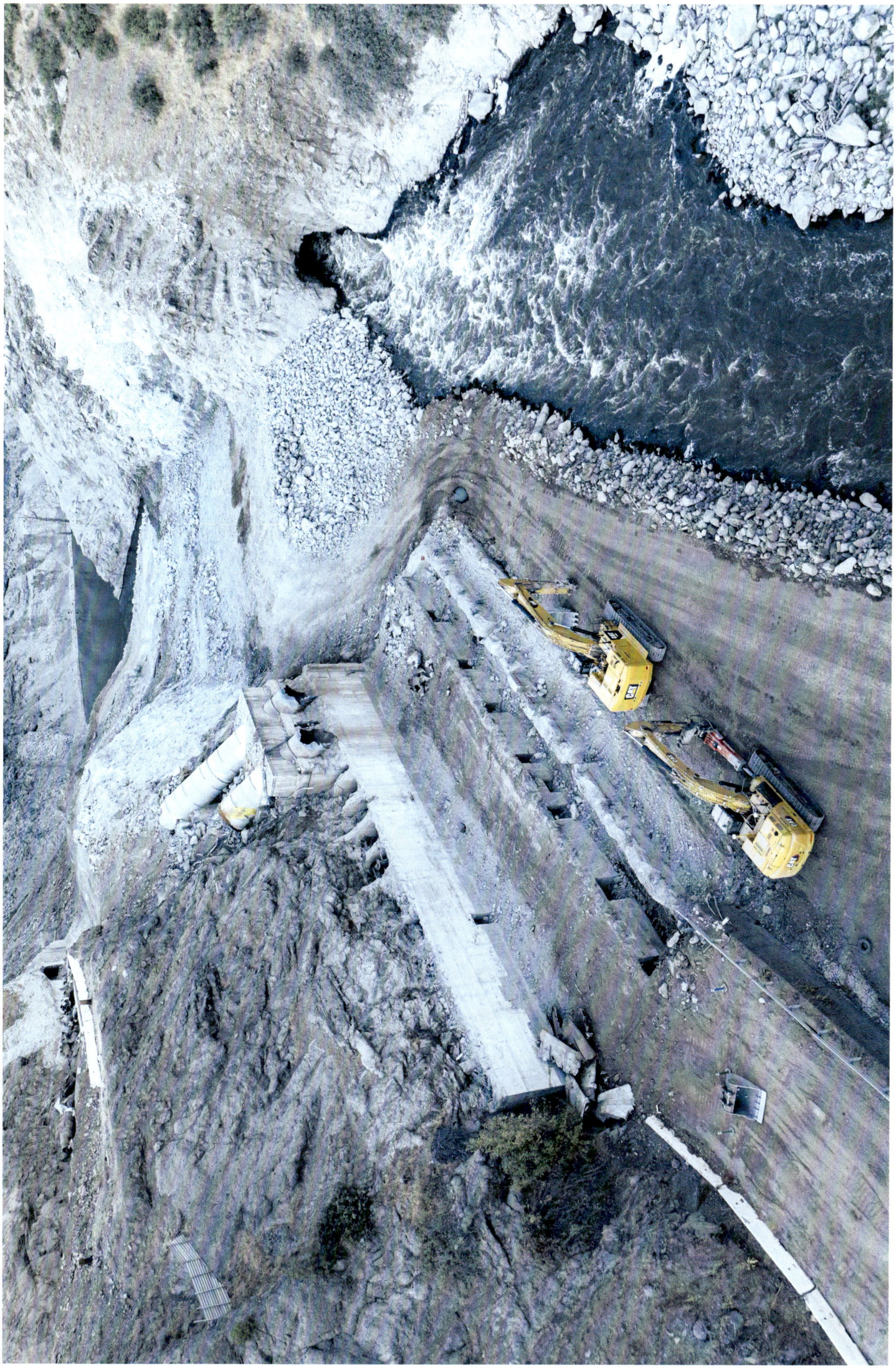

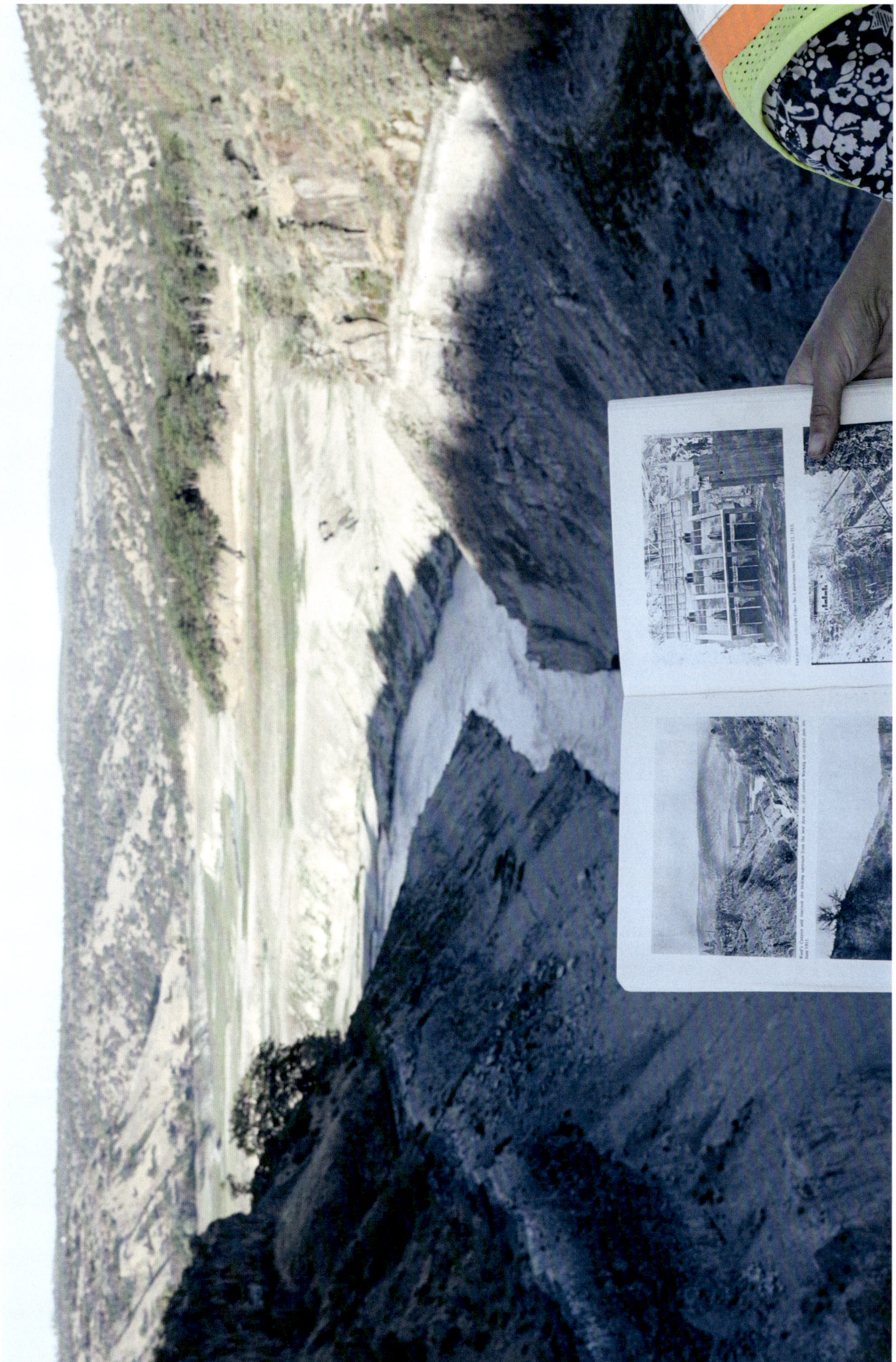

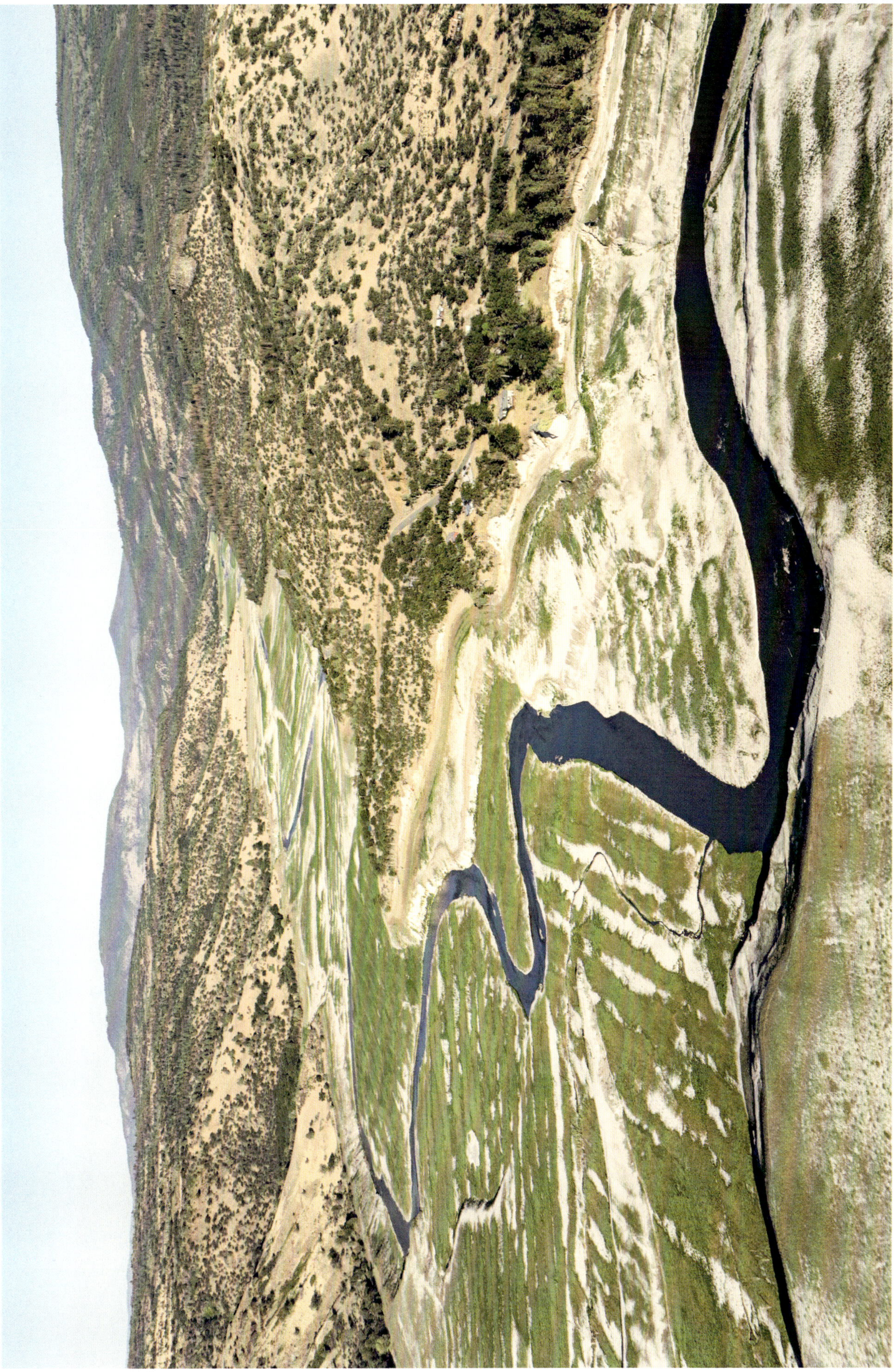

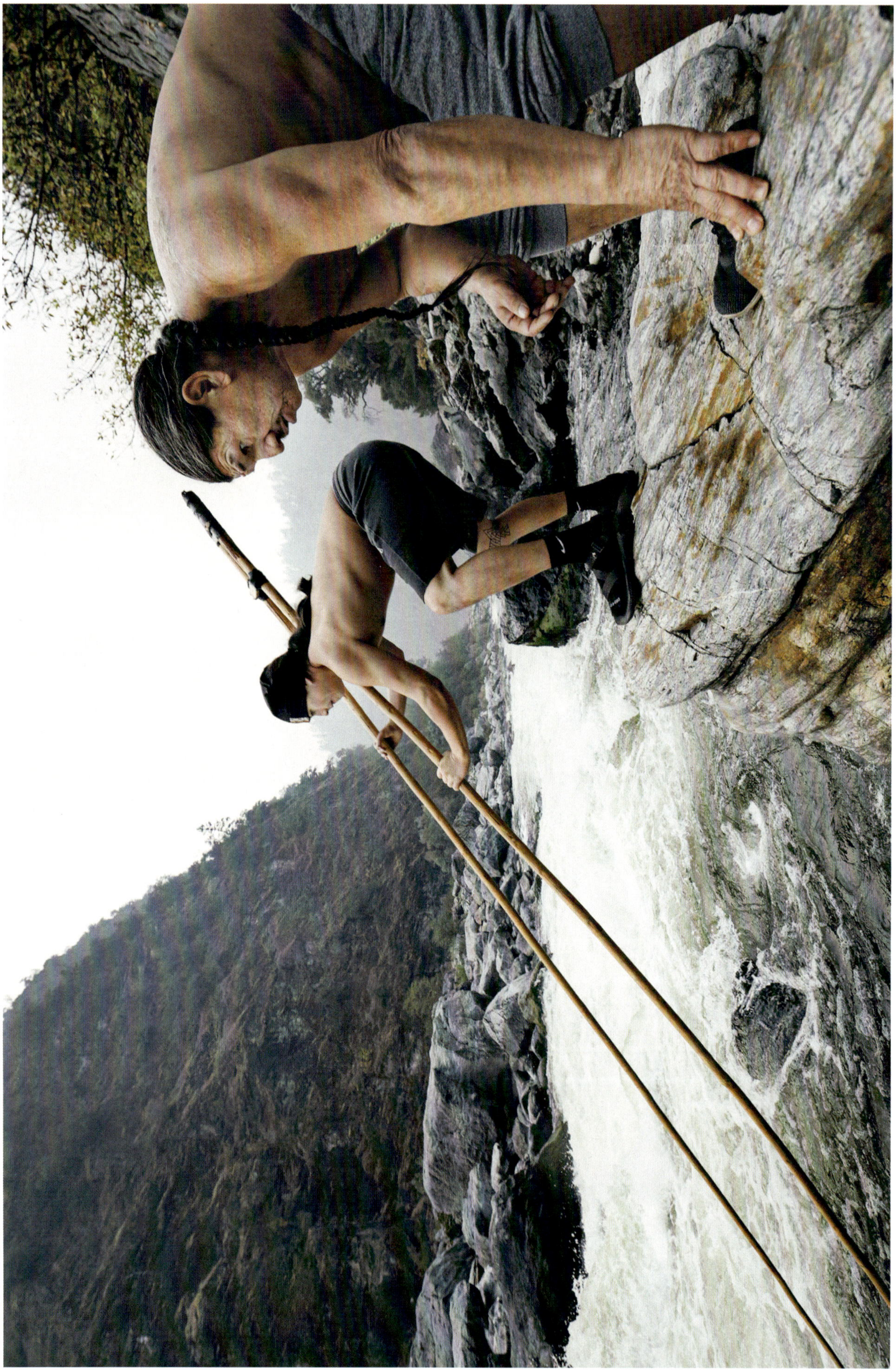

“Would fish that famously home to their birth streams swiftly find a stretch of river that had been foreclosed for more than a century?”

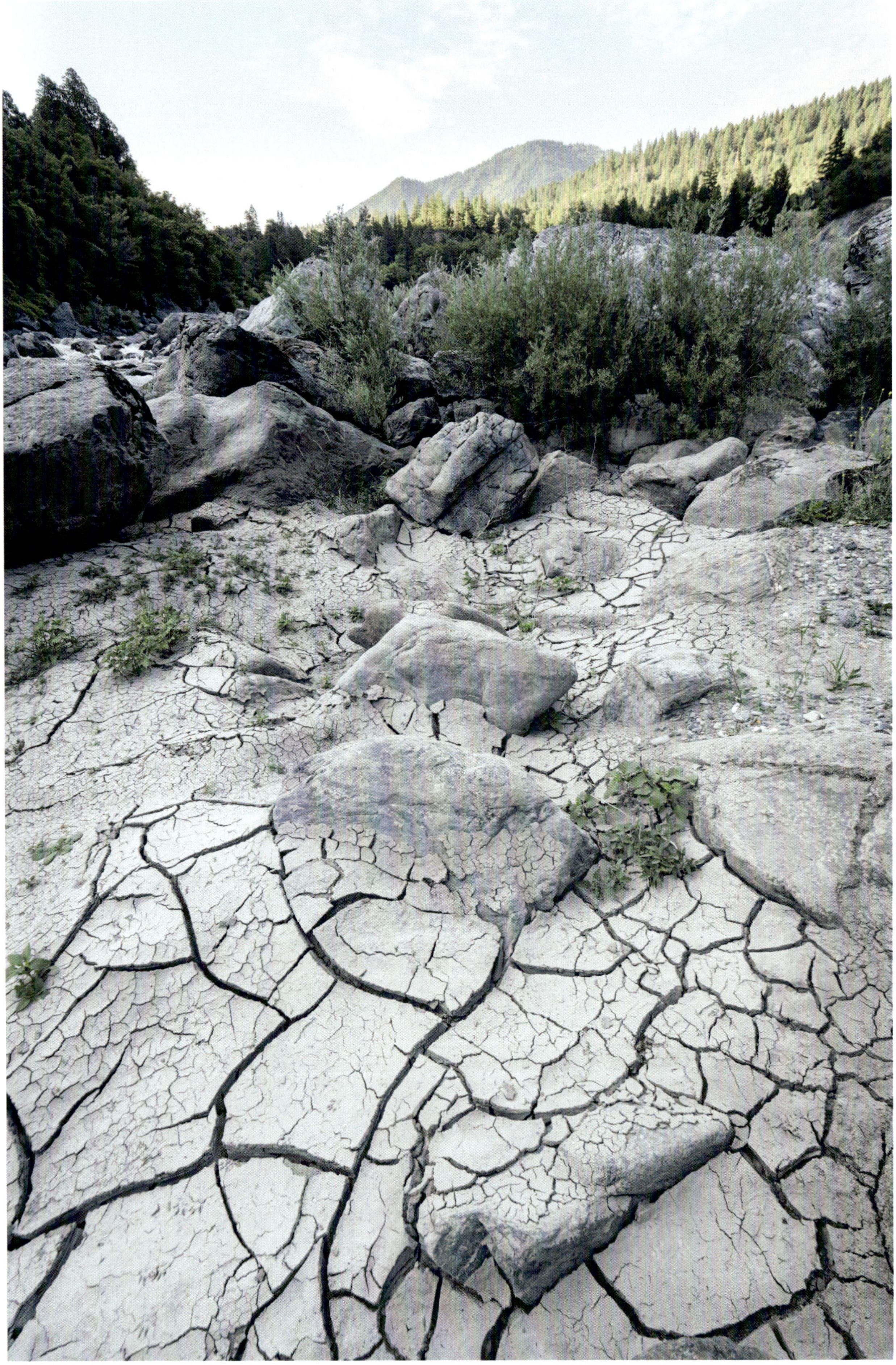

Marie Mutsuki Mockett
FIVE HUNDRED WORDS

"The real question isn't whether the essential words for nature will remain, but what we might do with them…"

ESSENTIAL JAPANESE KIGO
基本の季語

Translated by
Marie Mutsuki Mockett

SPRING
春 (haru)

BARELY SPRING
春浅し (haru asashi)

RETURNING COLD
冴かえる (saekaeru)

BUGS COME OUT
啓蟄 (keichitsu)

SERENE
麗か (uraraka)

TRANQUIL
長閑 (nodoka)

LINGERING DAY
遅じつ (chijitsu)

DEEP SPRING
春深し (haru fukashi)

FIRST SPRING GUST
春一番 (haru ichiban)

SHINING WIND
風光 (kaze hikari)

LAST FROST
忘れ霜 (wasurejimo)

BLOSSOM HAZE
花曇 (hanagumori)

SPRING FIELD
春の田 (haru no ta)

WATERS WARMING
水温む (mizu nurumu)

SPRING MUD
春泥 (shundei)

AVALANCHE
なだれ (nadare)

MELTING SNOW
雪解け (yukidoke)

ICE FLOES
流氷 (ryuuhyoo)

SOWING, PLANTING SEED
種蒔 (tanemaki)

HERB GATHERING
つみくさ (tsumikusa)

SPRING MELANCHOLY
春愁 (shunshuu)

TADPOLES
御玉杓子 (otamajakushi)

MANY BABY BIRDS
ももちどり (momochidori)

BUSH WARBLER
鶯 (uguisu)

PHEASANT
雉 (kiji)

SKYLARK
雲雀 (hibari)

SWALLOW
燕 (tsubame)

DEPARTING BIRDS
引鳥 (hitori)

BIRDS ENTER CLOUDS
とりくもにいる
(tori kumo ni iru)

TWITTERING
囀り (saezuri)

RISING CARP
のっこみぶな
(nokkomi buna)

SILKWORMS
蚕 (kaiko)

CHERRY BLOSSOMS
桜 (sakura)

WISTERIA
藤ふじ (fuji)

THE ONLY STORY I have about my Japanese great-grandmother comes from my American father. It was 1968 and my Japanese grandmother had been reluctant to introduce her son-in-law to extended family, since it was my father's country that had decimated the family home in Nagasaki. But at my mother's urging, the three of them trekked out to the tiny apartment where my great-grandmother lived alone—and their meeting was an instant success. They smiled at each other as they sat on the tatami floor, and despite the language barrier, instantly felt each other's warmth, kindness, and desire for acceptance.

And then, said my father, my great-grandmother turned and tossed out the beginning lines of a poem. My mother was supposed to be able to finish the poem to participate in an advanced game of exquisite corpse, but she couldn't think of what to say. My grandmother, still remembering her aristocratic upbringing on the island of Kyushu, chimed in, and then she and her mother went back and forth until the whole poem was complete, at which point the two women laughed, and then my great-grandmother gently scolded her daughter for not having taught my mother the art of Japanese poetry.

I know now that they were most likely engaging in *haikai*, which developed out of *renga*; the latter is a seven-hundred-year-old art which literally means "linked poetry," and the stanzas are very generally comprised of alternating lines of five or seven syllables. A descendant of this poetic form, *haiku* is today popular throughout the world.

The three women in my family who came before me were all artists. I am a writer too, but so much has changed between their time and mine that when I imagine being in the small apartment listening to them compose that poem, I see myself merely grasping at the edges of their conversation; even if I could be there, time, war, and my upbringing in America would render me a ghost of a figure. And yet, this story always fills me with longing to be able to join them, to mend the broken bridge of time.

ONE OF MANY THINGS these forms of Japanese poetry—renga, haikai, and haiku—have in common is that they must make mention of the season. Chances are my great-grandmother, grandmother, and even my mother studied something called a *saijiki*, a kind of encyclopedia which charts the words that are associated with each of the four seasons: spring, summer, fall, and autumn. Each seasonal word, a *kigo*, allows the poet to express a human feeling, conveyed via the natural world.

A subset of five hundred of these kigo has been listed by the scholar and haiku practitioner Kenkichi Yamamoto as essential, with subcategories for animals, plants, and other established topics.

When I look at this list, I recognize almost all of the words and can attach a memory to many of them: like the time my mother told me to look out the window at fields of rice pulsating with emerald light (summer); or the time we traveled to the ancient capital Nara in February, saw the sasanquas blooming in the cold (winter), and ate Japanese sweets shaped to look like those very blossoms. You may well be aware of some if not all of these words too.

Even though the most famous of the haiku poets, Basho, lived nearly four hundred years ago, his work in translation has arguably done more than anything else to influence a global understanding of what Japanese poetry can be. Here, for example, is one of his most famous poems, as translated by Donald Keene:

古池や
蛙飛び込む
水の音

furu ike ya
kawazu tobikomu
mizu no oto

The ancient pond
A frog leaps in
The sound of the water.

If, as I wrote, all haiku (and renga and haikai) utilize the seasons as a starting point to express an emotion, in what season would you place this poem? The frog, as a symbol of spring, is the giveaway, and a great deal of ink has been spilt over the deeper meanings contained in these three lines. For example, when we think of frogs making a sound, we usually conjure their springtime courtship calls, but Basho overturned this expectation, making the frog responsible for giving water a voice.

In addition to a seasonal word, haiku also include a "cutting term," which gives a poem breath—a kind of negative space in the middle of all the phonemes. In the case of this haiku, Basho has included the particle "ya," which functions as a beat so the reader will pause before continuing on. Knowing this, Alan Watts retranslated the poem like so:

The old pond,
A frog jumps in:
Plop!

Last spring, my friend Matthew and I took a quick trip to Jūniko Lakes in

WILD ROSE
山吹 (yamabuki)

TREE BUDS
木の芽 (ko no me)

MULBERRY
桑 (kuwa)

WILLOW FLUFF
柳絮 (ryuujo)

MUSTARD FLOWER
菜の花 (na no hana)

YOUNG GRASSES
若草 (wakakusa)

DANDELION
蒲公英 (tanpopo)

FIDDLEHEAD
蕨 (warabi)

REED EARS
茅 (tsubana)

WAKAME
和布 (wakame)

SUMMER
夏 (natsu)

SHORT NIGHT
短夜 (mijikayo)

HOT
暑し (atsushi)

SMOLDERING
もゆる (moyuru)

BURNING
灼くる (yakuru)

COOL
涼しい (suzushi)

CLOUD PEAKS
雲の峰 (kumo no mine)

SUMMER MOON
夏の月 (natsu no tsuki)

WIND IN THE VERDURE
青嵐 (aoarashi)

FRAGRANT BREEZE
薫風 (kunpuu)

EVENING LULL
ゆうなぎ (yuunagi)

MIDSUMMER RAIN
五月雨 (samidare)

EVENING DOWNPOUR
夕立 (yuudachi)

THUNDER
雷 (kaminari)

AFTERGLOW
夕焼 (yuuyake)

HEAT AT ZENITH
ひざかり (hizakari)

DROUGHT
旱 (hideri)

WATERFALL
瀧 (taki)

THIN CLOTHES
羅 (usumono)

SILKWORM COCOON
繭 (mayu)

SWIMMING
泳ぎ (oyogi)

COOLING ON THE PORCH
橋居 (hashi-i)

FAWN
かのこ (kanoko)

RIVER FROG
河鹿 (kajika)

Akita Prefecture, home of one of the world's largest remaining primeval beech forests; we were on the hunt for the rare Okinawa ruddy kingfisher. While I missed the kingfisher, I did come upon dozens of green frogs mating and reproducing in the branches of the thick trees above the blue waters. They hung onto foamy, oozing egg-filled balls of white goo, and every now and then a frog, presumably done with mating, would fall down into the water. Plop. The world felt sticky, and fecund. It is possible I would have noticed the frogs even without knowing the Basho poem, yet because of his haiku I found this compressed observation of nature in action riveting, my mind linking it to many other readers and writers of poetry across time, back to Basho.

IF SPRING SIGNALS birth and sex, autumn, with its fading light and drying grasses, often conveys longing. Here is another of Basho's famous haiku:

> 夏草や
> 兵どもが
> 夢の跡
>
> Natsukusa ya
> Tsuwamonodomo ga
> Yume no ato
>
> summer grass—
> all that remains
> of warriors' dreams

The ancient aristocrats, who helped to first codify the seasonal words, were writing about the natural world around them not so much to preserve nature, according to Columbia University professor Haruo Shirane in his book *Japan and the Culture of the Four Seasons*, but to advocate for imperial legitimacy. Their view of nature, which was greatly influenced by China, was of endlessly and predictably cycling seasons; nature, like imperial rule, was stable. The poetics of nature evolved, crossing the centuries in Japan, eventually codified into the saijiki. Such an attunement to seasonality is also expressed in Japan's social and material culture in what Haruo calls "secondary nature"—the tea ceremony, flower arranging, and poetry writing—and even today in the seasonal offerings of Starbucks, which in Tokyo includes a cherry blossom cake in the spring. As a young adult, I loved coming to Japan and seeing that cake everywhere starting in March. Never mind the Easter rabbit and Easter eggs! The Japanese love flowers! But I have had to face squarely that these aesthetics have not prevented the large-scale destruction of much of Japan's natural beauty. The aforementioned Jūniko Lakes or the Shiretoko Peninsula, two places where remaining native forests preserve wild bird and mammal habitats, are proportionally quite small to the rest of Japan's forests. I sometimes fret that the new practice of "secondary nature"—art installations like Team Lab Borderless which feature projected flowers and schools of fish into large rooms—gives viewers the sensation of being in harmony with a natural world that in reality is under continuous destruction.

Today, the distinctions between the four seasons in Japan are collapsing, so it is becoming increasingly difficult to align not only the anticipated festivals and décor to the seasons, but the lists in the saijiki with external reality. As I write this, in November 2024, Mt. Fuji remains snowless for the first time in over 130 years. The Soma Nomaoi horse festival, historically held in July in the Tohoku town of Minami-Soma and which I attended as a child, is now scheduled for May because the horses and the humans cannot cope with the dangerously high temperatures of summer.

Every time I hear about something traditional being lost or changing in Japan, I feel at least a twinge of sadness. I'm relieved the horse festival will be preserved, because its existence was greatly threatened by the 2011 earthquake and tsunami, but the change in date has upended expectations around seasonal preparation. So many precious cultural traditions feel endangered in Japan, and not just because of climate change. Many Japanese houses with traditional tatami mats now sit empty as young people understandably prefer more modern structures. My feelings toward my own mortality are of course bound up with the weightiness of such losses, but I suppose I feel an additional vulnerability where Japan is concerned. If only I could just have had enough time in "real" Japan, then perhaps I could have completed a chain from myself to my mother and back through time to my ancestors.

It's worth noting that a modern seasonal almanac, the *Nihon Dai Saijiki, Great Japanese Seasonal Almanac* (1983), includes the new words "short-sleeve shirts," "baseball night game," and "sunglasses" for summer. It seems inevitable that the saijiki, and its seasonal words, will only continue to change. The poet Natsui Itsuki anticipates this and has even written a book titled *The Dictionary of Endangered Seasonal Words* (*Zetsumetsu sunzen kigo jiten*) and in an interview gave a free verse–worthy answer when asked to predict how change will finally happen:

LITTLE CUCKOO
時鳥 (hototogisu)

OLD BUSH WARBLER
老鶯 (oiuguisu)

KINGFISHER
翡翠 (kawasemi)

FIREFLY,
LIGHTNING BUG
蛍 (hotaru)

CICADA
蝉 (semi)

CICADA SHELL
空蝉 (utsusemi)

FLY
蝿 (hae)

MOSQUITO
蚊 (ka)

ANT
蟻 (ari)

PEONY
牡丹 (botan)

MYRIAD GREEN
万緑 (banryoku)

SHADE OF A TREE
のこしたやみ
(konoshita yami)

WILD IRIS
あやめ (ayame)

PINKS
撫子 (nadeshiko)

MELON
瓜 (uri)

EGGPLANT
茄子 (nasu)

LOTUS
蓮 (hasu)

BARLEY
麦 (mugi)

AUTUMN
秋 (aki)

REMAINING HEAT
残暑 (zansho)

NEW COOLNESS
新涼 (shinryoo)

REFRESHING
爽やか (sawayaka)

CHILLY
冷ややか (hiyayaka)

SOAK TO THE BONE
身に入む (mi ni shimu)

AUTUMN DEEPENS,
AUTUMN IS DEEP
あきふかし (aki fukashi)

AUTUMN'S VOICE
秋の声 (aki no koe)

MACKEREL CLOUDS
鰯雲 (iwashigumo)

BRIGHT MOON,
HARVEST MOON
明月 (meigetsu)

AUTUMN WIND
秋風 (aki kaze)

FOG
霧 (kiri)

DEW
梅雨 (tsuyu)

LANTERN FLOATING
灯籠流し (tooroo)

SCARECROW
案山子 (kakashi)

AUTUMN CONTEMPLATION
秋思 (shuushi)

> Do you know a shell called "Akoya pearl oyster"? It is a shell that produces pearls, but if a foreign substance such as a stone gets inside this shell, it will be wrapped in multiple layers so as not to damage it. As a result, pearls are slowly made. The maturation of seasonal words is similar. It takes a long time to make one season word, and I think that period [of time] is what we call culture.

But she rejects the idea that old words need to be jettisoned. "There is no accreditation body [to determine which words are excluded]. It is not something that some kind of association recognizes, but something that naturally takes root in a long history."

I have said that I wished I could imbibe culture to complete myself. But Itsuki's point that culture is not about a set of rules one can memorize and master challenges this viewpoint. What matters, she says, is responding to living culture and thus making culture.

IN A BRILLIANT, intellectually challenging essay titled "Haiku, Time, Ecology"—too profound to completely unpack here—Hisao Suzuki, the poet and editor of the poetry magazine *Coal Sack*, reframes the question about seasonal words entirely. Traditional haiku has assumed a kind of timelessness in the world; climate change along with nuclear proliferation give the lie to such perfect circles. We do not, in fact, know that the spring grasses will always come and grow over the soldier's remains, and worse, we may be the architects of their demise. What is an artist to do? Suzuki foresees three options:

1. Remain true to the "fiction" of the seasonal calendar and pursue classical beauty.
2. Take "reality" and denounce the post–climate change world with realism.
3. Reimagine and reconstruct a new relationship between "fiction" and "reality."

I think sometimes that it is the child part of myself who doesn't want to let go of seasonal words as they have always been, and who wants to think of culture as something fixed to which I can always return. If the seasons stay the same, then I can always return to the memories of my mother, for example, eating the sasanqua sweets as a fixed point in time. I feel that Suzuki is speaking directly to all artists when he basically says it is not the saijiki we should be worried about, but rather whether or not we have fully realized the potential of our poetry. "Haiku is ecological literature. It teaches us how to live in surrender to the relationships and natural processes of nature." One of the reasons Basho remains such a great haiku poet is because his work *does* engage with ecology, even though he likely couldn't imagine what impact we would be having on the Earth hundreds of years later. Taken one way, Basho's haiku about autumn grasses and dead warriors can be read as a simple observation of the follies of man. But it could also be taken as a deeper philosophical observation about interdependence and the living relationships of all things—and the grave threat man's ability to wage war imposes on the world.

In her classic, visionary work *Tree Spirits Grass Spirits*, the bold, feminist writer Hiromi Ito meditates on the tensions between indigeneity and naturalization of both people and plants. She walks the wilderness around Mt. Aso on the island of Kyushu, noting the appearance and disappearance of both native and invasive plants, when she comes across a classic patch of Japanese flowers:

> I recalled the memories of my ancestors, for whom this profusion signaled the arrival of autumn. The ancient days of the poetry collection *Man'yōshu* and *The Tale of Genji*, and even further back. They must have been alive at that time, my ancestors' ancestors' ancestors, and their ancestors as well. While life loomed over them, while they lived and died, they saw them: these flowers of autumn.

This is not haiku, but in sensibility feels in communication with Basho, speaking to a deep longing for connection and the brief joy we feel at union across species, and across time. I think this is part of what Ito means when she states in an interview: "I have studied plants, I have seen that they have a system for living and dying that is not like the system of living and dying for humans. Plants can show us how to think in new ways when we are thinking about death."

Reflecting on the saijiki has made me think more deeply about the nature of culture, and what we expect from it. In childhood, Japan was my alternate reality, not in the video game sense, but a place powerfully different from and more real than the world of surfing, golfing, and shopping malls of my childhood

MIGRATING BIRDS
渡鳥 (wataridori)

RICE SPARROWS
いねすずめ (inesuzume)

SHRIKE
鵙 (mozu)

WAGTAIL
せきれい (sekirei)

QUAIL
うずら (uzura)

SANDPIPER, SNIPE
しぎ (shigi)

SALMON
鮭 (sake)

DRAGONFLY
蜻蛉 (tonbo)

CRICKET
蟋蟀 (koorogi)

WORMS CRY
みみずなく (mimizu naku)

PEACH
もものみ (momo no mi)

PEAR
梨 (nashi)

PERSIMMON
柿 (kaki)

CHESTNUTS
栗 (kuri)

RED LEAVES
紅葉 (momiji)

MAPLE
かえで (kaede)

WILLOW LEAVES FALL
やなぎちる (yanagi chiru)

NUTS AND SEEDS
木の実 (ko no mi)

TATTERED LOTUS
破れ蓮 (yare hachisu)

WIND IN THE REEDS
おぎのこえ (ogi no koe)

MUSHROOMS, FUNGUS
きのこ (kinoko)

WINTER
冬 (fuyu)

WINTER WITHERING
冬ざれ (fuyuzare)

CLEAR AND COLD
さゆる (sayuru)

FREEZE
いつる (itsuru)

NORTH WIND
きた (kita)

SLEET
みぞれ (mizore)

FROST
霜 (shimo)

FIRST SNOW
はつゆき (hatsuyuki)

ICICLES
氷柱 (tsurara)

QUILT
蒲団 (futon)

PORRIDGE
雑炊 (zoosui)

WINTER SECLUSION
冬籠 (fuyugomori)

BONFIRE
焚火 (takibi)

home in California. Japan was a solid place with rules I needed to learn, so my body and then my heart would bend into my own personal expression of being Japanese. But culture is a living thing, and it is somewhat childish to expect it to be infallible, always there to nurture and to care for us. As Itsuki, Suzuki, and others have suggested, the real question isn't whether the essential words for nature will remain, but what we might do with them, for culture is always ours to create. Might we learn to think and write and feel from the point of view of plants? Such a blurring of boundaries actually has a cultural precedent in Japan. The introduction of Buddhism to Japan included the idea that all plants and animals could attain enlightenment. By the fifteenth century, the occasional plant as character appeared in plays to remind audiences that all are capable of salvation. These playwrights doubtless were aware of the seasonal terms in Japan but expanded their work to address issues of justice and immortality. The real work of making Itsuki's "pearl" relies not on following and mastering rules, but on human compassion, daring, and imagination.

I think about my grandmother finishing her life in a small apartment in Nagoya, her home long ago destroyed in the war, and how she kept on making poems with her daughter. I wonder if these poems were a private way of keeping her home with her. When my grandmother died over a decade ago in April, my grandfather read a poem he had composed at the memorial service. I remember it had the line: *hira hara hanabira*. "*Hira hara*" was a play on my grandmother's maiden name, Hara, and on her married name, Hirabayashi. Taken together, the two words are an onomatopoeia for something falling or drifting; the third word, *hanabira*, means "cherry petal." He was trying to convey to us the sadness and the beauty of my grandmother softly fading away. He was saying that she is now in the petals of the cherry tree. He was writing a poem for her, or perhaps completed the poem she had started. I ask myself: how will I—how will we—respond?

SEARCHING FOR PLUM BLOSSOMS
探梅 (tanbai)

HAWK
鷹 (taka)

COLD SPARROWS
かんすずめ (kansuzume)

COLD CROW
かんがらす (kangarasu)

OYSTERS
かき (kaki)

FLOWERS OUT OF SEASON
帰り花 (kaeribana)

ONION
葱 (negi)

JAPANESE RADISH
大根 (daikon)

TURNIP
蕪 (kabu)

SNOW PELLETS
霰 (arare)

WATERFOWL
水鳥 (mizutori)

WILD DUCKS
鴨 (kamo)

PLOVERS, SANDPIPERS
ちどり (chidori)

GREBE
かいつぶり (kaitsuburi)

YELLOWTAIL
ぶり (buri)

COLD SILVER CARP
かんぶな (kanbuna)

CHARCOAL
すみ (sumi)

FIREPLACE
ろ (ro)

WATER DRIED UP
水涸 (mizu karu)

WINTER MOUNTAINS
ふゆのやま (fuyu no yama)

WITHERED FIELD
枯野 (kareno)

CLEAR WINTER DAY
冬晴 (fuyubare)

SEA CUCUMBER
なまこ (namako)

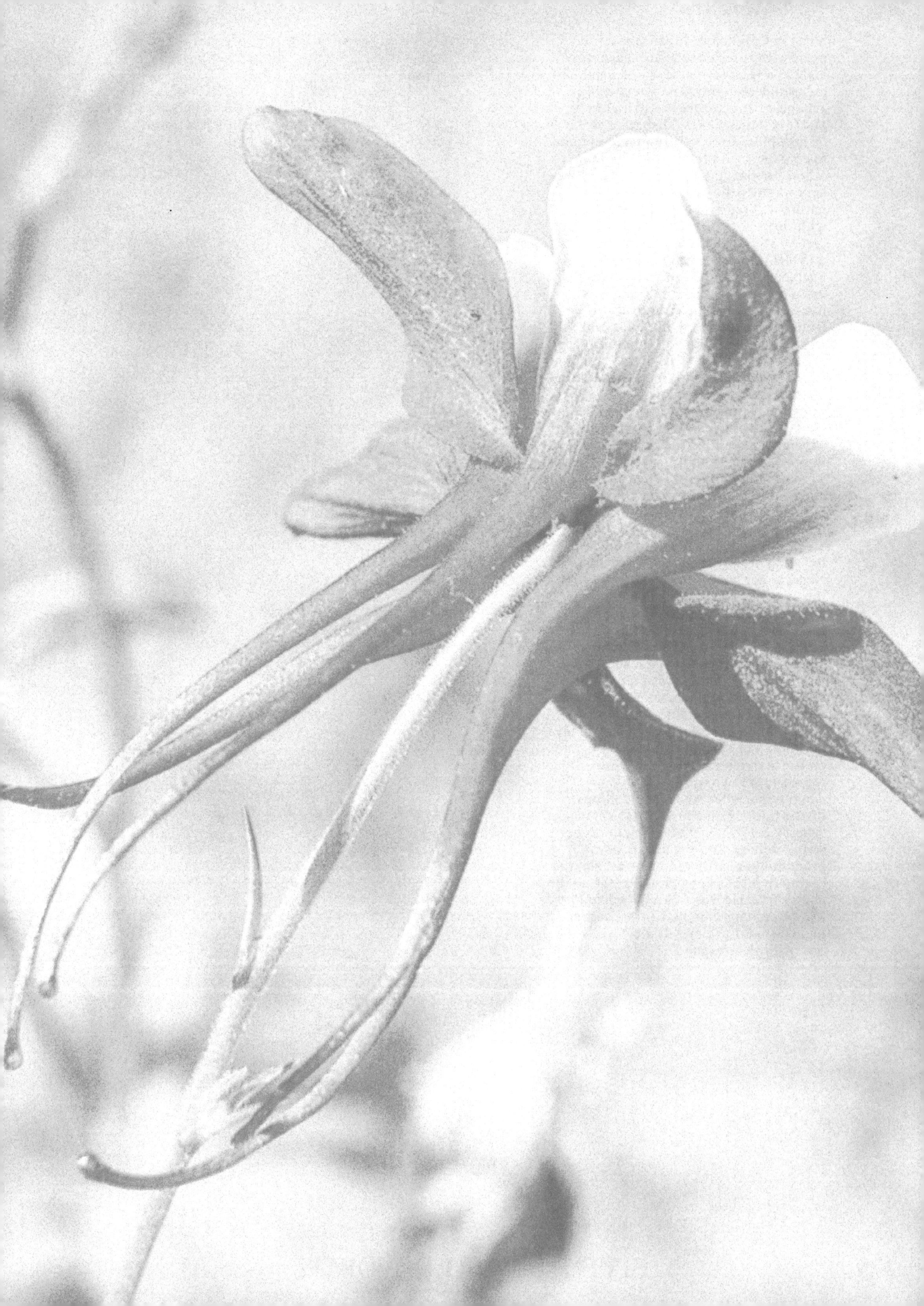

David George Haskell

WILDFLOWER BEAUTY AND THE SEARCH FOR HOME

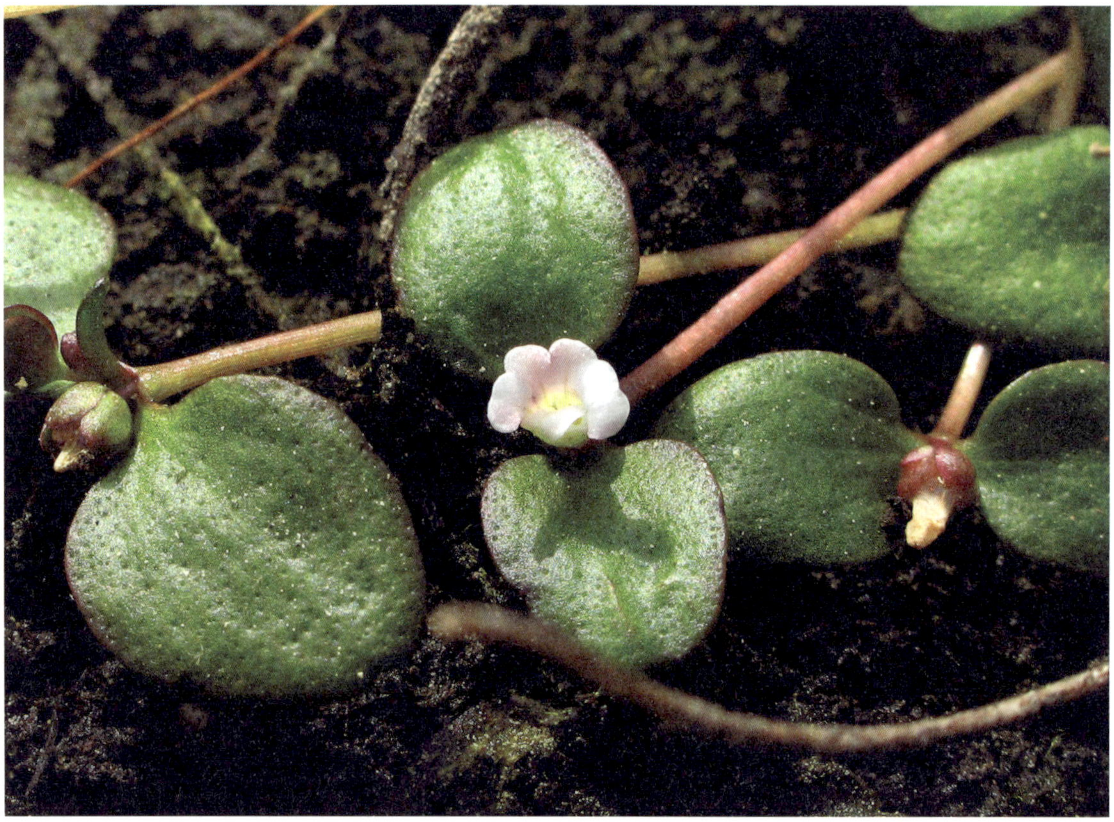

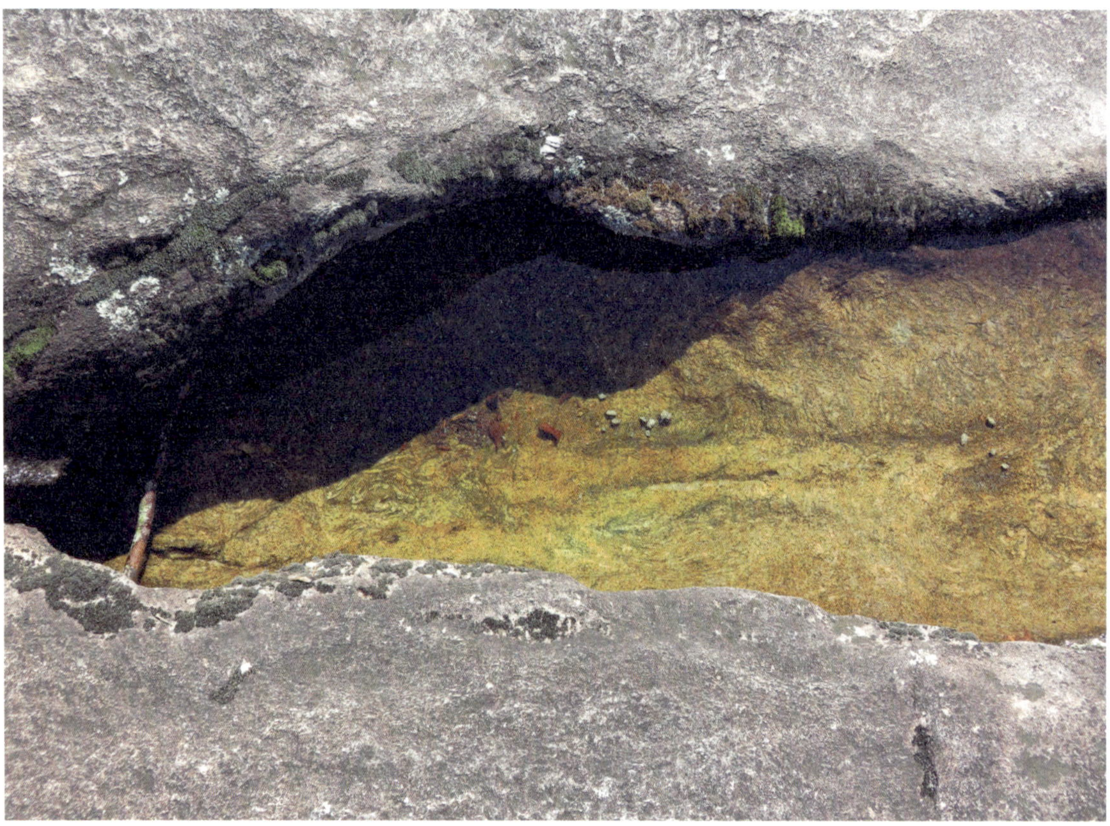

FIG. 27 *Aquilegia canadensis* (P. 280)
FIG. 28 *Gratiola amphiantha* / Allan Cressler (P. 282, above)
FIG. 29 Granite pool on Arabia Mountain (P. 282, below)

To know the seasons, look to plants. Wildflowers, especially, are excellent teachers. Their extravagant displays catch our attention. Their small, delicate bodies are beautifully, frighteningly permeable to the changing pulses of the world.

Plants feel seasonal changes in light, moisture, and heat like few other living beings. Plant cells feed on sunshine. Water wraps every root and coats the spongy interior of leaves. The body temperatures of plants fluctuate with those of their surroundings. This openness makes plants the primary interpreters of the seasons. The word "seasons" carries this knowledge in its origins. Descended from the Latin *serere*, meaning "to sow," the word changed from verb to noun and came to mean not only the act of sowing crops, but the right time to sow.

Today, the seasons are convulsed by change. The "right time" feels terrifyingly destabilized. If plants teach us about the seasons, what are they telling us now?

"What do plants do when life gets hard? Strew the world with floral beauty."

SNORKLEWORT

FOUR HUNDRED MILLION years ago, bubbles of magma pushed up through the Earth's crust in what are now the outskirts of Atlanta, Georgia. As the softer rocks around them eroded, the hard magma bubbles remained. From a distance they now look like giant whales surfacing, their bare, smooth skin gleaming against a dark sea of oak and pine forest.

On a spring morning, we climb a whale's back. The place is called Arabia Mountain, a name coined by quarry workers who compared the summer heat to the most sun-blasted place they could imagine. On a summer afternoon, the shadeless stone can reach 140 degrees Fahrenheit, too hot to touch. The sterilizing power of the sun keeps the whale's skin stony smooth and almost free of plant life. Yet, a few plants not only persist, but make this oven their only home.

In pockmarks on the whale's back, rain accumulates in puddles. These depressions were etched into the rock by millennia of slightly acidic rainfall. Most puddles drain or evaporate within days, but a few hold water throughout the winter and spring.

I lie down and peer through my hand lens: Paired oval leaves float on the water's surface, each leaf only as big as a small lentil. At the center of some of these pairs grows a white flower about half the size of a peppercorn. A thread tethers the floating leaves to a rosette of spiky leaves rooted at the bottom of the puddle. The soil at the bottom is thin, just a couple of millimeters of coarse sand and oozy muck. This is snorklewort, a plant that lives on the edge of impossibility.

Ephemeral pools in rocks are snorklewort's only home. The species lives on about three dozen rock outcrops in Georgia, Alabama, and South Carolina. Winter rain fills the pools and causes snorklewort seeds to germinate. The young plant grows into a submerged rosette, like a miniscule tuft of grass.

Rain and weak sunlight on warmer days sustain the growing rosettes through the early winter. As the days lengthen, the rosette grows its "snorkel," a thread leading to a bud on the water's surface. From the bud grow leaves and flower. The snorkel looks like a hose connecting a diver to the boat, but it carries no air and instead anchors the floating leaves, stopping breezes from washing them ashore. The flower is so small that my unaided eyes have trouble seeing it. On warmer days, tiny insects visit the blooms.

As spring progresses, the puddles dry faster in the ever-stronger sun, leaving a thin layer of damp, muddy sand. The flower matures to a tiny green fruit that encloses the seed, and the floating leaves lie prostrate in the muck. By early summer, the whole plant shrivels away. Mature seeds caught in the sand at the bottom of the depressions are snorklewort's only connection to the future. They wait all summer and autumn, surviving the heat by sending their embryos into deep sleep, a dried-up suspended animation. When summer rainstorms refill the puddles to overflowing, the seeds are not fooled into germinating. Emergence anytime before the cold rains of winter would mean certain death.

No one has studied how snorklewort seedlings know when to burst out of their seedcoats and greet what they hope is a welcoming puddle. But, we know from other plant species that seeds have lucid dreams during their slumbers. Cells at the tip of the sleeping embryo keep up hormonal conversations among themselves that track temperature, moisture, and the passage of time. Eventually the chemical whispers jolt the rest of the embryo: wake up, let's go, the world awaits!

Genes shape the seasonal chatter among plant cells. Every species has a different conversation underway in its seeds, each attuned to its home. The seasons live within, scribed into genes and physiology. Every species carries the pulse of home inside.

Snorklewort walks a fine line. If the pools dry out too fast, they cannot make floating leaves and flowers. If the pools hold too much soil, other plants like grasses and pine seedlings take over. If the pools contain too much dissolved minerals, algae grow profusely and smother the snorklewort. Yet, across millennia, snorklewort has yearly reseeded itself. In years when the rains are meager and pools do not fill, the rosettes grow backup flowers. These never open and instead self-fertilize and make inbred offspring. Not ideal, but essential insurance. Safeguards against swings in rainfall and heat caused by climate chaos will be harder to find.

Snorklewort is not the only flower on the whale's stony back. Elf orpine blazes its white flowers by the thousands from depressions that gather damp sand. Like

FIG. 30 *Aquilegia chrysantha* (P. 287)

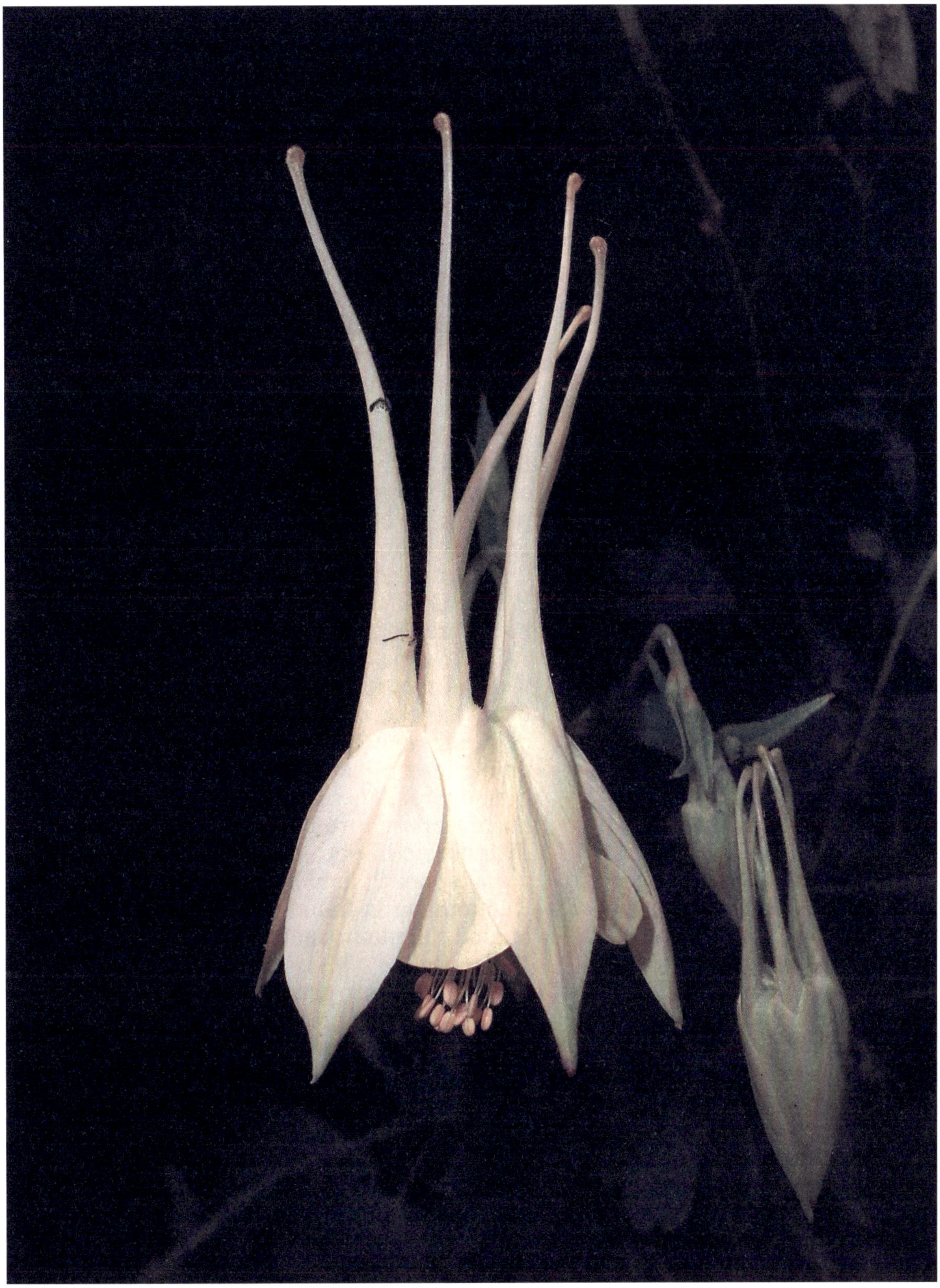

snorklewort, these grasshopper-high elves germinate in winter, bloom in spring, and wait out summer as seeds. Where a little more soil has accumulated, in stony cracks or deeper pits, wooly ragwort and blue toadflax add to the springtime bloom, usually by sprouting from roots stuffed with food carried over from the plants' germination and growth in the previous year. In autumn, Porter's sunflowers, which overwinter as seeds, turn the same soil-filled patches bright yellow, tens of thousands of flowers all emerging at once. What do plants do when life gets hard? Strew the world with floral beauty.

The plants at Arabia Mountain offer an extreme demonstration of a general truth. The seasons are polyrhythms. Although the seasons have their physical origins in the tilt of the revolving Earth, life has built millions of variations on this basic Newtonian beat. There are many ways to make a home in the seasons. Snorklewort and elf orpine have found one, tuned to winter rains. Ragwort and toadflax another, growing in one year and flowering the next. Porter's sunflower yet another, a burst of autumn flowering fed by summer growth. These different rhythms are created by the inner conversations that animate and modulate the timing of flowers, seeds, leaves, and roots. The seasons live inside every plant as green discourse.

COLUMBINE

ABOUT THREE OR FOUR million years ago, seeds from Asian columbine flowers somehow made it to North America. The tiny glossy black seeds might have drifted across the oceans on woody debris washed out from land. Or, perhaps, the travelers came in the gut of a bird or in the fur of a mammal. Once arrived, the seeds prospered and, eventually, their offspring founded a dynasty of some of America's most gorgeous and diverse flowers.

The columbines' success was built on their flexible relationships with the seasonal rhythms and body shapes of their pollinators. For flowers, the seasons are not just made by changing light and moisture, they are created by reciprocal relationships with animals. The freshly arrived flowers had stumbled into new animal seasons.

In Asia, bees were the partners of columbine flowers, a relationship that dates back at least seven million years and continues to the present day. In those ancient days, the ancestors of columbines evolved a key innovation: the nectar spur. They turned each of five petals into a tube leading to a drop of nectar. These spurs were ringed by another five petals that served as colored advertising banners. Bees loved it. They dipped their tongues into the spurs and drank the sweet reward. A happy bee is a loyal bee. The flowers' generosity ensured that the bees focused their attention on columbines.

To further entice the bees, ancestral columbines colored their petals blue and purple, the bees' favorite colors. They kept their nectar spurs short and curved to allow easy access by bee tongues. Next to the spurs, the flowers added bee landing platforms. The flowers came into bloom when the bees were active, especially at the height of summer. Columbine flowers became mirrors of bees. Evolution sculpted the columbines to fit the sensory preferences, body shapes, and seasonal timings of their pollinators. In reciprocity, bees and flowers thrived.

Columbine flowers found that American bees were ready to take up the work of their Asian cousins. The columbines spread out over much of the North American continent. As the plants expanded their range, they were visited by strange new pollinators, creatures entirely unlike any the plants' ancestors had encountered. These oddities hovered in front of the flowers on thrumming wings and dipped their needle-like beaks into the columbines' nectar spurs. Columbines, meet hummingbirds! Hummingbirds, found only in the Americas, offered columbines new possibilities for partnership.

Thanks to genetic variability within columbines, a few plants discovered that, although bees are nice, hummingbirds can be better. Genetic mutations in some of these plants turned columbine flowers from blue to red. Because hummingbird eyes are attracted to anything red, these new hues drew more pollinating birds. As they adapted to hummingbirds, the columbines lost their aromas, and petal landing pads for bees shrunk. The flowers also straightened and lengthened their nectar spurs to better accommodate hummingbird beaks.

In eastern North America, red columbines shifted their flowering season to match the seasonal migration of the

FIG. 31 *Aquilegia coerulea* (P. 289)

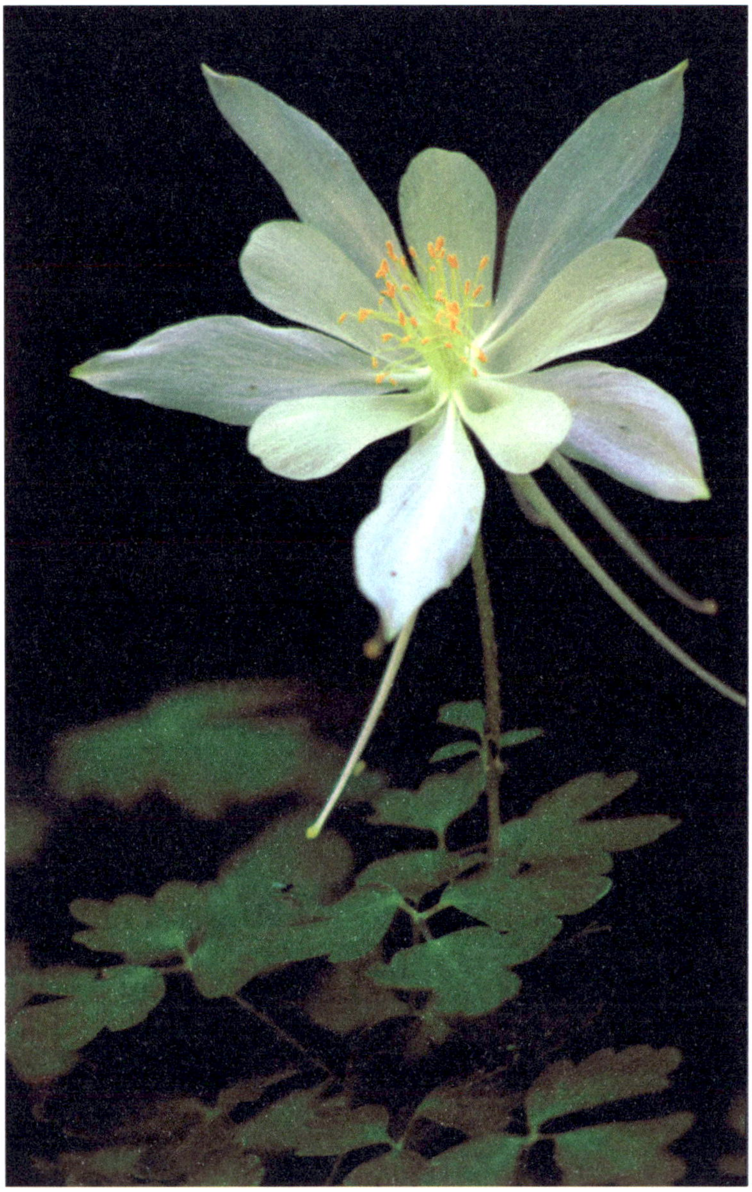

“For all our technologies and mobility, we still have a deep yearning to see and smell the blooms of home.”

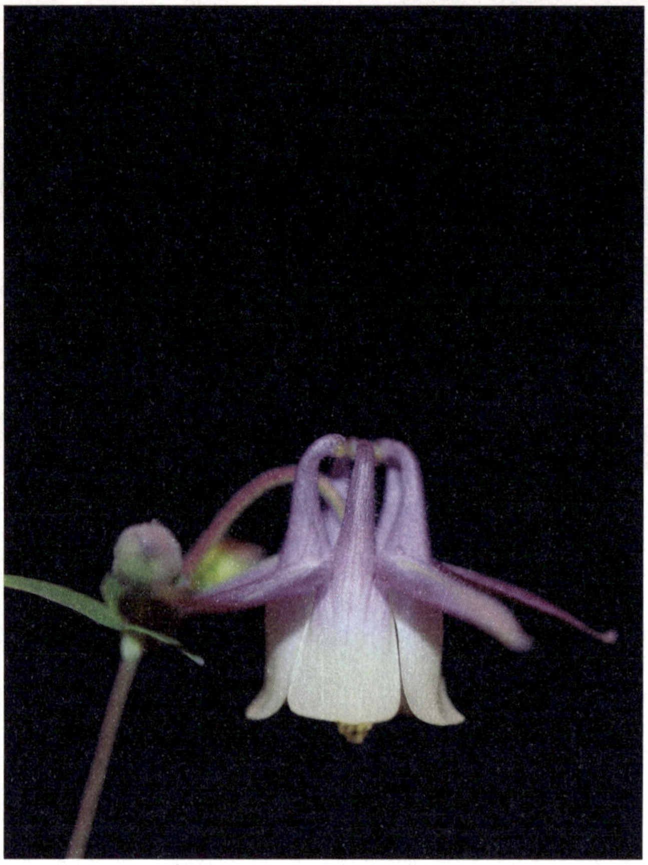

FIG. 32 *Aquilegia brevistyla* / Molly Edwards (P. 290)
FIG. 33 *Aquilegia canadensis* / Molly Edwards (P. 291)

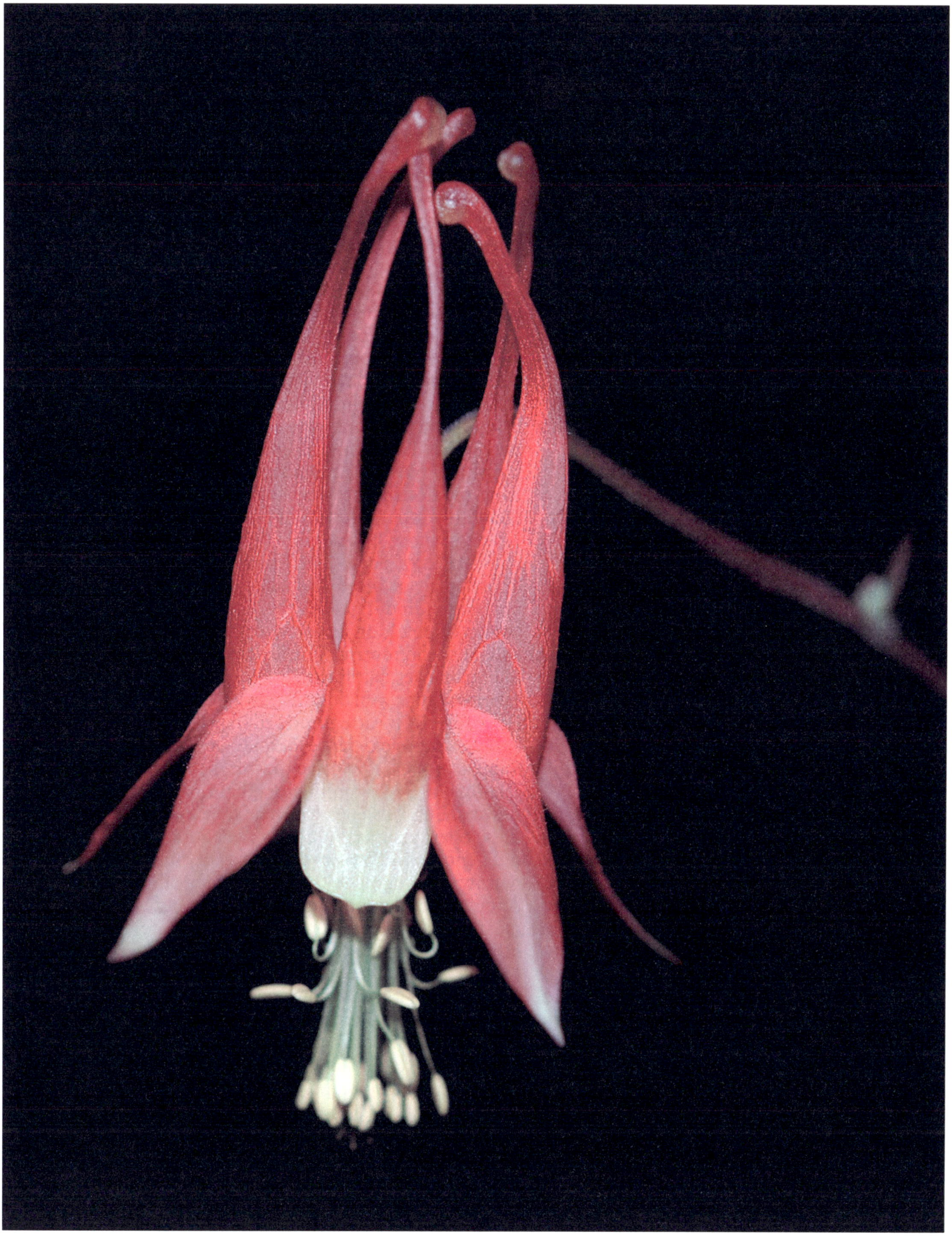

hummingbirds. In Atlanta, for example, the flowers come into bloom exactly when springtime waves of migrating ruby-throated hummingbirds pass through, the birds thrilling in sugar hits that will power their perilous northbound journeys. Farther north, where the wave of migrants is more modest and spread out, the red columbine waits to bloom until all the hummingbirds have settled on their breeding territories.

North American columbines remade themselves in the image of hummingbirds, an impressive innovation. But they were not done with genetic exploration. The longer nectar spurs of the hummingbird-pollinated columbines also attracted the attentions of hawkmoths. These large moths have proboscises many times longer than their bodies, making hummingbird beaks look puny. Another pollinator, another opportunity for evolution to get creative.

Using the hummingbird-lengthened spurs as starting points, columbines evolved even longer spurs. These eventually got so long that they now look like tresses flowing back from the blooms of species such as the golden and longspur columbines. To further encourage hawkmoths, the flowers tipped their faces toward the sky instead of hanging them down as they do for bees and hummingbirds. They also regained the floral aromas that had been useless for attracting hummingbirds. The petals changed from red to white, yellow, or sometimes blue, colors that hawkmoths love. Hawkmoths fly mostly at night and at dawn and dusk, so the flowers are nectar-filled and aromatic even at night and when the light is dim. They bloom when the hawkmoths are most active: mid-summer in the mountains and early spring in the deserts and along the coasts. Unlike other hawkmoth specialist flowers, such as some wild tobaccos, columbines do not open exclusively at night, perhaps to keep their options open with bumblebees and hummingbirds.

Hawkmoths also live in Asia and Europe, but no columbine there evolved superlong nectar spurs. Only in North America, where the hummingbirds served as an evolutionary stepping stone, did these long spurs appear. Sometimes one innovation leads to another.

Not all American columbines evolved to work with hummingbirds and hawkmoths. A few, like smallflower columbine in western Canada, stuck to the tried-and-true ancestral habit of working with bees and kept their short, often curved spurs and blue colors. A few, in one population of the Rocky Mountain columbine, have even lost their spurs. This makes the flowers less attractive to pollinators but is a good defense against excessive herbivory by deer and aphids. Today, twenty-five species and subspecies of columbines bloom all over North America, from the boreal forest, western coasts, desert southwest, to the forests of the east. Each columbine species has its own spur length and shape, color, and blooming time, matched to the preferences of pollinating and flower-eating animals.

For flowers, the seasons are made and marked by relationships with animal partners. These relationships involve timing but are also mediated by the match between the plants and their animals' bodies and senses. The genes that control the colors and shapes of flowers, then, have within them a memory or understanding of animals. The "other" is living inside, in the script of DNA. When humans get involved, these relationships can be severed or befuddled. Some cultivated varieties of columbine are mutants whose DNA causes the flowers to grow frilly stacks of petals, like Elizabethan ruffs. These cultivars often also lack nectar spurs. Pollinators find it hard to reach through the swarm of petals and, even when they do, often encounter no reward. The flowers are pleasing to human eyes, but for pollinators, many of them might as well be concrete garden gnomes. Horticulture, by attempting to improve on flowers whose existence long predates the human species, sometimes destroys the very relationships with pollinators that first built the flowers. But, gardeners can also tend and sustain these relationships. Planting or encouraging indigenous wildflowers is one way of cultivating our own belonging within the seasons of home. A few colorful gnomes are surely fine, but mostly our gardens should sustain local life, not offer empty promises.

I watch from my window in Atlanta as the first ruby-throated hummingbirds of the spring dip their beaks into red columbine blooms. The birds zip to the flowers, approaching from below. They hold themselves almost vertically and poke their beaks into the bell-like openings, finding a perfect fit between beak and the flowers' long petal spurs. I see hummingbird tongues flashing and throats pumping. The swollen tips on each petal are full of nectar. Their heads dusted with pollen, the hummingbirds move from bloom to bloom.

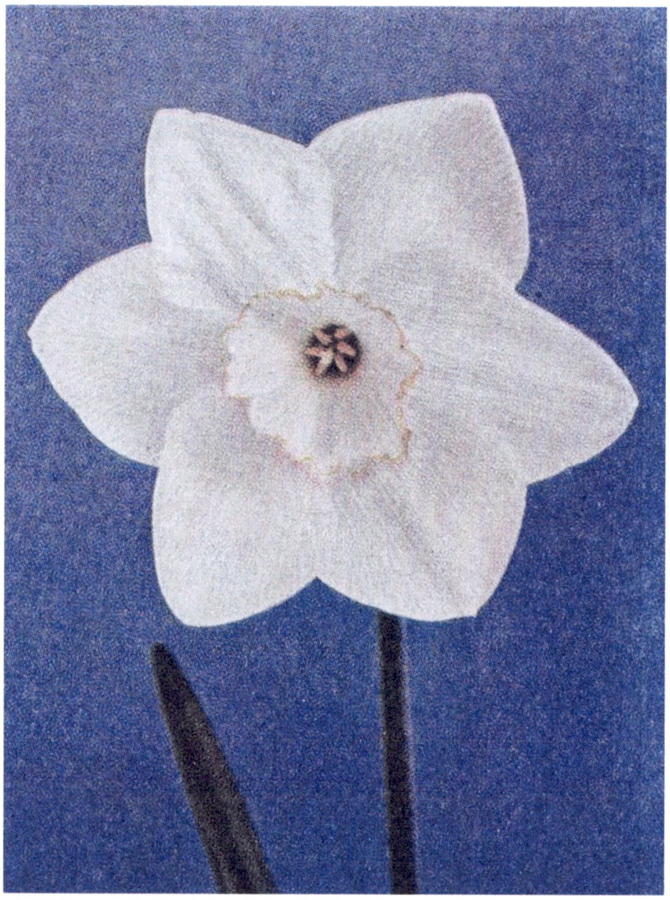
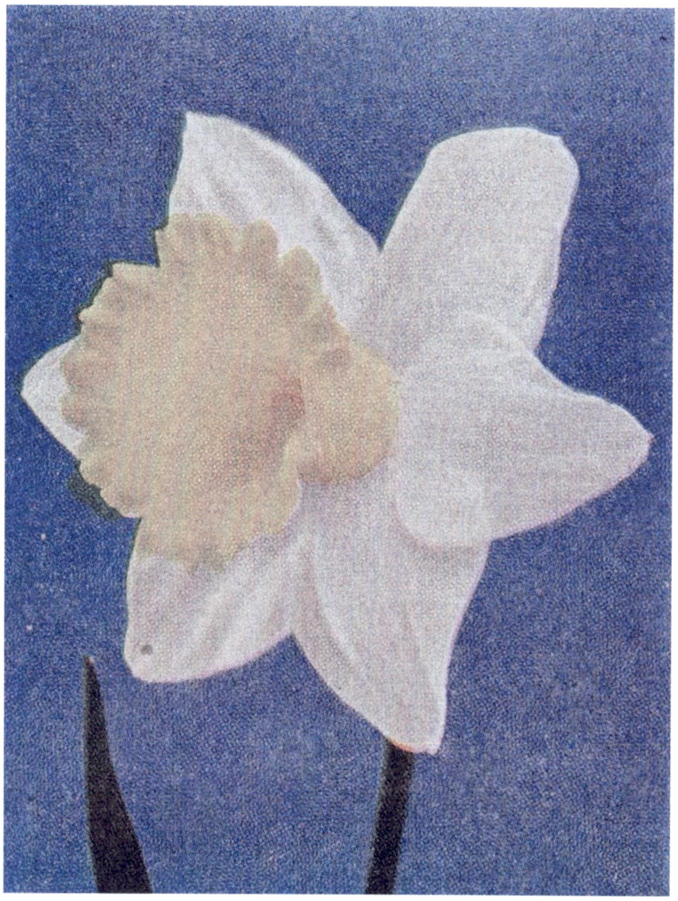
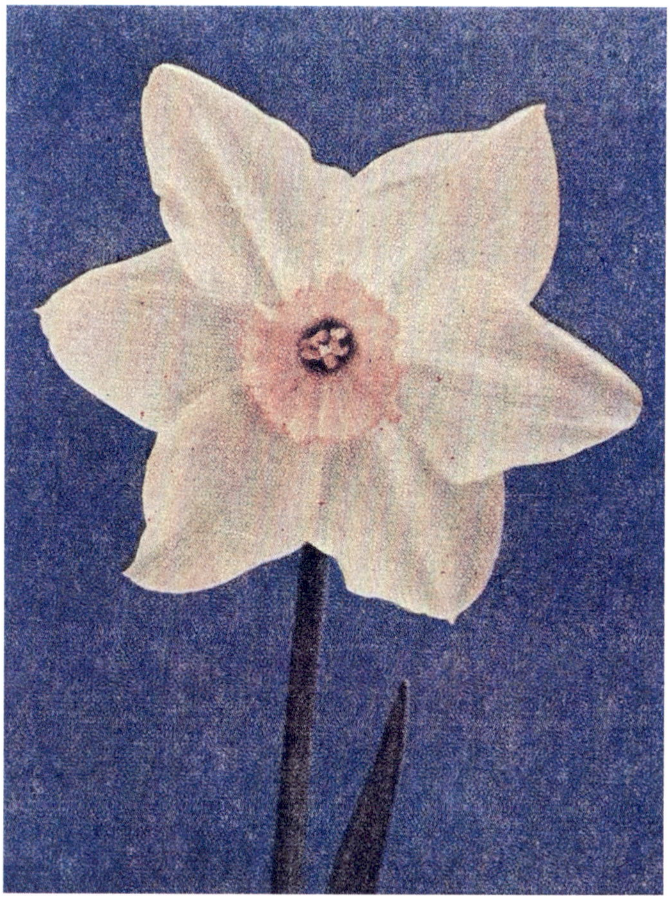
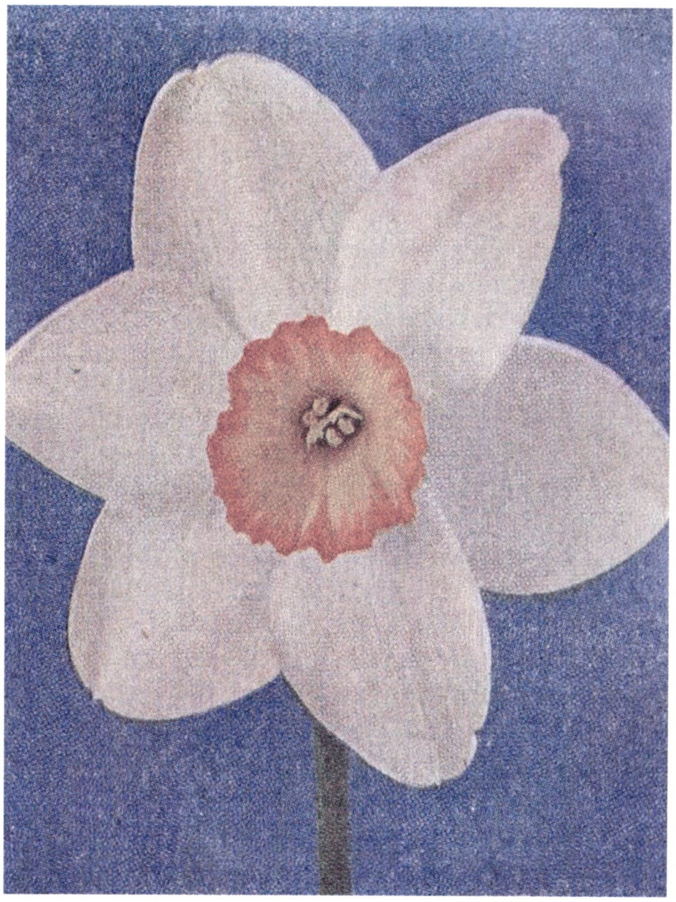

When night falls and the birds continue their migration north, they will be powered by columbine sugar, a gift from long-ago Asian immigrants who made new homes in the many seasons of the Americas. When the hummingbirds return in the autumn, their ranks swelled with the young birds hatched this summer, other flowers will emerge right as the birds pass through. Jewelweed and cardinal flower will proffer red and orange flowers and long nectar spurs, another season made from relationship.

DAFFODIL

DAFFODILS ARE SO WIDELY grown and used as symbols of springtime that they can seem caricatures of themselves. Yet, here they are, in lawns and woodland edges all over the temperate world, golden trumpeters in fussy collars, heralding the lengthening days. They have ancestral homes, growing wild in European, North African, and East Asian meadows, and they are especially diverse and abundant on the Iberian Peninsula. But, four hundred years of horticulture and colonialism have bred thousands of new varieties and carried them far beyond Europe. To their age-old connections with insect pollinators, daffodils added a new animal relationship, as signifiers of springtime in some human imaginations.

In Atlanta gardens, daffodils are among the very first blooms of the year. They daub sunny pigment over the otherwise muted color palette of early spring in yards and woodland fragments. No indigenous wildflower gives such a bold display. Harbinger-of-spring and liverleaf flowers sprout here in the New Year, but their creamy-purple blooms are tiny. Daffodils are more assertive, demanding attention. Not until Carolina jessamine vines deck themselves in yellow blooms in late spring can any indigenous flower compete for ebullience.

In North America, daffodils were among the plants brought by early European colonists. By the 1700s, vendors offered dozens of varieties for planting in gardens and meadows. This enthusiasm for plants from Europe was fed by nostalgia among settlers for the old seasonal rhythms of homes they had left behind. Individually and through the collective efforts of "acclimatization" societies, Europeans transported bulbs and seeds across the oceans to "recreate" familiar seasons. Even as they tried to remake seasons in colonized land in the botanical image of their former homes, colonists also shipped newfound green wonders back to Europe. Today, some of the oldest and largest trees in Paris and London are American—black locust and California redwood—and American goldenrod blooms all over Europe in the late summer. Botanically, colonialism is a mix of yearning for the old country and a fetish for sending exotica home. In many modern gardens, the seasons are now marked by blooms from many continents. With a global "palette" of seasonal flower rhythms to choose from, designers can create gardens where some plants are always in bloom.

European love of daffodils, now transplanted to other continents, is grounded in medicine as well as aesthetics. The fat bulbs and juicy leaves of daffodils are steeped in poison. Like many soft-tissued wildflowers with no woody defenses, daffodils deploy an impressive chemical arsenal. Over one hundred different alkaloids have been found by scientists in daffodil flesh, and most of these chemicals can sicken animals. As an added precaution, daffodils lace their leaves and bulbs with spiky crystals of oxalate. Bite into daffodil and you get a mouthful of poison and needles. In low doses, though, poisons can be healing. From antiquity, daffodil extracts have treated tumors and nervous system disorders, and one alkaloid extract is used in a modern drug to treat dementia.

Once arrived in the Americas, the daffodil found itself well prepared. A plant that can fend off the abundant and diverse voles and other tunneling rodents of Europe can thrive in American woodlands. Even hungry deer leave the foliage alone. Daffodils' persistence is evident not only in manicured landscapes, but also in less intensively managed places like woodlands. In eastern North America, haloes of daffodils growing in the middle of the woods reveal the sites of long-decayed homesteads abandoned a century or more ago. Nothing obvious remains except daffodils and perhaps some yucca, with forest regrowing all around. Planted by human hands into cultivated soil, these plants now persist and spread on their own. Botanists call them "naturalized," but the human desire to see the flowers of our homelands, however misguided and founded on colonialism, is surely also natural, part of our own wild nature. Indeed, the desire reveals that,

FIG. 34 Daffodil varieties from a 1946 catalogue clockwise from top left: 1 Hera, 2 Silvanite, 3 Alcida, 4 Yellow Poppy (P. 295)
FIG. 35 Mrs. Nette O'Melveny (P. 297)

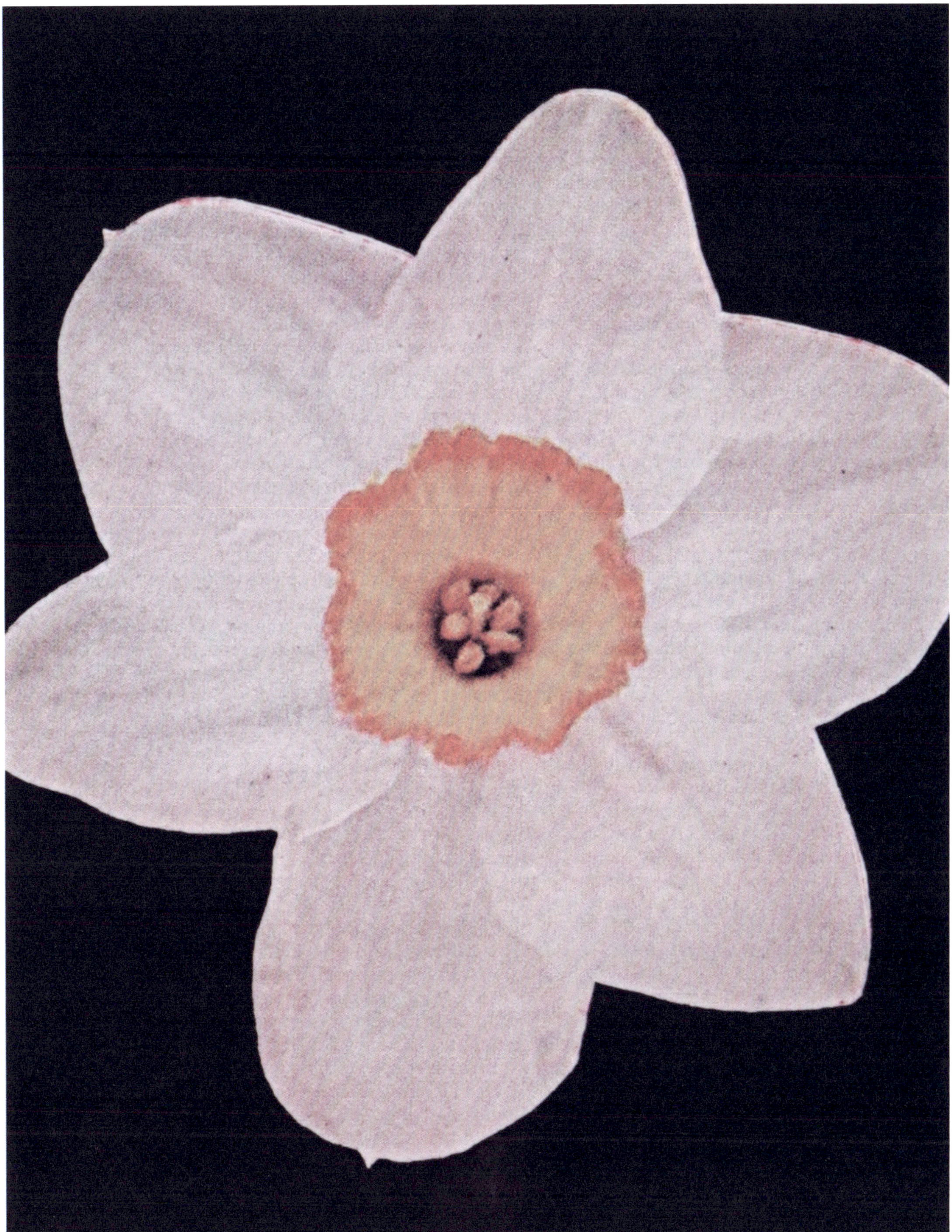

WILDFLOWER BEAUTY

for all our technologies and mobility, we still have a deep yearning to see and smell the blooms of home.

As is true for so many transcontinental transplants, daffodils are out of synch with local ecological rhythms. Their pigmented horns blare but summon few pollinators. In Atlanta, I see a scant few queen bumblebees, newly emerged from their winter dens, clamber into daffodil blooms. Eurasian honeybees, too, will sometimes ferry daffodil pollen. But daffodils lack the hum of miner and other bees that gather around indigenous blooms like spring beauty flowers and blueberries. Unlike columbines, these newly arrived flowers have yet to co-evolve with local animals and find their place.

As humans moved them around the world, daffodils took on new symbolic roles. The Daffodil Project, based in Atlanta, aims to plant 1.5 million daffodils worldwide, one for every child murdered by Nazis and their collaborators. The yellow, starlike faces of the flowers echo the color and form of the badges that Nazis forced Jews to wear. Now, blooming flowers reclaim the hateful symbol and turn it into an expression of remembrance and hope for the future.

In other places, daffodils are intertwined with the colonization of human imagination. Jamaica Kincaid recounts being forced, as a child in school in Antigua, to learn Wordsworth's *I Wandered Lonely as a Cloud*, a poem that features a "host of golden daffodils." She was repulsed by the poem's disconnection from her home, where daffodils do not grow. The "fluttering and dancing" daffodils represented the "tyrannical order of a people, the British people, in my child's life." The curriculum forced British ideas of floral seasons onto the imaginations of children in colonized lands. In the name of canonical literature, daffodils became tools to ignore or denigrate local seasons, plants, and people.

Kincaid later flipped the narrative, refusing to let colonial curricula define for her either springtime or her relationship to poetry. She engaged with daffodils and Wordsworth on her own terms, planting ten thousand daffodil bulbs in her garden in Vermont. "Sometimes," she told Hayoung E. Ahn in an interview for *The Harvard Crimson*, "I have friends come over and we have a daffodil party, and we recite Wordsworth and drink champagne."

As we move flowers around the world, we reshape not only the colors of seasonal blooms, but the very idea of springtime. Inherent in this process is power over human imagination. Who gets to choose which springtime blooms are quintessential? In colonized lands, how do we respond to the cultural and ecological narratives of the seasons that we inherit?

Kincaid's champagne toast restores her agency, refuses to blame the plants or Wordsworth, yet grows from a full acknowledgment that colonial literature and horticulture can unroot us from home. As was true in Antigua, daffodils never grew in Vermont until immigrants imported their bulbs. Her work also, I think, offers questions and invitations. How do we celebrate the cycles of the seasons when our homes and cultures are complex and often troubled weaves of immigrant and indigenous? How do seasonal blooms orient us toward or away from home? What stories of seasonality and floral belonging are we offering to others, especially young people seeking their way? A meadow of questions blooms every spring.

When I ask my North American students to name a local spring wildflower, most tell me *daffodil*. In the Anthropocene, it's not just the seasons that are changing, but what we imagine the seasons to be. To notice and celebrate flowers, and to seek out their stories, to toast them, is to reorient ourselves to the seasons in all their beauty and brokenness.

SPRING BEAUTY

FROM A DISTANCE, the flowers look like the aftermath of a late spring snow squall, thousands of big snowflakes strewn across the leaf litter of the forest. Seen close up, each bloom is a porcelain teacup glazed with pink piping. These are the flowers of *Claytonia caroliniana*, a spring wildflower so extravagantly gorgeous that its common name is spring beauty. The flowers are not just pretty, but generous. They are fonts of nectar at a time when many other wildflowers in the forests of eastern North America—liverleaf, rue anemone, bloodroot—offer only meager pollen and no sugar. On a warm day, pollinators swarm spring beauty flowers.

A springtime ritual of mine is to lie down next to a patch of spring beauty flowers and peer at them through my hand lens. The first thing I notice is the white gloss of the petals, almost silvery when seen close up. This polished ivory is striped with pink from the top to the bottom of each petal. Any insect winging past sees radiating pink lines. Bees and other pollinators have good memories, recalling for weeks the appearance and aromas of rewarding flowers, so they know what nectar riches lie at the confluence of these guidelines.

As I watch, most of the visitors to spring beauty flowers are small black bees with a fuzz of white hair on their faces, thorax, and legs. These are all members of a single species, the spring beauty miner bee. The bees move frenetically but systematically in the flowers, circling inside the bowl of petals to sup at nectar. Many of them also paw at the pollen-producing anthers that sprout from the center of each flower, swiping the pollen onto their hind legs. Spring beauty pollen is pink, so after visiting a few flowers, the ebony and silver bees are thoroughly dusted in pink, often with large pink pollen balls on each hind leg. Magnified in my lens, the effect is like a carnival or birthday party, pink confetti feting the arrival of spring.

For these bees, the pollen party is the source of life. This bee species feeds entirely on spring beauty flowers. The bees time their emergence from underground tunnels to coincide with the bloom. The adult bees feast on spring beauty nectar and pollen. Female bees dig tunnels in sandy soil and provision egg chambers with nectar-sweetened pollen balls. They lay their eggs inside the tunnels, then female and male adults die as the spring beauty flowers fade. The young hatch later in the year, eat the entombed spring beauty pollen, then pupate and wait until spring. The aboveground life of the bees amounts to a month each year, at most. All their food comes from spring beauty flowers.

Other pollinators also feast at the spring beauties but have more diverse tastes. Bee flies, bee-mimicking flies that look like flying feather dusters, in particular, love to dip their pole-like proboscises into the flowers. They, too, get dusted in pink, although their long, inflexible proboscis means that the dusting is slight compared to the bees. Bee flies feed on many other flowers, so their fate is not tied to just a single plant species. But, like the bees, they have a narrow window to complete their lifecycles. They rely on the springtime burst of wildflowers to get nectar and pollen to fuel their mating and egg-laying. Female bee flies lay their eggs in the nests of other pollinators, spring-flying bees and wasps. Once hatched, the young flies are horrible guests and eat the hosts' young. This parasitic breeding method only works if the bee flies are synchronized with the seasonal cycles of their victims.

Ants take over when the bees and bee flies are done and the spring beauty flowers mature to fruits. A tiny fatty attachment on every spring beauty seed attracts the attentions of ever-hungry ants. Lofting the seed in their mandibles, the ants carry it back to their nest. There, they slice off the juicy lure and carry the unwounded seed to their colony's compost heap. That soft duff is a perfect place to germinate. In this way, the seeds of many wildflowers are carried away from their parents and are sown in nutritious soil. Other seeds are eaten by deer who, by passing seeds intact in their droppings, carry them much farther than do the ants.

Like columbines, the spring beauty's seasons are partly made from relationships with animals. Trees, though, lay down the fundamental seasonal beat. For most of the year, it is gloomy on the forest floor. As soon as the tree leaves unfurl in late spring, the ground below falls into deep shade. Only in early spring, around the equinox and just after, do the plants on the forest floor get enough light to feast. In this narrow time window, the sun is high and strong but the tree leaves are not yet out. Light intensity on the forest floor in springtime can be ten or more times what it is for the rest of the year.

Spring beauties have learned, through natural selection, how to time their emergence to fit their relationships with trees and pollinators. In just a few springtime weeks, they flower then grow their fruit and seeds. They also stuff as much food as they can into corms, swollen underground stems. These provisions will keep the plants going through the long lean months of summer, autumn, and winter. Spring beauties then drop their leaves as summer arrives, waiting underground for the arrival of the next year's spring. Other species in the eastern forests do the same. A few, like trillium and liverleaf, keep their leaves through the summer, feeding on the occasional burst of sunshine when a sunfleck hits them, but others, like harbinger-of-spring and rue anemone, are aboveground for just a few weeks. We call them "ephemeral wildflowers," although their underground stems and roots may be as old as the trees around them.

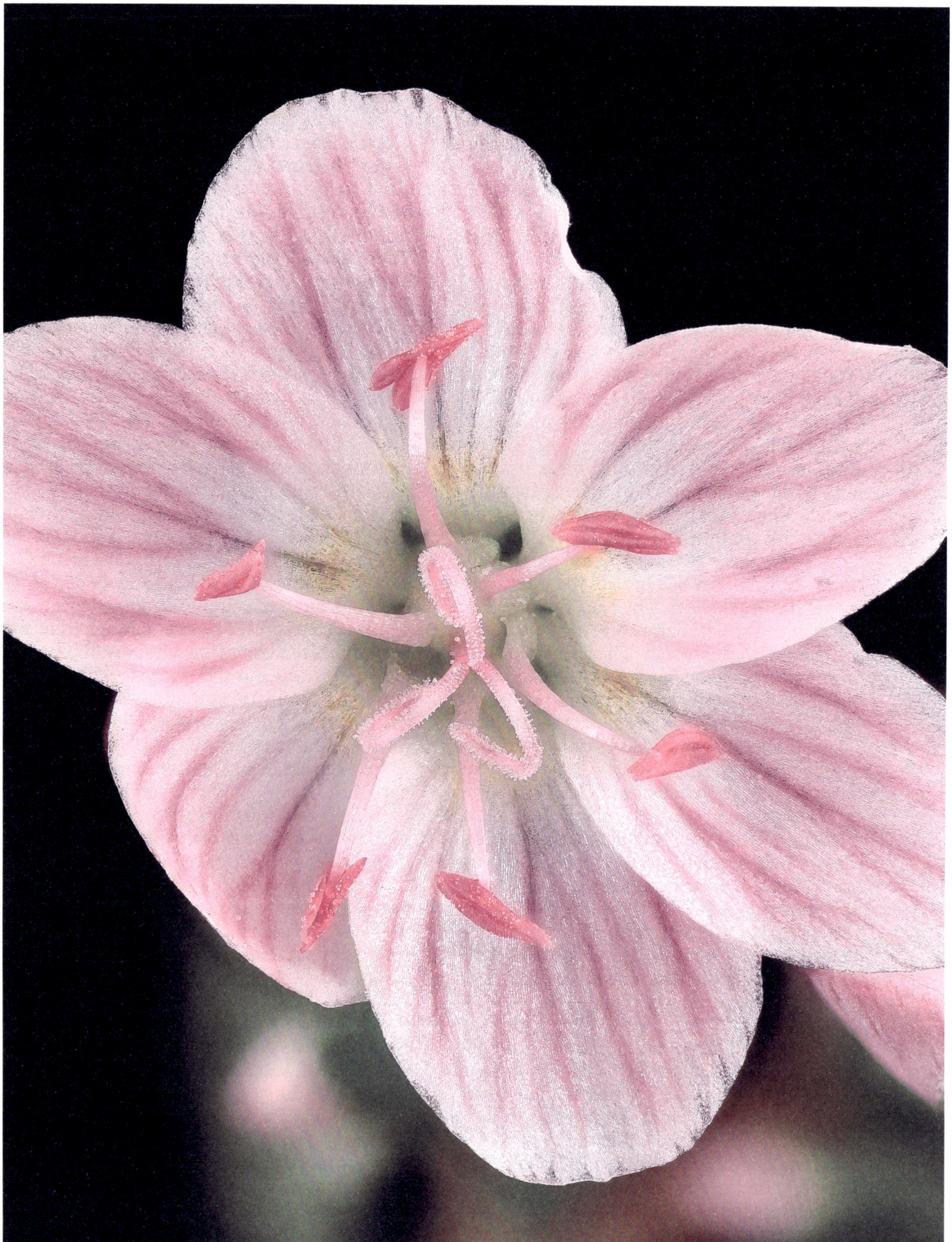

FIG. 36 *Claytonia virginica* / Helen Lowe Metzman (P. 300)
FIG. 37 *Claytonia umbellata* / Thomas Stoughton (P. 301)

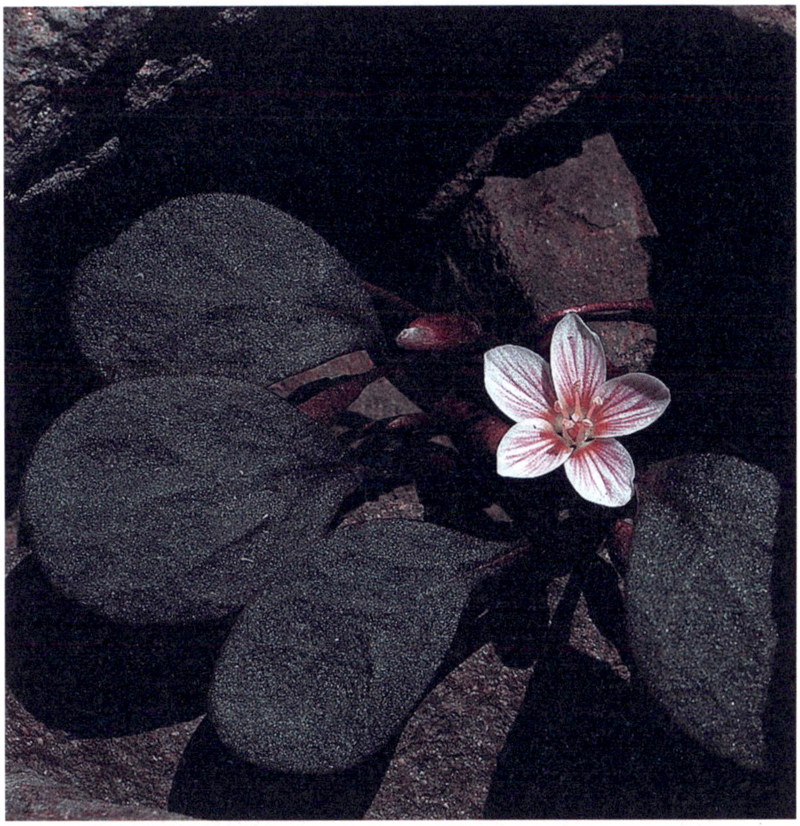

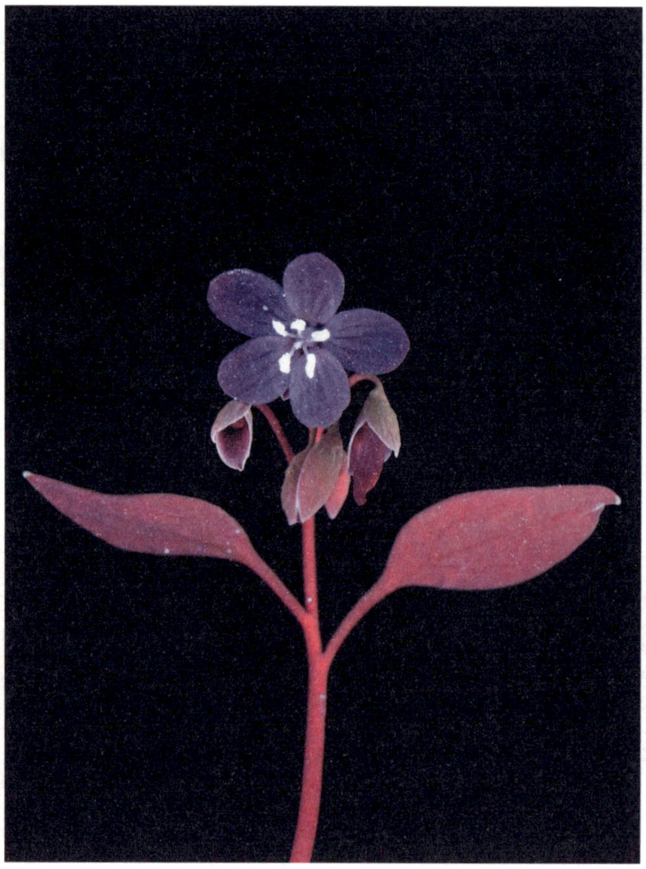

FIG. 38 *Claytonia caroliniana* / Byron Meade (P. 302)
FIG. 39 *Claytonia virginica* / Charley Eiseman (P. 305)

These seasonal rhythms are now getting desynchronized by climate chaos. Trees are leafing out weeks earlier than they did a century ago, especially beech and red maple trees. The trend toward earlier tree leaf-out dates has accelerated in the last thirty years. These changes partly close the precious window of sunlight for spring wildflowers. Because shade arrives early, the wildflowers get hungrier, meaning that they grow more slowly, invest less in seeds, and struggle to store up food for the rest of the year. At its most extreme, earlier tree shade can nearly halve light-feeding opportunities for wildflowers on the forest floor.

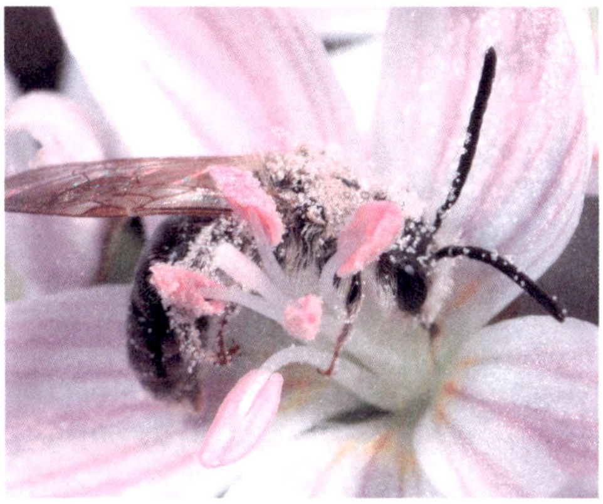

Wildflowers are sliding their emergence dates earlier, too, but not as fast as the trees. Snow cover and cold constrain them. Only when the soil warms enough can the wildflowers grow. The divergence between trees and spring wildflowers seems to be expanding, but only in some regions. In the southeast of the United States, trees are surging into springtime and wildflowers are lagging. In the colder north, the trees are also edging earlier, but at half the rate of warmer regions. In Asia and Europe, spring wildflowers are keeping pace and even outstripping trees in their shift to earlier emergence. If these trends continue, the season of woodland wildflowers will shrink in parts of North America but expand in Asia and Europe.

In many areas, bees and other pollinators are, so far, keeping up with the shifting seasonality of spring wildflowers. Because most of these pollinators overwinter in the soil, they experience similar temperatures as wildflower roots and buried buds. For both insects and wildflowers, soil temperature is a major trigger for spring emergence, whereas for trees air temperature, especially daytime temperature, is more important. In most years, pollinators and wildflowers stay in synchrony. But, very early warm spells or early snowmelt can cause flowers to open long before pollinators emerge, leaving bees and other insects with scant food for the next generation. In the future, mismatch between the timing of pollinator and wildflower emergence may become a more severe problem.

These interlocking rhythms of wildflowers, trees, and insects are mediated by genetic pacemakers in each species. Evolution has scrawled wisdom about the best time to emerge into the script of genes that shape the physiology of cells. Fortunately, genes evolve. New synchronies can develop. At the end of the last Ice Age, for example, most of the trees and wildflowers that now live all over eastern North America lived piled together in refugia in the Deep South, away from glaciers and chilly weather. In the last ten thousand years, they have spread across the continent, interconnecting their seasonalities as they move.

But genetic nimbleness is not guaranteed. Evolution works best when populations are large and freely mixing, giving natural selection plenty of raw material and scope for experimentation. Today, most spring wildflowers and their pollinators live in disconnected small populations, assailed by habitat loss. Even when forests persist or have regrown, their soil is often impoverished, as are their wildflower and pollinator populations. Introduced species get in the way of adaptability as plants from other continents smother the growth of indigenous wildflower species and fire ants eat seeds without dispersing them. Herbicides and pesticides are so widely used that they come down in the rain and blow in dust from fields, weakening plants and insects. In imposing these changes, we suppress the creative potential of the living Earth, making it harder for the inherent flexibility of evolution to express itself.

Yet, the carnival goes on. Not just in woodlands, but even in wilder, unsprayed lawns, spring beauties and their pollinators continue the celebratory feast of sugars and sex. Witnessing this springtime exuberance teaches us to give space to others—to use fewer poisons, to find better ways of living in relation to forests and other habitats, to burn less fossil fuel—so that the seasonal rhythms can not only continue but find their new pulses.

I lie down and peer through my hand lens not just to see a colorful spring party, but to taste the nectar of reality. Pink-dusted bees ply generous wildflowers. Here is part of the antidote to algorithm-shaped lies. Celebrating wildflowers is not an anesthetic—attentiveness reveals loss as well as beauty—but a grounding in the world as it is. Because flowers so entrance our senses, they offer memorable lessons, reorienting us back to the living Earth.

What will we tell future generations about our time? Imagine telling our descendants, students, and neighbors about our experiences of wildflowers. How the blooms opened. How we felt and acted as we witnessed the bloom. What the bees did. This will be worth knowing. To have something true to tell the future, let's pay attention to flowers today.

LATE SUMMER THEN BLINK AND IT'S FALL

—for Callie, moving out at fourteen

I gathered the flowers
that leaned over
our walkway

like some drowsy
headstrong child.
I thought I would build

a bouquet
to grace
our kitchen table.

But then I saw a nest
those two wrens wove
this spring

sagging off a branch
in the cedar. Empty
now. Already

I have changed
my mind.
I gave them away.

Every bloom.
Every flower.

An Interview with Robin Wall Kimmerer PRACTICAL REVERENCE

Interviewed by
Emmanuel Vaughan-Lee

EVL Robin, it's such a pleasure to be in conversation with you today. Welcome.

RWK Thanks for inviting me.

EVL I've just finished your new book, *The Serviceberry*, which grew from an essay you wrote for *Emergence* in 2020 by the same name. It was the most read essay we've ever published, which I think points to the chord it struck with people. This new book expands on the essay and is not only a wonderful celebration of the generosity of the land but a really powerful manifesto on abundance and reciprocity as models for a new economy that operates in right relationship with the Earth. But before delving deeper into that, I wondered if you could introduce us to the book's namesake, the serviceberry. Who is this plant and what kind of relationships do we have with it?

RWK I'd love to start there. The serviceberry is a plant with so many different names: juneberry, saskatoon, sarvis, shadblow, shadflower. It has so many names because it has so many relationships. And if you were to meet a serviceberry, that would likely be along a wood's edge, near water. It's a small tree, a little bit shrubby in nature, and in a way quite unremarkable looking: just oval leaves, smooth gray bark. You might just walk by it without thinking too much about it, unless it was springtime, in which case there's just this explosion of bloom before anything else in the woods is in flower. So some of its relationships are associated with those early spring pollinators.

In July or June, depending on where you live, there are these heavy clusters of delicious berries that hang from the branches. And then it surely draws your attention. And even then, if you missed it, the cedar waxwings and the robins would let you know, because they're just calling and chattering and saying, *Berries, berries, berries. Everybody, come feast.* So your attention would be drawn when it's in fruit.

EVL In the book, you share that in the Potawatomi language, the word for serviceberry is a revelation, because it is also the root word for "gift."

RWK Yes. That little word *min* means "berry" in my language, but it is also the root word around "gift-giving," and "a gift." And I love the poetry of that, because, of course, berries feel like a gift, don't they? There they are, just presenting themselves, hanging there all red and blue and sweet and juicy. We didn't earn them. We don't deserve them. We don't own them. And yet there they are, like an offering from the tree. And so, I love that that's present in our language as well.

EVL Berry picking is a hugely seasonal act, and it is for many a ritual of the warmer months that embodies the gift of summer. Across your work, and particularly in *The Serviceberry*, you write about how the summer proliferation of berries and flowers, fruit and vegetables, leads us to characterize this season as one of deep abundance, of plentifulness—although abundance can be found and felt across all seasons in different ways. And in *The Serviceberry*, you reorient us to look at this seasonal abundance differently, introducing us to how it can be pivotal in reimagining an economy that is currently based on scarcity. I wonder if you could speak to this.

RWK You know—back to the language—our word for summer, *niben*, means the time of plenty, it means the time of abundance. And I think about the abundance being provided by the plants, not only in berries, but in medicines for us, in materials for us, basket plants—all the kinds of things that the plants create in abundance for us, if we know them, if we know their gifts, if we are paying attention to them. And I like what you said, that it's not just in the summertime: even in deep mid-winter, the plants are offering us medicines and teachings and materials.

EVL In the book, you point towards a need to shift our ideas about consumption, to learn to see that most of the time we already have what we need. And you write that recognizing *enoughness* is a radical act in an economy that is always urging us to consume more.

RWK Yeah, for sure. You know, think of all the messages that we get relentlessly from media, from advertising, saying: *Well, you know, if you only bought this, then you'd be happy. You need to consume this.* In fact, our very measure of a successful economy is one that is always growing, which means always consuming more. Right? Whereas the notion of enoughness— Doesn't it just make you feel content to think of enoughness? To say: *I have what I need. I have everything that I need provided for me by the land.* And to me, that just awakens gratitude and a sense of sharing: to say, I have enough. And so that means if I have enough, the rest, the surplus, can be shared. And that notion of enoughness as a radical act really can put the brakes on consumption. And we know that it is hyper-consumption that has us poised at the brink of climate catastrophe, right? And so it's not only a radical act in an economy, it's a real act of healing for the land and for people, as well, to say: *I have enough. I don't need to take any more.* Which then liberates that abundance for others so that they can flourish too.

EVL Well, what you're talking about is radical, particularly in the framework of the capitalist economy that we operate in. It also isn't, in many ways, because this way of living in accordance with abundance and an ethic of sharing has been around for millennia practiced by cultures that live in close relationship with the land the world over. And in both *The Serviceberry* and *Braiding Sweetgrass* you talk about a canon of principles that govern this practice in many Indigenous cultures, including your own, called the Honorable Harvest. Could you talk about this?

RWK Thank you for recognizing that this isn't new and radical. These are in fact the fundamental principles of how one lives sustainably in place, which we have forgotten, which we have been made to forget by an economy that doesn't want us to have enough, that always wants us to consume more. And in order to talk about the Honorable Harvest, what I also have to talk about is that the stuff that the Western extractive economy wants us to consume is understood as material. It's just stuff, right? It's objects. And so if we're just consuming objects, and if those objects belong to us, if they're our property, we don't really need any ethical guidelines about consumption, because it's just stuff.

But an Indigenous worldview sees those plants, those

“What is the gift that I could give you in return for water or berries or birdsong?”

animals, Mother Earth, as our relatives, as our kinfolk—now we’re talking about eating our relatives in order to live, right? They’re not “natural resources,” but our relatives, our kinfolk, who are giving us gifts. And so that creates both a pragmatic and an ethical imperative to have guidelines that regulate how we consume, and those guidelines are what are known collectively as the Honorable Harvest. They were taught to me in picking berries and digging medicine roots, et cetera, sort of piece by piece. We’re always taught responsibility before we’re taught the taking. Right? And the Honorable Harvest begins with the fact that we never take the first one; whether it’s berries or firewood or basket plants, you never take the first one. And this self-restraint means that you’re never going to take the last one, so it has an inherent conservation ethic.

And, you know, different cultures have different ways of thinking about it, but sometimes the rule is you don’t harvest until you see four, or you see seven, or you see ten—whatever your family’s guidelines might be. And then, you never take more than half, because you always have to leave some for the thriving of the plant, but also for the other beings who want and need berries or medicines too.

When we see the fourth one, let’s say, we also ask permission of that plant. I will quite literally introduce myself. In fact, I was just doing this the other day, harvesting some mosses for my upcoming Ecology of Mosses class, and I had to talk to those mosses and ask them: Would you come into my lab and teach my students? Is that okay? And that step of asking permission recognizes their sovereignty. It recognizes that the plants don’t belong to us; they belong to themselves. And so if we’re going to ask permission, we have to listen for the answer as well. And there are a lot of ways to do that. We can use Western science to do that and look at the demographics of the population. Look at its health, look at its vigor, look at the soil quality. Is it thriving? And if it is, you say, well, yeah, I think they have enough to spare. But if it’s weak, if it’s chlorotic, if there aren’t any young ones, you would say, no, I can’t harvest here because this population doesn’t have enough to give.

But if it does, then as I said, you take only half, and less than; you take only what you need. And you take it in such a way that you do as little harm as possible. Don’t disturb the whole place in order to get what you need. There’s a long protocol for picking berries, for taking from the Earth, as opposed to the Western mode of going in and just grabbing what you need. When you harvest, you take only what you need and give thanks. You stop and pay gratitude to those plants, because, after all, they’ve just given you their bodies, in some cases it’s their offspring you’re taking home in your basket. And so you really pay gratitude, not just with a sort of flippant “thank you,” but with a real recognition that your life is inextricably tied to theirs. A deep kind of gratitude.

And then, I’m told that we never go home with our basket without reciprocating the gift, giving back to those plants. We’ve taken something; they’ve given us something. So how will we pay them back? Sometimes it’s with a spiritual gift. In fact, it’s always with a spiritual gift, but also a material gift. Maybe they need a little more sun. Maybe you should weed around them. Maybe you should sprinkle some fertilizer there if they’re looking like they need it. So you need to know the plants; you need to know what they want and to help them out. And then, you have done right by the plants. It is an Honorable Harvest because you have been given what you need, you haven’t done serious damage, and, in fact, some of the ways that we’re taught to harvest actually help the plants to multiply. If that reciprocated gift is carrying some of these roots to another place where that plant could flourish, well then, I’ve just used my gift of mobility to complement the gift of the plant making medicine. So oftentimes the ways that we harvest actually multiply abundance.

EVL You’ve previously written that this knowledge has continued forward in stories, and that these stories help us to restore balance and locate us once again in the circle. Can you speak a bit about this circle?

RWK The circle that I’m referring to is a circle of mutual flourishing with our kinfolk. These stories remind us that the Earth doesn’t belong to us, that we are blessed to receive the gifts of the Earth, and that we have to give our gifts back in return. That's the circle, right? It's a circle of giving and receiving that recognizes that everybody in the circle has a gift. And it's our responsibility to use whatever our gift is to support the flourishing of our kinfolk: leafy ones, the feathered ones, the furred ones.

EVL Throughout *The Serviceberry* you refer to a way of thinking that understands the currency of the gift economy to be relationship, which you express perhaps most directly in the line, "I store my meat in the belly of my brother." And I love this line. Could you talk about this?

RWK It is the heart of the book and of the essay, isn't it?

EVL Yeah.

RWK It comes from the explorations of a linguist who was working in Amazonia with Native peoples there. And in his reports, he tells this story of how a hunter and his family were really successful on a hunt, and they brought back some big game. And as they were preparing it, the anthropologist and the linguist who were observing said: Well, what will you do with the surplus? How will you store it? Because clearly it was way more meat than the family could consume. And the hunter said, "Store my meat?" He didn't quite understand it. And the interviewer said, "Well, you know, dry it or smoke it, or put it away for a time when you need it." And the hunter said, "I store my meat in the belly of my brother," meaning he had a surplus, he had an abundance of food, and so he was holding a feast. And in the village, all his family and friends and neighbors were all invited to come partake of that feast. So the storage of that meat was in good relationships, in the feasting, in the storytelling, in the singing that accompanied his sharing of the gift of the forest with the people.

And this notion—"I store my surplus in the belly of my brother"—means, of course, that you're creating relationships of reciprocity and that those reciprocal relations will manifest themselves in food security down the line. Because abundance isn't guaranteed, right? There are going to be scarce times too. And in those scarce times, you then have the sense that the people who came to your feast will share with you. When they have a big net full of fish, you're going to be invited to their feast. And so, the food security comes from good relationships with your neighbors and a trust that abundance will always be shared.

EVL You write about how our current economic model is rooted in projects of colonization, and how the dispossession of Indigenous people was designed to eradicate the notion of land as a source of belonging and to replace it with the idea that land is nothing more than a source of belongings, which you pointed to a little bit earlier. And that this, in turn, narrowed the definition of well-being from commonwealth to individual wealth, and from abundance to scarcity, which really gets to the heart of the crises that we're experiencing.

RWK: You know, the idea that the land is a gift that we harvest honorably and that we hold land in common, not as individuals, runs completely counter to the Western notion of property law and prosperity, where the gifts of the land go to make individuals prosperous and wealthy as opposed to the whole community. That land should be held in common, held as sacred, was a very dangerous notion to the colonizers, particularly those who came to North America expressly for land. That's what they wanted.

And so when we look at the projects of violent assimilation—through the boarding schools, for example, and other tools of cultural erasure—much of that, including the attempted erasure of our language, was in large part to replace, in this imperialistic way, the notion of common land with the notion of private land and private property. This enables the commoditization of land, the commoditization of forests and water and wildlife, so that the benefits all accrue to individuals. And now, of course, corporations are viewed as persons. So we're basically talking

about the replacement of the Indigenous view of commonwealth with the notion of private wealth.

EVL You talk about how the equations we use to measure economic value like GDP only account for that which can be bought and sold. And there is a great line in the book that speaks to this: "There is no room in these equations for the economic value of clean air and carbon sequestration and the ineffable riches of a forest filled with birdsong. Where is the value of a butterfly whose species has prospered for millennia and lives nowhere else on the planet? There is no formula complex enough to hold the birthplace of stories." I was very moved by that line, and especially the last sentence: "There is no formula complex enough to hold the birthplace of stories."

RWK You know, economists, particularly ecological economists, are trying to quantify the values of clean water, air quality, forests, et cetera, through this language of ecosystem services. And the idea is that if you could put a monetary value on ecosystem services, then you could factor them into that equation. There's absolutely merit in that way of thinking. But the problem is that when we try to put economic valuation on birdsong and water, it converts the gift to a commodity.

EVL Right.

RWK Monetizing it takes away from its inherent value. It says that the value is in the dollars associated with it, not its intrinsic, indeed sacred, nature. And so there's quite a bit of resistance, on philosophical grounds, to valuation of ecosystem services. But it's also true that it's an attempt to put those things back in the equation.

EVL I want to talk a little bit more about the notion of gift, which we've touched on already, because this model of harvesting only what you need to live is really an example of a gift economy. And I wonder if you can talk a bit about the sorts of ethical constraints a gift economy encourages around the accumulation and distribution of things.

RWK So the ethical constraint around not converting a gift to a commodity, to me, is best exemplified in thinking about water. You know, maybe when you turn your faucet on you just think it's this fluid that's coming to you from public works. But if you focus on really understanding what's coming out of your faucet, that beautiful water, finite in quantity—we will never have any more than we do today—that falls freely from the sky and waters our gardens and makes food grow and makes flowers bloom. This water that can be dew, it can be clouds, it can be snow; this long traveling molecule that animates life all over the planet, without which life simply would not exist. Oh, now you start looking at water and saying, it's a lot more than this clear substance flowing out of my faucet. It's not an object anymore. It is a gift. And when you think about this gift of water—it belongs to all of us. The rain falls on all our heads, right? So why does a corporation have the right to say, I am going to take this freely distributed gift and filter it and put it into plastic bottles and sell it at a price that's higher than gasoline? That they will make all kinds of money over a freely given gift seems an ethical travesty. And, of course, think of all the environmental damage that is done by privatization of water, in single-use plastics, et cetera. But to me, the real crux is that water should be a public good, a common good, and not privatized. So that's just one example of the ethical jeopardy of privatizing a freely given gift.

EVL You write that "to name the world as gift is to feel your membership in the web of reciprocity," which really challenges what you just described as the way we currently perceive water, for example.

RWK Yeah, exactly.

EVL You look at the serviceberry plant itself as a model of gift exchange, how it participates in hundreds of gift exchanges before you even put a berry in your mouth. The plant is accepting things from different parts of the ecosystem so that it can grow, and giving many other parts of the ecosystem what they need in return. And you speak about how this is a big part of the gift economy ethos, keeping the gift in motion so that it does not stagnate.

RWK Yeah. When we look at the economy, if you will, of the serviceberry, it's a circular economy. It's an economy in which the production of that wonderful plant is in circulation. It's not hoarded. It's given away when the pollen on those beautiful, frothy white flowers in the springtime feed those early season bees, right? It's given away. When we think about the foliage, those beautiful solar panels of leaves that are fueling the growth of that tree, that are the sole food for certain kinds of caterpillars—that production is being given away, as it were, released to those caterpillars. When it comes time for the ripening berries, everybody shows up—all the birds, all the small mammals, and the people too—to share in this abundance. So the plant is making these baskets full of berries, and they're heading out in all kinds of other directions, not to be accumulated, but to become part of life: to make more birds and more birdsongs and more meadow voles and jumping mice and everything up and down the food chain. And then when fall time comes, the leaves fall to the ground and feed that whole web of detritivores that make the soil that allows more serviceberries to grow. And so it's a circular economy. Everything that is made is given away, is sent off to support other lives. But then those lives support the serviceberry. So it's a model of circulation and circularity.

We know that these circular regenerative economies are the ways that nature provides abundance, and for the most part, our industrial economies are quite the opposite. They're just these short industrial pipelines that go from production to waste with amazing efficiency. But in a natural economy, there's no such thing as waste: a waste product becomes a resource for someone else's life. And in that way, I mean, the whole point of the book is this idea of biomimicry. Could we look at how nature delivers goods and services in this regenerative way? And why is it that we create our human economies to wreck nature rather than to emulate nature?

EVL You say that in response to gifts, our first intuitive response should be gratitude. And not just surface-level manners, the simple vocalized "thank you" that we are often accustomed to. It's more about a recognition of indebtedness that brings you into the realization that your life is nurtured from the body of Mother Earth. Can you speak a little bit more about the recognition of indebtedness that lies at the heart of gratitude?

RWK Yeah. And what converts it from being just this ritual of saying "thank you" is the recognition that our lives are intertwined, that our physical lives are intertwined. If not for you, I would not live. And so that's a powerful kind of gratitude, right? To say, *without you, I could not be*. And really what it takes is that attention and a kind of humility, the beautiful kind of humility. Oftentimes in the Western world that idea of humility comes to mean a kind of meekness or self-effacement. But in the teachings that I've been given, humility—in Potawatomi language the word is *edbesendowen*—means the recognition that I am not more important than you. Which doesn't mean that I'm not important. It means that you're important too, that we are important to each other. So it's a way of lifting up all lives to say we are all important to each other. Without each other, we would not be. And that's a really deep kind of gratitude that makes you feel so fortunate, right? It creates a really different orientation to the world: not that I'm going to try to take more, but that I'm going to respect what has been given to me.

EVL You echo this thought in *Braiding Sweetgrass*, writing that the expression of gratitude for what the Earth gives us is revolutionary in a consumer society. That contentment is radical. Gratitude creates an ethic of fullness, and we live in an economy that thrives on emptiness.

RWK Yeah, exactly. And that's why the notion of gratitude, enoughness, and abundance feels so important as an antidote to the endless need to consume. The idea of contentment. And we're back to the notion of enoughness, aren't we?

EVL Yeah.

RWK It just makes you say, I have everything that I need.

EVL You also say we need to go beyond gratitude and that we need to become a culture of reciprocity. What do you mean by that?

RWK You know, gratitude feels like we are expressing our thankfulness for our lives, et cetera. But then, you know, when someone gives you a gift, you want to give *them* something. You are in their debt, in a way, and you want to honor them and respect them in the way that you've been respected. And so that opens the door to reciprocity, to say, well, what is the gift that I could give you in return for water or berries or birdsong or whatever it is that we're talking about? And that requires a deep self-examination, to say: *Well, what is my gift? And which of my gifts are what the world needs in this moment?* And now we're talking about a purpose-driven life, right? To say: *Oh, I matter too. I matter too. My participation, my gifts need to be in the world in order for the world to thrive.* And then that converts our sense of ourselves far beyond just a consumer, right? We've been sold this narrative that we humans are just takers, just consumers, that's all that we do. But in reciprocity, we can reclaim our sense of ourselves as givers, as well; as full participants in the flourishing of the world. And that's joyful. It gives you a sense of kinship and purpose and agency that rivals this sense of agency and purpose that the birds and the trees have.

EVL As the currency of the gift exchange, gratitude and reciprocity are a truly renewable resource. And you write that every time gifts are given, their energy concentrates as they pass from hand to hand. Can you speak a little bit more about what you mean by this and what is enlivened within both the giver and the recipient in this exchange?

RWK There's some beautiful writing around this in Lewis Hyde's beautiful book, *The Gift*, and other philosophers and anthropologists talk about this. But let's say, for example, I wanted to just give you a teacup. I could go down to the local store and buy a teacup and give it to you. But what if the teacup that I gave you was my great-grandma's, and she brought it with her from a long journey, and she had told stories and had tea parties? They're both vessels for holding hot water, but one of them has been exchanged so many times, has so much more resonance, so much more meaning, so much value and honor. And that's the way that relationships kind of burnish the gift and make it even more valuable. And if you then took that gift and gave it, and said, this was given to me by Robin in honor of our friendship, and she gave it to me in honor of her grandmother—all of that story keeps going, right? And so the gift as it is passed on, in the sense of a material gift, gathers the nonmaterial value and stories that go with it. In an ecological sense, gifts also get more concentrated when they go up the food chain.

EVL Right.

RWK And that's another element of ecological gifts. Plants, for example, are harvesting abundant sunshine, but when they make berries that are then eaten by the birds, the birds are only concentrating about ten percent of the energy that the tree produced in those fruits. And so the birds are a more concentrated form of that energy. And whoever eats the bird—say the fox that just picked that robin off the ground—is getting only ten percent of that. So now it's a hundredth of what the plant produced. As you go up the food chain, energy also becomes much more concentrated. And that's another way to think about how, as gifts are passed on, they become more valuable. I mean, it's why there are fewer birds in the world than grasshoppers, because that energy is concentrated. That gift becomes in a sense more valuable as it is passed up the food chain. So it's both cultural and ecological.

EVL Yeah. I liked what you said about how the material gift holds the story when given to others. And it also makes me think about the spiritual exchange: the energy that's present within the story that is allowed to become more concentrated as it is used and enlivened, as the exchange passes it on. And that when we stop it by saying, no, it's mine, it's like we stop the flow of everything that's happened up until that point.

RWK Absolutely. Right? Yep. Exactly.

EVL One of the main questions now being asked in relation to the gift economy model is, how do we take it and scale it up so it can be feasible within societies at large? But you challenge this notion and you say that you're not sure that's the right question, because it is the small scale and the community context that makes the flow of gifts meaningful.

RWK Yeah. Gift economies occur all over the world; they occur in small, close-knit communities. And there's a very good reason for that. Gift economies rely on trust. They rely on being known. They rely on saying, *You invited me to your feast, so I'm going to invite you to mine.* In a society which is too big and too complex, you can be anonymous, right? And anonymity creates the opportunity for cheating in the system. But where everybody is known and related to through gift exchange, there's a high level of trust. So this diffuse reciprocity can work.

And so it could be said, well, gift economies then can never prevail in a society like in the United States today. But I don't think that's true, because what we as individuals crave is community and a sense of belonging. So gift economies are not going to replace extractive capitalism, right? But I think they can exist within it as we create and value these small-scale communities. And we saw that happen during the pandemic as mutual aid societies in neighborhoods grew, as community gardens grew. People found ways to create these small, very local webs of reciprocity and care. And that, I think, is the invitation: to do those things that allow us to honor a currency of relationship rather than a currency of money. And so when I say, well, I don't think we should scale them up, I really mean they probably wouldn't work at a scale of five hundred to a thousand people; but they work really well at two hundred people.

And so, how do we, again, invest in our neighborhoods in our communities to create opportunities for things like tool sharing and community gardening and food sharing? And I think about the buy-nothing networks, for example, that are deeply community-based. Those are gift economies. And we get the benefits of, I suppose, the goods and services that come through those exchanges, but we also get the benefit of human relationships and mutual respect and the sense that you matter, that that network needs you and what you bring. And in a society where I think people are longing not only for community but for purpose—oh, those are pretty good benefits.

EVL I want to talk a little bit about the deeper spiritual values present in this book, and of course your work overall, that your exploration of the gift economy seems to be pointing towards. There is this crisis of a lack of respect for the Earth as a spiritual being, one might say; we don't value Her and all She brings because of the systems that have removed us, sometimes very, very violently. And your work is very much about inviting people to transform this and to want to change the bleak future that is often promised to us and to mend this relationship. So I wonder if you might speak a little bit about the deeper spiritual values that a gift economy could really lead us towards and help us learn to reembody.

RWK This is, of course, work that transcends human communities and the exchange of goods and services. What it means is that we are investing again in communities of care and compassion, not only for one another, but for the Earth. I think what we're really leaning toward is a kind of interspecies justice, to say that this mutual responsibility that we have for one another is our primary spiritual responsibility. It's not just pragmatic, it's "practical reverence."

EVL Oh, I like that.

RWK Because this is deeply practical, but it has sacred dimensions, doesn't it?

EVL Yeah.

RWK Of caring for one another and honoring the gifts that come to us. To me, our responsibility to participate in the gift economy is very much tied to our spiritual responsibilities. In teachings that have been shared with me, and that guide me, is the notion that, in return for life in this beautiful, complicated place, we bring a gift here that was given us. Each of us is to bring that gift. And to not give the gift is a betrayal of a kind of spiritual responsibility, a spiritual equation, in a way. And so gift economies offer an opportunity for individuals to say, *Here is the gift that I carry, and I'm going to share it with you to enliven our community, to enliven life around us.* And that deep sense of purpose is a spiritual one as well.

EVL You know, to me the immense popularity of both *Braiding Sweetgrass* and "The Serviceberry" essay speaks to a deep-rooted hunger people have for this way of being rooted in reciprocity, for this sense of practical reverence, for being in caring, mutual relationship with all that's alive around us; and that we are craving models and pathways into once again living in spiritual connection with the Earth. I wonder if you could speak a little to this hunger that is apparent, this innate desire that remains—although often buried in us—to be in conversation with this Earth.

RWK Oh, yes. You know, one of the joys of the work that *Braiding Sweetgrass* in particular has done in the world is an almost daily flow of messages from readers who convey just what you're talking about: longing, longing to be in right relationship with the Earth. And in the face of all the stories around us that divert us from that—that say, well, no, that doesn't really matter, that's not what you're here for—*Braiding Sweetgrass* has given permission, I think, to many of us to feel that longing. And the idea of being in right relationship with land, given the way that our species—particularly in this country and in industrial economies—has inflicted so much harm on the marvelous creation around us, can also create this sense of shame and dishonor. You think: That's not who I am. That's not who I want to be. And practical reverence offers almost a notion of redemption: *No, you are not just a taker, you are not a despoiler. You can be medicine, you can be medicine for the Earth. You can be a healer. You can participate in regenerative economies. You can participate in ecological restoration. You can contribute to justice within our own species, and interspecies justice.*

People are longing for a kind of permission to really be their authentic selves in right relationship to land. And I've been so gratified to see the ways in which people are taking this on, feeling liberated to say: *Oh, I could be a giver. Well, here's what I want to do.* You know, somebody said, I'm going to this education system that teaches us just to be consumers. I don't want to participate in that. I'm starting a school, or I'm writing curriculum. Another person wrote me and said, I've been in finance on Wall Street for most of my professional life, and now I can't do it anymore; and I'm going to take my wealth and go create a regenerative farm. You know, there are just so many stories of people feeling liberated to be in right relationship with the land, which for some reason they had just felt wasn't even possible. And that's the power of collective storytelling, isn't it?

EVL Yeah.

RWK Because when one person says, *Here's how I'm looking at this*, it's contagious and gives people agency and permission to take those steps so that we are not complicit in destruction. Because that complicity weighs on us, doesn't it? It weighs on us heavily. And to be able to take those steps in a gift economy, in regenerative economies—to step outside of that complicity and resist it in any way—really gives a sense of power and agency and rightness.

EVL You offer a lovely example in the book of how intuitive and innate a gift economy is to us as humans. That gift-giving is a primal element of human relationships. And you point to the "maternal gift economy" here: the giving of milk from a mother to a baby, which really is "pure gift." Mothers don't sell their milk to their babies. The currency of this economy, this exchange, is gratitude and love in support of continued life.

RWK Isn't that a powerful idea? Genevieve Vaughan was the first to talk about this. And I've only scraped the surface of trying to understand the work that's being done around maternal gift economies. I want to learn more. And I plant that as a seed for readers to learn more as well, to say, *What would that look like to live in a way that honored these exchanges of life?* What those thinkers, those wonderful feminist thinkers, are arguing is that gift economies are a biological imperative. If we didn't do this, we simply wouldn't be. So how could that translate into means of social and economic organization based on blurring the boundary between me and we? That's part of the beauty of the maternal gift economy: the boundary between mother and child is so porous, right? It really is an exemplar of this idea that all flourishing is mutual. Our lives are so linked. And when we start to think about the ultimate mother from whose body we are fed—Mother Earth—what does a maternal gift economy look like in that realm? It's a really exciting arena of thought.

EVL Hand in hand with what's shown by the maternal gift economy, you go on to suggest that like the sun is "the source of flow" in the economy of nature, perhaps the source that replenishes the flow of gifts in the human gift economy is love.

RWK In the maternal gift economy, I think there's no argument about that, right?

EVL No.

RWK But it's a kind of, again, practical reverence of love and milk. We need both. Love alone is not going to nourish that infant. And, again, when we think about the story of the hunter who says, *I store my meat in the belly of my brother*—isn't that love, isn't that love for your people? And there, the boundary between me and we is also blurred: the gifts of the Earth—that hunted food—don't just belong to me, they belong to all of us. And I can be an agent of distributing that abundance to the we. And I think all of this really leads us to that acknowledgment that we live in a society that is so hyper-individualistic that we think all of the benefits are to accrue to individuals and their tight circles. Whereas what would it be like to think about where the benefits could flow within the whole community, as in an ecological system?

Sandor Ellix Katz
A SEASONAL PRACTICE OF FERMENTATION

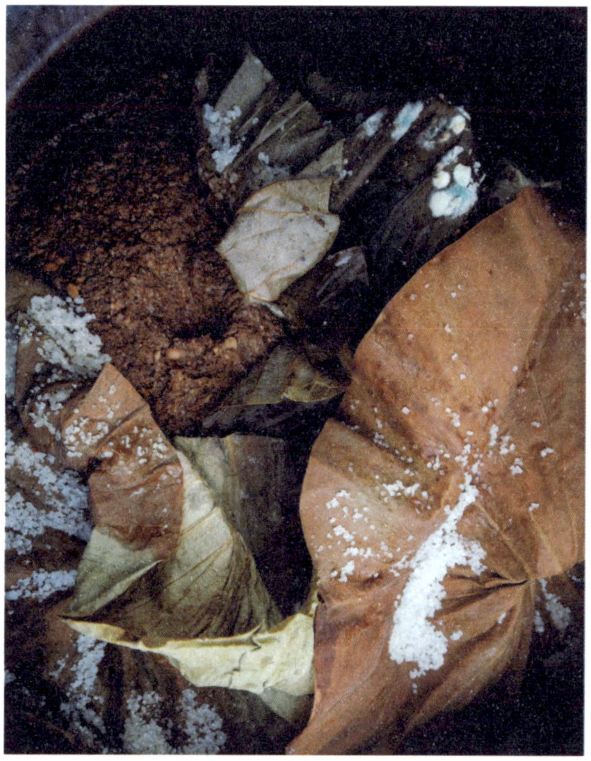

I GREW UP EATING SAUERKRAUT on street vendor hotdogs and loved it as a salty, sour, juicy condiment. Little did I know how important sauerkraut was as a survival food, enabling people in temperate climates with long winters to survive by providing them with a stable and reliable source of vitamin C. Yet I vaguely understood that sauerkraut had something to do with preserving cabbage and found a recipe in the cookbook ubiquitous in twentieth-century American kitchens: *The Joy of Cooking*. I couldn't quite believe how straightforward the process was: shred cabbage; lightly salt and gently massage the cabbage until it gets juicy; add seasonings if desired; then stuff the juicy salted cabbage into a crock or jars until it is submerged under its own juices; and wait while bacteria on the cabbage ferment carbohydrates into acids, which preserve it and protect it from pathogens.

Once I made that first batch of sauerkraut, I started experimenting and learned that I could ferment almost any firm vegetable or combination of firm vegetables in the same way; I could do it with less salt or more; I could shred finely, chop coarsely, or even leave vegetables whole; and I could season the vegetables any way I like. Since that first batch more than thirty years ago, I've had kraut going continuously, and have eaten it with almost every meal (even breakfast).

Wherever you live, and wherever your ancestors came from, fermentation is part of your cultural legacy; it's as integral to how people everywhere use food as cooking and drying. Yet most of us have become removed from the cycles of growing foods and fearful of traditional processes such as fermentation that transform them. Do not let the "war on bacteria" scare you into believing that fermentation requires microscopes, laboratories, and specialized knowledge! Disparate fermentation processes were developed hundreds and thousands of years ago, with tools much more limited than those found in any contemporary kitchen. Consider this an invitation to celebrate the seasons by developing an annual fermentation practice in your kitchen.

WHERE I LIVE IN TENNESSEE, early spring brings tender young asparagus shoots and luscious juicy strawberries; in high summer you'll find tomatoes and okra; and in autumn, hearty root vegetables. Though our globalized economy has promised transcendence from the limitations of geography and season—for instance, tomatoes available on demand, all year round—it cannot alter the inherent specificity of food production: what grows where, and when. Fermentation has been used for ages as a strategy for preserving seasonal abundance, catching foods at their ripest and most flavorful, so they can be enjoyed throughout the year.

Wine, for example, is fermented from fresh, ripe grapes and is generally made near where the grapes are grown. There is great variability from place to place, and season to season, in terms of soil, topography, and climate, which affects the growth and specific qualities of the grapes, as well as the microorganisms and conditions of fermentation. After the fermentation, wine can be aged and stored for long periods, but it is not something that can be made at any time. The same can be said for cider fermented from pressed apples, or any fruit-based alcohol. (In contrast, beer and other alcohol based upon grains—which are dry at harvest and can be stored for many months—can be fermented later, as needed.)

Many ferments are little known beyond the places where they are made. In Colombia, I tried a fizzy, delicious lightly fermented pineapple beverage called *guarapo de piña*, made by a man named Pacho, who belongs to an Indigenous Amazon group called the Matapi. He demonstrated how he makes the guarapo, and it is deceptively simple. Pacho grates ripe pineapples (skin and all), and lets the mash spontaneously ferment, meaning it ferments without added starters or intervention, driven by yeasts and bacteria indigenous to the pineapple itself. The fermentation requires just a day or two in the tropical heat, then Pacho strains the liquid and serves it. Guarapo de piña requires an abundance of pineapples, and it is made only where they grow and in the season when they are most abundant. Interestingly, in the Matapi culture guarapo de piña plays an important role in an annual ceremony marking the passage of the seasons and celebrating reciprocity with other life-forms. For days, participants dance and sing, foregoing all food and beverage except for guarapo de piña. As my Colombian host Esteban Yepes Montoya explained it to me, this brings them into a trance state, in which they "surrender to the here and now of the season" and "bow to the sacred essence of the pineapple."

Another approach I've encountered for

FIG. 40 Photo by Kristin Teig (P. 321)

fermenting pineapples is perhaps more suitable for those of us living far from where pineapples grow: Mexican *tepache*, made from the skins and cores, the parts typically discarded when you eat a pineapple. Tepache exemplifies the potential to apply fermentation as a strategy to reduce and make use of food waste. Flavor, sugar, and acidity in the pineapple flesh that is inevitably cut away with the skin are infused into a sugar-water solution, as microbes in the skin begin to ferment it. Tepache is pretty straightforward to make and takes just a few days, so try it the next time you eat a pineapple!

Growing up in New York City, the fermented food I loved as a kid was pickles—fermented cucumbers—though I couldn't have told you back then that they were fermented. My grandparents and great-grandparents came to New York from Belarus and Lithuania, and the pickles that my family ate (not homemade but bought from a delicatessen) were the Eastern European style: cucumbers fermented with garlic and dill. We knew these pickles as "sour" or "half-sour," depending on the intensity of their acidity, which I later came to understand as an expression of time. The longer the cucumbers ferment, the more lactic acid is produced.

It turns out that cucumbers can be among the most challenging vegetables to ferment. Cucumbers and other watery hot-weather vegetables, such as summer squash, have high concentrations of enzymes that break down the pectin that makes vegetables crispy and crunchy. Many of the fermentation traditions used to preserve cucumbers come from places with relatively mild summers, like Belarus and Lithuania. In hot environments, it's easy for fermented cucumbers to get soft and mushy; and nobody likes a mushy pickle! I've learned a number of techniques to help keep pickles crunchy, and I'm happy to report that despite the intensely hot summers where I live in Tennessee, I've learned to make consistently crunchy pickles.

Most other vegetables are easier to ferment than cucumbers, and pretty much all vegetable fermentation traditions are seasonal. My first fermentation experiences were driven by the realities of the garden. When I started gardening after I moved from New York City to rural Tennessee, I was such a naïve city kid that I hadn't considered that in a garden, all the

TEPACHE

Tepache is a wonderful, effervescent, lightly fermented pineapple beverage popular in Mexico. It is made from the skin and core of a pineapple; so you can enjoy the pineapple flesh while it's fresh and also make use of the parts you would typically discard to enjoy it over a longer period of time.

TIMEFRAME:
- 2 to 5 days

VESSEL:
- Wide-mouth vessel of at least ½-gallon / 2-liter capacity

INGREDIENTS (for about 1 quart / 1 liter):
- ½ cup / 100 grams sugar, or more, to taste (ideally piloncillo, panela, or another unrefined sugar, but any type of sugar will work)
- Skin and core of 1 pineapple (eat the rest!) cut into 1- to 2-inch / 3- to 5-centimeter pieces
- 1 cinnamon stick and/or a few whole cloves and/or other spices (optional)

PROCESS:
- Dissolve the sugar in about 1 cup / 250 milliliters of water.
- Place the pineapple skin and core and optional spices into the vessel.
- Pour the sugar water over the pineapple, then add additional water as needed to cover the pineapple.
- Cover with a loose lid or cloth and stir daily.
- Ferment for 2 to 5 days, depending upon temperature and desired level of fermentation. It will get fizzy, then develop a pronounced sourness after a few days.
- Taste each day after the first few to evaluate developing flavor.
- Strain out the solids.
- Enjoy fresh or refrigerate for up to a couple of weeks.
- If it gets too sour, do not despair! After straining out the solids, leave it with the surface exposed to the air, and it will become pineapple vinegar after a week or two.

SOUR PICKLES

TIMEFRAME:
· About 2 weeks

VESSEL:
· 1-liter jar (or for larger batches a larger jar, ceramic crock, or small wooden barrel)

INGREDIENTS (for 1 liter):
· 500 grams small unwaxed pickling cucumbers, the fresher the better
· 25 grams sea salt, about 1½ tablespoons
· 1 or 2 heads fresh flowering dill, or 1–2 tablespoons dill seeds
· 1–2 heads garlic
· 1 small handful fresh grape, cherry, oak, and/or horseradish leaves (if available)
· 1 pinch whole black peppercorns
· 1–2 dried chilis (optional)

PROCESS:

· *Prepare the cucumbers.* Rinse the cucumbers, taking care to not bruise them and making sure their blossoms are removed. Scrape off any remains at the blossom end. If you're using cucumbers that aren't fresh off the vine that day, soak them for at least a half hour in ice water to freshen them.

· *Mix the brine.* Dissolve the sea salt in 500 milliliters of dechlorinated water to create a brine solution. Stir until the salt is thoroughly dissolved. Use sufficient salt, as the salt slows the enzymes that break down pectin.

· *Fill the vessel.* Clean the vessel, then at the bottom of it place dill, garlic, peppercorns, and fresh grape leaves (or other tannin-rich leaves; the tannins also slow down the enzymes). Pack whole cucumbers in the vessel, tightly to help them remain submerged under the brine.

· *Add the brine.* If the brine doesn't cover the cucumbers, add more brine mixed at the same ratio. If the cucumbers are floating at the surface, an easy solution is to cut a chunk of a bigger cucumber to hold the others down, or cut the lid of a plastic food container so it's just a little bigger than the mouth of the jar and squeeze it in, using it to hold the cucumbers submerged. If you're using a crock, use a plate to weigh down the cucumbers and cover it with a cloth to keep out dust and flies. If using a jar, loosely seal the jar with its lid.

· *Ferment.* Leave the pickles to ferment until the color of the cucumbers changes from bright green to a duller olive green. Sourness will develop over time, how fast depending primarily upon temperature. These pickles are traditional mostly in places with cool summers, enabling long fermentation times and long-term preservation. The process can be adapted to warmer locales or shifting climate patterns with the help of refrigeration. If your kitchen is hot, transfer pickles to the refrigerator within a week and continue to ferment there for a couple more weeks. If any white surface scum appears, skim it from the surface. Taste pickles after a couple of weeks. If they are sour enough for you, eat and enjoy them; if not, continue to ferment and check them regularly.

cabbages or all the radishes are ready at about the same time. Faced with a glorious abundance of cabbage the first year I was gardening, I turned to making sauerkraut, using fermentation as a strategy to preserve the harvest and extend the season.

While I continue to enjoy traditional cabbage kraut, I've come to make my biggest batches of kraut from daikon radishes, which a farmer friend grows as a soil-improving cover crop. Each autumn, in late October, I drive a pick-up truck to his farm and fill up the truck with hundreds of pounds of daikons, along with some cabbages. Friends help scrub, chop, and salt the veggies, and then pack them into a hundred-liter vessel. We enjoy radish kraut all autumn, winter, spring, and into the early summer.

As with other vegetables, there are actually many different ways you can ferment a daikon. You can do it Korean style, as *kimchi*. You can do it Japanese style, as *takuan*, *nuka*, or other types of *tsukemono*. You can do it Sichuan style, as *pao-cai*. Or you can do it Taiwanese style, as *cai bo*, aged for years or even decades. (I tried some that had been aged for more than forty years!) Or, you can use your imagination and create your own innovative style of pickling; my Tasmanian friend Adam James used an abundance of turmeric to create a turmeric-based paste which he uses as a perpetual pickling medium, and daikon pickled in that turn bright yellow (on the outside). All of which is to say: there is no limit to the possible approaches to fermenting! Do not be afraid to experiment.

And it's not only fruits and vegetables that give rise to seasonal fermentation traditions. Many of Korean cuisine's most distinctive flavors come from *jangs*, seasonings fermented using *meju*, a starter which is itself fermented from a block of soybeans. The whole process begins with the soybean harvest, typically in October. The beans are cleaned, soaked, cooked until soft, and then mashed and pressed into brick-like blocks. The first few days of the fermentation, while the blocks are very moist, they are kept on a mat of rice straw in a heated space and turned periodically so that every side of each block comes into contact with the straw, an important source of bacteria and fungi, as well as with the air, so the blocks become dry enough to hang. During this initial stage, the fermentation is dominated by bacteria known as *Bacillus*.

After a few days in this warm environment, the exteriors of the blocks become dry enough that they can be handled. They are then tied and hung in an open-air environment where they continue to develop in fluctuating temperatures, protected from rain. The meju-maker I visited, Bong Rok Oh, hung his meju in an open-ended plastic-covered hoop house. Here, diverse molds flourish, typically dominated by the genus *Aspergillus*. According to Mr. Oh, the more diverse the fungi, the more complex the flavor profile of the meju. He hangs the blocks of meju in the hoop house for two to three months and begins to harvest them after the lunar New Year in February.

Meju is not eaten as a food; rather, it is the starting point for *doenjang*, *ganjang*, *gochujang*, and other jangs, which are used as building blocks of flavor in Korean cuisine. I'm making my first batches of doenjang (soy sauce) and ganjang (soy paste) from a block of meju that I was gifted by Mr. Oh. The two products are made in tandem, beginning with a single process: covering the meju with a salty brine. Mr. Oh was vague about his salt proportions, except to say that due to warmer temperatures, he had been forced to increase the salt in recent years, as salt inhibits putrefying bacteria and other undesirable organisms that are more prolific at warmer temperatures. Climate change impacts everything in fermentation, from what plants thrive where, to the dynamics of microbial growth and accordingly to details such as salt proportions and timing. I mixed my brine at 18 percent salt by weight (180 grams salt per liter of water)—extremely salty—knowing that the salt would be diluted by the mass of the meju. I used enough brine to allow the meju to float in it.

The meju absorbs brine, softens, and gradually breaks apart into the brine. Mr. Oh's fermentation vessels were stored outdoors, with glass covers to allow for sun exposure while still protecting them from rain. I stored my crock in the house but brought it outside and opened it on sunny days to give it sun exposure, stirring it regularly. The meju is fermented in the brine for about three months, then the liquid is strained and pressed from the solids, and the two distinct products begin to diverge: the liquid is further fermented to become ganjang, and the solids are further fermented to become doenjang. These final fermentations take a minimum of one year, but ideally several. One fermentation master I met in Korea has a vessel full of 129-year-old soy sauce, and he adds a little of that to each of his contemporary batches.

An inheritance like this really highlights the generational continuity of seasonal food preservation traditions, which sadly few of us have carried on. Yet, if we are to be more connected to the lands where we live, and to the plants, animals, and ancestral processes that enable us to survive and thrive, we must find ways to reestablish these seasonal traditions. I call myself a fermentation revivalist, because my work aims to empower people to revive fermentation as a living tradition in our homes and communities.

All around the world, fermentation is an essential part of how people make effective use of food resources. It is both a strategy and a celebration, engaging us more intimately with plants, invisible forces such as bacteria, and other relationships that connect us, through the rich transformations of the seasons, to the Earth. Incorporating a simple fermentation practice into your kitchen routine will enable you to produce foods or drinks that you can enjoy and share with others, inviting them to join in these ancient processes, which are still as important and relevant as ever.

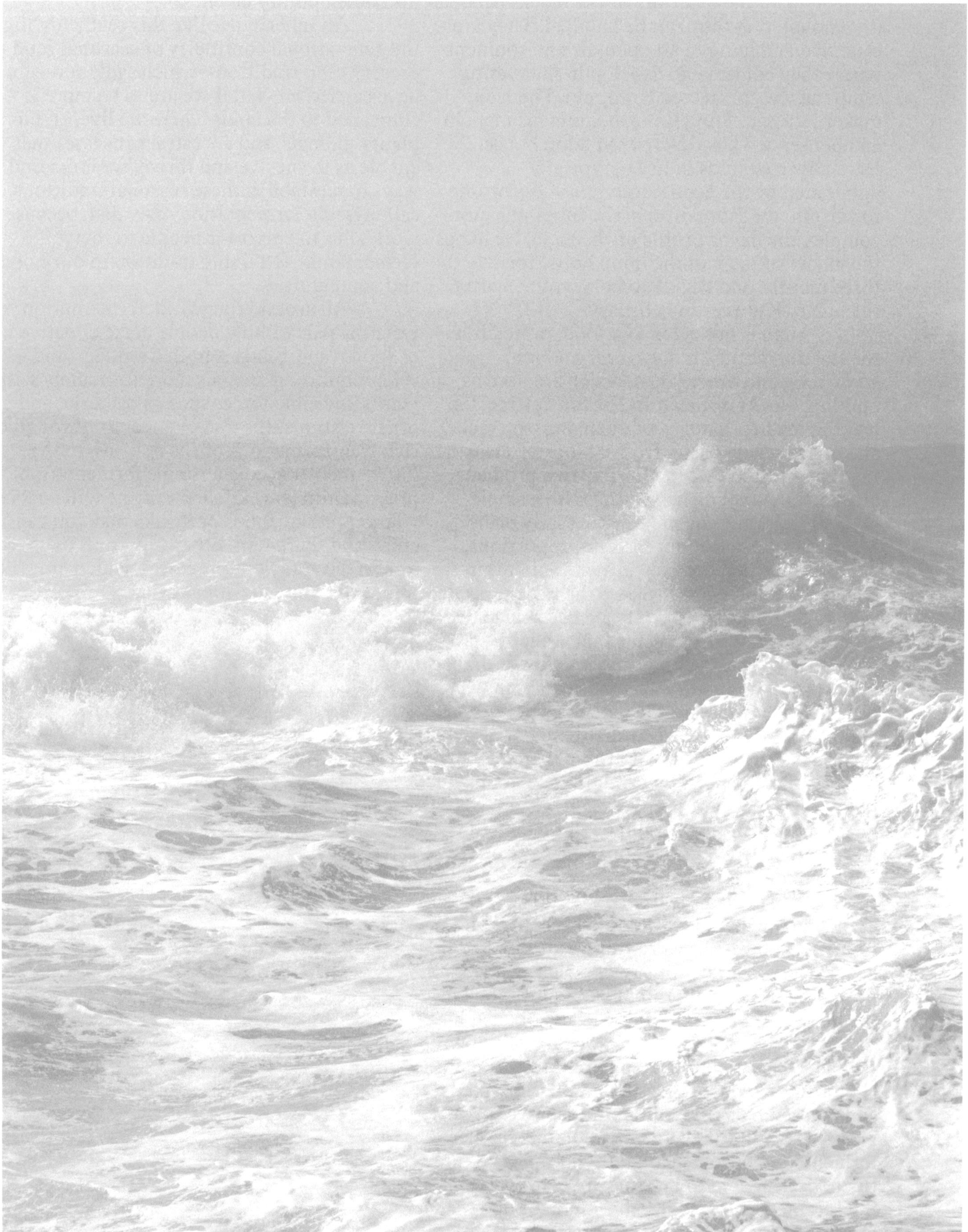

 FIGS. 41-46 Photos by Ron Jude (PP. 328, 336-342)

David James Duncan
HOW THE PACIFIC MAKES LOVE TO THE ROCKIES

“These places, forces, and spiritual mysteries, to put it the ancient way, are our Mother; the living terrain her body; the flora her clothes; the lakes, rivers, rills her blood and arteries; the seasons and weathers her moods; the birds, fish, fauna, humans *all*, *equally*, her offspring.”

I. "THE ENVIRONMENT" IS NOT THE GUARDIAN HOLINESS

Emergence has invited me to explore, in their words, "spiritual traditions tied to the seasons that have been broken and must be remade." I chose the above title because I've spent seven decades immersed in the ways the Pacific Ocean makes love to the Rocky Mountains, and my title is not a fanciful poetic flourish. Based on my lifelong immersion I'm here to tell you that most of this lovemaking is a literal, mutual, two-way giving and receiving involving thousands of interwoven species of flora and fauna, but the spiritual traditions tied to that interweaving have been *very* broken by the "free market" delusion that Earth is an infinite "resource" to be exploited for financial gain regardless of the cost to life. My lifelong familiars, the states of Oregon, Washington, Idaho, and Montana, are a tapestry of extremely varied and vulnerable landscapes, weathery forces, living beings, and wild intricacy to which people from all over the world flock like grateful birds simply to see Earth being Earth; see wildness intact; see the beautiful creations of the Divine Female properly known as *Sophia*—not Rome's masculinized "Holy Ghost" —dreamt up before our eyes.

We call these landscapes ours, but the Pacific Northwest and Northern Rockies are a web of life-forms and mysteries we did not create, and cannot regenerate once the wild's ability to sustain life has been savaged. What we currently call "North America" is pre-American and will be post-American, and it is not even vaguely described by the pitiful term "the environment." If the Bible began with the words "*In the beginning God created the environment*," it would be out of print. The lovemaking between the Pacific and the Rockies is a guardian holiness that enables biodiversity to diversify, natural selection to naturally select, and generation after generation of kids to muck around in river shallows playing with frogs, fingerlings, and caddis fly casings, and it is governed not by such creatures as "governors," but by elemental and celestial harmonies as powerful as Earth's spinning, yet as delicate as an orb weaver's dew-bedecked web. These places, forces, and spiritual mysteries, to put it the ancient way, are our Mother; the living terrain her body; the flora her clothes; the lakes, rivers, rills her blood and arteries; the seasons and weathers her moods; the birds, fish, fauna, humans *all*, *equally*, her offspring. And every man, woman, and child striving to defend the life and lives she supports —even in poverty and political impotence; even against monstrous power and seemingly hopeless odds—is not only a hero but an integral part of her, hence every bit as holy as she whom they seek to defend.

II. CEASELESS FLOW

The Native salmon tribes of the 258,000- square-mile Columbia River Basin did not measure the passing of time with calendars that divide the flow of seasons into linear months, weeks, days, digital minutes, seconds, and nanoseconds. Judging by the tribes' twelve-thousand-year-old artifacts, surviving languages, and remnant myths and legends, they experienced the flow of seasons by tracking the copious number of fish species that came charging up the rivers of the Basin, affording the tribes and hundreds of other species unsurpassed protein and Omega-3 fatty acids as the vast forests of the same region throve on marine nitrogen distributed over thousands of riparian miles by the salmon-eaters' scat.

Is it possible for those of us measuring our lives with computer digits and procuring our food at chain supermarkets to track the eternal Now by turning our attention to migratory species arriving by rivers and skies many fossil-fuel-sucking miles from our urban and suburban homes? The answer "*Not likely*" probably goes without saying. So what *can* we do to deepen connection to a cosmology based on literal and spiritual life-forms?

In *Thoughts in Solitude* the great Trappist contemplative, Thomas Merton, put it like this:

> Our destiny is to live out what we think, because unless we live what we know, we do not even know it. It is only by making our knowledge part of ourselves, through action, that we enter into the reality that is signified by our concepts. . . . Living is the constant adjustment of thought to life and life to thought in such a way that we are always growing, always experiencing new things in the old and old things in the new. Thus life is always new.

This is a way of understanding time's flow that I can get behind. My main method of experiencing new things in the old and old things in the new has been intimately entwined, lifelong, with what began as fishing to catch fish, but long since evolved into friendships with rivers and streams, where the main attraction is intimacy with the hosts of birds, fish, aquatic insects, and riparian flora and fauna that thrive thanks to rivers and creeks. Catching fish has become secondary.

In the last stanza of "Cabin Poem," my esteemed friend, the poet Jim Harrison, said he yearned to finish his life "disguised as a creek, / an eddy, joining at night the full, / sweet flow, to absorb the sky, / to swallow the heat and cold, the moon / and the stars, to swallow myself / in ceaseless flow." Like Jim, I've had hundreds of strange and wonderful encounters with the denizens of creeks, rivers, and riparians over the thousands of days I've spent on, and literally *in*, flowing waters. An uncanny example of "strange and wonderful": Listening to one of Emmanuel Vaughan-Lee's talks on *Emergence* last year, he asked his listeners, referring to the Earth, *"How would you walk across a lover's back?"* His question set off wild resonations in me when it summoned from memory how, in my late twenties, to reach my favorite high-desert Oregon river from Portland I had to get up in pitch darkness and drive so far that, after just half a day spent fly fishing in desert heat, I'd nap to be rested for when the trout would rise to evening caddis hatches.

After one such nap I woke in the shade of the towering canyon walls and noticed my back felt oddly cool. Sitting up, I removed my shirt—and burst out laughing. Field mice had tiptoed onto my back and eaten a 12-by-18-inch hole in the flannel! What a reply, nearly fifty years later, to Emmanuel's uncanny question! I'd given the mice the shirt off my back, passing a gift on to their offspring in the selfless way Earth, day and night, gifts us all.

As said, the Native tribes who inhabited this region celebrated the flow of seasons by preparing for precisely which anadromous fishes would next arrive in their customary fishing places. There were a plethora of species and subspecies in the historic Columbia Basin's dam-free rivers, about which we know almost nothing today. My river-brother, the writer and sage Barry Lopez, tapped into a version of this preparedness

1 Wang Wei, from *Mountain Home: The Wilderness Poetry of Ancient China*, trans. David Hinton (New York: New Directions, 2005).

during the fifty years he spent observing spawning Chinook salmon on Oregon's McKenzie River. "The world of variables salmon are alert to, to which they respond, is astonishingly complex," Barry wrote. "The closer we look the more we see the individual animal is a reflection of the organization of the energy around it. To try to understand the animal apart from its background—except as an imaginative exercise—is to risk the collapse of both."

To closely witness the Chinooks' epic migration, redd-building, and total self-sacrifice to create tiny silver offspring is to experience salvific wisdom alive and well in running water; it's the Pacific making love to mountains before our eyes. Barry felt this so strongly he couldn't sleep during the McKenzie's modest fall salmon run if he didn't first check on the adult Chinook that reproduced in the side channel closest to his home.

Because I've known my favorite eight or ten rivers so intimately, I too know what has gone missing from them. Essential Indigenous food traditions have been devastated globally in a multi-century disaster larger than any mind can track. This might be the place to admit that educating one's wild heart teaches, in the words of William of Saint-Thierry, that "*Amor ipse intellectus est*, love in itself is already the beginning of knowledge." But it's also the place to admit that love for Chinook salmon and orcas in the Columbia River's compassion-stripped corridor teaches, as the American poet laureate Stanley Kunitz wrote, that *in a murderous time / the heart breaks and breaks / and lives by breaking.*

III. STREAMS CASCADING EMPTY TOWARD HUMAN REALMS

So many beautiful things happen in even the smaller streams blessed with runs of salmon and steelhead. In the November creek I lived on near the Oregon coast I have sat, buddha-style, in neoprene waders, watching two otters not twenty feet away share an adult coho's entire body, discussing its complex flavors in urbane otter chitter. I once fished the headwaters of a coastal salmon and steelhead stream so fog-bound and so seldom visited by humans that a blacktail doe stepped out of the gray a few feet from me, stepped even closer to sniff the tip of my fly rod as if to ascertain whether I was real, strolled fifty feet upstream, gave the same sniff to my fishing partner's rod, then melted back into the gray. I've watched water ouzels stroll the massive, rotting backs of still-living still-spawning Chinooks, singing blithely as they danced upon the salmons' very death. I've watched scores of coho salmon arrive in my home river, spawn for long, exhausting days, then weaken, drift downstream, and die; watched their carcasses hang from branches or flutter from the torn metal of drowned cars; watched them lie inert in the quietest water, turning black for days, white for a few more, before sending out pale clouds of a ghostly green growth that let me see decomposition as a kind of blossoming. I've watched swarms of the ghost cohos' two-inch offspring nibble those blossoms the way the faithful nibble the body of Christ. Like all who worship on salmon rivers, I've witnessed in water the death, the resurrection, and the life.

When I moved to Montana in 1993, I became intimate with the longest wild salmon migration route on Earth, and caught and released Idaho salmon and steelhead that had come six hundred miles inland and six thousand feet above the Pacific, climbing the most powerful river of its size in North America with no help from legs or feet.

A dozen years into that fishing I began losing sleep over the spring and summer Chinook that should have been coming home to their high-elevation birth houses on the Montana border, but whose young were being slaughtered annually by a migratory passage chopped into 450 miles of overheated desert reservoirs by eight gigantic dams. For millennia Idaho's Chinook salmon, born in Columbia and Snake River headwaters, all turned north at the mouth of the Columbia, becoming the main food source of the Puget Sound orcas living fifteen hundred or more miles away. Those orcas still teach their young an ancient word for this largest of salmon species. Orcas literally leap for what a child would call joy as the Interior West's last few Chinook reach the Sound. But a feeble remnant of formerly abundant salmon is not enough. Extinction now speeds toward the Sound's dwindling orca pods. If you have not made a study of the grief-shattered orca mother, Tahlequah, who with the help of her pod carried her dead and disintegrating calf a thousand miles through the Salish Sea for seventeen days as millions of people, globally, tracked her sorrow, you have missed a tragedy more poignant than any by the ancient Greeks or Shakespeare.

How to bear the emptiness of the Interior West's headwaters as they flow all those miles to the starving orcas of Puget Sound? Cormac McCarthy's novel *The Road* ends with a staggeringly beautiful description of wild brook trout in a post-apocalypse world that could no longer sustain trout. If Cormac had lived in wild Idaho, his famed final paragraph may have read more like this:

> Once wild salmon defined
> these mountains. You could
> see them holding in the strong,
> clear currents, the edges of
> their fins trembling in the flow.
> They were wounded silver,
> massive, muscular, torsional,
> their ancestral wildness
> blessing every high-elevation
> stream. They smelled of ocean
> in our hands. On their sides
> gleamed maps of the Pacific in
> its becoming. On their backs,
> mazes of the ways by which
> they'd come. Maps and mazes
> of things that could not be put
> back. Not be made right again.
> In the birth houses where, for
> eons, they had sacrificed their
> lives that their kind might live,
> all things hummed of
> mysteries older than man.

How to part with creatures so perfectly self-giving? What to pray for as I wander tributaries stripped of their keystone species in just two purblind human generations?

I pray thanks to salmon and steelhead for the treasure it's been to know their impossible strength via a rod that carried me across the species barrier as I played them. I pray thanks to have held, loved, and released each one. I pray thanks that their lovemaking has for millennia wed mountains to ocean as no other creature's has, or can, or shall. I pray that, like the speaker of the Gospel words "*It is finished*," crucified salmon will one day rise from the dead. I pray their spirits, lifted by tree roots from the riparians, migrate up the trees' torsos to keep company with owls in the canopies, and with higher mysteries in the canopy of stars. I pray their beauty and self-sacrifice remain so alive in my heart and hands that, even now, spirit salmon will guide me on the shores of what remains:

Streams cascading, empty, toward human realms. (1)

IV. OTHER WORLDS IN THIS ONE

Before I submit to the mournfulness of what I've written, I confess I feel far less devastated by the havoc being wreaked upon this world when I bear in mind that the world I seem to see daily may not be the only world. I have many times experienced glimpses of what some Tibetan Buddhists call "the view." In Ani Tenzin Palmo's *Reflections on a Mountain Lake*, a wisdom book I've carried into the Rockies to add Tibetan resonances to my mountains, she writes,

> [W]e are so fixated on things being solid. . . . But even physics tells us that matter consists mostly of space. The actual solidity here is minute, and maybe that isn't really solid, either. But we think that the way we perceive things is the way they really are.
>
> There are many layers of perception. Each one of us believes that our way of perceiving is the only way. But that's not so. . . . Dilgo Khyentse Rinpoche said that he first started [meditating] when he was eight years old. He saw the walls and all the furniture begin to quiver and become transparent. . . . [And] the fact is that that kind of perception, seeing things as if they were made of wisdom light, is actually more akin to reality than our normal ways of seeing things as solid. . . . [W]e have the impure perception which says, "Things are like this, and they couldn't be like anything else" . . . . That's our ignorant mind. Vajrayana [meditation] is trying to align us with the way things really are . . . [to get us] closer to the inherent nature of things than our usual perceptions, which is why it can affect us very deeply. . . . [A]t a very profound level, we recognize it. We know that it is true.

I've had many glimpses and dreams of deeper realities and have kept an ongoing spiritual journal about them for decades. In 2008 for example, in the last hour before dawn, I had an enlightenment dream that, when I woke from it, left me feeling that I'd fallen out of my real existence. My waking life now felt like an unenlightened dream from which I try daily to wake, grateful for glimpses of deeper realities that pierce days of "unenlightenment."

The original dream unfolded like this:

> A woman standing at the front of a small classroom has an intelligent and pretty face, a white blouse, dark skirt, dark hair, and I'm concentrating on her so hard that I don't know whether there are even other students in the room.
>
> Suddenly she says, "Consider this equation."
>
> Extending her right arm and hand, she points at the air in front of her, and the word "Atom" appears in blue letters, hovering before her as a holograph. In one continuous sentence, which I'll break into paragraphs to convey what I felt as she spoke, she continues,
>
> "The word 'Atom' means 'I am' . . ." And I feel a shockwave of bliss.
>
> "And the words 'I am' mean 'The King.'" Another bliss-wave.
>
> "Be that!" she concludes. "*Only that!*" And the bliss, truth, and simplicity of her equation seizes me so completely that the quotation marks should be removed from the pronoun "I." I sit in the classroom as The King Himself now, and it seems impossible that I could fall out of this eternal state back into ordinary "I"ness.
>
> But alas, within seconds the classroom, teacher, equation, and King begin atomizing into a mist till I'm lying in a night-blackened bed by a creek in Montana beyond reach of the bliss, truth, and simplicity that just subsumed me.
>
> "Even so," the now-imperceptible King somehow assures me, "if, come dawn, you remember the world inside your world in which you have *been* Me, I, the King Himself, will remain closer to you than your inmost thoughts and breath.
>
> "*I am the Inmost*," He whispers as He retreats into the eternal world inside my mortal realm, leaving "me" to marvel, which all these years later I continue to do:
>
> "I" am Perfection's illusory son.
>
> The King in me is the reality.
>
> Every atom means *I am*.
>
> An equation in the air of a dream classroom once proved it.
>
> Everything in my undreamt Montana world except "*Be that!*" is illusion, and every day and night is Perfection disguised as a chaos of confusions waiting to *stop* waiting, and be as Perfect as the days, nights, and atoms truly are.

V. WATER MEETS SOUL

Turning back to how the Pacific makes love to the Rockies, but bearing in mind that I had dreamed something, as Tenzin Palmo contends, much closer to the inherent nature of things than my workaday perceptions, I can't shake the feeling that, at a profound level, I know this dream to be true.

A related set of intuitions I've had in connection with my love for mountains and rivers: certain mythic things in our world strike me as being so close to omnipotent that I feel they deploy *us* to achieve *their* ends, not the other way around. Even the names of these things strike me as so mountainous they generate weather systems, sending forth thunderhead-energies that blast my attempted definitions to pieces.

Soul is such a name. *Water* is another. And to complicate matters, these two names strike me as profoundly interrelated. *Water* and *soul* both link the natural to the supernatural. By "supernatural" I don't mean the weird, the occult, the unnatural. I mean the *inexpressibly natural*, which in my fiction I have sometimes called "the *extra* extra-natural."

Water links us to the extra-natural because it's crucial to the creation and continuation of all earthly life, and communes with us through life-forms in an infinite number of ways. Water covers four-fifths of our planet, it pervades all flora and fauna, humans included, and its pervasiveness is reflected in world wisdom traditions and scriptures. As a river worshipper I relish the fact that the word *theology* occurs nowhere in the concordance of my *King James Bible*, whereas the words *fish* and *rivers* occur 180 times, and the varied

forms water can take occur close to a thousand times. I also love it that the primary realm of the gods in Northwest tribal, pre-Christian European, and many other aboriginal mythologies is not celestial: it is *submarine*. Pre-industrial Finnish, Celtic, Haida, Druidic, and neo-Druidic lovers of wild water didn't yearn for a "heaven above": they worshipped a fathomless Ocean hidden inside the oceans of Earth—and within *us*, if we consider Rumi's lines, "When the Ocean comes to you as a lover, / Marry her at once for God's sake!"

Every drop of rain and fresh melted snow shares this oceanic yearning and acts upon it in obedience to the form of love we call *gravity*, setting out at once in search of ever-greater bodies of water. This is why the spirituality of the Watershed-Aware is so much more holistic, alive, and literally *baptized* than the spirituality of such people as Baptists. Water, as Henry David Thoreau put it, is "the Earth's eye; looking into which the beholder measures the depths of his own nature," and in these depths I sense something so *extra-natural* about this wondrous liquid, *and* my essential self that water strikes me as not just *resembling* the indweller we call "soul," but as being powerfully linked to it.

Perhaps my favorite definition of soul is Lord Krishna's in the Bhagavad Gita. Krishna tells Arjuna: *The soul is not born, it does not die. Having been, it will never not be. Unborn, enduring, constant, primordial, it is not killed when the body is killed. . . . Weapons do not cut it, fire does not burn it, waters do not wet it, wind does not wither it. . . . Fools pass blindly by it, and of its majesty know nothing. It is nearer than knowing.*

Substitute "water" for "soul" and much of Krishna's definition holds. Water is not killed when the body is killed; it evaporates as a body desiccates, but evaporation isn't death.

Can fire burn water? Let's be scientific about this. Extreme heat changes water from liquid to steam that returns to the atmosphere, but changing form is not the same as burning up. Burning is an exothermic, self-propagating oxidation reaction that usually gives off flames. Extreme heat causes water to decompose by reducing its hydrogen atoms to H_2, but decomposition is not the same as burning. Is water then "deathless," like the soul? A tricky question. If our sun eventually becomes a nova, Earth's waters will become a fleeting cloud of H_2 and O and disappear, but disappearance may not be dying.

I've seen five streams and rivers firsthand that were pronounced dead, but then sprang back to life once the industrial madness of humans stopped "killing" them. Just this year, in October 2024, Chinook salmon returned to Northern California's Klamath River less than one month after four dams were removed. In June of 1999 a trout and salmon stream in Bellingham, Washington, Whatcom Creek, was assaulted by 330,000 gallons of gasoline spilled from a broken pipeline. The gas was then accidentally ignited by two boys playing with a bottle rocket, causing an extended explosion that killed the two boys and a young fly-fisher farther downstream, burning the creek deep into its stone substrata, killing every fish, insect, and riparian creature in a single terrible day. Just four years later I waded that same creek, found a plethora of healthy nymphs in its waters, and learned from biologists and friends working on restoration that nearly every life-form the stream formerly supported had already returned.

"I pray thanks to salmon and steelhead for the treasure it's been to know their impossible strength via a rod that carried me across the species barrier as I played them. I pray thanks to have held, loved, and released each one. I pray thanks that their lovemaking has for millennia wed mountains to ocean as no other creature's has, or can, or shall."

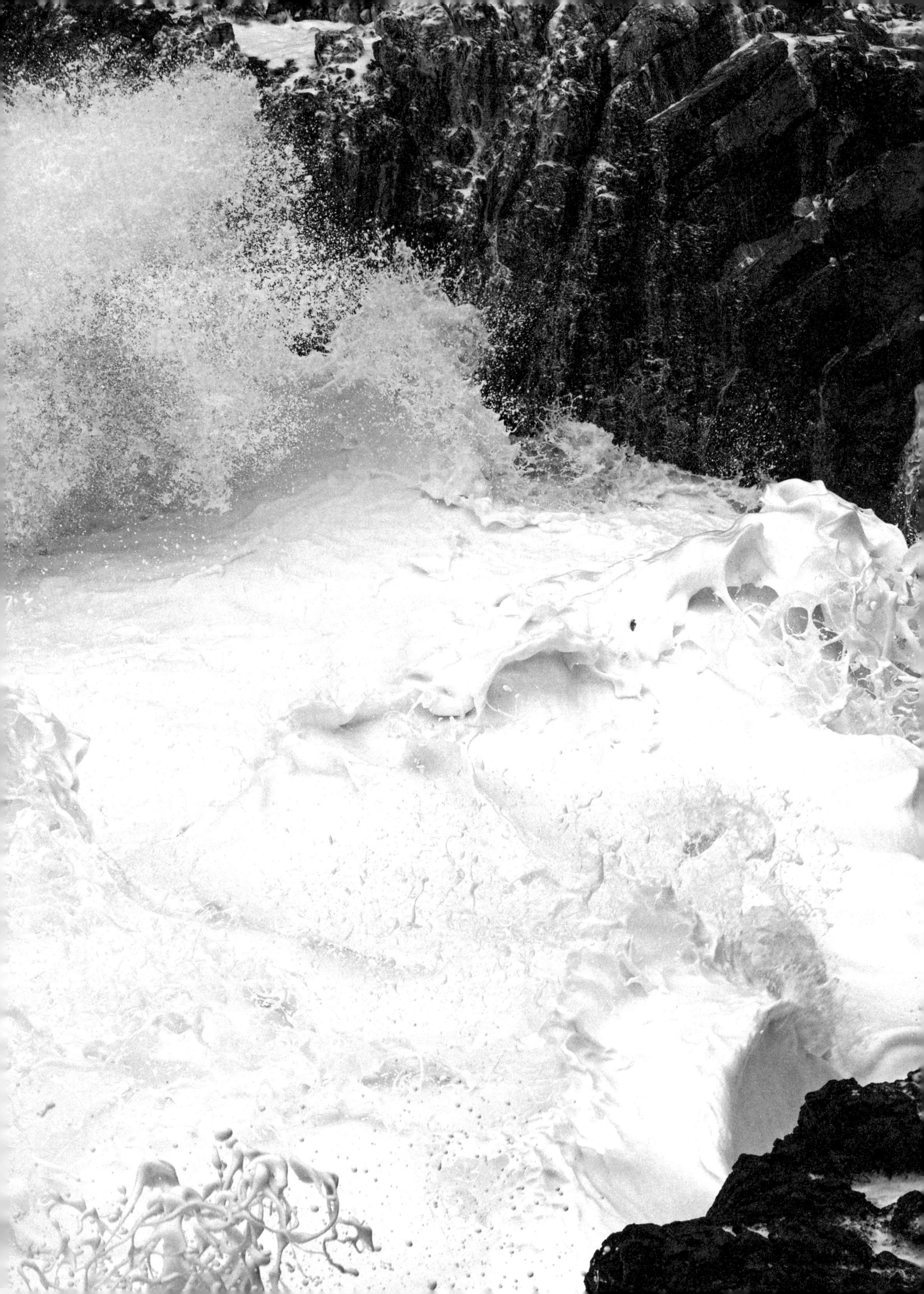

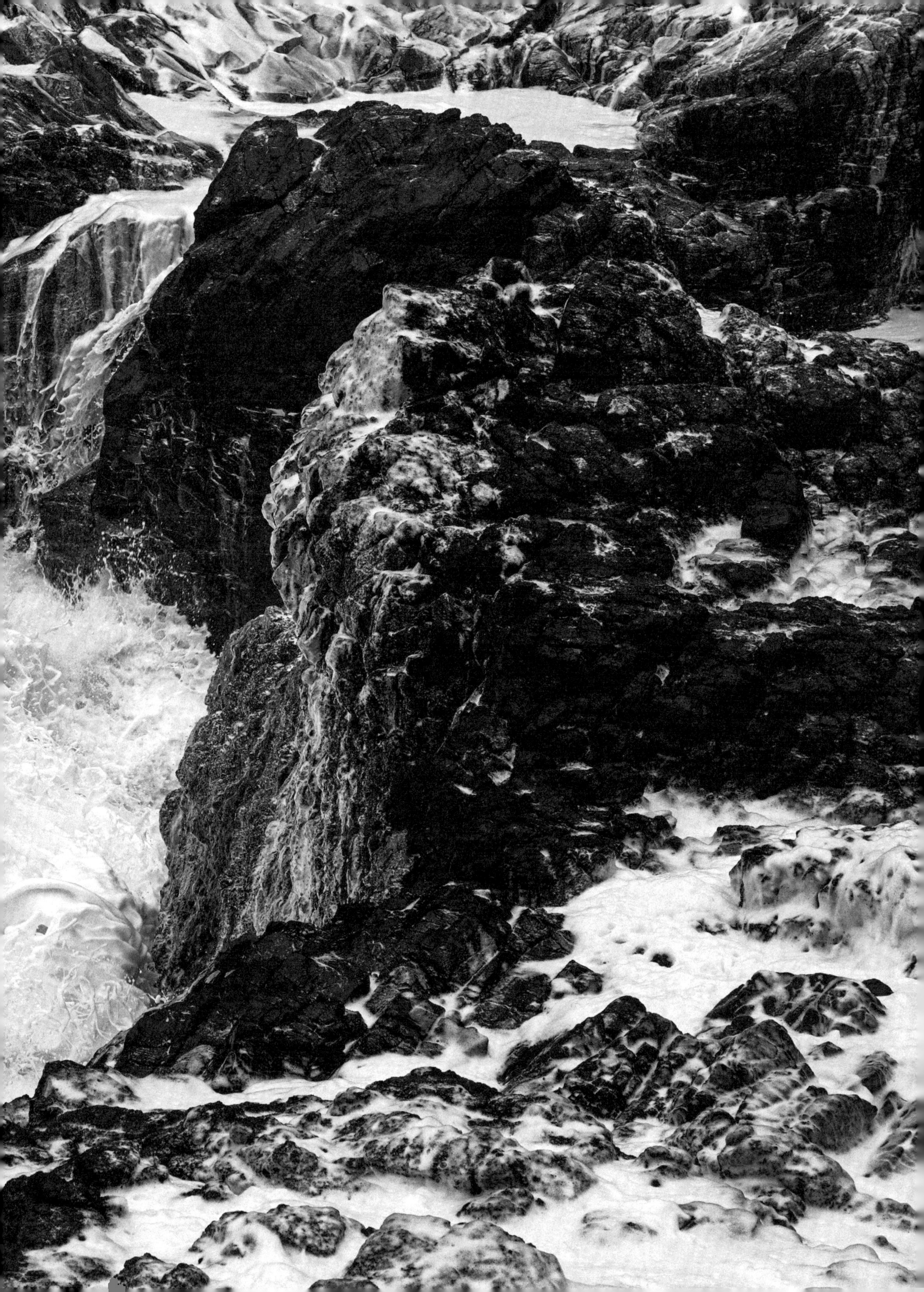

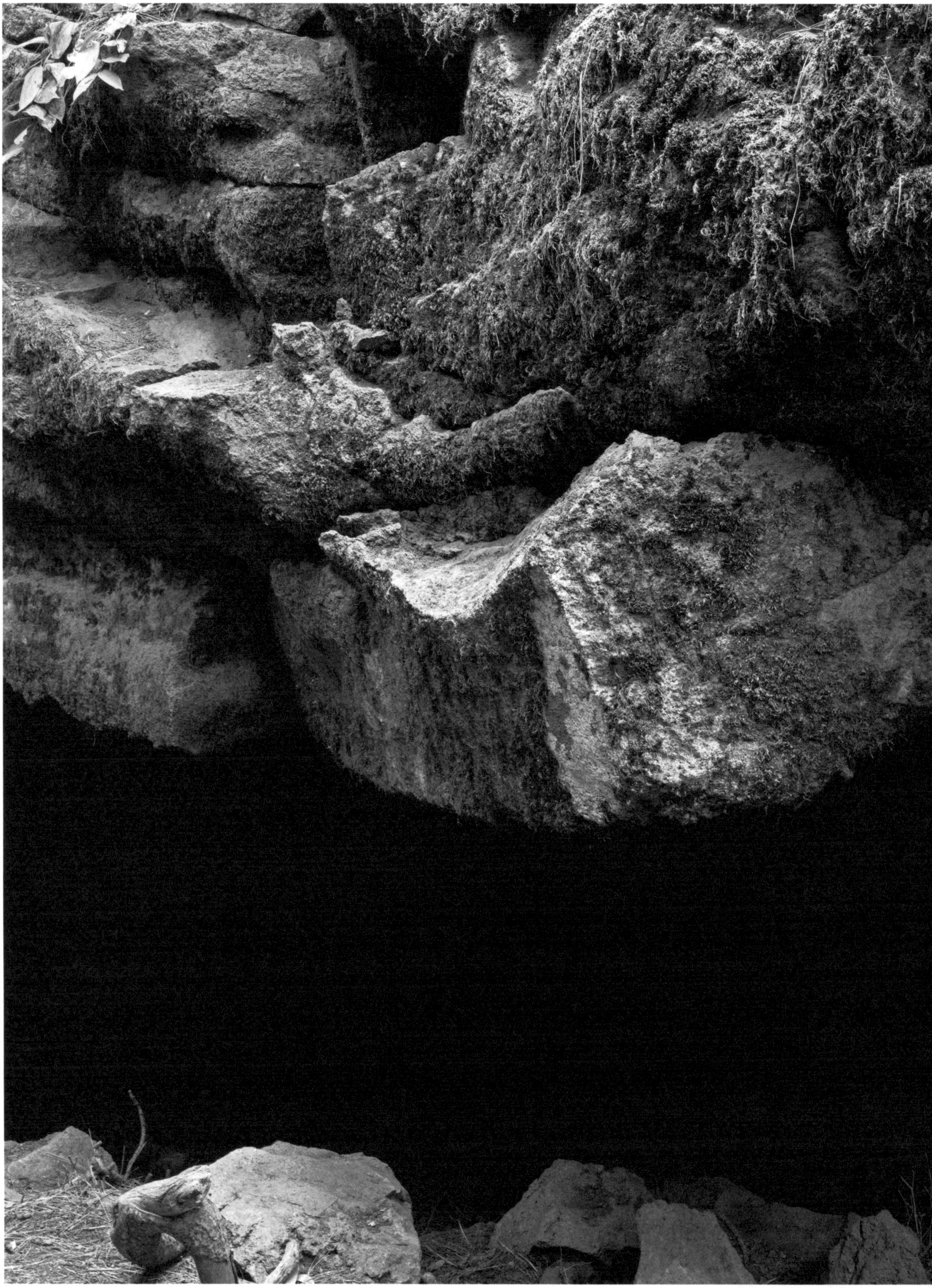

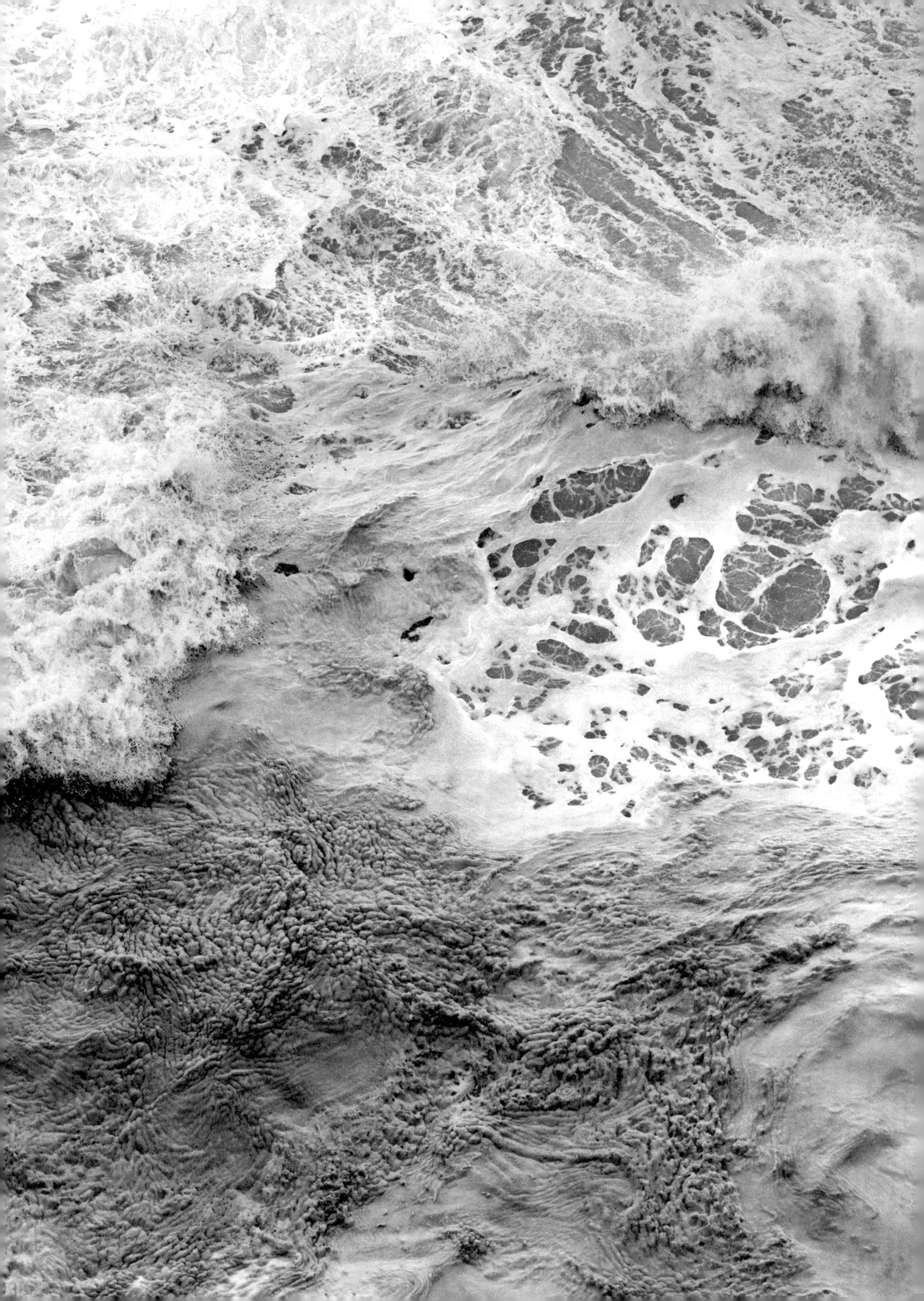

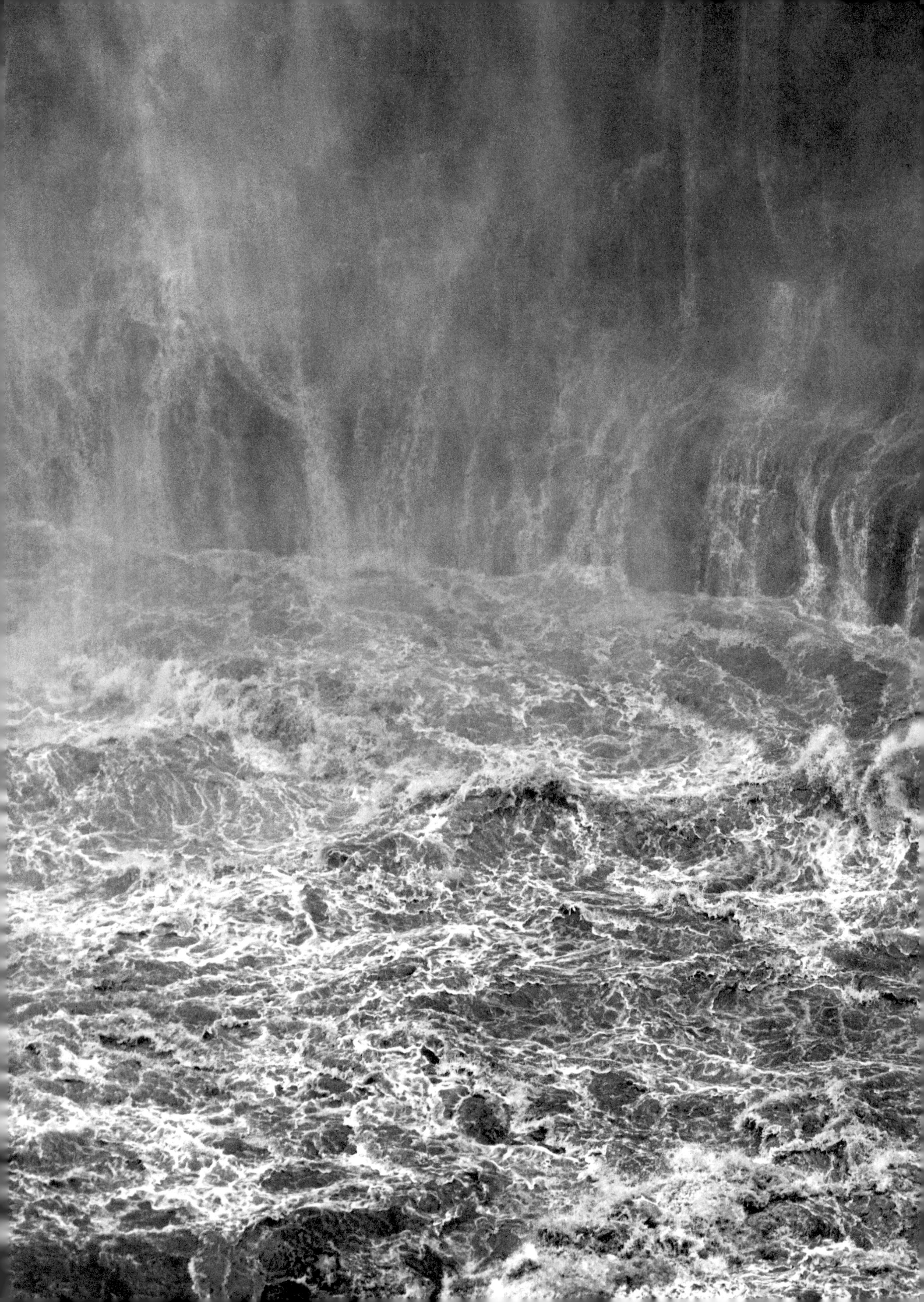

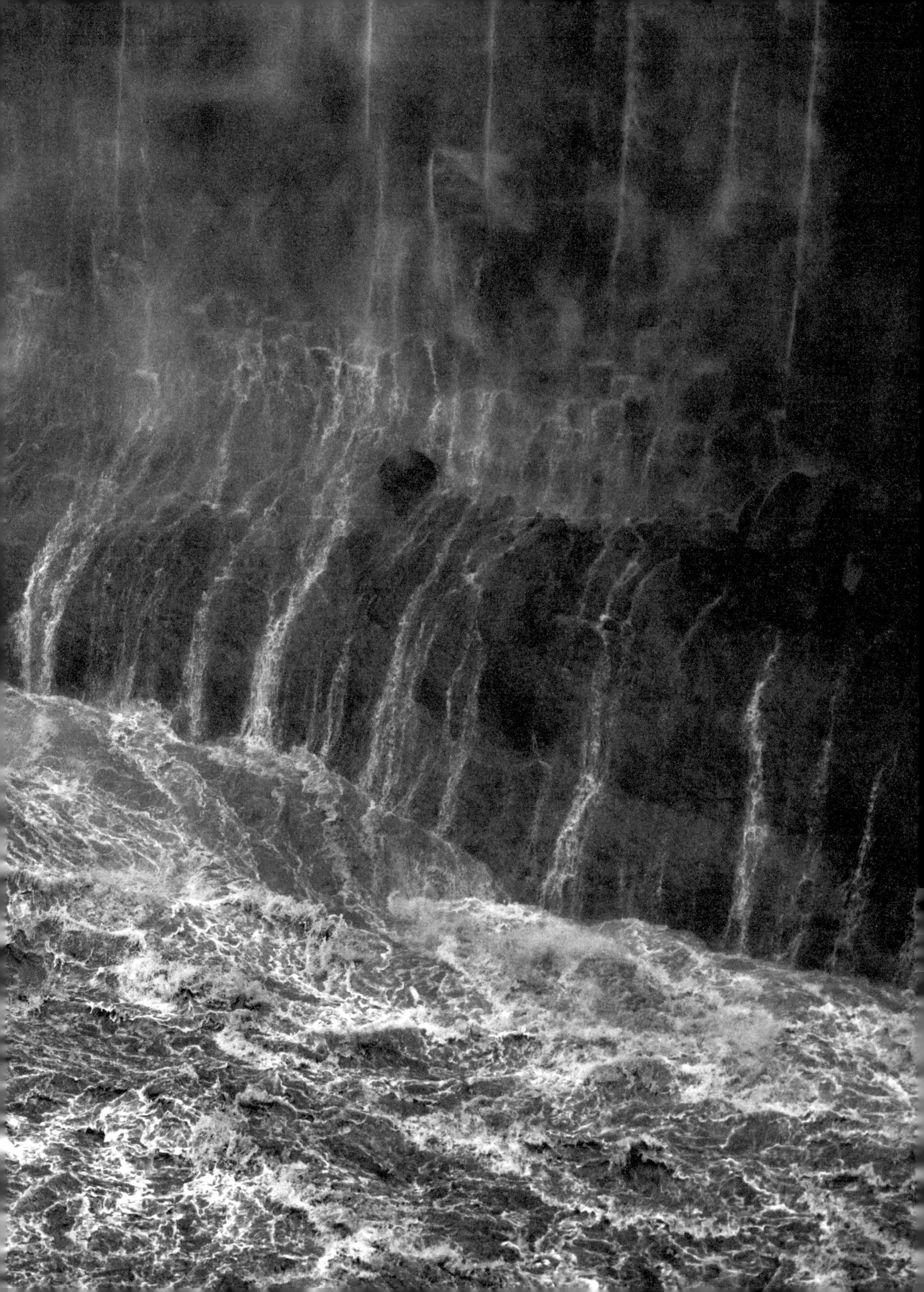

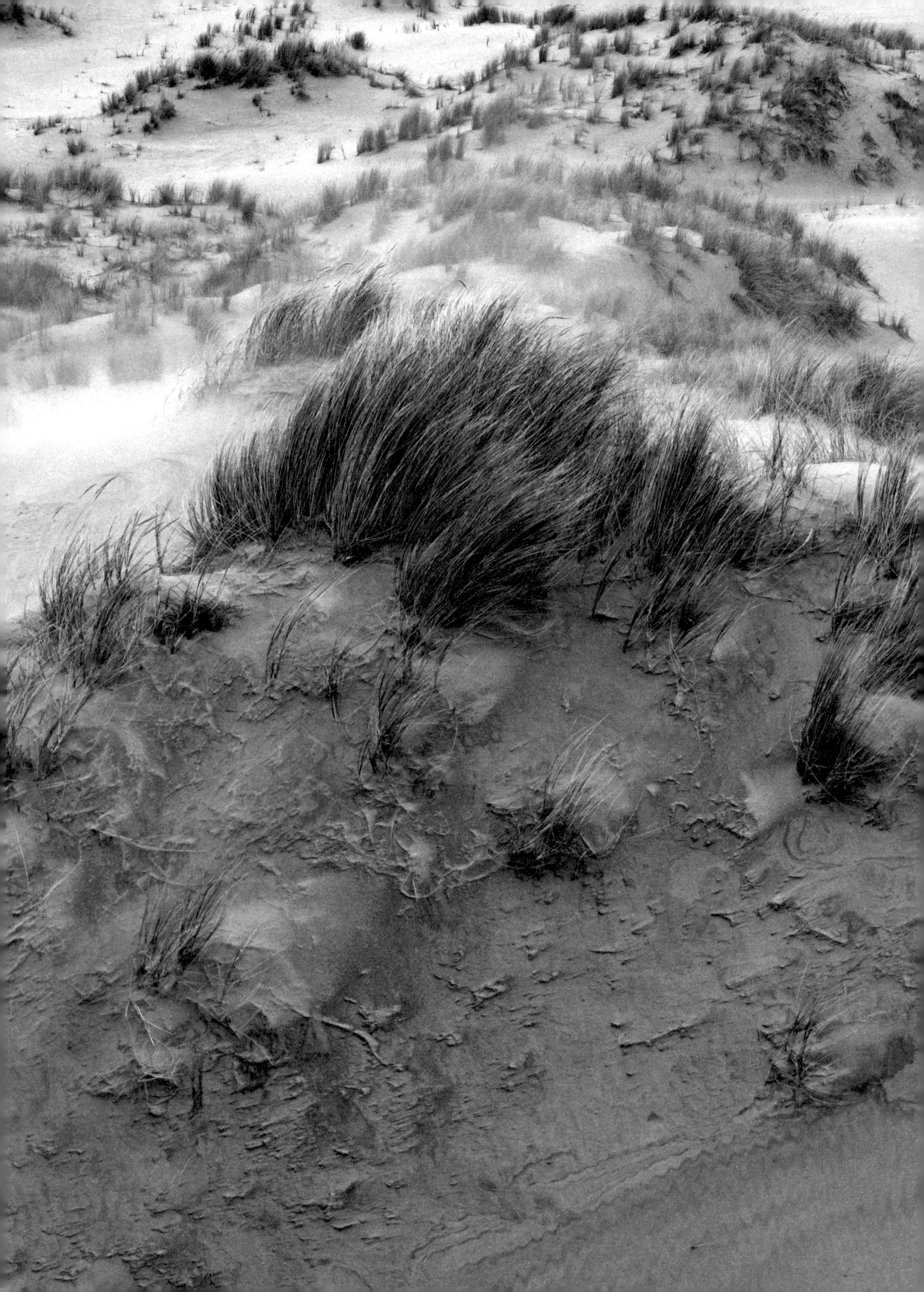

So could water, like the soul, be *unborn* and incapable of dying? To possess this eternal attribute water would have to precede creation. Impossible as this sounds, some of our most respected wisdom traditions suggest that water was indeed here before any other describable beings or stories began.

"In the beginning," say the ancient rishis of India in the *Brihadaranyaka Upanishad*, "there was nothing here at all. . . . Death alone covered this completely, for what is nothingness but Death? Then Death thought: 'Let me equip myself with a body' (Sanskrit: *atma*). So Death undertook a liturgical recitation (Sanskrit: *arc*), and as Death was reciting, water (Sanskrit: *ka*) suddenly sprang from it. Amazed, Death thought: *Recitation caused water to spring from me!*" This is what gave the name to and discloses the true nature of recitation (*arc-ka*). "Recitation is running water." And we're back to the wonder-inducing fact that "running water" is hidden in the bodies, breath, words, imagining brains, and beating hearts of every user of human languages. I adore the depth of mystery here. In this ancient account of life's beginnings, water springs from Nothing before the first body, or anything else, even exists. In this sense it is indeed "unborn."

And the book of Genesis reinforces this contention. As Genesis has it, "In the beginning, God created the heaven and the earth. And the earth was without form, and void; and darkness was upon the face of the deep. And the Spirit of God moved upon the face of the waters. And God said, 'Let there be light': and there was light."

If we carefully consider this familiar text, it's not familiar at all: it's *mind-bending!* Before the first instant in Time or point in Space from whence the Creator began to fashion our world by *letting there be light*, Genesis is saying water was *already here*, already *deep*, already had a *face*, and it feels safe to say this face was wet. Is the Bible then declaring that water is the one element the Creator did *not create*, implying that water is as old as, or even coequal to, the Creator herself, latent in the "dark energy" physicists say was here before the universe burst into existence? In water's solid forms, no two snowflakes or ice crystals are alike. Does this mean water is infinitely creative due to its *extra-natural nature?* Being unborn, deathless, and primordial, might water be the pellucid "paint" the Unseen Painter uses to place life on the canvas of our entire universe?

Though I can't answer such questions, I can't help but marvel at them. My lifelong love of flowing water links me in the most natural way I've found to the marvelous, the mysterious, the *extra* extra-natural, and the Genesis and Upanishad authors and I are far from alone in having noticed this.

"Wisdom begins in wonder," says Socrates.

"From wonder into wonder, existence opens," adds Lao Tzu.

To bring all this home to the true nature of a "you" or "me," when water is so mysterious, essential, and possibly deathless, comprising 60 to 70 percent of our bodies and 75 percent of a brain, continuously flowing between what science calls "different compartments and cell types during physiological and pathophysiological processes," how scientific is it to define this process as *pathophysiological*—which means *abnormal*—when a wondrous extra-natural watershed is flowing through our bodies and brains at all times?

For all I know (and don't laugh: the watershed in my head is being serious!), it could be *the soul's own autobiography* that makes me feel I was once an iota of a life-form floating on the face of dark and silent deeps, when a Voice arose, saying, *"Let there be a firmament in the midst of the waters, and let it divide the waters from the waters,"* and my iota-self watched the waters swell, roil, and divide till a firmament of heaven burst into being. For all I know, I could be the Alpha and the Omega wading through a literary fly-fisher's life due to a hilariously low self-esteem problem! For all I know I could be the Almighty Herself, stuck in the throes of a *"Hi! My name is David"* dream that will one day burst like a bubble in a Bitterroot River foam line, leaving the Creator of the Universe standing, radiant, in Burst-Bubble-David's place.

VI. THREE IMPROVISATIONS ON SEASONS AND TIME

The countless things that fit inside our minds and imaginations do so because they are abstract. Abstraction, in this sense, is highly useful, making memories and knowledge portable, art, science, and stories possible, and music, images, and experiences had by one person able to move through time and space into many persons.

The danger of abstraction is that the matter and life-forms that sustain us are not abstract. Our actions unleash forces latent in abstract concepts into the realm of matter and living forms. If insufficiently faithful to life, abstract concepts can then cause harm. This is why we need cosmologies. Cosmology is creation and abstraction engaged in imaginative negotiation; it is mind, matter, and spirit at play.

When the cosmos speaks to us, it does not use words. We are all involved, daily, in translating creation's nonverbal messages into abstract thought and language. To live in harmony with other life-forms our translations must be accurate. If, for instance, we flout the cosmologists known as meteorologists and wear shorts and a tank top at ten below, we suffer hypothermia; if we defy the cosmologists known as soil scientists and irrigate with alkaline water, our gardens wither; if we flout the cosmologists who study pollutants and power our cities with coal-fired electricity, we fill the air, clouds, rain, soil, rivers, and foods with mercury, and thousands unnecessarily suffer and die.

Moses was a living man, not an archaic list of dos and don'ts. His cosmology was an ongoing series of creative responses to ever-changing circumstances. But for all his wisdom, Moses had a famously short fuse. When I picture him learning that human industry is spewing so much heat into the atmosphere that we're destroying both the polar caps and the life-sustaining ocean gyres that give us viable seasons, setting off planet-heating chain reactions that could make Earth uninhabitable to every life-form Moses pronounced "very good" in *Genesis*, it's hard to imagine he wouldn't storm into corporate boardrooms, turn his staff into a wizard's wand, turn fossil fuel spreadsheets into clouds of locusts, and issue a fresh list of thou-shalt-nots that would leave coal plants, Tar Sands, and runaway internal combustion to be dealt with as the abominations they've become.

Informed in part by scripture and tradition, a cosmology is a living relationship between humans and the universe that envelops us, inhaling what's fresh, exhaling what's obsolete, cross-pollinating, reasoning, intuiting, imagining, and responding as needed. The best cosmological speculation is therefore more like an improvised Indian raga or American jazz tune than a classical recital. A jazz pianist or sitar player can, on any given occasion, pull trained instincts from their fingers, pull structures from their imagination, and interact with their keys or fretboard to perform extempore music utterly unique to time and place. Shouldn't the possessor of a viable cosmology be able to do the same?

I live in the extreme upper Columbia River drainage in the Bitterroot Mountains' rain shadow on a cottonwood- and willow-lined creek between six-thousand-foot pine-covered, fire-vulnerable ridges. We call the current year 2025 and the current season "spring." Can I extemporaneously pull trained instincts from my fingers and structures from my experience and imagination to produce a series of cosmological improvisations in response to this time and place?

Assignment to self: find out. Sit down, place fingers on keys, and see if you can improvise three cosmological riffs based on what is materially and spiritually perceptible; what is moving through time and space with me; what I see, hear, touch, smell, dream, and intuit to be true in this ever-changing Season and Time . . .

IMPROV I: THE SEASON OF TWO SEASONS

It is March in Montana and the door between winter and spring is swinging violently open and closed. For days a sometimes-gentle, sometimes-brutal southwesterly wind has been breaking over the Bitterroot Range, bringing walls of cloud so towering and dark they look world-ending. But no sooner does each dark wall dump its wintry load than the seasonal door swings back open to spring, an impossibly blue sky breaks out, the snow swiftly melts, birds burst into arias, summer feels just round the corner; and then—tied to the balm like an anti-proverbial March lion to its lamb—the next cloud-wall arrives, briefly hurtling us back an entire season.

Studying this weather after dropping my daughters off at school, I return home, go to my desk to capture what I've been seeing, but instead see that after a long winter of writing my study looks as if the schizoid weather has been blasting through indoors.

Grabbing a vacuum and cleaning products, I set out to restore order, but an hour into this work I start to recycle two old magazines (a *Time*, a *National Geographic*), open the *Time* to save a nice grouse feather bookmark, and the page the feather marked stops me in my tracks:

It's a Hubble Space Telescope photo of clouds in the Orion Nebula, 1,500 light-years away—that's 10,000,000,000,000,000 miles from Montana and me—and these clouds are made not of ice crystals like the clouds outside, but of superheated hydrogen that lights them up from within. In color they range from orange to gold to rosewood brown, pierced here and there by tiny flares of bright pink. In form they're flagrantly phallic, reminding me of stalagmites, velvet moose antlers, coral formations, and, begging your pardon, one of the exceedingly odd parts of Everyman. In size, however, the Orion clouds annihilate all earthly analogy: they are *six trillion miles long.*

There are projections coming off them. Shaped like animal ears, bean sprouts, the antennae of slugs (some artfully tipped by the pink flares), the protuberances are minuscule compared to the masses out of which they grow. Yet even the smallest protrusions, the Hubble astronomers tell us, are as wide as our entire solar system, and even the smallest contain something astounding: *stars.*

Those piercingly pink flares? Fetal stars, every one of them, caught by the Hubble in the very act of being born. What's more, the astronomers say, our sun, solar system, Earth, its waters, life-forms, and selves are all the offspring of pink flares such as these and their clouds.

In other words, the Sun, Earth, and us humans are siblings, for we're all the progeny of these stupendous clouds. Here at my Montana window I'm seated on the lap of an Ancient Sister, enjoying the light of an Ancient Brother, looking as if in a family album at a photo of our Heavenly Father/Mothers, experiencing waves of feeling so paradoxical they make me dizzy. I'm so tiny and short-lived compared to my parent-clouds! Yet I share a progenitive shape with them, I have conceived offspring as have they, and my offspring shine like stars to me.

IMPROV II: TRUE WILDERNESS

Recalling why I saved the dusty *National Geographic* as well, I open it—and am again struck dumb by a Hubble Space photo even grander than the one of the Orion Nebula. To capture this image the Hubble was aimed, the astronomers explain, at one of the darkest parts of space, focused on an interstellar region "the size of a grain of sand held at arm's length," and 276 exposures were taken over ten days "to gather as much distant light as possible." The result is a photograph not of layers of stars, but layers of literally thousands of galaxies in this single image, stretching "as far as the Hubble's eye can see."

Feeling my mind bend severely, I circle slowly back through what I'm seeing. Here is a mere *speck* of our universe, a sand-sized grain of it, yet when a 276-exposure jury turns in its verdict, this grain is seen to contain a vast field of jeweled galaxies glittering in blankness and blackness. The physical gaze of this photo has penetrated so deep it tells a story too vast for thought or word, yet here it sits on a page, speaking a beyond-language of spheres, swirls, colors, light. Even the tiniest points in this image, astronomers say, are not stars but entire galaxies. The light from some, traveling at 186,000 miles per second, takes *eleven billion years* to reach Earth.

This is what I call *a Roadless Area!* This is true *Wilderness*. But how to even partially describe its relationship to Time and Seasons? The number of stars, star-birthing nebula-clouds, solar systems, planets, moons, mineral-forms, life-forms, dead-forms implied by this photo stop my mind and leave me hearing music. If we could look back toward ourselves from some bright point here pictured, our entire Milky Way would be a single shining dot, our sun a nothingness lost in the deeps of that dot, and our Earth and selves a dream within those depths.

Another fact that stuns and consoles me is the realization that Earth is at one not with industrial humanity, but with this photo's multi-galaxied swirl. Lacking some unthinkable sci-fi miracle such as "warp speed" that would let us travel millions of times faster than light, not a molecule of this vastness will ever be disturbed, colonized, debated, exploited, degraded, or even touched by our too-often insanely manipulative species. Human-caused havoc has knocked our planet terribly out of balance, creating extinctions that throw the evolution of life-forms eons backward in time, but the birthing of stars, cooling of stars into planets, and evolution of planetary life-forms are so inexorable they've recovered tremendous biodiversity after all five of the great extinctions we know of. Earth will swirl on. It's only a self-obsessed species known as "terrestrial humanity" that may not. The wilderness in this photograph contains us the way a shoreless ocean contains a drop. Even at our worst, we're a negligible jot of darkness in a boundlessness filled with symmetries, mysteries, colors, creations, and heavenly lights.

IMPROV III: ASSAILED

On a five-foot shelf within reach of my desk I keep thirty or so books I love so much that their imaginative flights and insights now bleed into my own. Turning from the Hubble photo to this shelf, my eyes alight on Annie Dillard's *For the Time Being* as I try to remember words spoken by Annie's hero, the French paleontologist, priest, and mystic Pierre Teilhard de Chardin, words that once left me hearing the same inward music that spring snow clouds and Hubble images are playing now. I page through Annie's masterpiece till Teilhard's words and the inward music mesh:

> *By means of all created things, without exception, the divine assails us, penetrates us, and molds us. We imagined it as distant and inaccessible, whereas in fact we live steeped in its burning layers.*

My God! I whisper as the words somehow reverse the Hubble image, throwing the swirl of galaxies into my interior. I'm covered instantly with goosebumps. It seems an unneeded act of cosmic exhibitionism when, out the window, sunlight bursts forth, finches, crossbills, grosbeaks, and siskins burst into song, and the swirling snowflakes turn blindingly bright.

Turning from snow to the galaxies to embryonic pink stars to a desk photo of my daughters, I am assailed. In the photo my youngest oh so carefully holds a single petal of a living sunflower between her thumb and index finger. The same flower's blind eye followed the sun across the sky every day last summer, in autumn bowed low, and in winter fed its great eye to the siskins, juncos, and chickadees who repaid the gift by planting black bits of the eye in the snow-softened soil. Tiny green sprouts now unfurl all over the yard. While our sun is burning four million tons of itself per second to enliven this world of bird-sustaining sunflowers and snow, countless agèd suns are exploding like spent blossoms, scattering fragments throughout their solar systems, falling into orbits, becoming planets, as future suns gestate in fiery phallic clouds.

This sunlit snow is a falling Milky Way. The cells of my body are another. We are born of, fed, and assailed by a sacrificial burning. We live steeped in its layers. My daughters' brown eyes burn so serenely in the photo—yet they burn. The music of Teilhard's words rises. Tears rise. I turn from stars to sunlight to sunflowers to snow to my children's faces. I feel us steeping in the sacrificial layers. How gorgeously the Pacific makes love to the Rockies!

I start plundering my journals for quotes to enhance the explosion of feelings assailing me:

Albert Einstein: *In the new physics, there is no place for both field and matter, because field is the only reality.*

Jalal al-Din Rumi: *Out beyond ideas of right-doing and wrong-doing there is a field. I'll meet you there.*

Willigis Jager: *There aren't two kinds of laws: matter and mind. Rather, there is a single continuous law for both matter and mind. Matter is the domain of space in which the field is extremely dense.*

Pierre Teilhard de Chardin: *Concretely speaking, there is no matter and spirit. There exists only matter that is becoming spirit.*

Frederick Sommer: *Spirit is the behavior of matter. Perception does not take spiritedness into a state of affairs that does not already have it.*

Stephen Hawking: *What is it that breathes fire into the equations and makes a universe for them to describe?*

St. John of the Cross: *The fire! The fire inside!*

Julian of Norwich: *We shall be tempested, we shall be travailed, we shall be dis-eased, we shall pass through death, but we shall not be overcome, and all manner of wounded and vanished things shall be well.*

Thich Nhat Hanh: *Tomorrow, I will continue to be. But you will have to be very attentive to see me. I will be a flower, or a leaf. I will be in these forms and I will say hello to you. If you are attentive enough, you will recognize me, and you may greet me. I will be very happy.*

Think about it, you who fear the swift passing of seasons out of yearning for an immortal life: the simplest way to begin living forever is to remember you already have!

Light is in everything we see, yet its nature is elusive. As a wave of light interacts with the world, it scatters, diffuses, becomes absorbed, and transforms. And what appears as white light is, in fact, composed of seven distinct colors—red, orange, yellow, green, blue, indigo, and violet.

It is light, in its many permutations, that gives form to the cycle of Earth's seasons. As our planet tilts and orbits around the Sun, the shifting angles of light create rhythms that shape temperature and weather, and beyond that, entire ecosystems, human cultures, and our deepest sense of time and place.

Variation—and its absence—is central to our experience of these rhythms. The changing light of the seasons is more than a visual phenomenon; it is a cosmic metronome. Without these fluctuations, time would feel adrift, and the intricate ecological, emotional, spiritual systems built on light would begin to unravel.

As light changes throughout the seasons, we encounter how the nature of light determines what we see—for it is only through the instruction of light that we can perceive the world. We experience how light bounces, bends, diffuses, and disperses; how it creates shadow and saturates color; how the quality of light at dawn differs from that at dusk; how the absence or presence of light alters the human experience at its most fundamental level.

These studies on light explore not only the elements of light at play throughout the seasons, but also the very nature of light itself. They are invitations to meet each of light's faces; to move with it as it evolves.

L:100, A:0, B:0

Appendix: Five Studies on Light

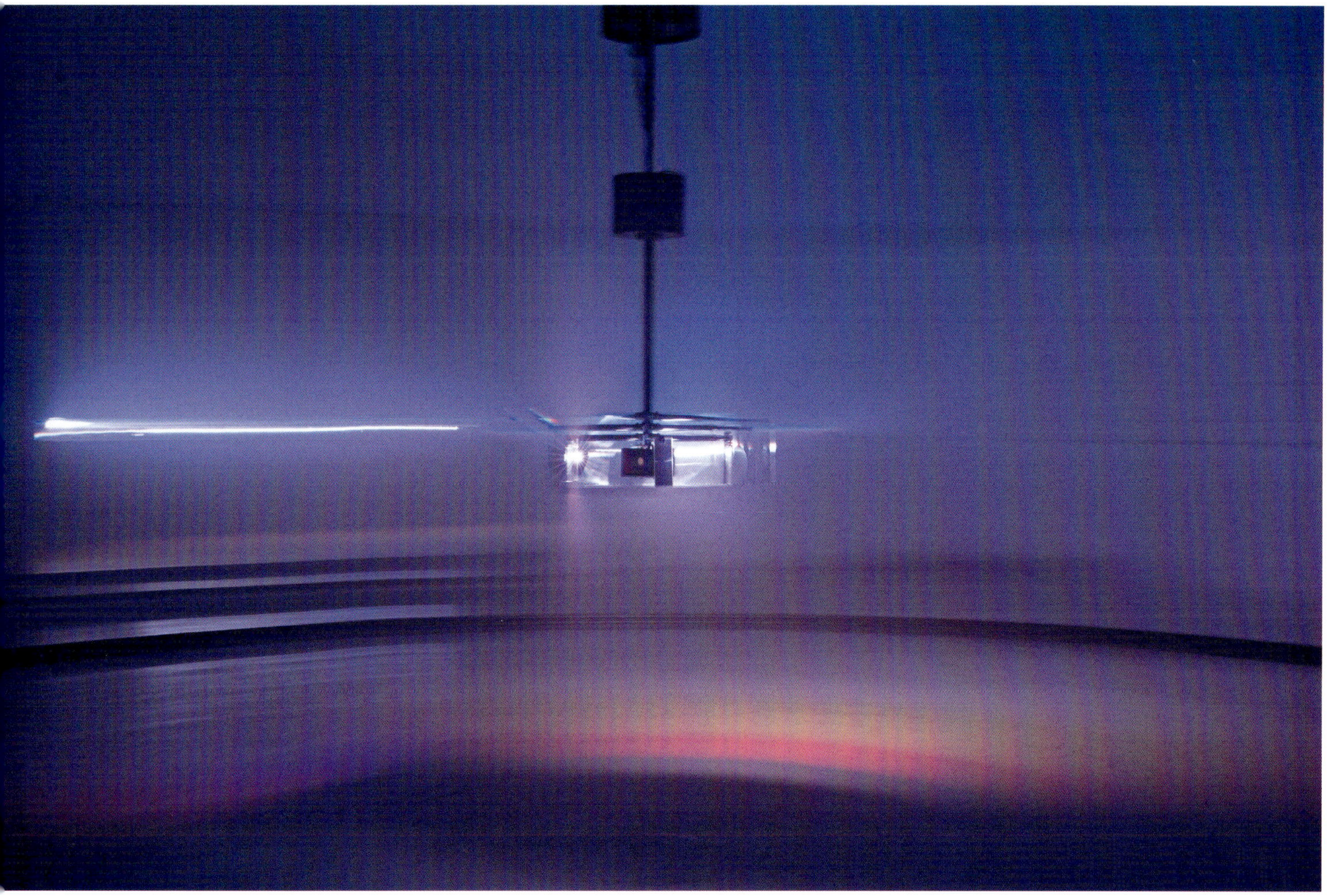

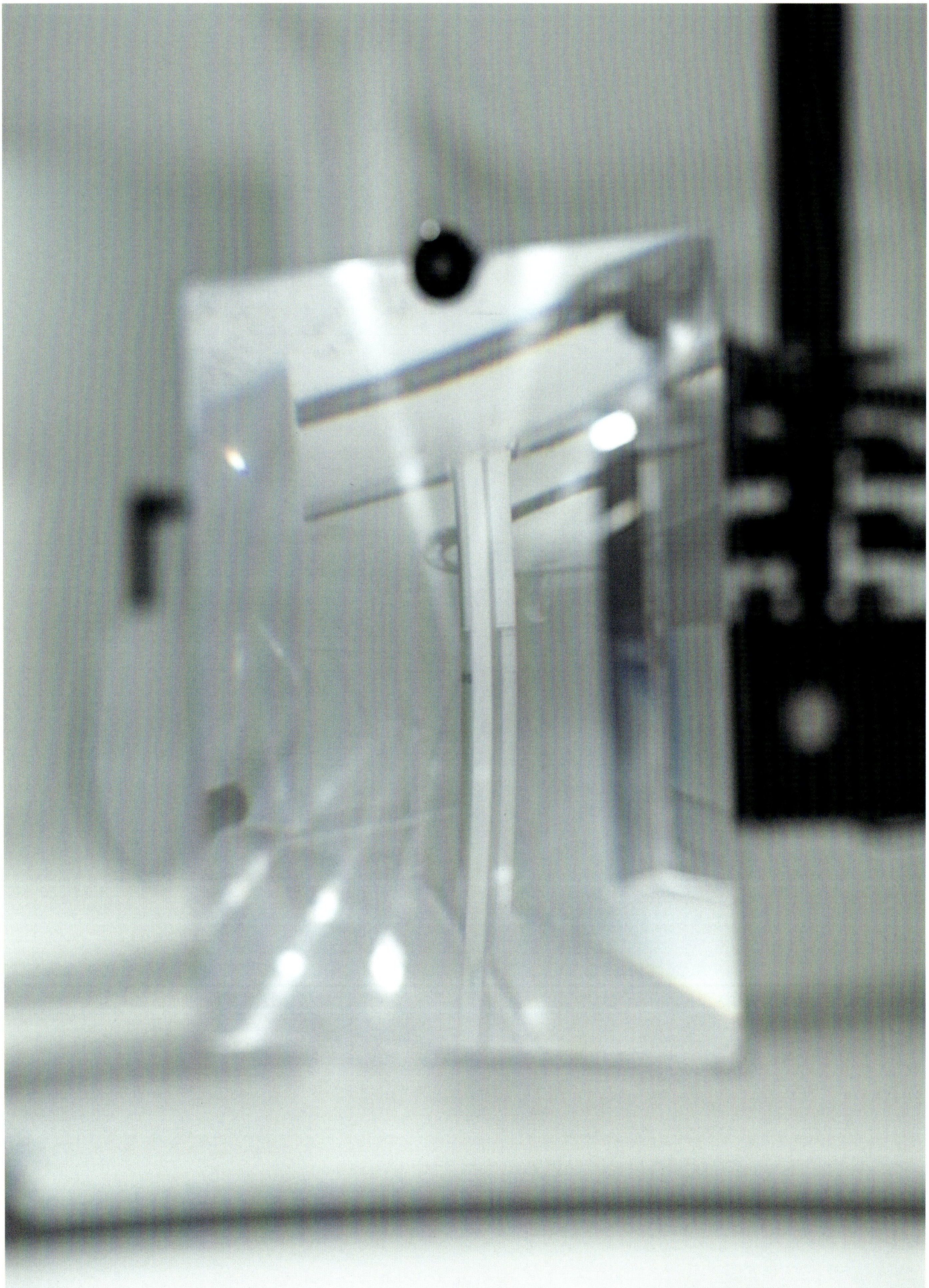

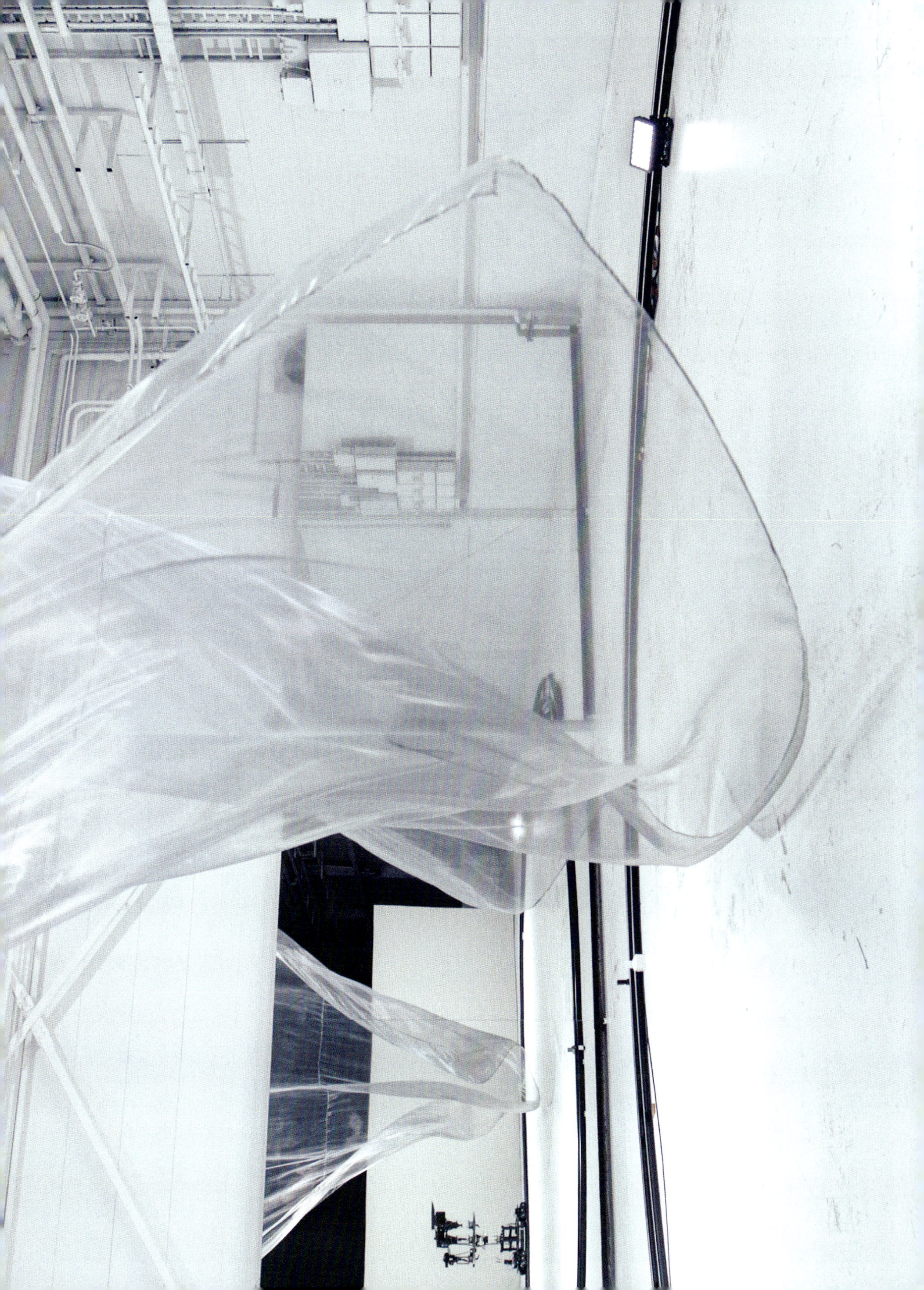

Does darkness have a shape?

Does light?

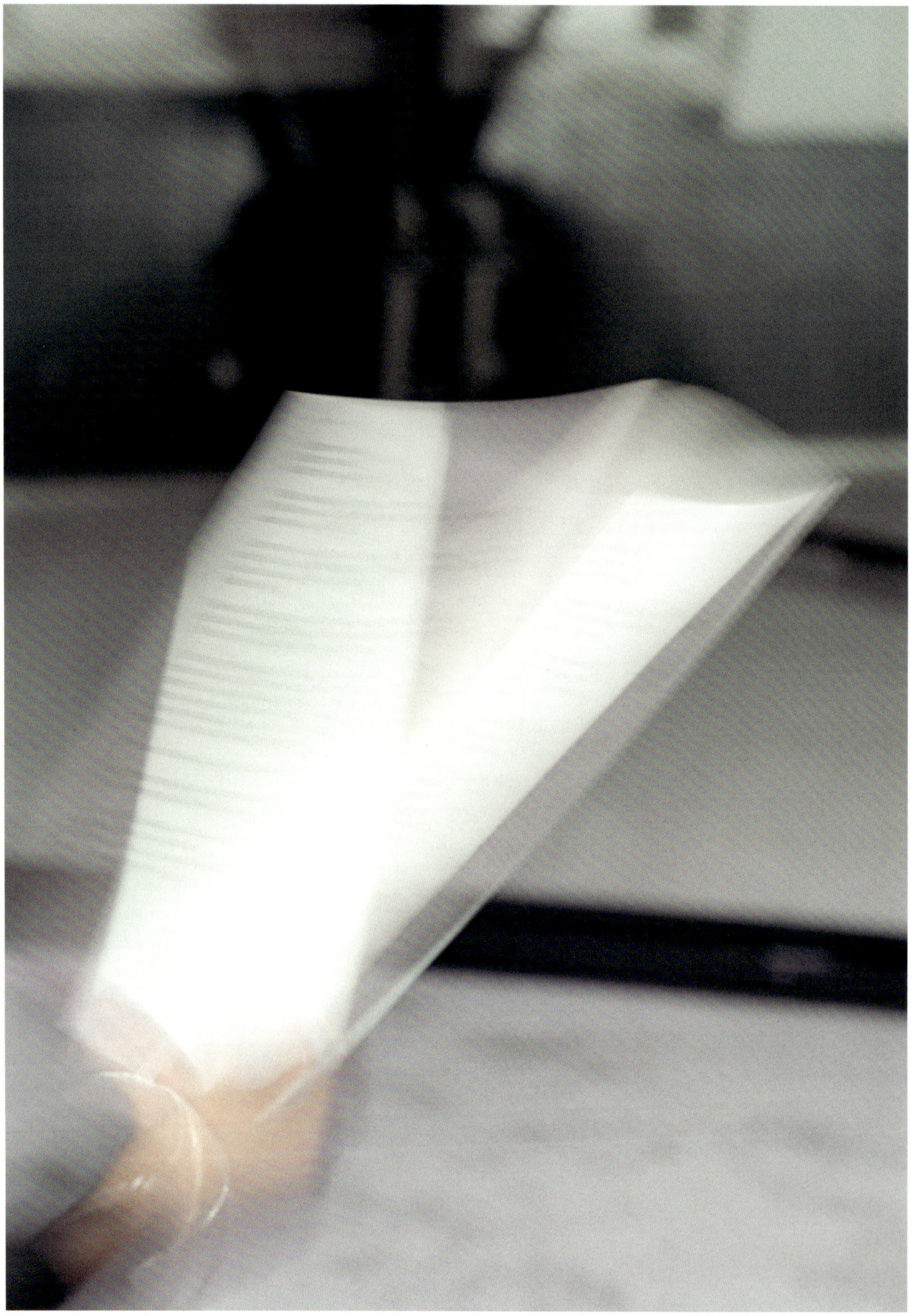

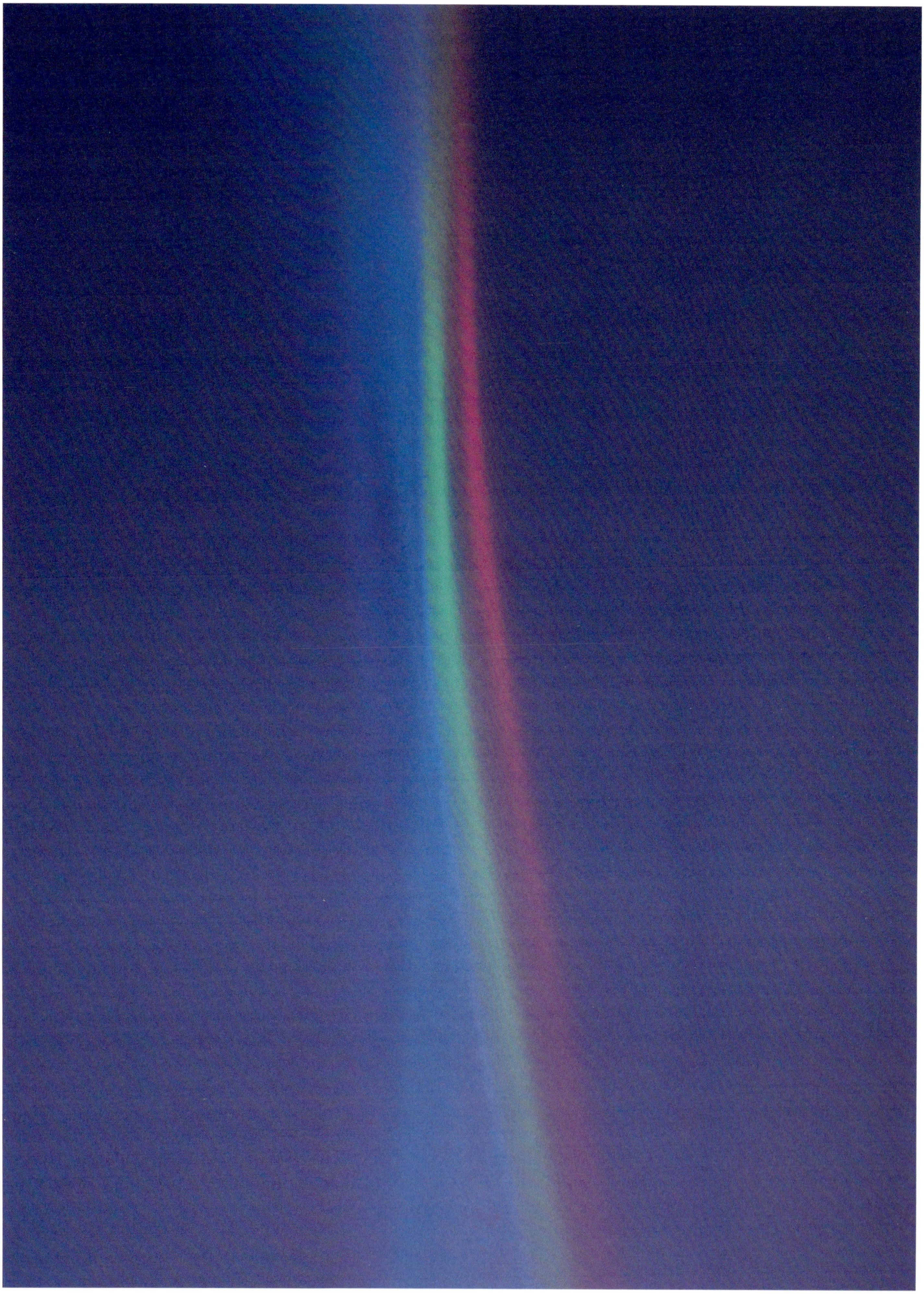

DIFFUSION & SCATTERING—Light rarely travels untouched. Scattered by particles or surfaces, its path is broken into many directions. The wave is sent astray. A clear beam becomes a soft glow. Blue skies and red sunsets are born this way. Diffusion is a more delicate scattering. On matte surfaces or through clouds, light is scattered evenly, erasing glare, softening shadows. The world becomes quieter, less defined, but more forgiving.

(1)

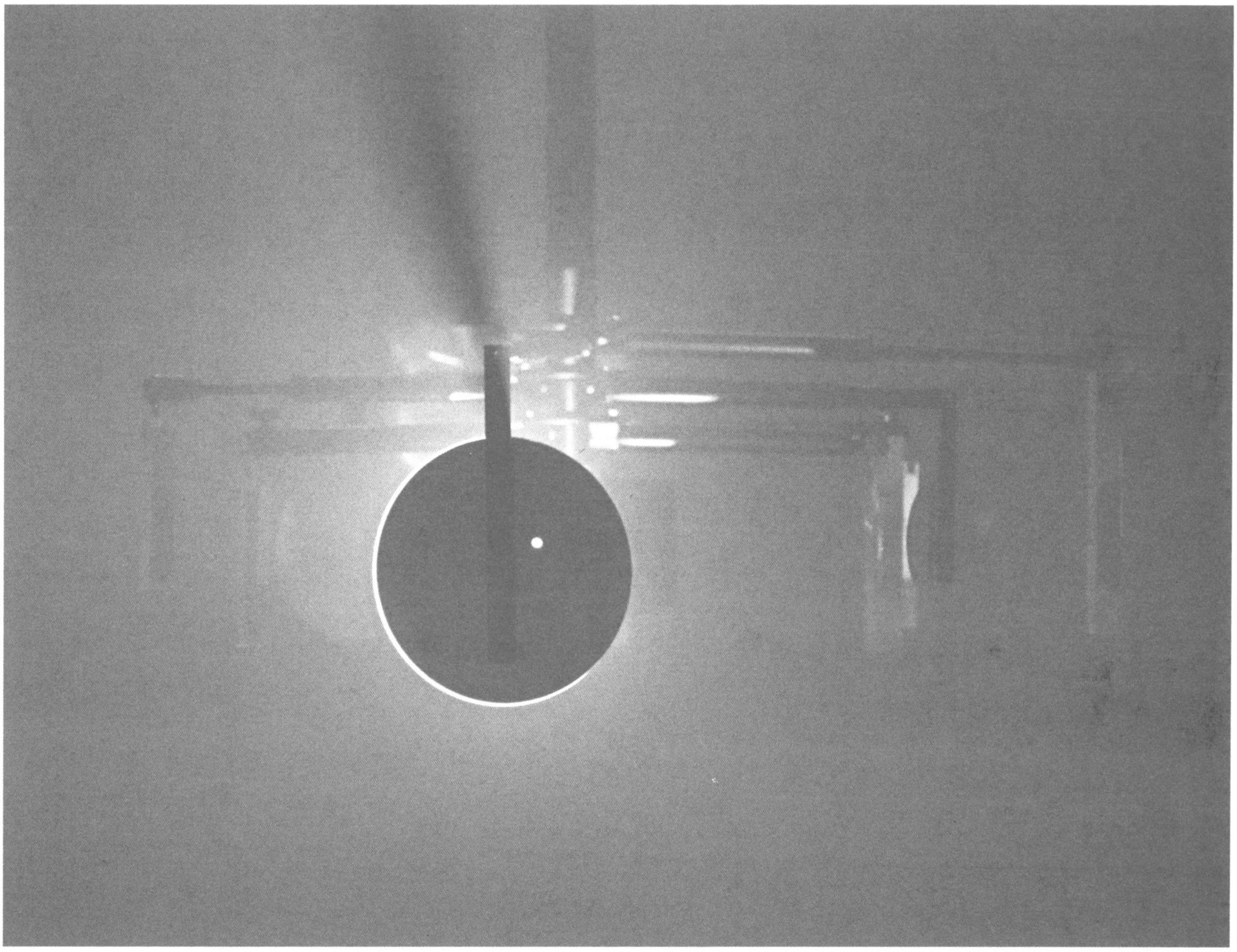

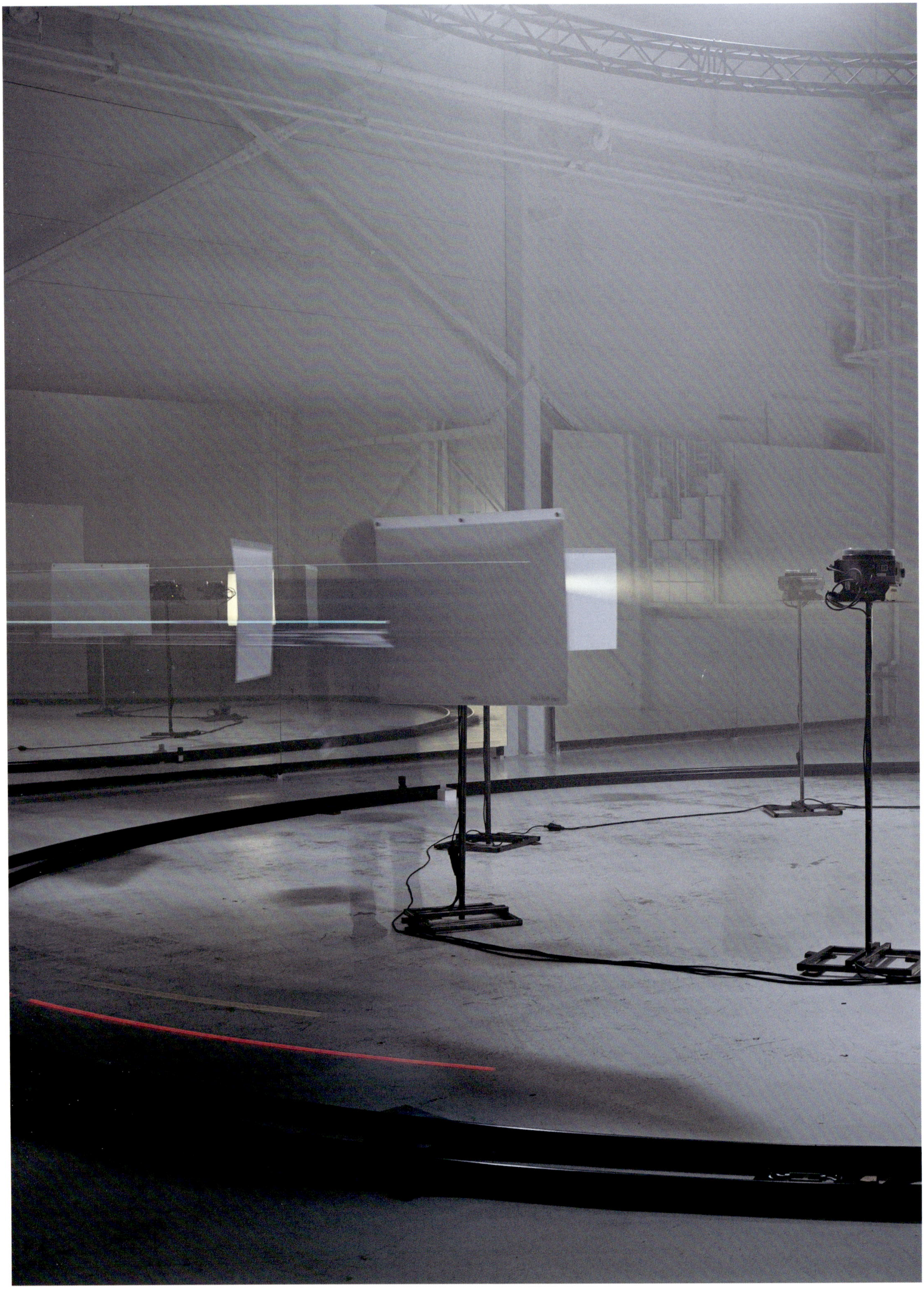

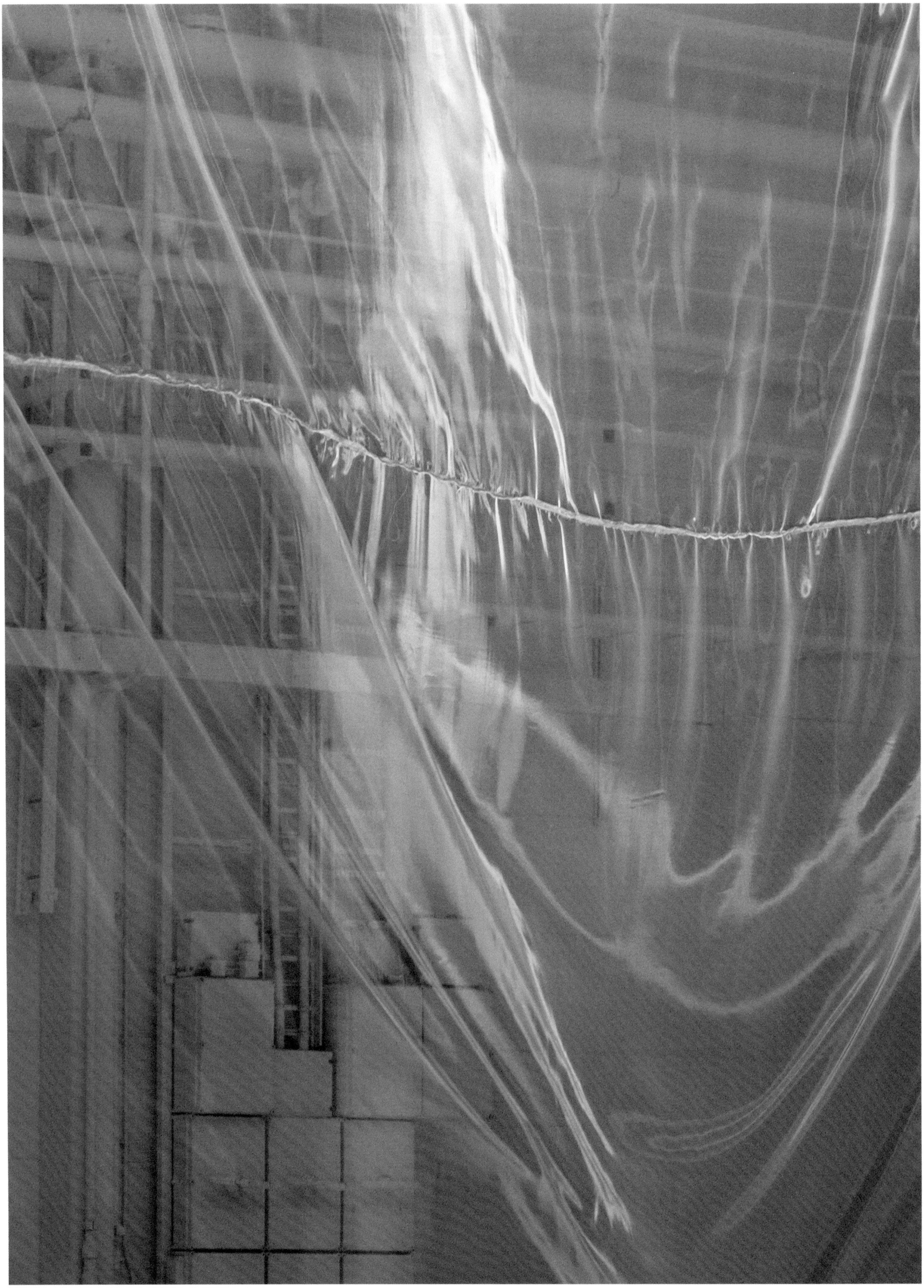

DIFFRACTION—Light finds its way through the cracks. It bends around edges and slips through narrow openings. This is diffraction. The wave spreads, creating patterns of light and dark, ripples of energy beyond simple lines. It reveals light's true nature: a wave that cannot be confined. Diffraction is light's gentle bending, a reminder of its fluid form.

(2)

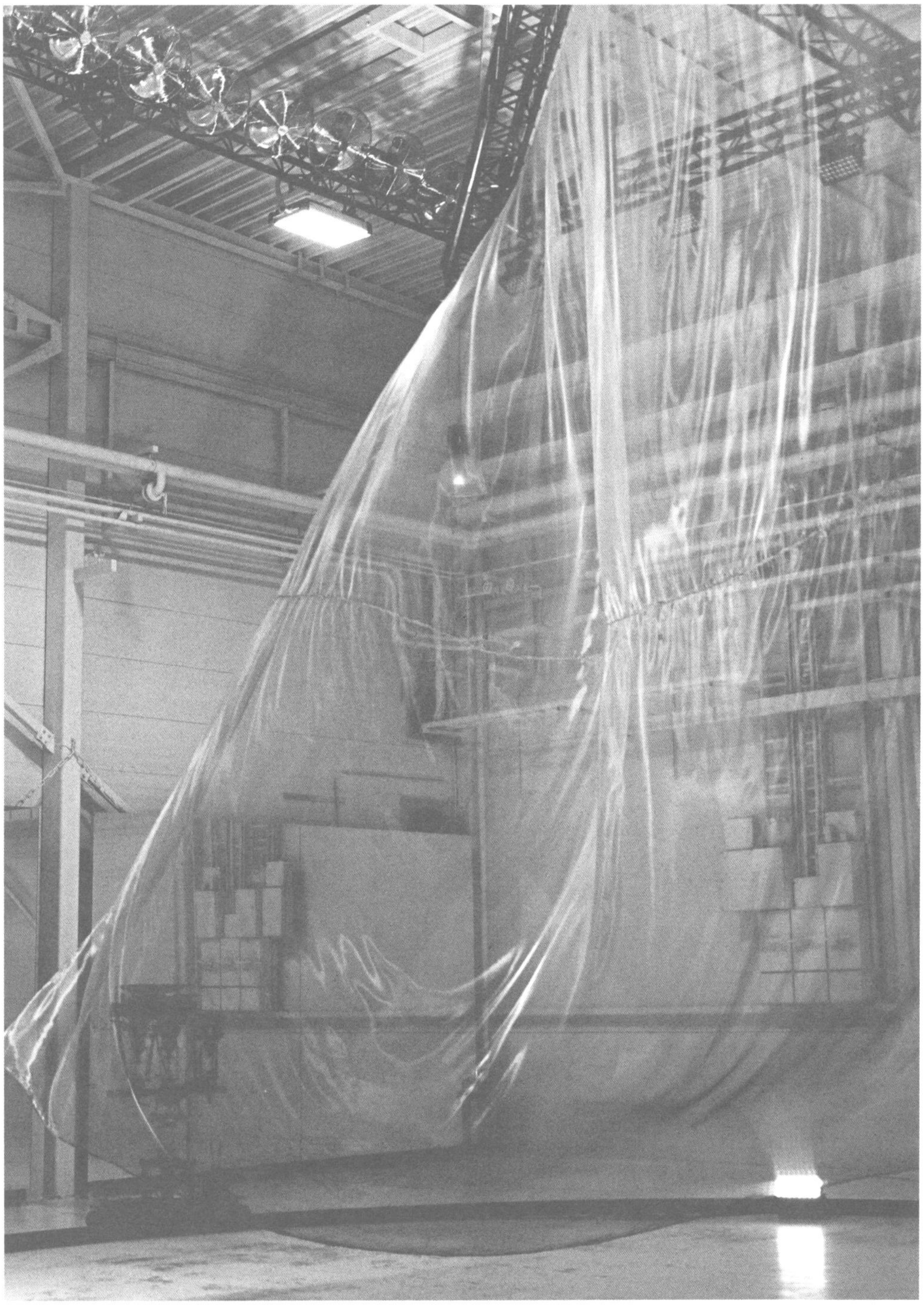

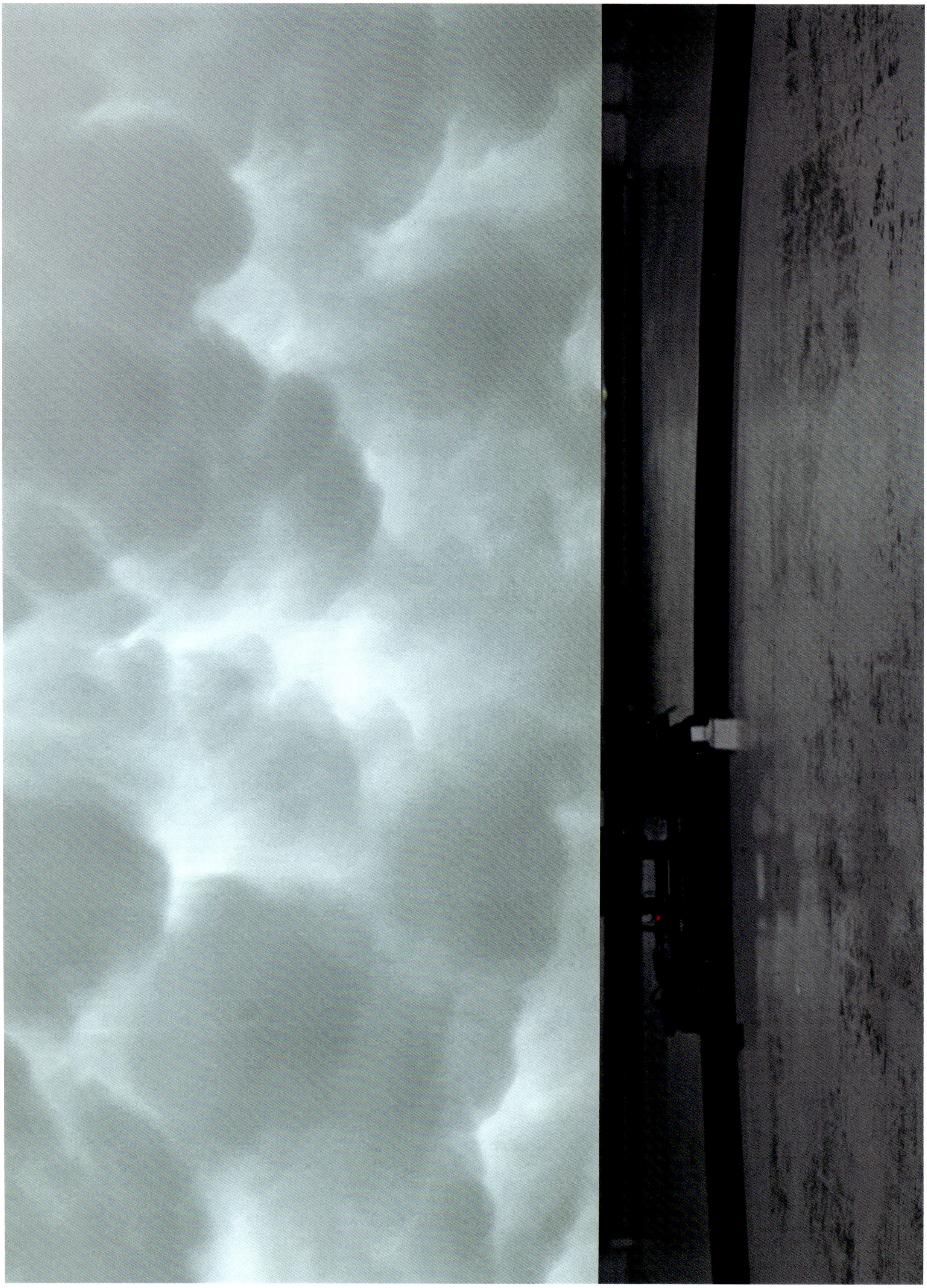

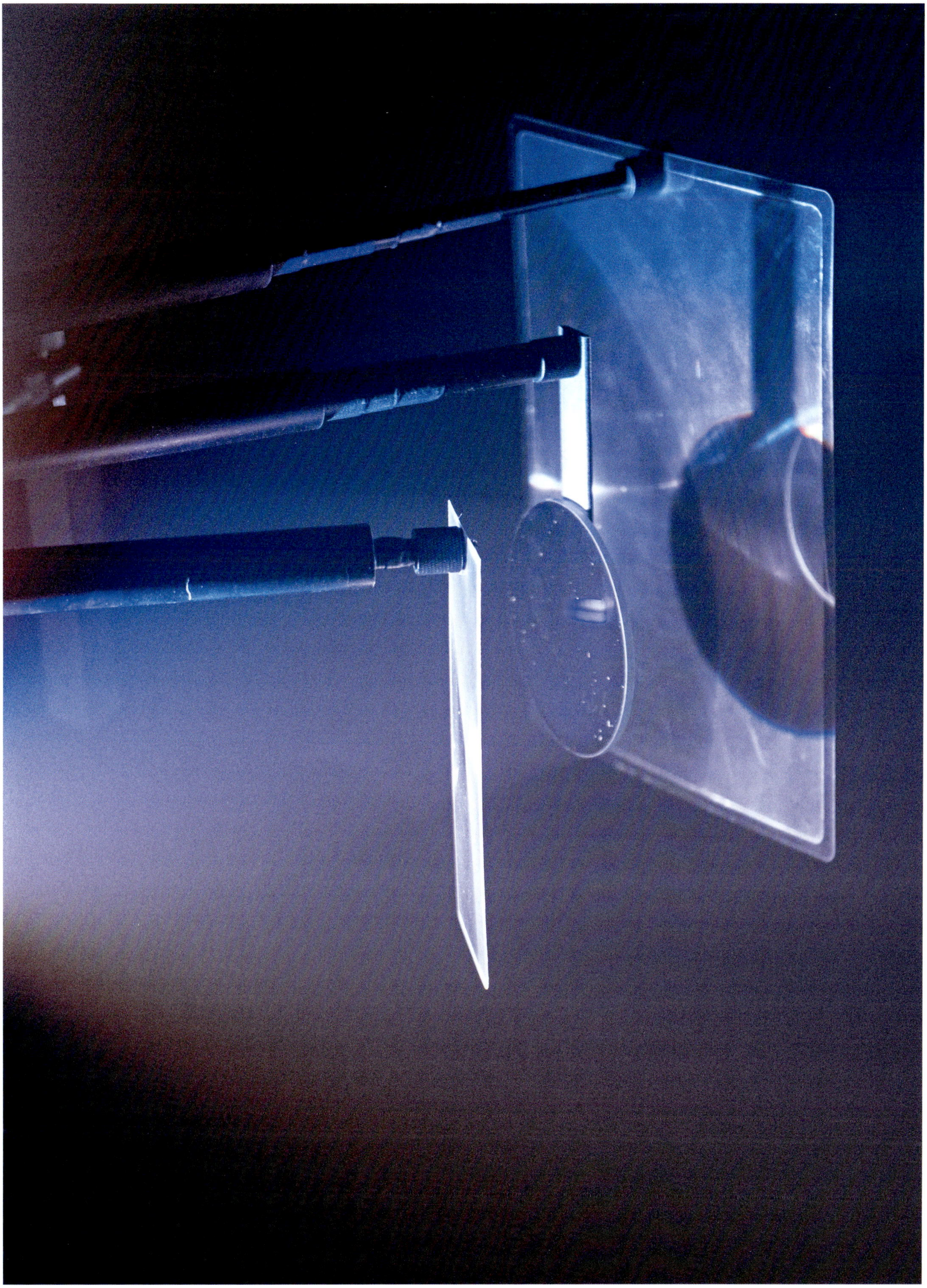

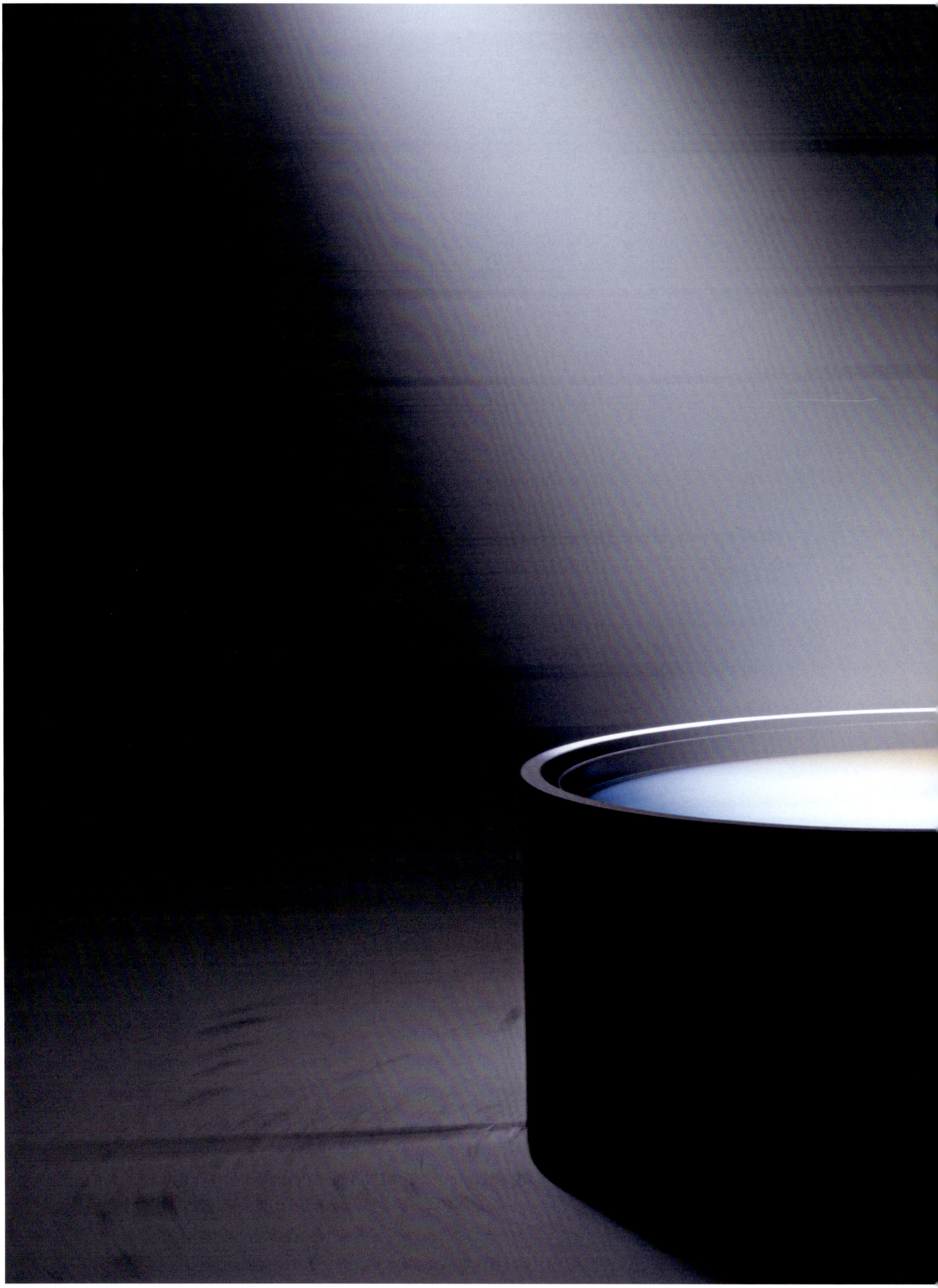

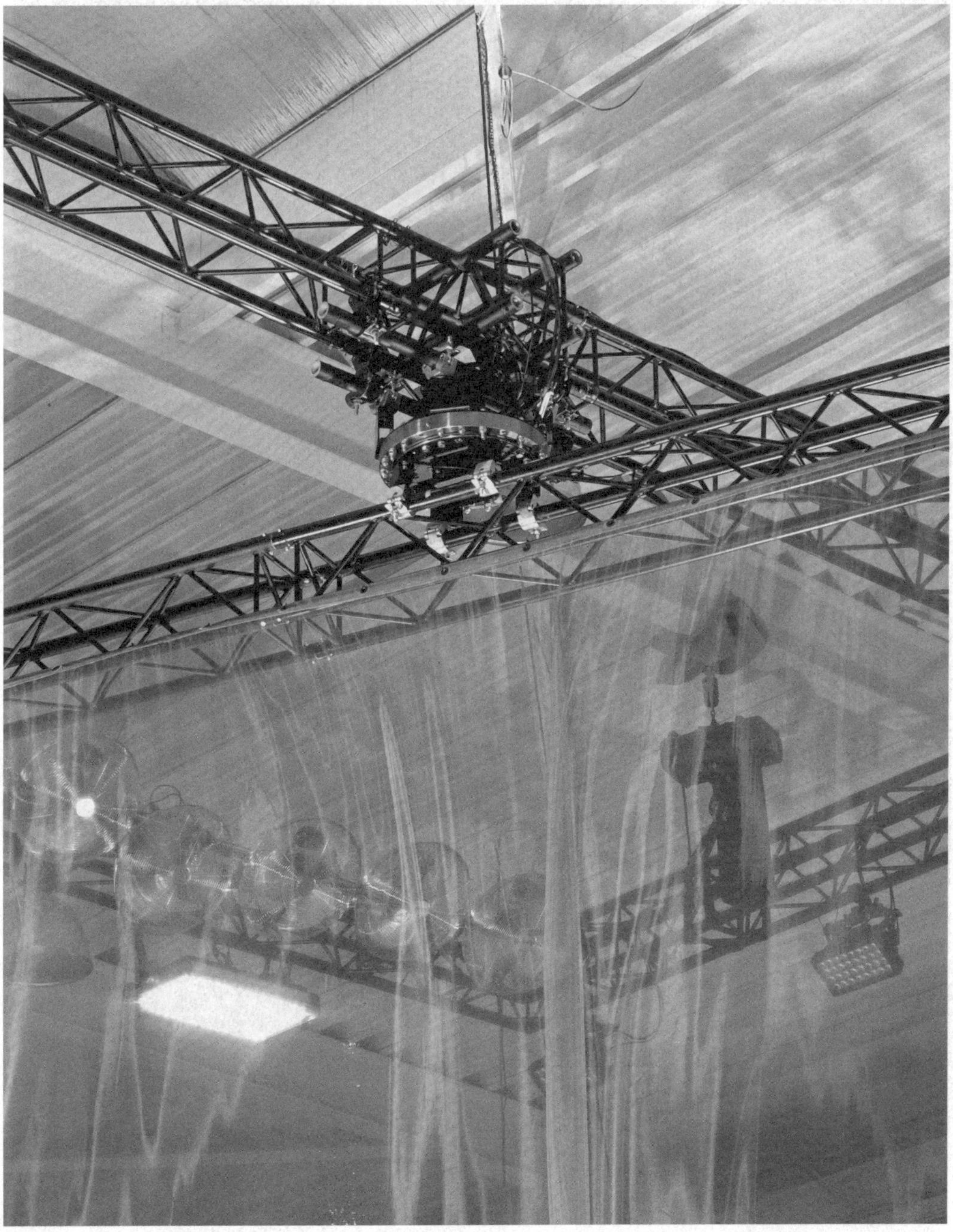

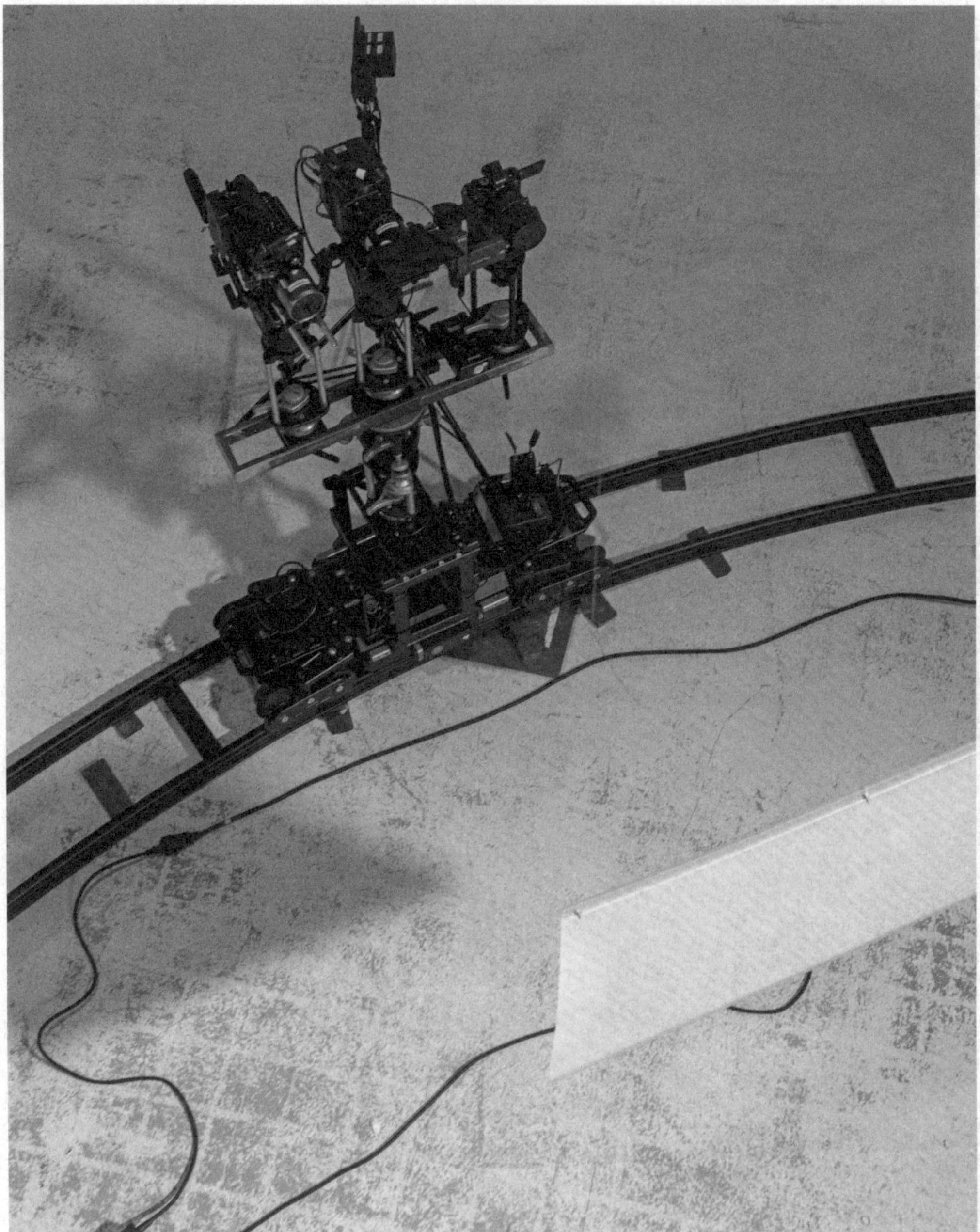

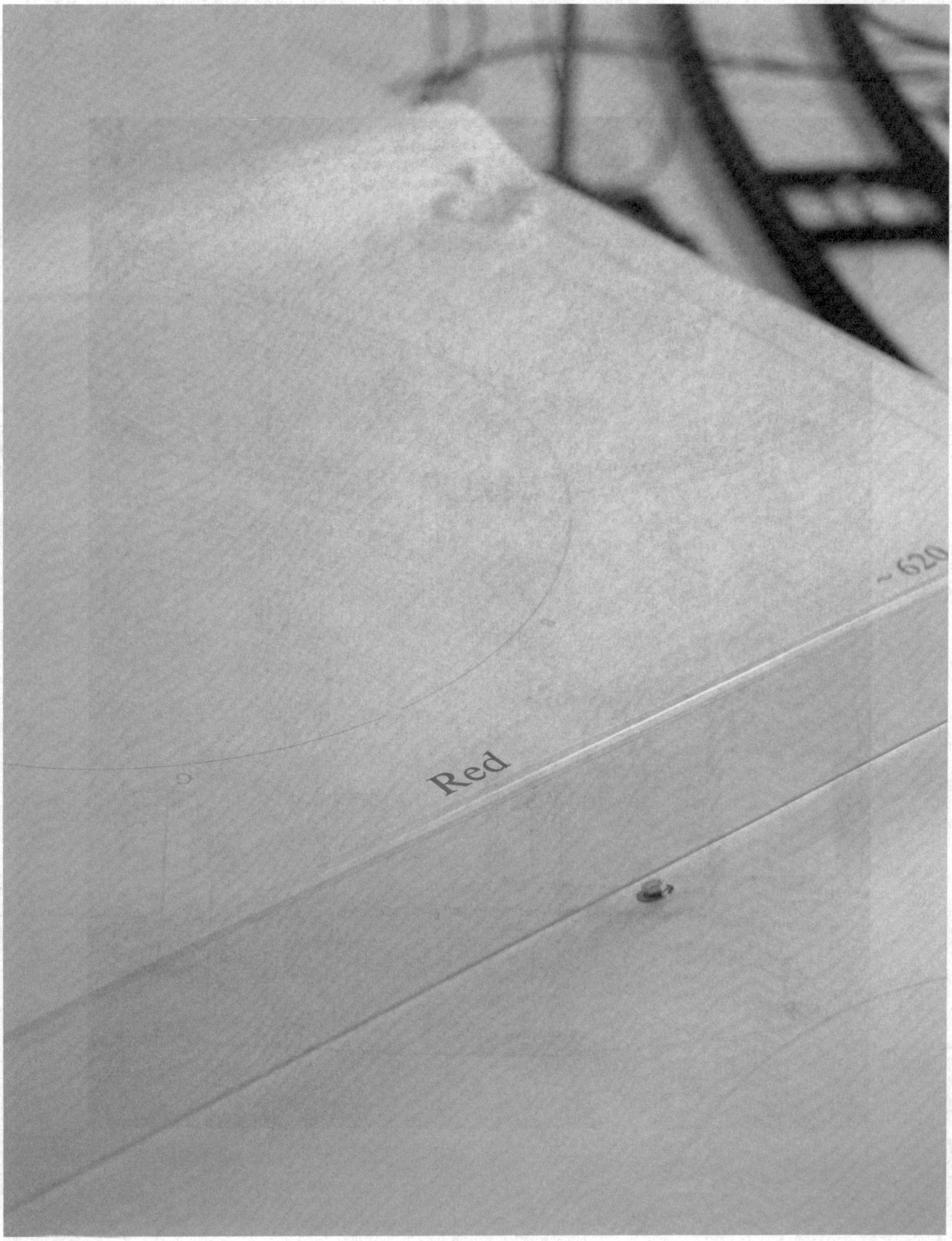
~620
Red

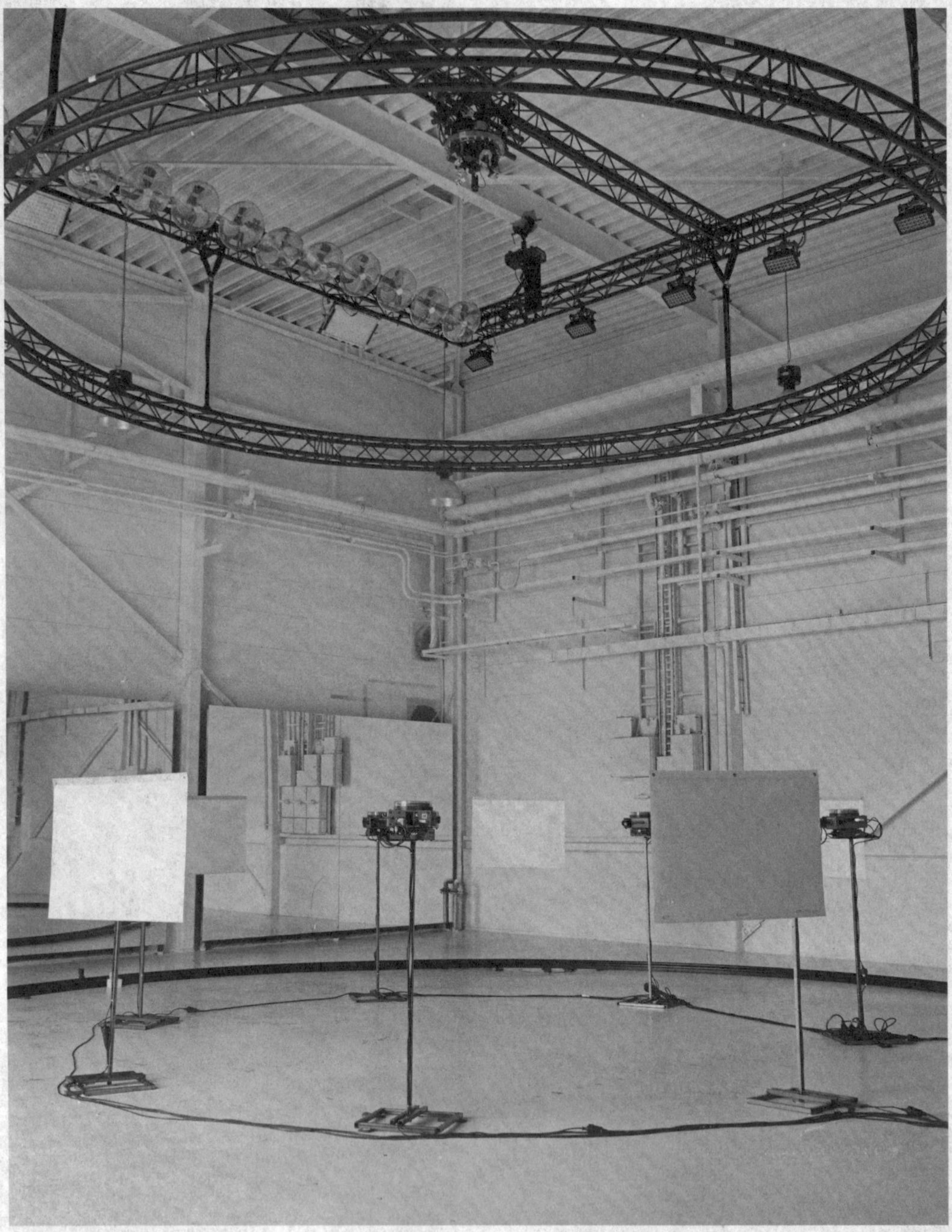

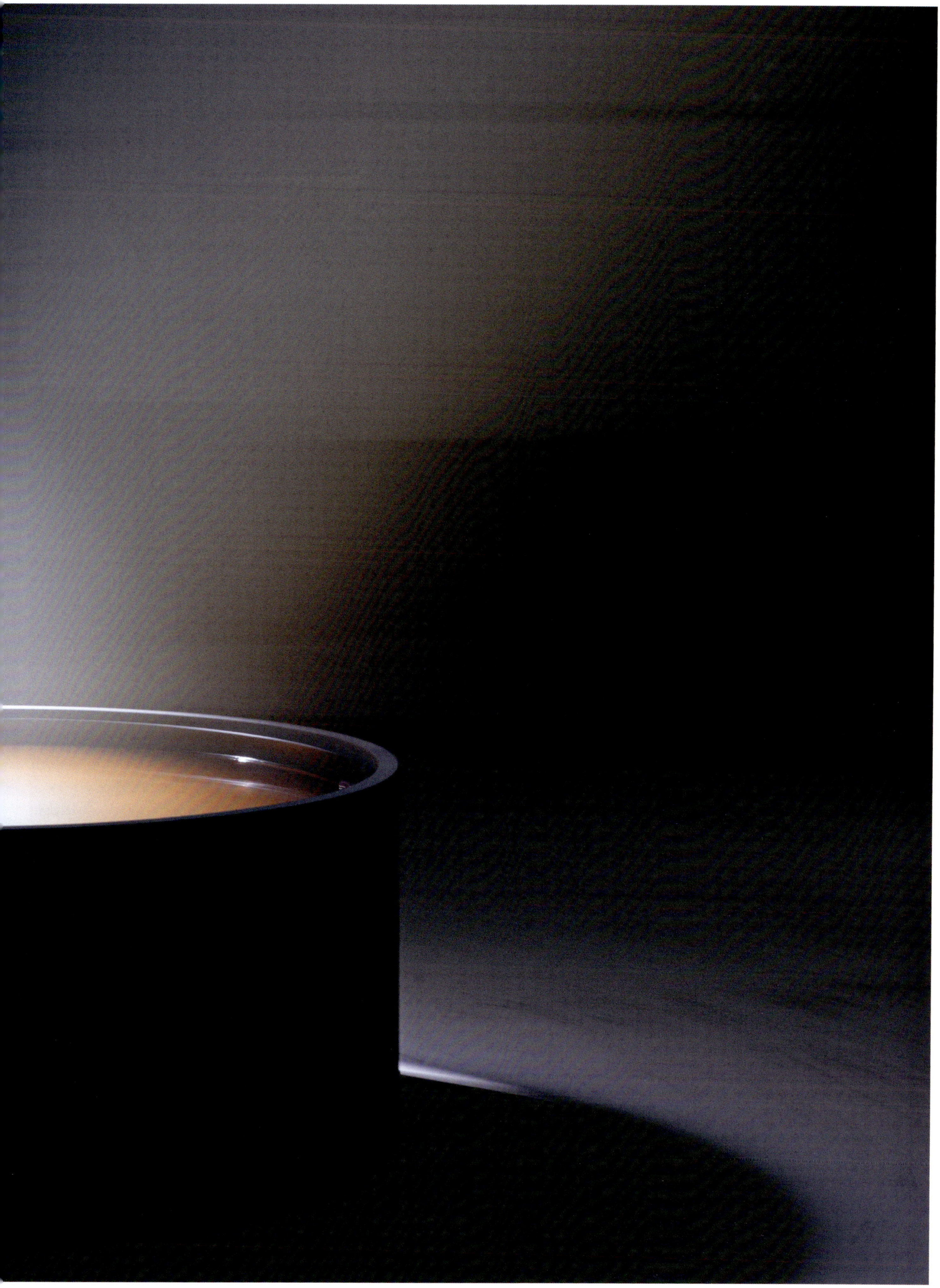

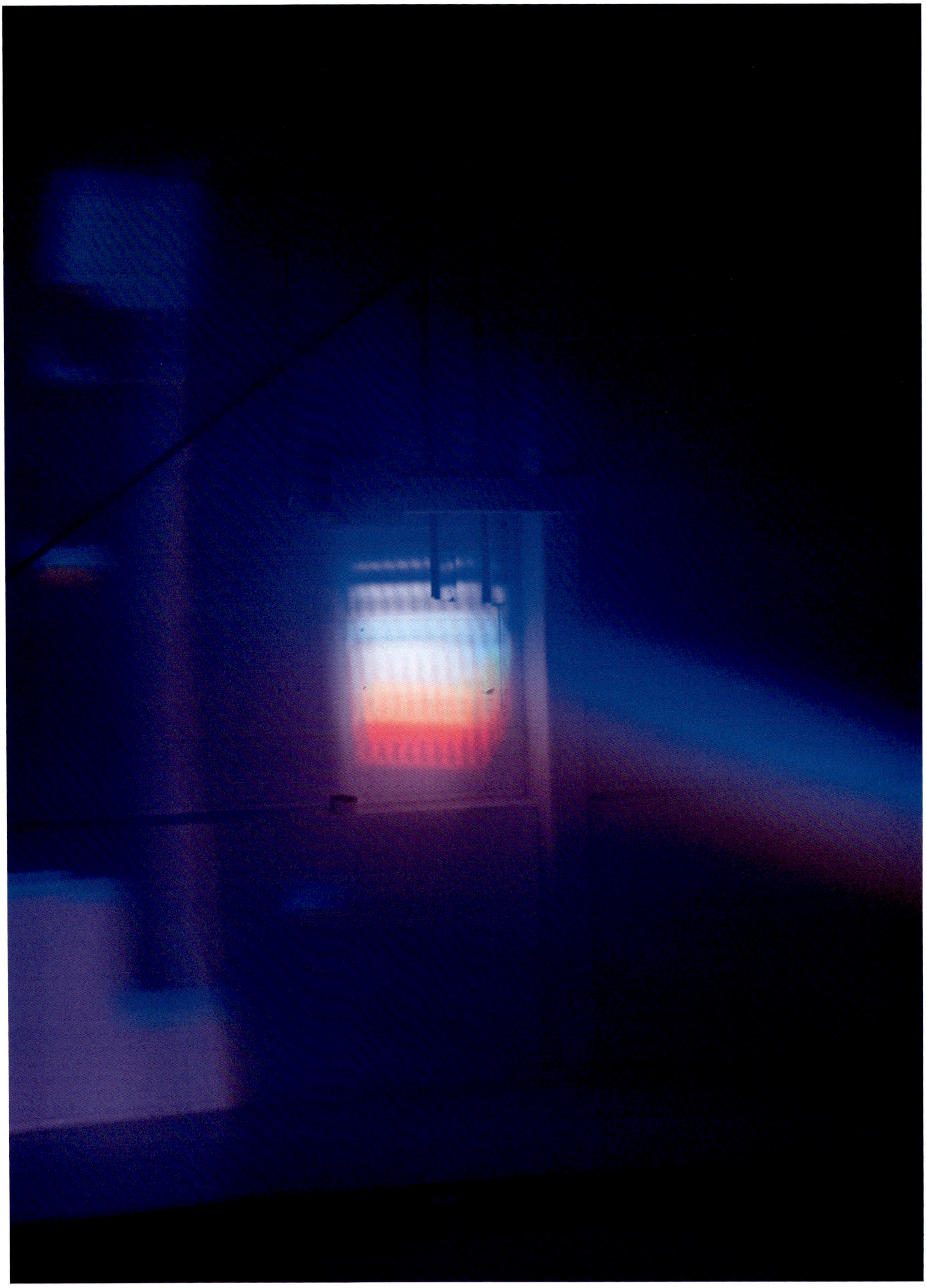

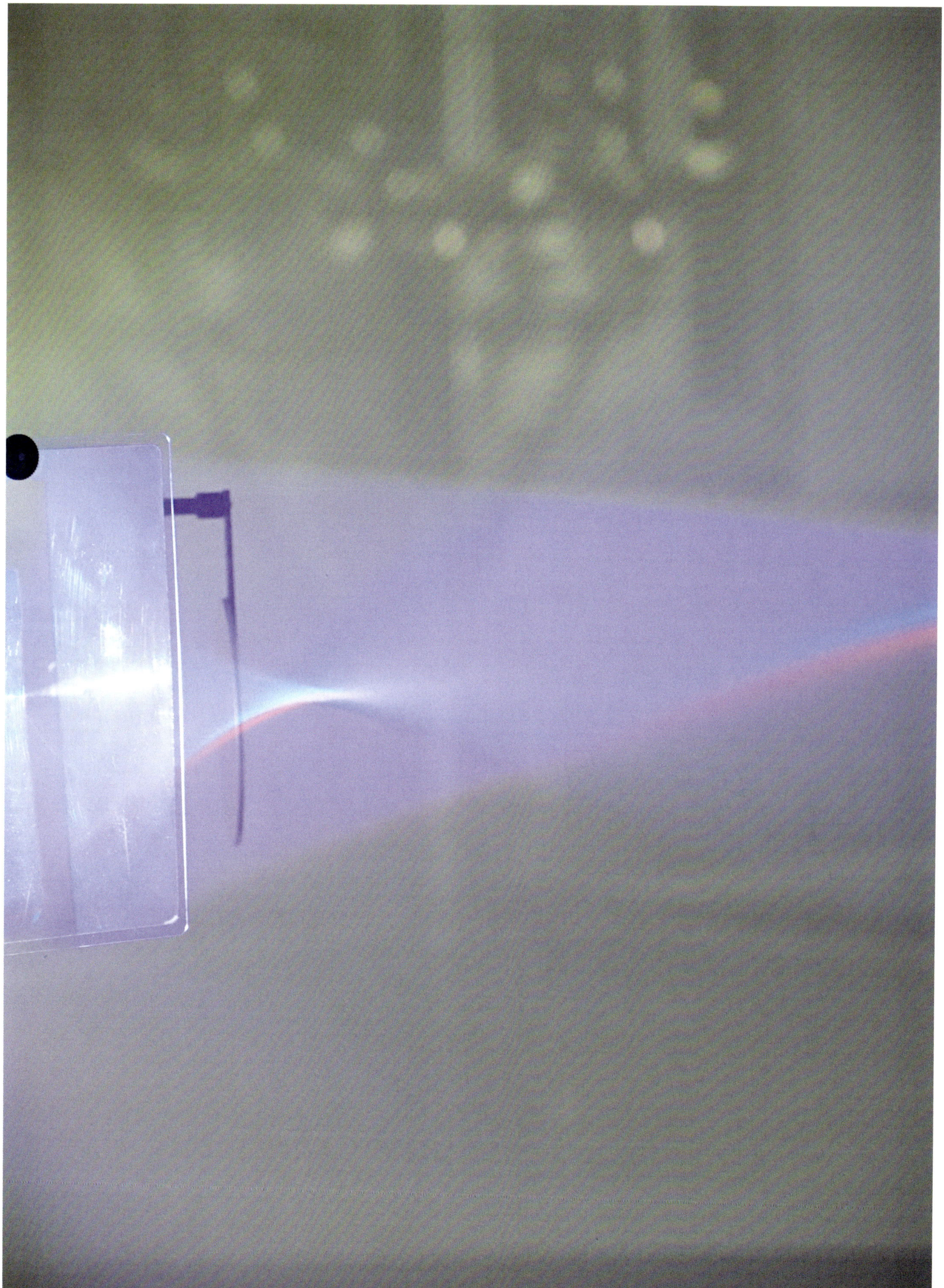

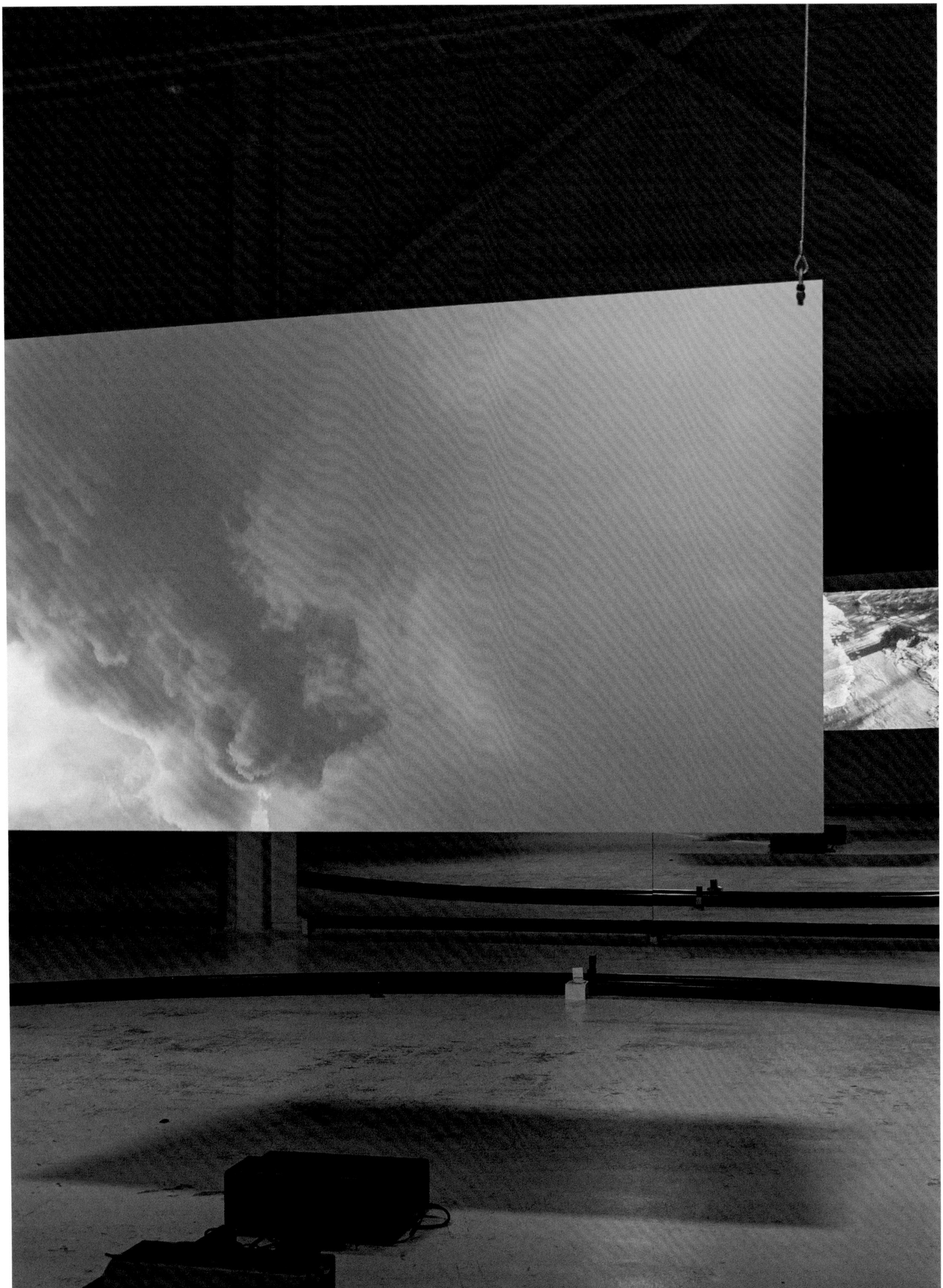

TRANSPARENCY & TRANSLUCENCY—When light passes through a material, its path reveals the nature of what it meets. Transparent mediums—clear glass, still air, pure water—allow light to travel with little interference. The wave continues onwards sharp and undistorted; detail and direction are preserved. That which is translucent, however, scatters light. It enters, but its course is blurred—like the glow of mist hanging in the morning air, flower petals, the wing of an insect. Shapes lose their edges; the strength of light diffuses into softness, much like sunrays filtered through drifting clouds. Both let light through, but only one lets it through unchanged.

(3)

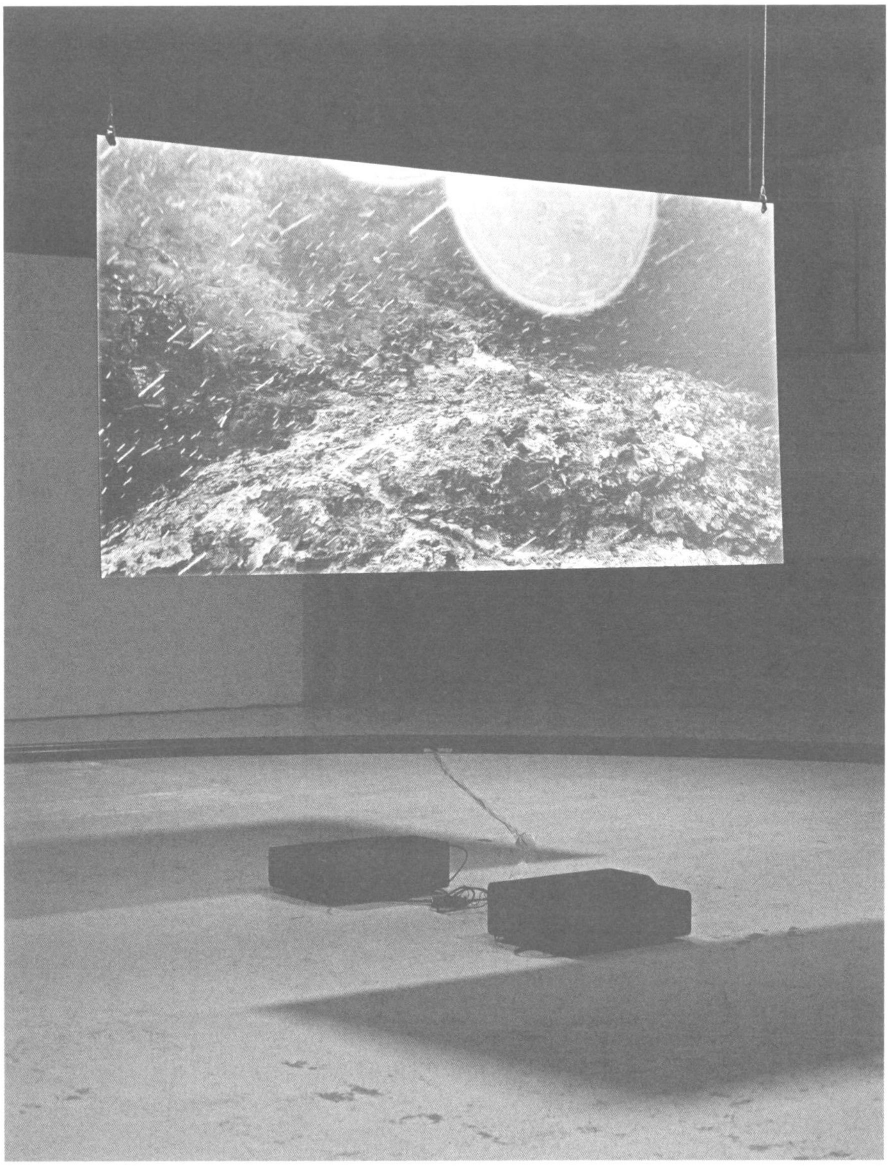

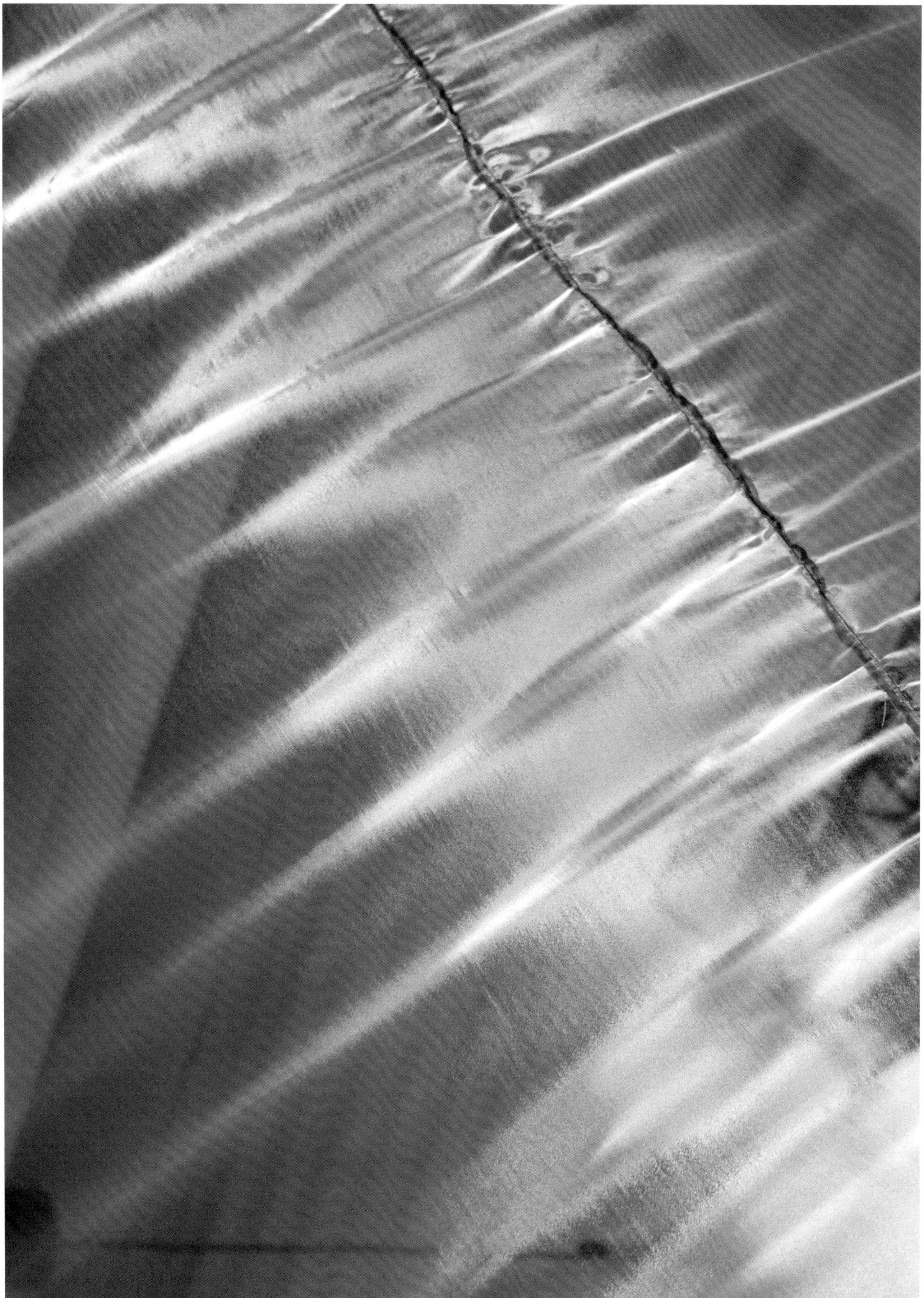

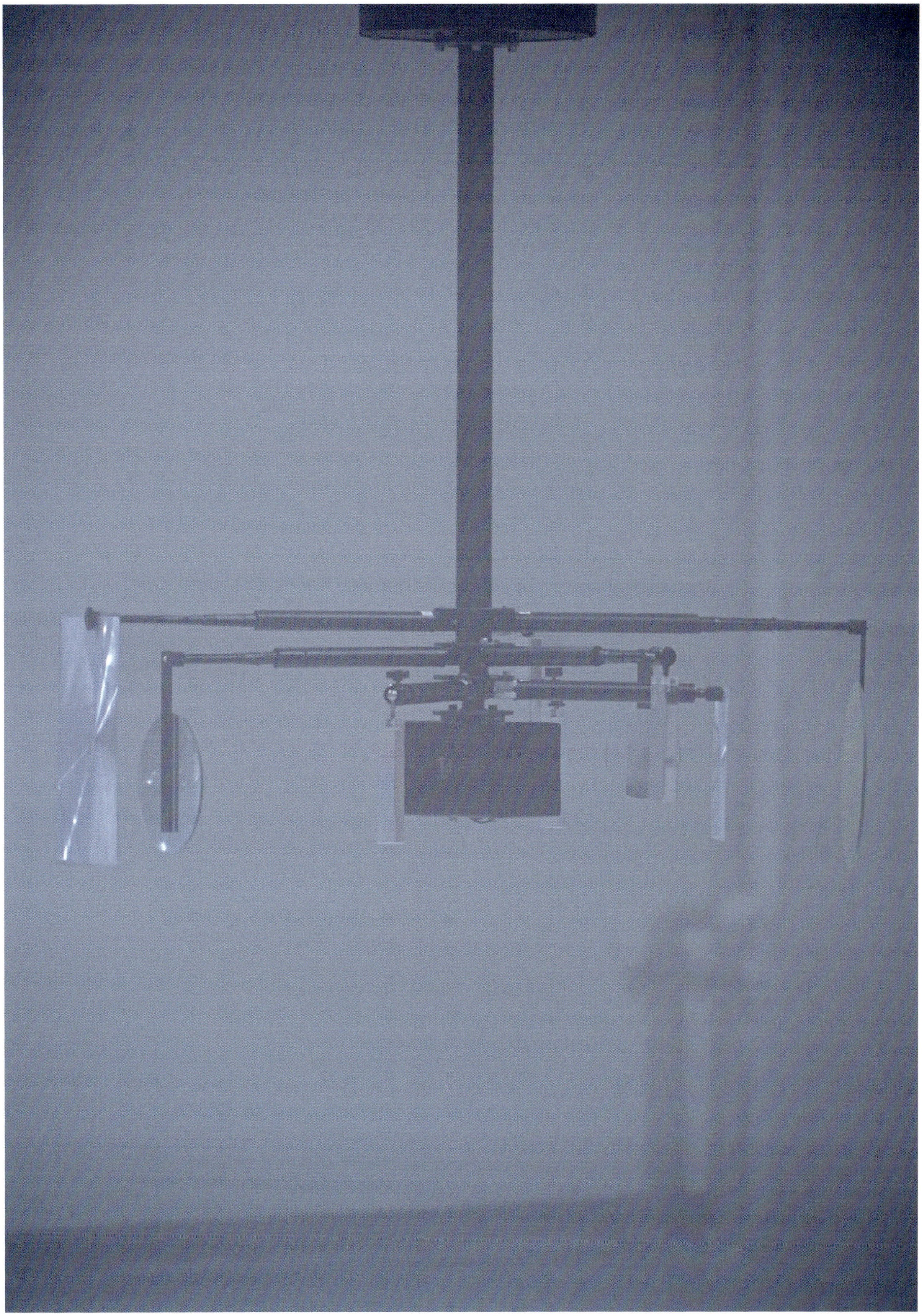

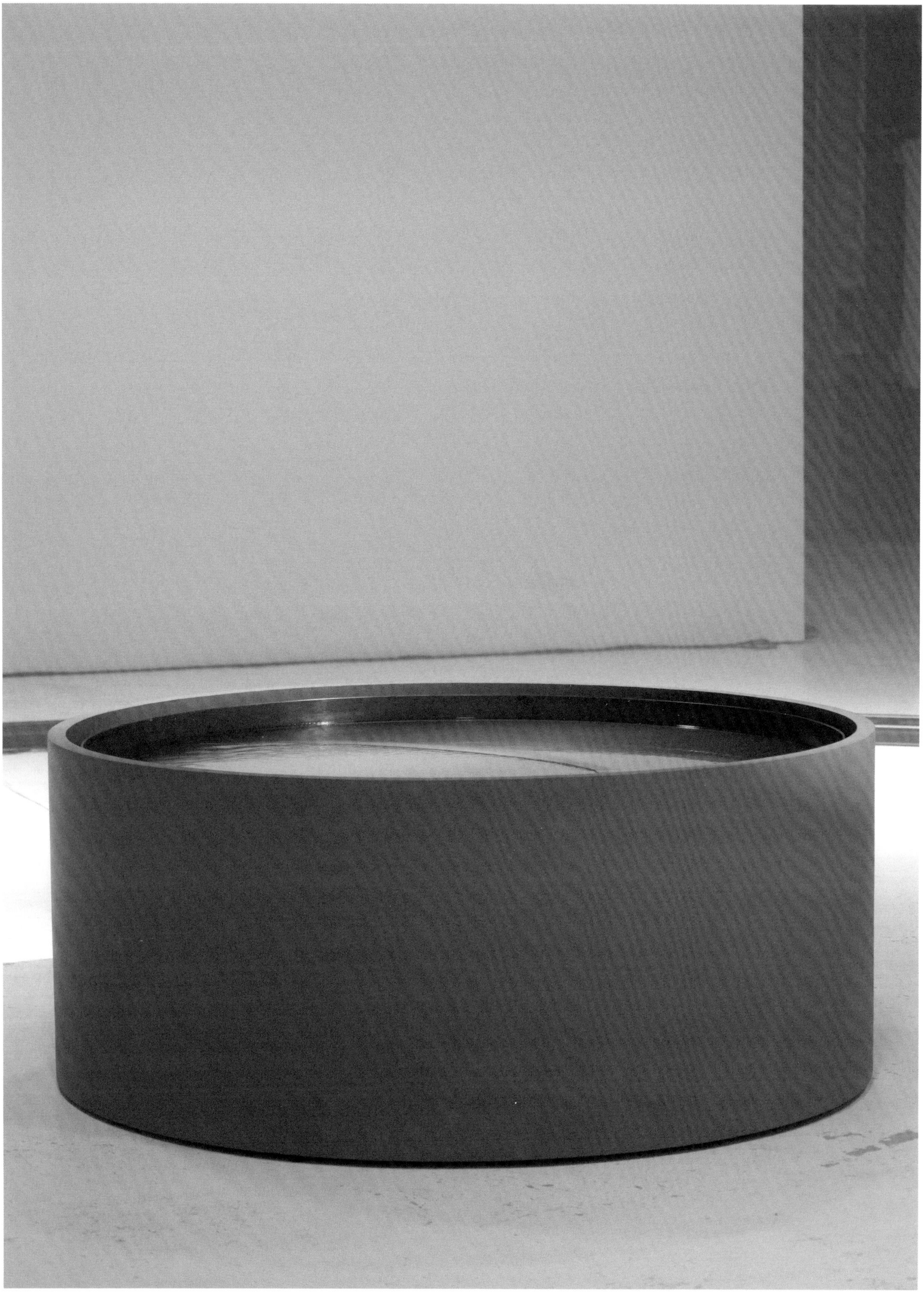

REFLECTION & REFRACTION—Light moves until it meets a boundary. Reflection turns the light back. A mirror sends the wave away at the same angle it arrived in—direction reversed but form intact. Reflection is light's echo—crisp and predictable. Refraction bends the wave. As light enters a new medium—air to water, glass to air—it changes speed, and with it, direction. The path curves. A straw in a glass appears broken; a setting sun shifts position. Reflection preserves the light's path. Refraction reshapes it.

(4)

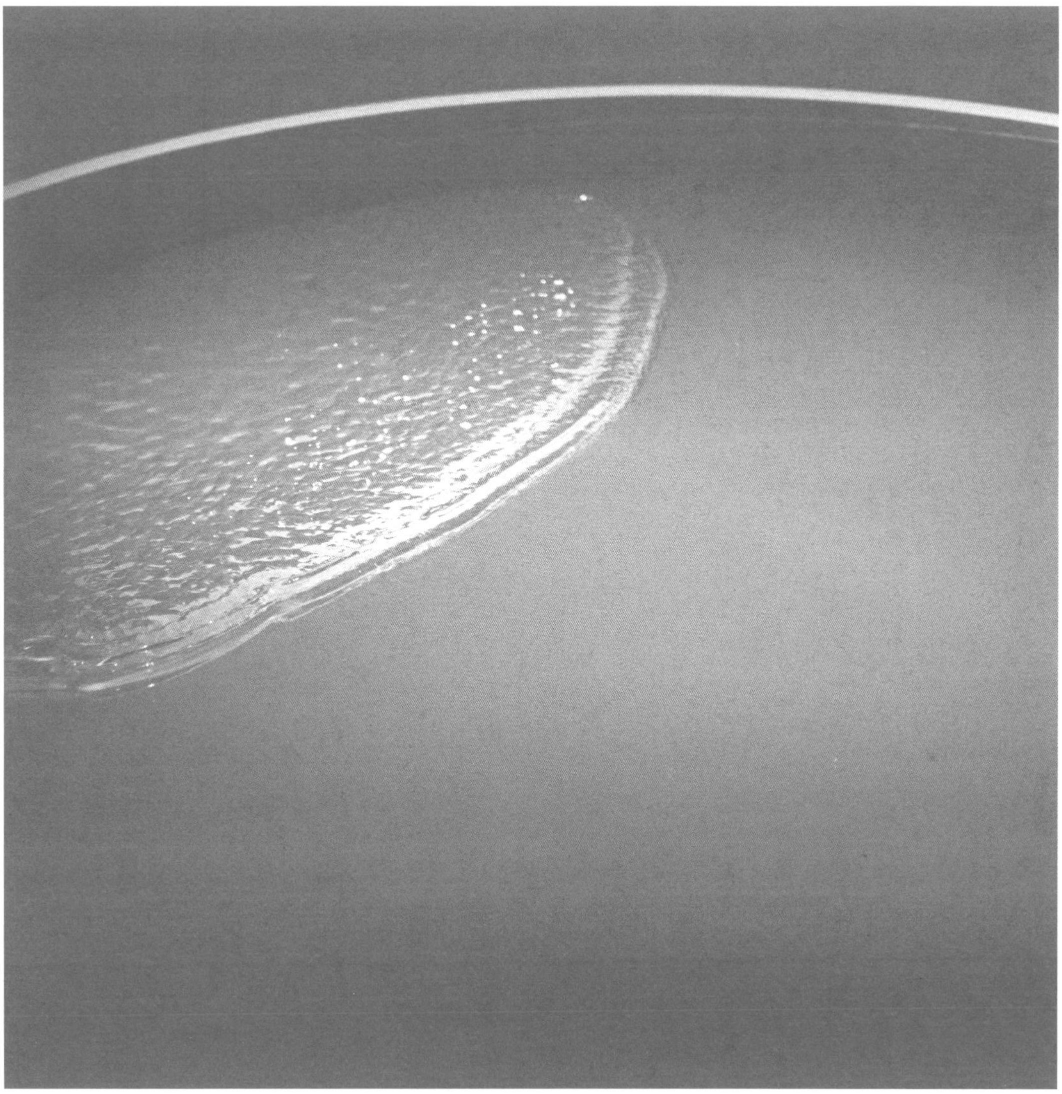

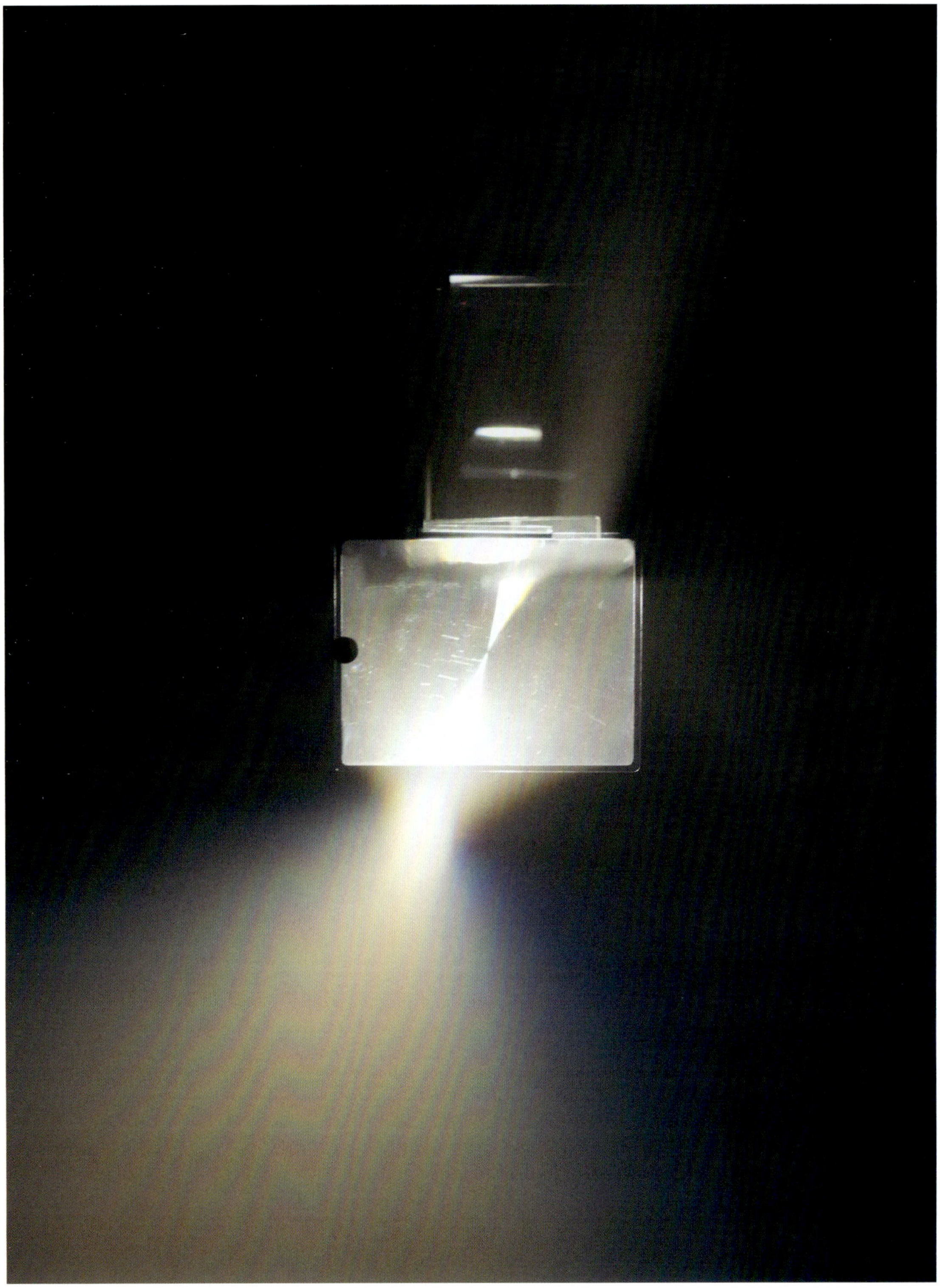

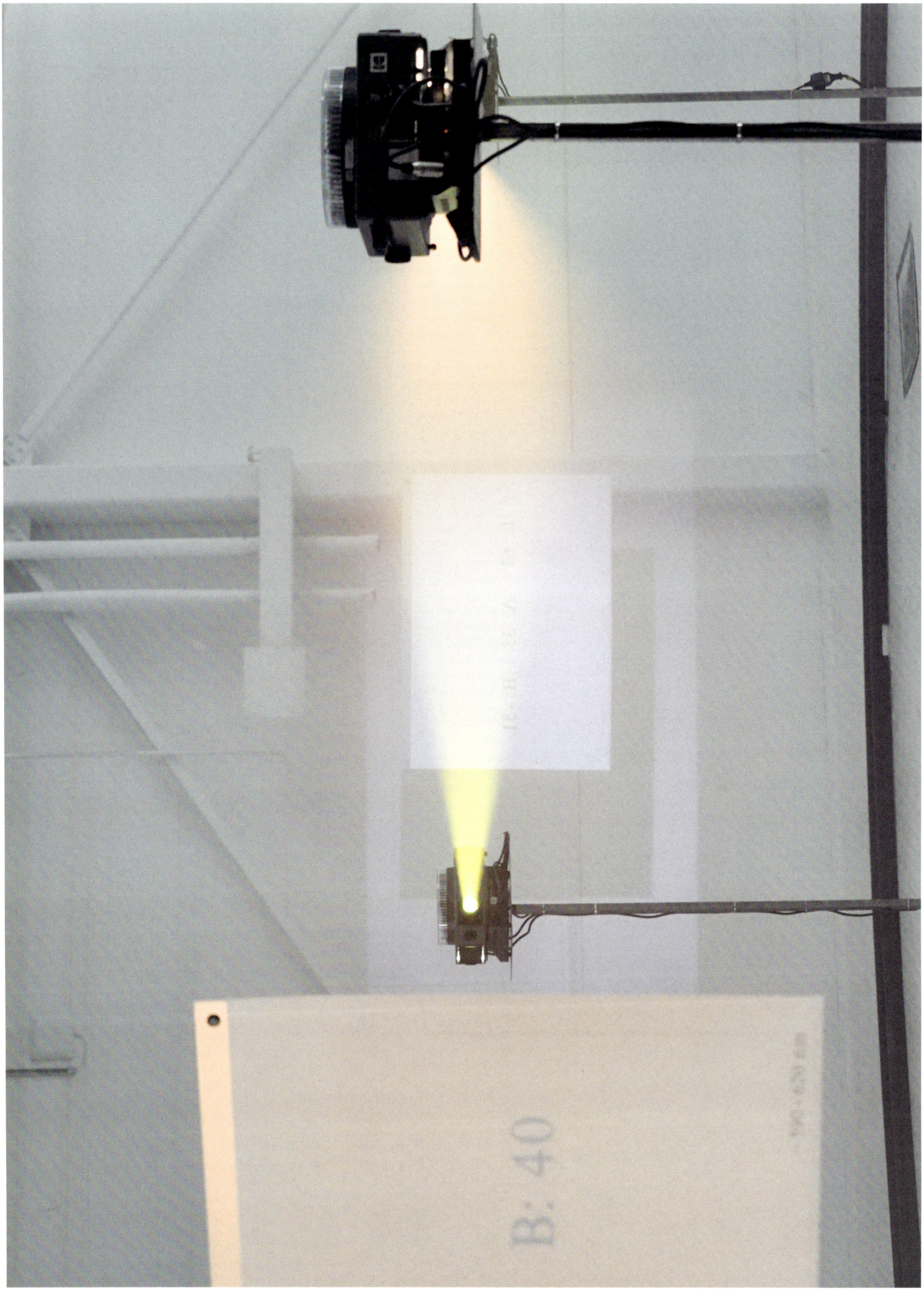
B: 40

HUE SPECTRUM—Light has no inherent color—hue is not a property of light, but a product of our perception. Light travels as a wave and variations in these wavelengths are what we see as hues, like the hidden color spectrum revealed when white light passes through a prism. As light enters our eyes, the mind assigns meaning to its rhythm. Longer wavelengths appear as red, while shorter ones shift towards violet. Color is not in the light but in the looking—the trace light leaves in us.

(5)

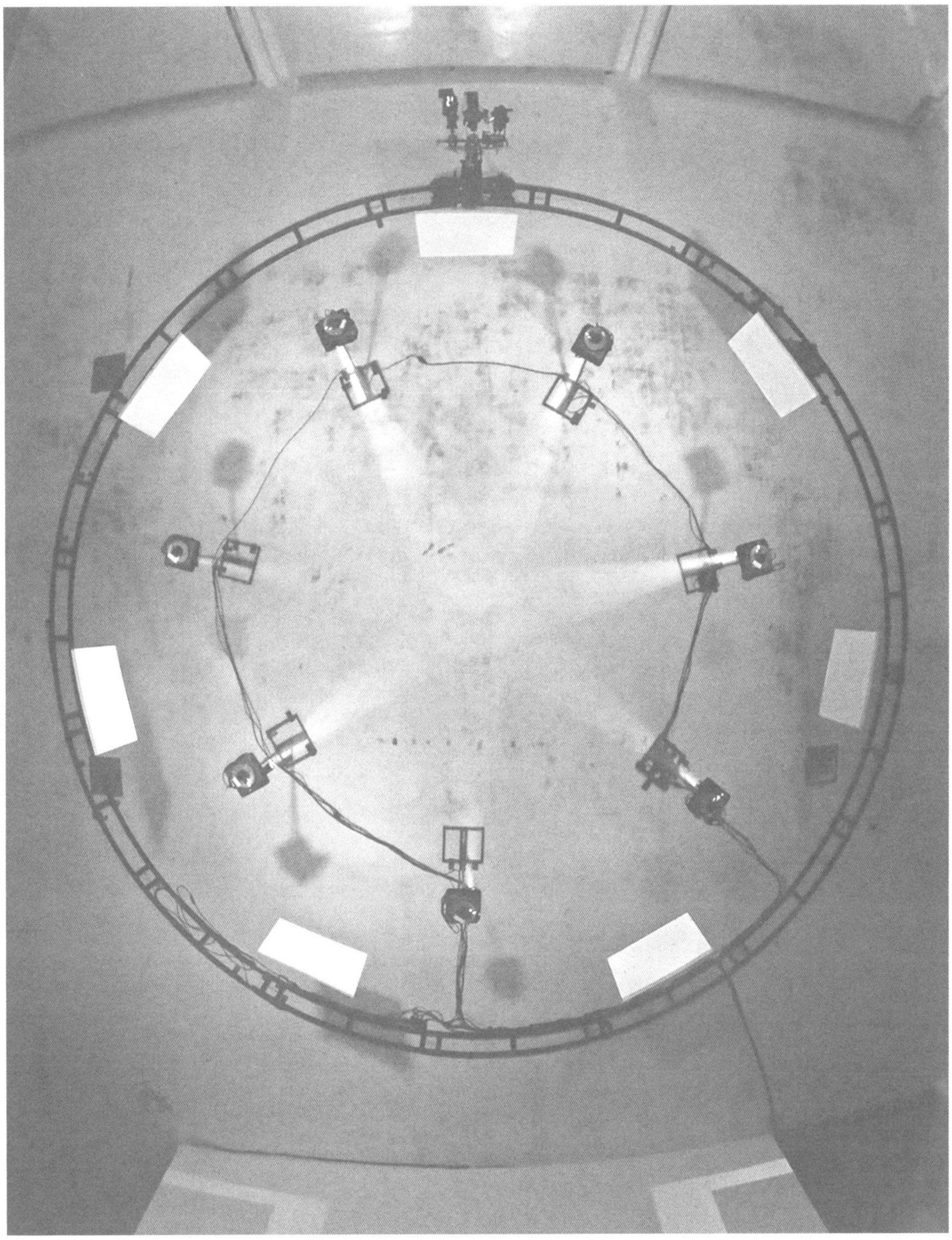

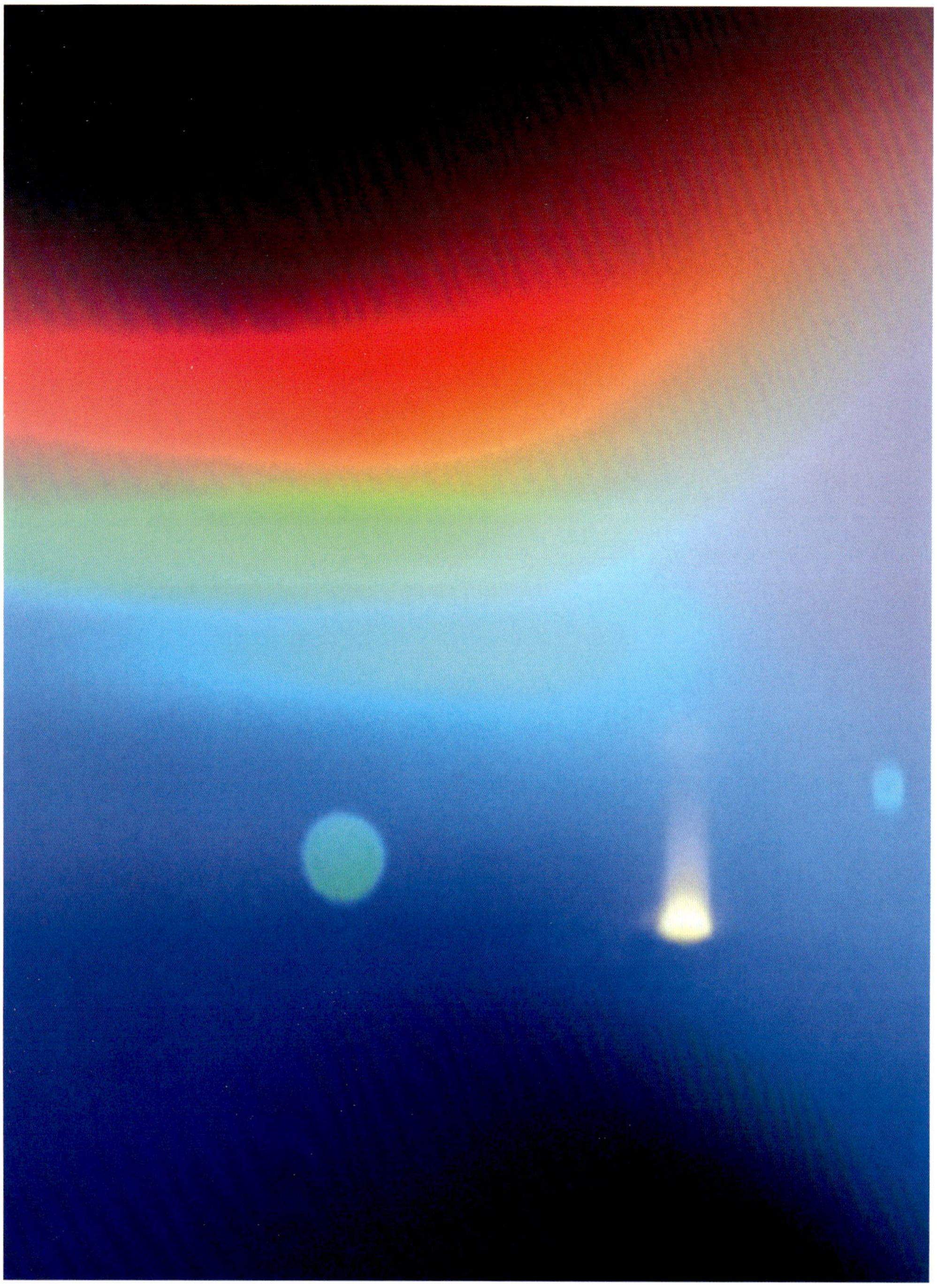

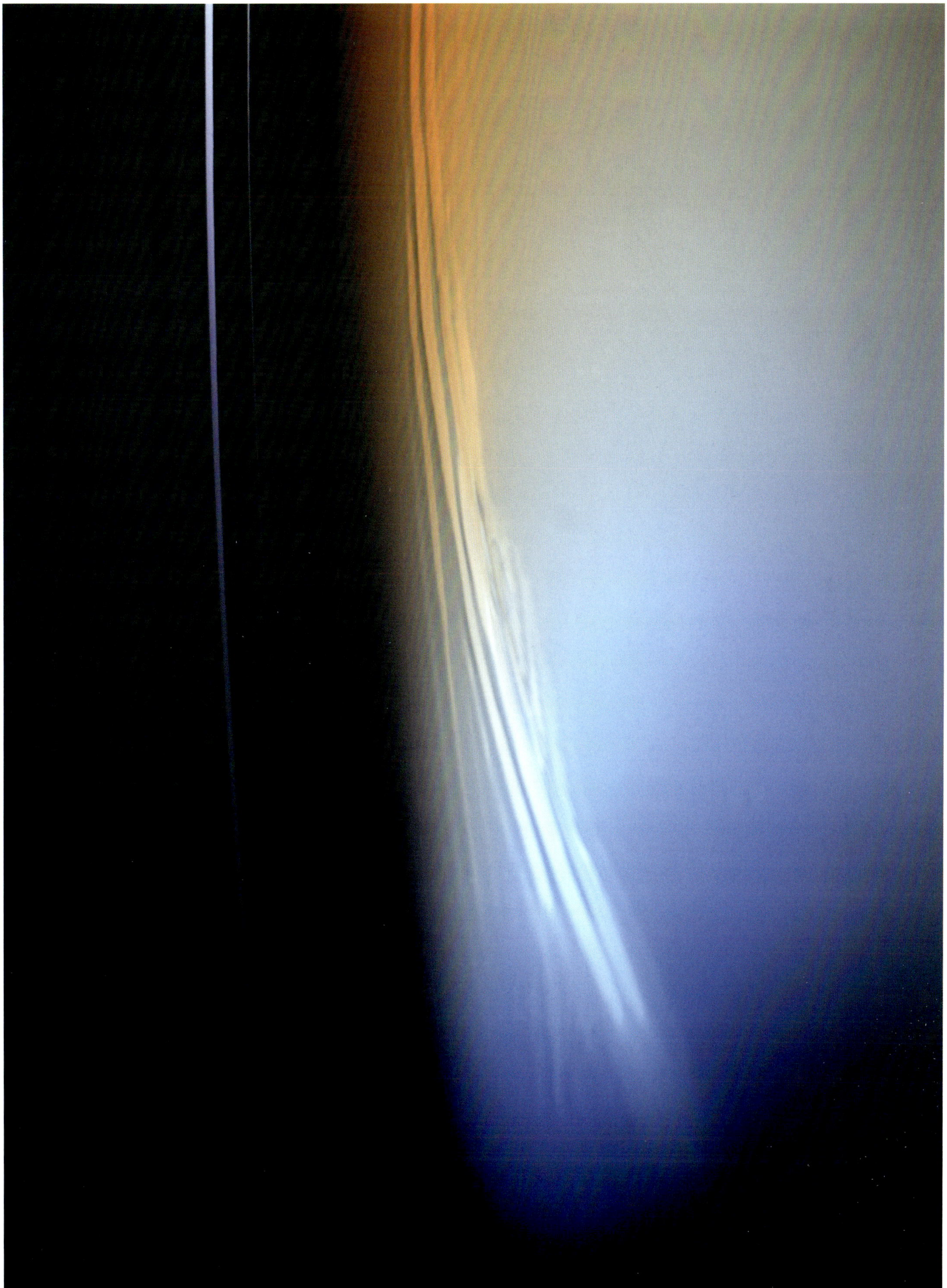

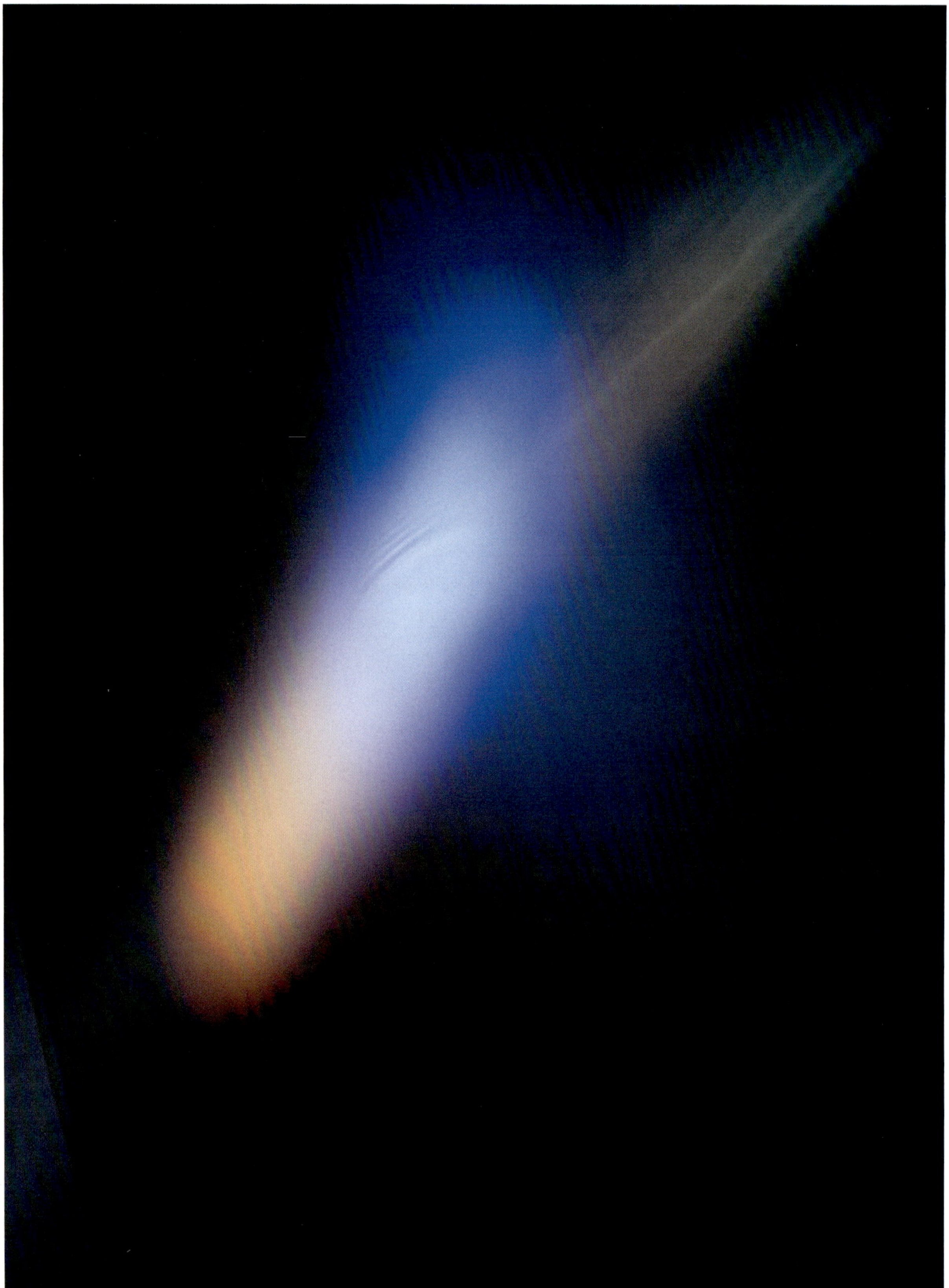

The entities were all colored windows upon which fell the rays of Being's Sun. In every window—red, yellow, blue— the Light appeared in the window's color.

—Jami

Five Studies on Light
by Studio Airport & Boris Acket

This appendix is an adaptation of the interactive film *Five Studies on Light*.

emergencemagazine.org/seasonsfilm

Creative Directors
Bram Broerse
Maurits Wouters

Visual Artists
Boris Acket
Sabine Marcelis

Engineer
Merijn Versnel

Director of Photography
Luuk de Kok